Corporate Takeovers

A National Bureau
of Economic Research
Project Report

Corporate Takeovers: Causes and Consequences

Edited by Alan J. Auerbach

The University of Chicago Press

Chicago and London

ALAN J. AUERBACH is professor of economics at the University of
Pennsylvania and a research associate of the National Bureau of
Economic Research.

The University of Chicago Press, Chicago 60637
The University of Chicago Press, Ltd., London

Library of Congress Cataloging-in-Publication Data

Corporate takeovers: causes and consequences / edited by Alan J.
Auerbach.
    p.   cm. — (National Bureau of Economic Research project
report)
    Papers originally presented at a National Bureau of Economic
Research conference in Feb. 1987 in Key Largo.
    Bibliography: p.
    Includes index.
    Contents: The impact of firm acquisitions on labor / Charles
Brown, James L. Medoff — Breach of trust in hostile takeovers /
Andrei Shleifer, Lawrence H. Summers — The effect of takeover
activity on corporate research and development / Bronwyn H. Hall—
Characteristics of targets of hostile and friendly takeovers /
Randall Mørck, Andrei Shleifer, Robert W. Vishny — Do target
shareholders lose in unsuccessful control contests? / Richard S.
Ruback — The effects of taxation on the merger decision / Alan J.
Auerbach, David Reishus — Share repurchases and acquisitions /
Laurie Simon Bagwell, John B. Shoven — Means of payment in
takeovers / Julian R. Franks, Robert S. Harris, Colin Mayer — A
time-series analysis of mergers and acquisitions in the U.S. economy
/ Devra L. Golbe, Lawrence J. White — Panel Discussion /
Joseph A. Grundfest, Gregg Jarrell, Steven C. Salop, Lawrence
J. White.
    ISBN 0-226-03211-6
    1. Consolidation and merger of corporations—Congresses.
2. Consolidation and merger of corporations—United States—
Congresses. I. Auerbach, Alan J. II. National Bureau of
Economic Research. III. Series.
HD2746.5.C675 1988
338.8'3'0973—dc19   87-37497
                                                            CIP

Relation of the Directors to the
Work and Publications of the
National Bureau of Economic Research

1. The object of the National Bureau of Economic Research is to ascertain and to present to the public important economic facts and their interpretation in a scientific and impartial manner. The Board of Directors is charged with the responsibility of ensuring that the work of the National Bureau is carried on in strict conformity with this object.

2. The President of the National Bureau shall submit to the Board of Directors, or to its Executive Committee, for their formal adoption all specific proposals for research to be instituted.

3. No research report shall be published by the National Bureau until the President has sent each member of the Board a notice that a manuscript is recommended for publication and that in the President's opinion it is suitable for publication in accordance with the principles of the National Bureau. Such notification will include an abstract or summary of the manuscript's content and a response form for use by those Directors who desire a copy of the manuscript for review. Each manuscript shall contain a summary drawing attention to the nature and treatment of the problem studied, the character of the data and their utilization in the report, and the main conclusions reached.

4. For each manuscript so submitted, a special committee of the Directors (including Directors Emeriti) shall be appointed by majority agreement of the President and Vice Presidents (or by the Executive Committee in case of inability to decide on the part of the President and Vice Presidents), consisting of three Directors selected as nearly as may be one from each general division of the Board. The names of the special manuscript committee shall be stated to each Director when notice of the proposed publication is submitted to him. It shall be the duty of each member of the special manuscript committee to read the manuscript. If each member of the manuscript committee signifies his approval within thirty days of the transmittal of the manuscript, the report may be published. If at the end of that period any member of the manuscript committee withholds his approval, the President shall then notify each member of the Board, requesting approval or disapproval of publication, and thirty days additional shall be granted for this purpose. The manuscript shall then not be published unless at least a majority of the entire Board who shall have voted on the proposal within the time fixed for the receipt of votes shall have approved.

5. No manuscript may be published, though approved by each member of the special manuscript committee, until forty-five days have elapsed from the transmittal of the report in manuscript form. The interval is allowed for the receipt of any memorandum of dissent or reservation, together with a brief statement of his reasons, that any member may wish to express; and such memorandum of dissent or reservation shall be published with the manuscript if he so desires. Publication does not, however, imply that each member of the Board has read the manuscript, or that either members of the Board in general or the special committee have passed on its validity in every detail.

6. Publications of the National Bureau issued for informational purposes concerning the work of the Bureau and its staff, or issued to inform the public of activities of Bureau staff, and volumes issued as a result of various conferences involving the National Bureau shall contain a specific disclaimer noting that such publication has not passed through the normal review procedures required in this resolution. The Executive Committee of the Board is charged with review of all such publications from time to time to ensure that they do not take on the character of formal research reports of the National Bureau, requiring formal Board approval.

7. Unless otherwise determined by the Board or exempted by the terms of paragraph 6, a copy of this resolution shall be printed in each National Bureau publication.

(Resolution adopted October 25, 1926, as revised through September 30, 1974)

Contents

JUL   1989

Preface

The papers and discussants' comments that follow were originally presented at a National Bureau of Economic Research conference in February 1987 in Key Largo. The reader should keep this date in mind in light of whatever may have happened since in the rapidly evolving market for corporate control. This volume represents a part of the NBER project on Mergers and Acquisitions, which was generously funded by the Seaver Institute.

The conference participants are already aware that the meticulous planning and organization of the meeting by Kirsten Foss Davis and Ilana Hardesty of the NBER made it possible (and indeed necessary) for them to worry only about the quality of their own contributions to the conference. After the conference the task of preparing this book for publication has been organized by Mark Fitz-Patrick and Annie Spillane of the NBER Publications Department. I am also grateful to Henry S. Farber and another, anonymous internal referee for reviewing the entire manuscript.

The opinions expressed in this volume are those of the individual authors and not necessarily those of the NBER, the Seaver Institute, or any other organization.

Introduction

Alan J. Auerbach

During the mid-1980s the U.S. economy experienced the highest level of corporate takeover activity since the late 1960s, perhaps even since before the Great Depression. As with the takeover boom of the sixties, the recent one has brought after it a tide of legislation aimed at correcting the perceived abuses and societal ills generated by the acquisitions.

It is natural to seek simple, common explanations for the different waves of mergers the U.S. economy has experienced, but obvious differences in the characteristics of these periods make such an effort inadvisable. The recent takeover boom has exhibited many phenomena not observed in the trust building of the early 1900s or in the conglomerate mergers of the 1960s, in particular, hostile takeovers and takeover defenses, the acquisition of companies ranking among the largest in the country, and the prevalence of cash as a means of payment for acquired targets. Legislative initiatives have also changed, moving away from concerns for competition and efficiency to concerns for the stability of the financial and tax systems and for the competing rights and interests of shareholders, managers, employees, and other "stakeholders" who are interested parties to the takeover process.

One of the clearest lessons of the recent period is that, whatever the social gains generated by mergers and acquisitions, large redistributions are occurring simultaneously. It is therefore unrealistic to expect a social consensus regarding whether mergers are "good" or "bad," but it is also extremely important that "all" the costs and benefits of mergers be evaluated if their overall value is to be understood. Weighing the rights of different parties in a changing economic environment poses such difficult problems of analysis that it is important to avoid the additional burden of faulty information. Toward this goal of providing better information about a broad range of issues concerning mergers and acquisitions, the National Bureau of Economic Research launched a project on this subject in 1985. This volume reports the results of much of the research that project has generated.

Much of the empirical research to date on mergers and acquisitions has focused on the financial aspects of takeovers. This research, with its disinterested perspective, has offered a comprehensible version of the story told in the popular business press through the experiences of the managers and investors involved in the takeover process. This is one of the merits of such research. But most citizens are neither economics professors nor CEOs or arbitrageurs, and the common view of the takeover process is a very different, negative one that is dominated by very different issues and concerns. The first two chapters of this volume are devoted to these questions, foremost among which is the impact of takeovers on the employees of acquired companies.

Charles Brown and James L. Medoff consider the impact of acquisitions on the wages and employment of workers in a comprehensive sample of Michigan companies during the years 1979–84. The authors identify three main classes of changes in business control: changes only in the identity of the company's owner ("simple sales"); outright sales of the company's assets ("assets-only sales"); and mergers, by which two preexisting companies form a combined entity. Over the five-year period 16 percent of all workers sampled were touched by one of the three types of transactions, although only 4 percent experienced a merger. Moreover, the average number of employees of the combined entity after merger was only 268 in 1984. These findings remind us that there are many types of potentially disruptive business restructurings besides mergers and acquisitions, and that the typical companies involved are relatively small.

For each of their three samples Brown and Medoff find that wages and employment change in opposite directions around the event of business ownership change, with employment increasing and wages declining in simple sales and mergers and the opposite pattern being observed in the case of assets sales. Perhaps most important for the current debate, however, is the relatively small magnitude of these changes. Among the mergers that occurred in 1981–82, for example, the wages of the combined work force fell by about 4 percent and employment rose by about 2 percent. This is not the stuff of which plant-closing laws are made.

Andrei Shleifer and Lawrence H. Summers argue in their chapter that the large hostile takeovers that have been the subject of much publicity in recent years are of a qualitatively different character than the mergers in the sample studied by Brown and Medoff, and that their effects on labor are likely to be quite different, too.

Shleifer and Summers make two basic points. First, the gains to target shareholders so well documented as occurring at the initiation of a takeover bid (discussed in chapters 5 and 8) need not signal a pure efficiency gain, but may well incorporate a large transfer component from other stakeholders in the firm, such as employees who take pay cuts or suppliers who are forced to renegotiate contracts. Second, hostile takeovers may generate efficiency losses of two types in addition to whatever efficiency gains they achieve through the restructuring of company operations.

The first type is the ex post inefficiency of increased transactions costs incurred in reorganizing the company. The second is the ex ante inefficiency associated with the reduced ability of a firm to participate in long-term implicit contracts with its stakeholders because a raider may violate the contracts if it is in the interest of the shareholders, ex post, to do so. This second type of inefficiency is potentially more serious than the first because of the spillover effects that a single, well-publicized hostile takeover can have on the ability of other firms to effectively commit themselves to honoring implicit contracts. The authors use the acquisitions of Trans World Airlines and Youngstown Sheet and Tube to support their propositions.

A frequent argument against hostile takeovers is that the threat of takeover attempts forces incumbent managers to shorten planning horizons that may already be too short from a social perspective. The logic of this position is that the stock market undervalues long-term projects, particularly research and development, so that firms undertaking such projects in the long-run interests of shareholders will suffer low stock prices and be ripe for takeover attempts. A response to this argument is that the stock market is rationally valuing the shares of firms whose managers are expanding operations by reinvesting the shareholders' money in projects with negative present value. It is difficult to evaluate these alternative views because the payoff to R&D expenditures comes only after many years and is difficult to measure. Nevertheless, the next two chapters do provide insight into this important question.

Examining a sample of all publicly traded U.S. manufacturing corporations acquired between 1976 and 1986, Bronwyn H. Hall considers the role played by R&D activity in the takeover process. Of 603 corporations taken over, 332 were acquired by other U.S. firms, 199 were taken private, and 72 were acquired by foreign parents. In recent years acquisitions have been concentrated in low-technology industries. Hall finds that there is no difference discernible in R&D expenditure levels (relative to firm size) of firms acquired and firms not acquired by public domestic corporations and that firms acquired by foreign or private parents are likely to have lower than average R&D activity. Although parent companies tend to have lower R&D expenditure levels than their targets, there is no evidence of a drop in the combined levels of R&D expenditures after the merger occurs.

Randall Mørck, Andrei Shleifer, and Robert W. Vishny also relate the characteristics of firms to the likelihood of acquisition. Their sample is the 454 publicly traded companies on the Fortune 500 list in 1980. The authors find that 82 of these companies were acquired or taken private between 1981 and 1985, and they classify 40 of these takeovers as hostile and 42 as friendly, based on the way in which the takeover process began. They do find that the companies subject to hostile acquisitions had low ratios of market value to assets, both in absolute terms and relative to other firms in their industries. But these firms had a lower average growth rate and rate of investment than both the sample of all firms and the subsample of firms acquired in friendly transactions. Slow growth is certainly not a characteristic one associates with high R&D expenditures.

Mørck, Shleifer, and Vishny also find that targets acquired in hostile transactions had a lower fraction of equity ownership by the top two officers and a smaller likelihood that a member of the founding family was on the management team than firms not acquired. On the other hand, ownership by the top officers, ownership by the board, and the presence of a founding family member were all much more common in friendly transactions. These findings suggest that firms whose managers' interests are more closely aligned with those of their shareholders are less likely to be the targets of hostile acquisitions.

Whatever their effects on the behavior of corporate managers, hostile takeover attempts have a clear and immediate impact on the well-being of shareholders. Richard S. Ruback presents in his chapter an analysis of 33 failed takeover attempts between 1963 and 1979 of firms listed on the New York and American stock exchanges. Some of these firms were ultimately acquired by other bidders, others were not. Ruback finds that the average gain in share prices associated with initial bids was about 31 percent. (An interesting aspect of this gain is that nearly one third of it accrued during the nine-day period ending a day *before* the public announcement of the takeover bid, indicating a substantial amount of "leakage," as the use of inside information has euphemistically been called.) This percentage is consistent with earlier findings about takeover premia. Ruback also finds, however, that the subsequent announcement of a takeover bid termination results in a loss in share prices averaging 11 percent for the sample as a whole.

Why don't share prices drop by the full amount of the original takeover premia? Two additional pieces of evidence are that, for firms not eventually acquired, the loss with a terminated bid is larger, 17 percent, and that, after the termination announcement, share prices continue to fall over a longer period of time. These findings suggest that one reason for the incomplete drop in share prices upon a termination is that shareholders expect that the firm, once "put in play," may remain so. Firms less likely to do so experience a larger drop in price. Several important questions remain unanswered. First, what fraction of the share price gains are "permanent," that is, not associated with increased residual takeover prospects but perhaps with managerial improvements initiated in response to the initial, unsuccessful bids? Second, does resistance to takeovers increase shareholder wealth, ex ante, by increasing the price of successful bids by a greater proportion than it reduces the likelihood of success? One cannot know by looking only at the "failures."

An argument against takeovers is that they are often tax driven, that the private gains realized by investors may be at the expense of other taxpayers. The Tax Reform Act of 1986 reduced two of the important tax incentives to merge: the ability to use the accumulated tax losses and credits of acquired companies to shield a company's own taxable income; and the opportunity to step up the bases of depreciable assets for tax purposes without paying capital gains taxes. Despite the enactment of this legislation, however, there has been an absence of empirical evidence on the importance of these and other tax benefits in driving merger activity.

In the chapter written by David Reishus and me, we compare a sample of 316 mergers and acquisitions involving large public corporations with a random sample of similar-size companies that did not merge, over the years 1968–83. We find that the average estimated tax benefits from combining were similar in the two samples, which constitutes fairly strong evidence that tax factors were not the major force driving the mergers. Only in cases in which companies with unused tax losses and credits acquired taxable companies (takeovers that were generally unaffected by the provisions of the 1986 act) was there a discernible impact of taxes on merger activity, but the impact was small relative to the aggregate level of mergers. In addition, we did not uncover significant changes in combined debt-equity ratios among the merging firms in our sample, relative to the changes observed in our control sample. This suggests that, at least until the past few years, the tax advantage associated with interest deductibility did not play an important role in fostering takeovers by large public corporations.

Beginning in 1984 a startling phenomenon arose in the U.S. nonfinancial corporate sector. In that year (according to statistics compiled by the Federal Reserve Board), and in 1985 and 1986 as well, net issues of new equity were markedly negative, as share repurchases exceeded new issues by about $80 billion in each year. Those alarmed by this process have called it the "deequitization of America," although the coincident rise in corporate debt-equity ratios over these same years was muted by the rising stock market.

Share repurchases are rising not only because more firms are purchasing their own shares, but also because more purchases of shares in corporate acquisitions are being cash-financed. The growth of these activities in recent years is explored in the chapter by Laurie Simon Bagwell and John B. Shoven. As they discuss, a well-known puzzle is why firms subject their shareholders to ordinary income taxes on dividends when they could use other methods to distribute cash from the corporate sector at favorable capital gains treatment. A possible explanation for cash-financed acquisitions has been the "trapped equity" view stating that firms encounter difficulty repurchasing their own shares and are therefore led to repurchase the shares of other firms instead. Yet some firms do engage in massive purchases of their own equity, and so it is important to understand what leads some firms to do this and others to engage in cash acquisitions.

Bagwell and Shoven analyze repurchase and acquisition behavior in both 1976 and 1984. Among other results, they find that in both years firms with low ratios of market to book value and high ratios of cash flow to assets were more likely than other firms to repurchase their own shares, and that a low market to book ratio is also important in explaining acquisitions. Perhaps most important, however, are their findings that the most important predictor of whether a firm will engage in either activity is whether it did so in the previous year, that having previously engaged in one activity increases the predicted probability of engaging in the other as well, and that the behavioral equations for the 1976 and 1984 samples are not statistically different, even though aggregate behavior changed in the intervening years. Future research must gain a better understanding of the underlying factors causing persistent differences in the behavior of firms that the authors refer to as the "habit formation."

Evidence on the changing use of cash to finance mergers and acquisitions is provided by Julian R. Franks, Robert S. Harris and Colin Mayer, who study a sample of over 2,500 takeovers in the United States and the United Kingdom over the years 1955–85. The cross-national comparison is also valuable because the two countries differ in their tax treatment of cash acquisitions and in other laws regarding takeovers. The authors confirm that the use of cash as a means of payment in U.S. mergers and acquisitions has exhibited a strongly increasing trend over time, but that has not been true in Great Britain. The authors argue that the pattern of cash acquisitions in Britain has not been consistent with the predictions of the "trapped equity" view of cash-financed merger activity, even though that the government's historical prohibition of own-share repurchases makes this view more plausible for Britain than for the United States.

Franks, Harris, and Mayer uncover several interesting patterns in their sample. They find that, in both countries, cash acquisitions carry a higher average premium for target shareholders than do stock acquisitions. This result may be explained by tax or nontax factors. The authors also discover that the shareholders of acquiring U.K. firms generally receive no benefit (or loss) as the result of the acquisition, but that acquiring U.S. shareholders gain in cash acquisitions but lose in stock acquisitions. These findings defy simple explanation, but they raise important questions about the economic motivations of takeover activity.

An even longer historical perspective is offered by Devra L. Golbe and Lawrence J. White, who compare the intensity of merger activity in the 1980s to that in earlier periods of high activity. The authors reject the argument that there have been no merger "waves," but at the same time suggest that the current wave is not large by historical standards. Relative to the size of the economy, the current wave is about as large as that of the late 1960s. A much larger wave of activity emerged between the end of World War I and the Depression, and an even larger one took place around the turn of the century. Unlike the experience during the earliest of these periods, no noticeable change in industrial concentration has accompanied the recent merger waves. From 1963 to 1982, for example, the fractions of value added accounted for by the largest 50, 100, and 200 manufacturing companies were nearly constant. And the results are similar for the private sector as a whole.

Golbe and White attempt to explain the recent peak in merger activity using a variety of hypotheses. They find, however, that the only important explanatory variable for the aggregate level of activity, given the size of the economy, is the value of the stock market relative to book value.

The final contribution to this volume is a panel discussion by economists who have participated in U.S. policymaking in recent years. Leading off the discussion of the implications for the economy of recent policy actions, Joseph A. Grundfest and Gregg Jarrell review the recent insider-trading scandals and speculate about the effects of pending changes in securities regulations. Steven C. Salop explores the rationale of recent antitrust policy, as does Lawrence White, who also looks at the special problems in the banking and thrift industry.

Together the contributions in this volume present many important findings about the causes and consequences of takeovers. Perhaps the most important message they convey is that one should not look for a simple "bottom line" result from a class of transactions that vary so much in their size, method of financing, motivation, overall economic impact, and distributional effects.

1 The Impact of Firm Acquisitions on Labor

Charles Brown and James L. Medoff

1.1 Introduction

The impact of firm acquisitions on the value of both the acquiring and the acquired firm has been the subject of a large and growing body of research (see, for example, Asquith, Bruner, and Mullins 1986; and in this volume, Franks, Harris, and Mayer; Hall; and Ruback). But there are no similar systematic investigations of the impact of corporate acquisitions on labor. A lack of concern about how labor fares in a takeover cannot be the reason for the absence of statistical analysis of this question; indeed, the popular press (and, presumably, its readers) are fascinated by the subject.

The public's perception is conditioned by a relatively small number of highly publicized and extremely hostile takeovers. What comes to mind immediately is the elaborate history of Carl Icahn, Frank Lorenzo, and the airline industry. Also widely covered was the extensive employment loss—estimated at 25,000 jobs—associated with the takeover attempts made on two major food store chains, Safeway Stores and Lucky Stores.

Organized labor has explicitly stated its concern that acquisitions are bad for workers (AFL–CIO 1987, E1):

Charles Brown is professor of economics, Department of Economics, and program director, Survey Research Center, Institute for Social Research, at the University of Michigan, and a research associate of the National Bureau of Economic Research. James L. Medoff is professor of economics at Harvard University and a research associate of the NBER.

The authors are grateful to Judith Connor, Steven Heeringa, John Jackson, and Charles Lake for help with the MESC data; to Judith Connor for skillful programming; and to Marsha Silverberg for research assistance. They also acknowledge helpful suggestions by Geoffrey Carliner and Henry S. Farber, the commentators, and by several other conference participants.

Workers and their unions have a vital interest in the corporate take-over issue. Corporate mergers, takeovers, and leveraged buy-outs often have serious effects on jobs, wages, and working conditions.

The general public exhibits similar concern. A recent survey by Louis Harris and Associates revealed that 58 percent of the sample believes that hostile takeovers do more harm than good. Moreover, when respondents were asked which *one* group they thought ought to be protected most from being hurt in a hostile takeover, 63 percent said "employees" (Louis Harris and Associates, 1987).

Despite these fears, it is not obvious that acquisitions necessarily lower wages and employment. One reason for being skeptical about any widespread injury to workers from acquisitions is the highly unrepresentative set of takeovers that has received the most publicity.

Another reason for skepticism lies in an understanding of the various motives for acquisitions. First, acquisitions may occur because of differences in opinion, with the buyer thinking the acquisition more valuable than the seller. Second, acquisitions may occur because a group outside the firm believes it can manage the firm more efficiently than current management (Jensen 1984). Third, acquisitions may occur because the sale may permit the abrogation of rules governing employment and earnings at smaller costs to employee morale and the firm's reputation (Shleifer and Summers, in this volume).

The first possible reason for an acquisition does not imply impending disaster for labor: to the contrary, if the acquiring optimist is correct, increased prosperity for workers might be just around the corner. The second reason also need not be a harbinger of bad times: better management might lead to more and better jobs. This is particularly true if the new managers have better access to capital markets for expanding the operation. The third reason, however, can be expected to be associated with worse conditions for workers. Although these worse conditions are usually blamed on the acquiring owners or managers, they typically reflect some significant change in market conditions, such as deregulation in the airline industry. Indeed, if the acquisition shocks the workers into accepting changes in work rules, employment and wages could actually be improved by the acquisition.

When the dust settles, does labor win or lose from the typical acquisition? In particular, what happens to wages and employment? In this paper, we address these questions. To do so, we use data on the employment and wages of firms in Michigan compiled from unemployment insurance (ES202) records kept by the Michigan Employment Security Commission. The MESC data file has several useful characteristics: consistent longitudinal data for six and one-half years (1978:III–1984:IV); the inclusion of small firms likely to be absent from other data files; and the identification of acquisitions as part of the bookkeeping needed to run the unemployment insurance (UI) system. Its disadvantages are the result of its being limited to a single state: Michigan is not representative of the entire nation, the data do not reflect what is happening in other locations of multistate companies, and the data chart relatively few of the mega-acquisitions which dominate public attention. The data also do not allow us to distinguish between friendly and hostile takeovers. Hence, our findings apply to acquisitions in general, and not necessarily to hostile takeovers.

In section 1.2 we describe the data in greater detail. Our twin goals here are to specify the issues that arise in distinguishing between mergers and other sorts of acquisitions and to give an overview of the characteristics of firms that were and were not involved in acquisitions in the years in question. In section 1.3 we describe our methods of analysis. Sections 1.4 and 1.5 document our measures of the impact of mergers on wages and employment. In the case of mergers we compare post-merger wages and employment to the wages and employment of the two partners taken together. The longitudinal data provide several years of preacquisition information to serve as a base for the analysis and several years of subsequent data to go beyond the very short-term effects. In general, we find small (and sometimes positive) changes in wages and employment following an acquisition. In section 1.6 we summarize our findings and discuss options for future work.

1.2 The Data

The file of MESC records available at the Institute for Social Research at the University of Michigan includes data on over 200,000 firms over the period 1978:III through 1984:IV.[1] Employment data are calculated monthly, and total payroll (*not UI-taxable payroll*) data are calculated quarterly. As part of the normal bookkeeping of the UI system, MESC identifies situations in which the assets of one firm (a "predecessor") are acquired by another (a "successor"). The file used in this paper does not include predecessors as separate firms, but it includes predecessor employment and payroll prior to the acquisition in separate "predecessor" fields on the successor firm's longitudinal record.[2]

In thinking about the impact of acquisitions on employment and wages, it is important to distinguish among several different types of acquisitions:

1. Firm A changes ownership without being integrated with any other firm;
2. Firm A purchases the assets of firm B without absorbing its work force;
3. Firm A purchases firm B and (at least initially) absorbs (most of) firm B's workers, or firm A and firm B combine to form firm C,

with (at least initially) firm C including (most of) the workers of firms A and B.

The key to distinguishing among these types of acquisitions is the pattern of predecessor (P) and successor (S) employment over time. Let T be the period of the acquisition, the last period in which P is positive. In situation 1 we would observe this pattern:

Month	1	2	...	$T-1$	T	$T+1$	$T+2$	$T+3$	...
Predecessor employment	P_1	P_2	...	P_{T-1}	P_T	0	0	0	...
Successor employment	0	0	...	0	0	S_{T+1}	S_{T+2}	S_{T+3}	...

We might expect $S_{T+1} = P_T$ if the firm's employment was stable. In any case, the pattern of zero employment for the successor through T makes this case easy to distinguish from the others.

In situation 2 we should observe:

Month	1	2	...	$T-1$	T	$T+1$	$T+2$	$T+3$	...
Predecessor employment	P_1	P_2	...	P_{T-1}	P_T	0	0	0	...
Successor employment	S_1	S_2	...	S_{T-1}	S_T	S_{T+1}	S_{T+2}	S_{T+3}	...

Because the successor is acquiring the assets but not the workers of the predecessor, we expect $S_{T+1} \simeq S_T$.

Finally, situation 3—at least mergers of two firms doing business in Michigan—should generate this pattern:[3]

Month	1	2	...	$T-1$	T	$T+1$	$T+2$	$T+3$	...
Predecessor employment	P_1	P_2	...	P_{T-1}	P_T	0	0	0	...
Successor employment	S_1	S_2	...	S_{T-1}	S_T	S_{T+1}	S_{T+2}	S_{T+3}	...

Unless employment is growing or fluctuating significantly, S_{T+1} should approximately equal $P_T + S_T$.

There are three problems in classifying acquisitions with these data. First, we have no information on mergers between in-state and out-of-state firms. When an in-state firm is acquired by an out-of-state firm, there will be no record of the successor prior to the acquisition, and so it will look like a type 1 acquisition. Conversely, when an out-of-state firm is acquired by an in-state firm, there is no record of the merger at all.

The second problem lies in distinguishing between acquisitions in which the successor acquires the predecessor's workers and acquisitions in which the successor does not. The only evidence to distinguish between cases 2 and 3 is whether $S_{T+1} \simeq S_T$, or $S_{T+1} \simeq P_T + S_T$. If P_T and S_T are unstable and/or P_T is small, it will be hard to identify true mergers. To see this, consider this record:

Month	1	2	...	$T-1$	T	$T+1$	$T+2$	$T+3$	...
Predecessor employment	4	3	...	5	4	0	0	0	...
Successor employment	100	101	...	105	107	110	110	110	...

One interpretation is that the two firms merged in month T, creating a firm with 111 employees, all but one of whom was employed in the next month. The other interpretation is that the successor expanded by 3 workers at the same time as it acquired the assets (but not the employees) of the predecessor.

In the tables below we identify as type 3 acquisitions or "mergers" those records that have positive successor employment prior to T and

(a) $\dfrac{S_{T+1} - (S_T + P_T)}{P_T} > -0.50$, or equivalently, $\dfrac{S_{T+1} - S_T}{P_T} > 0.50$

(b) $P_T > 10$

Condition (a) says the successor must grow by at least 50 percent of the predecessor's employment. Condition (b) requires that the predecessor be large enough that condition (a) is practically meaningful.[4] Conditions like these are needed if artificial inflation of the merger count is to be avoided.[5] The particular cutoffs are, to be sure, arbitrary.

A third problem is that the predecessor-successor relationship applies to reorganizations as well as to acquisitions. It is difficult to distinguish reorganizations from type 1 acquisitions (simple sales) because the pattern of predecessor and successor employment would be exactly the same. A "type of business" (for example, proprietorship, partnership, corporation) field is available, however, and we can distinguish cases where the type of business changes. We call cases that otherwise look like simple sales but show a change in the type of business code "reorganizations." The distinction between "simple sales" and "reorganizations" is not as clean as we would like, since some restructuring does not involve a change of business type while some sales are accompanied by such a change.

To summarize, type 1 acquisitions are those for which there is no successor employment prior to T and for which the "type of business" remains the same. Type 2 acquisitions are those for which there is positive successor employment prior to T but which do not satisfy the two conditions (a) and (b) above. Type 3 acquisitions are those for which there is positive successor employment prior to T and which do satisfy those two conditions. We will sometimes refer to types 1, 2, and 3 as "simple sales," "assets-only sales," and "mergers," respectively. We treat "reorganizations" as a separate category, though they are not our primary focus. We ignore those acquisitions that occurred in 1978 or 1984:IV because the predecessor and successor data on them are scant.

Because acquisitions—and especially mergers—are fairly rare events but the MESC file is enormous, we constructed an "extract file" consisting of *all* firms with nonzero predecessor fields and a 20 percent sample of other firms. Most of our analysis, however, is based on a smaller file, consisting of observations that had relatively complete data. More specifically, we included an observation in what we call the "clean-data file" only if there was *some* employment and payroll data in *each* year.

Table 1.1 offers an overview of the extract file and the clean-data file. Two findings shown in the table are striking. First, even remembering that the "no predecessor" cases represent a 20 percent subsample, the relative frequency of "reorganizations" compared to no-predecessor firms over the six years 1979–84 is striking. (We also found the frequency of type 2 (assets only) acquisitions surprisingly high.) The second striking finding in the table is that the clean-data file is so much smaller than the complete extract. There are two reasons for this. First, birth and death rates of firms are quite high, and they show up as "missing" data in the years before a birth or after a death. Connor, Heeringa, and Jackson (1985) note that both births and deaths are very common in these data. We will have a little to say about deaths later in the paper. Second, there are some missing data, although we have somewhat reduced their influence by eliminating only observations for which the data are missing for an entire year.

Table 1.2 divides the extract and clean-data files by broad industry type. The distribution of observations in the two files is quite similar,

Table 1.1   **An Overview of the Extract File and the Clean-Data File**

	Number of Observations in:	
Type of Firm	Complete Extract File	Clean-Data File
No predecessor	34,689	14,005
Type 1 acquisition: simple sale	7,905	4,055
Type 2 acquisition: assets-only sale	3,138	2,391
Type 3 acquisition: merger	479	438
Reorganization	17,578	9,363
1978 or 1984:IV acquisition†	4,155	0
Total	67,944	30,252

†This category also includes a small number of acquisitions for which missing data made it difficult to code the type of acquisition.

Table 1.2   MESC Records, by Industry

Industry Group	Complete Extract File	Number of Observations in: Clean-Data File					
		Total	No Predecessor	Type 1: Simple Sale	Type 2: Assets-Only Sale	Type 3: Merger	Reorganization
Agriculture	1,108	469	236	53	24	2	154
Mining	172	76	34	11	14	1	16
Construction	6,990	2,211	1,272	130	108	12	689
Durable manufacturing	3,782	1,982	1,117	187	156	61	461
Nondurable manufacturing	1,322	735	391	80	74	30	160
Transportation and public utilities	2,034	812	405	101	62	26	218
Wholesale trade	5,229	2,501	1,447	222	324	61	447
Retail trade	20,798	9,473	3,162	1,839	681	130	3,661
Finance, insurance, and real estate	3,916	1,824	971	188	281	31	353
Services	22,593	10,169	4,970	1,244	667	84	3,204
Total	67,944	30,252	14,005	4,055	2,391	438	9,363

Table 1.3   **Average Firm Employment, by Type of Acquisition**

	Average Number of Employees			
	Extract File		Clean-Data File	
Type of Acquisition	1978	1984	1978	1984
No predecessor	22	20	29	27
	(284)	(233)	(350)	(296)
	[21,535]	[23,186]	[14,005]	[14,005]
Type 1 acquisition: simple sale	17	17	21	20
	(114)	(97)	(140)	(110)
	[6,166]	[5,376]	[4,055]	[4,055]
Type 2 acquisition: assets-only sale	114	99	130	109
	(1,672)	(1,082)	(1,813)	(1,142)
	[2,815]	[2,665]	[2,391]	[2,391]
Type 3 acquisition: merger	255	262	264	268
	(740)	(708)	(758)	(717)
	[462]	[451]	[438]	[438]
Reorganization	9	10	10	11
	(65)	(61)	(74)	(72)
	[12,814]	[13,194]	[9,363]	[9,363]

Note: Standard deviations are in parentheses and sample sizes in brackets below the means.

with the clean-data file having proportionately fewer construction firms and more manufacturing firms than the extract file from which it was derived. The three types of acquisitions are also spread broadly across industries.

Table 1.3 shows the average level of employment in the firms in the two files, categorized by the type of acquisition. Our employment variable includes the employment of both partners in cases where an acquisition occurred. The mean value for 1978 excludes those cases in the extract file where employment in 1978 was zero (missing); the mean value for 1984 similarly excludes observations with zero (missing) 1984 employment.

A comparison between the mean levels of employment in the extract file and in the clean-data file shows that average firm size is larger in the latter. This is exactly what one would expect, because births and deaths are more common among small firms than among large ones. Comparing the number of firms and the mean employment by type of acquisition brings out an important but less obvious fact. Although the average size of firms in type 1 acquisitions is small (17 workers, in the 1984 figures from the extract file), there are many such firms. Type 2 firms are larger, but there are proportionately fewer of them. Type 3 acquisitions (mergers) involve still larger firms, and here there are far fewer of them. Overall, the 1984 data from the extract file show there were roughly 85,000 workers employed in firms involved in type 1 acquisitions; 265,000 workers in type 2 acquisitions; and 115,000 workers in type 3 acquisitions (mergers). After taking account of the fact that the no-predecessor firms in table 1.3 are a 20 percent sample, we calculate that roughly 3, 9, and 4 percent, respectively, of workers in Michigan worked for firms involved in the three types of acquisitions in this period.

Finally, table 1.4 presents information about employment levels at the predecessor and successor firms, measured three months before the acquisition, and at the combined entity one month afterward. Three conclusions stand out. First, the predecessors in type 1 and type 2 acquisitions are small (averaging 20 workers and 11 workers, respectively), while the acquired firms in type 3 acquisitions (mergers) are on average medium-size (78 workers). Second, as one might expect, the successor (acquiring) firms are typically larger than the predecessors. Third, on average type 2 successors do not grow ($S_{T+1} - S_T = -2$), despite having acquired the assets of predecessors with an average of 11 workers, whereas type 3 successors grow by nearly all the employment at the acquired firm ($S_{T+1} - S_T = 79$; $P_T = 78$). In part, this last contrast follows from the definition of type 2 and type 3 acquisitions, but it is sharper than one might have guessed on purely definitional grounds.

1.3 Method of Analysis

To assess the relationship between changes in ownership and changes in wages and employment, we will compare firms involved in acquisitions in year T with the much larger set of firms that were not involved

Table 1.4   **Average Employment at Predecessors and Successors**

	Average Employment		
Type of Acquisition	P_{T-3}	S_{T-3}	S_{T+1}
Type 1 acquisition: simple sale	20 (126)	—	21 (120)
Type 2 acquisition: assets-only sale	11 (57)	107 (970)	105 (931)
Type 3 acquisition: merger	78 (169)	199 (707)	278 (781)
Reorganization	10 (65)	—	11 (71)

Note: Standard deviations are in parentheses below means.

in any acquisitions (that is, that had zero predecessor employment) throughout the sample period.[6] Our wage equation is:

$$(1) \quad \ln W_{T+j} = \sum_{t=1978}^{B} \alpha_{jt} \ln E_t + \sum_{t=1978}^{B} \beta_{jt} \ln W_t + \sum_{k=1}^{4} \gamma_{jk} D_k + \epsilon_j,$$

where W is the payroll per worker (per month); E is employment (averaged over all months where positive employment is reported); B is a "base year" either one or two years prior to T; and D_k is a dummy variable that equals one when the firm is involved in a type k acquisition ($k = 1,2,3$) or reorganization ($k = 4$) in year T, and zero otherwise. Not shown explicitly in equation (1) are one-digit industry dummy variables, which are added to each equation. For each acquisition year T, separate equations are estimated for each year $T + j$, for $j = 0$ through $T + j = 1984$ (for example, for $T = 1981$ we have four equations, one for each of the years 1981–84).

Our employment equation is slightly more complicated:

$$(2) \quad E_{T+j} = \sum_{t=1978}^{B} \alpha'_{jt} E_t + \sum_{t=1978}^{B} \beta'_{jt} \ln W_t + \sum_{k=1}^{4} \gamma'_{jk} D_k \bar{E} + \epsilon'_j$$

where $\bar{E}$ is the firm's average employment in the years prior to the merger. Interacting D_k with $\bar{E}$ means that the impact of the various types of acquisitions is proportional to the premerger level of employment rather than being a fixed number of workers for all firm sizes.[7] We weight the observations to produce a homoskedastic error term.[8] We use E rather than $\ln E$ as our dependent variable because it allows us to consider (in section 1.5) the impact of adding to the clean-data sample those firms that appear to have "died" after year T, by treating them as having $E_{T+j} = 0$.

The ideas underlying these equations are borrowed from the literature that evaluates the impact of employment-training programs on individuals' earnings and employment (see, for example, Bloch 1979). Holding constant the history of the firm prior to T, we ask whether firms involved in changes of ownership had significantly different wages (or employment) j years thereafter.[9]

Using $T - 1$ as the base year is the natural choice in our framework. The choice of year $T - 2$ is motivated by the possibility that firms involved in mergers in year T were subject to unusual transitory shocks in the previous year, from which they would anyway recover. Using $T - 2$ as the base year ignores those shocks in predicting outcomes in $T + j$ and so essentially treats the $T - 1$ shock as transitory (Ashenfelter 1978).

In the results reported in the next section we study (separately) firms involved in acquisitions in 1981 and in 1982. These middle-of-the-sample years were chosen to ensure several years of data after T (to evaluate the consequences of acquisitions) and several years before T (to control accurately for prior conditions). In each case our "control group" consists of the firms not involved in an acquisition at *any* point between 1978 and 1984; we exclude altogether those firms that were involved in acquisitions in one of the other years.

1.4 Wage Equations

The key results from estimating equation (1) for $T = 1981$ are presented in table 1.5. The top half of the table uses 1980 as the base year, while the bottom half uses 1979. Each column of the table represents the predicted employment for the year shown. Only the coefficients of the four dummy variables are reported, although each set of four coefficients comes from a (separate) equation with lagged wages and employment and the industry dummy variables included.

Table 1.5   **Average-Wage Equations for the 1981 Acquisitions**

Control Variable	Base Year	Acquisition Variable†	Proportional Effect on Average Wage in:				
			1980	1981	1982	1983	1984
ln W_{-78} . . . ln W_{-80}	1980	D_1 (SS)		−.029	−.031	−.039	−.055
ln E_{-78} . . . ln E_{-80}				(.009)	(.012)	(.014)	(.015)
		D_2 (AO)		.012	.061	.048	.032
				(.012)	(.016)	(.017)	(.019)
		D_3 (M)		−.015	−.041	−.035	−.083
				(.029)	(.037)	(.041)	(.046)
		D_4 (R)		.051	.170	.164	.162
				(.007)	(.009)	(.009)	(.011)
ln W_{-78} ln W_{-79}	1979	D_1 (SS)	−.020	−.045	−.046	−.054	−.069
ln E_{-78} ln E_{-79}			(.009)	(.011)	(.014)	(.015)	(.016)
		D_2 (AO)	−.000	.014	.065	.053	.037
			(.012)	(.014)	(.017)	(.019)	(.020)
		D_3 (M)	−.028	−.030	−.051	−.044	−.089
			(.027)	(.034)	(.041)	(.044)	(.049)
		D_4 (R)	.005	.054	.174	.167	.165
			(.006)	(.008)	(.010)	(.010)	(.011)

Note: Standard errors are in parentheses.
†SS = simple sale; AO = assets-only sale; M = merger; R = reorganization.

The choice of base year makes little difference to the results, and so our discussion will focus on the equations with 1980 as the base year. In the three years after the acquisition (1982–84), wages at firms involved in type 1 (simple sale) acquisitions averaged about 4 percent lower than one would otherwise predict from their pre-1981 wages and employment. Similarly, wages were about 5 percent higher in firms involved in type 2 (assets-only) acquisitions. Firms involved in mergers had wages about 5 percent lower than we estimate they otherwise would be. But in contrast to the previous coefficients, the standard errors of these estimates are sizable. It is worth emphasizing that these last results refer to the average wages in the postmerger firm, controlling for the (weighted average of) premerger wages at both the predecessor and the successor.[10]

Analogous results for the 1982 acquisitions are presented in table 1.6. Although the "control groups" in tables 1.5 and 1.6 are the same, the firms involved in acquisitions are completely different, so that table 1.6 is a nearly independent replication of the previous table. The most important difference is that the coefficient of D_3 is now tiny (averaging −1.5 percent for 1983 and 1984).

We also reestimated equation (1), restricting the sample to firms employing at least 50 workers. Overall, the coefficients were similar

Table 1.6   **Average-Wage Equations for the 1982 Acquisitions**

Control Variables	Base Year	Acquisition Variable	Proportional Effect on Average Wage in:			
			1981	1982	1983	1984
ln $W_{\cdot78}$ . . . ln $W_{\cdot81}$	1981	D_1 (SS)		−.035	−.053	−.049
ln $E_{\cdot78}$ . . . ln $E_{\cdot81}$				(.010)	(.012)	(.014)
		D_2 (AO)		.001	.042	.049
				(.012)	(.016)	(.018)
		D_3 (M)		.005	−.005	−.025
				(.028)	(.035)	(.041)
		D_4 (R)		.034	.114	.112
				(.007)	(.009)	(.011)
ln $W_{\cdot78}$ . . . ln $W_{\cdot80}$	1980	D_1 (SS)	−.011	−.043	−.061	−.056
ln $E_{\cdot78}$ . . . ln $E_{\cdot80}$			(.009)	(.012)	(.013)	(.015)
		D_2 (AO)	.005	.009	.049	.058
			(.011)	(.015)	(.017)	(.019)
		D_3 (M)	−.034	−.011	−.016	−.031
			(.026)	(.033)	(.038)	(.043)
		D_4 (R)	−.012	.026	.108	.106
			(.007)	(.009)	(.010)	(.011)

to those in tables 1.5 and 1.6 but somewhat smaller. They averaged
−1, 0, and −2 percent for type 1, 2, and 3 acquisitions, respectively.
We conclude, therefore, that the impact of acquisitions on wages in
our sample is small.

1.5   Employment Equations

The results of estimating equation (2) for $T = 1981$ are summarized
in table 1.7. Once again, the choice of base year—1980 (top half of
table) or 1979 (bottom half)—has little effect on the results, and we
therefore focus on the coefficients from the 1980 base-year equations.

Firms experiencing a simple sale in 1981 had employment in 1982–
84 about 3 percent higher than one would otherwise have predicted.
Those involved in assets-only acquisitions had employment about 5
percent lower than would be expected. The employment at firms that
merged was indistinguishably different from what we estimate it would
have been in the absence of the merger.

Analogous results for the 1982 acquisitions appear in table 1.8. Unfortunately, there are appreciable differences between the coefficients
in table 1.8 and those in table 1.7. The effect of a simple sale is now
15 percent (rather than 3 percent), and the effects of the other two

Table 1.7   Employment Equations for the 1981 Acquisitions

Control Variables	Base Year	Acquisition Variable	Proportional Effect on Employment in:				
			1980	1981	1982	1983	1984
$\ln E_{\cdot78} \ldots \ln E_{\cdot80}$ $\ln W_{\cdot78} \ldots \ln W_{\cdot80}$	1980	D_1 (SS)		.028 (.008)	.026 (.011)	.041 (.014)	.039 (.019)
		D_2 (AO)		.017 (.006)	−.024 (.008)	−.048 (.010)	−.073 (.014)
		D_3 (M)		.037 (.007)	.036 (.011)	−.019 (.013)	−.020 (.017)
		D_4 (R)		−.011 (.010)	−.010 (.014)	−.060 (.018)	−.092 (.024)
$\ln E_{\cdot78} \ln E_{\cdot79}$ $\ln W_{\cdot78} \ln W_{\cdot79}$	1979	D_1 (SS)	−.004 (.009)	.012 (.013)	.016 (.015)	.032 (.017)	.021 (.022)
		D_2 (AO)	−.003 (.007)	.022 (.009)	−.017 (.011)	−.041 (.013)	−.065 (.016)
		D_3 (M)	.014 (.008)	.054 (.012)	.051 (.014)	−.007 (.015)	−.005 (.020)
		D_4 (R)	−.063 (.012)	−.065 (.015)	−.075 (.019)	−.124 (.022)	−.143 (.027)

types of acquisitions are also a bit larger (-6 percent and 3 percent, respectively) when one averages over the two postacquisition years (1983 and 1984). Moreover, the merger effects (the coefficients of D_3) are sensitive to the choice of a base year, reaching 8 percent when 1980 rather than 1981 is the base.

This instability across years—and the fact that the results were also sensitive to whether we specified the equation as logarithmic, linear, or (as in tables 1.7 and 1.8) weighted linear—makes us less confident about these results than about the wage results in tables 1.5 and 1.6. Averaging across base years and across the two tables, the three employment effects are roughly 9 percent (simple sales), -5 percent (assets only), and 2 percent (mergers).

As noted in section 1.2, our results use a sample of firms that reported wages and employment in each year. Thus, firms are deleted if they "were born" or "died" during the sample period or if for some reason a whole year's data were missing. To explore the consequences of deleting "deaths" from the sample, we considered a slightly different sample-inclusion criterion. We reran our analysis of employment at firms involved in acquisitions in 1981 (table 1.7), including firms that reported zero employment in 1982 or 1983 through 1984 (in other words, firms that disappeared for at least two years after 1981 and did not

Table 1.8   **Employment Equations for the 1982 Acquisitions**

Control Variable	Base Year	Acquisition Variable	Proportional Effect on Employment in:			
			1981	1982	1983	1984
$\ln E_{\cdot 78} \ldots \ln E_{\cdot 81}$	1981	D_1 (SS)		.067	.142	.156
$\ln W_{\cdot 78} \ldots \ln W_{\cdot 81}$				(.008)	(.010)	(.013)
		D_2 (AO)		.056	$-.061$	$-.067$
				(.005)	(.007)	(.008)
		D_3 (M)		.007	.046	.015
				(.007)	(.009)	(.011)
		D_4 (R)		$-.078$	$-.128$	$-.174$
				(.009)	(.012)	(.016)
$\ln E_{\cdot 78} \ldots \ln E_{\cdot 80}$	1980	D_1 (SS)	.010	.077	.157	.163
$\ln W_{\cdot 78} \ldots \ln W_{\cdot 80}$			(.006)	(.011)	(.013)	(.017)
		D_2 (AO)	.009	.082	$-.045$	$-.057$
			(.004)	(.007)	(.008)	(.010)
		D_3 (M)	.029	.051	.094	.071
			(.005)	(.009)	(.011)	(.013)
		D_4 (R)	.024	$-.073$	$-.119$	$-.141$
			(.008)	(.013)	(.016)	(.020)

reappear). Even though this loosening increased the sample considerably (from about 17,000 to about 20,000), the coefficients of our acquisition dummy variables did not change appreciably. The largest change was for D_3, whose coefficient moved from zero (averaging 1982–84, top half of table 1.7) to 3 percent with the expanded sample.

1.6 Conclusions

Based on our analysis of the MESC data, we find that firms that are part of "simple sales" have postsale wages about 5 percent lower than they would otherwise be, but employment roughly 9 percent higher. Firms that are part of "assets only" acquisitions[11] have wages about 5 percent higher than they would otherwise be, but employment about 5 percent lower. Mergers are associated with wage declines of about 4 percent and employment growth of about 2 percent.

Two qualifications are in order in viewing these results. First, as we noted in section 1.5, the estimated employment effects are sensitive to which year's acquisitions we study, and to other specification details. Second, our wage measure is the average payroll per worker, and it will therefore deviate from a more ideal wage measure if composition of the work force is changing. In particular, if (as is usually the case) newly hired workers earn less than others in the firm, our wage changes will tend to be negatively related to employment changes. The fact that the effect of each type of acquisition on wages is opposite in sign from its effect on employment is consistent with this interpretation. The estimated effects of mergers on wages are also subject to a different composition effect. If the (relatively high paid) head of the acquired firm leaves following the merger, average wages will fall. Given the small size of our typical firms, a nontrivial share of our estimated wage decline from mergers may be due to such compositional effects.

At this early stage of our research, is difficult to be certain whether these patterns are consequences or merely correlates of the acquisitions. But, at least in our sample, the common public perception that acquisitions provide the occasion to slash wages and employment finds little support.

Notes

1. For a description of the construction, characteristics, and availability of this file, see Connor, Converse, Heeringa, and Jackson (1984).

2. Predecessor data are aggregated in the relatively rare case of multiple predecessors. Thus, if firm A acquires firm B and later firm C, the predecessor

field on A's record includes the sum of B and C's employment and payroll up to the time when B is acquired, and then only C's employment and payroll until C is acquired. After C is acquired, succeeding months' (quarters') employment (payroll) data are blank.

3. If the two firms form a new firm, which firm is called the successor is, for our purposes, arbitrary.

4. In scanning the raw data, we noticed that in some cases P fell and S rose just before P became zero. If P in month T was less than half of its value three months earlier, we used P and S in month $T - 3$ instead of month T in the above tests. This led to a slight increase in the number of type 3 cases and a corresponding reduction in the number of type 2 cases.

5. Even with the relatively conservative definition of type 3 acquisitions and therefore relatively broad definition of type 2 acquisitions, 20 percent of the type 2 firms in the clean-data file had S_{T+1} exactly equal to S_T, and another 20 percent had S_{T+1} less than S_T. The phenomenon of acquiring the assets but not the workers of the predecessor appears, therefore, to be real.

6. To simplify notation, we suppress a subscript for individual firms, but our unit of observation is, of course, firms.

7. We estimated the unweighted equation and then regressed the absolute error on a constant term and premerger employment. We found that both coefficients were consistently positive, suggesting that the error variance increased, but less than proportionately, with the size of the firm.

8. We also interacted the industry dummy variables with $\bar{E}$.

9. One could, of course, hold constant employment and wages through year $T + j - 1$ in the equation with year $T + j$ as the dependent variable, but that significantly complicates the interpretation of the results. With that specification, the impact of, say, D_k on $\ln W_{T+1}$ would depend on the coefficient of D_k in that year's equation *plus* the indirect effects of D_k on $\ln W_T$ times the effect of $\ln W_T$ on $\ln W_{T+1}$ and of D_k on $\ln E_T$ times the effect of $\ln E_T$ on $\ln W_{T+1}$.

10. One might expect that wages at the postmerger firm would move toward the wages at the premerger successor, since the successor has acquired the predecessor. We added a term reflecting the difference in ln-wages between predecessor and successor to the equation (1) specification, but it was never significant. Basically, we cannot tell whether our conjecture is true because of the limited number of mergers in the data.

11. Recall that this category includes mergers involving tiny predecessors, as well as cases in which the predecessor's work force is not acquired.

References

American Federation of Labor and Congress of Industrial Organizations (AFL–CIO). 1987. "Statement" before House Government Operations Subcommittee on Employment and Housing, in *Daily Labor Report*, 1 April, E1–E2.

Ashenfelter, Orley. 1978. Estimating the effect of training programs on earnings. *Review of Economics and Statistics* 60, no. 1, 47–57.

Asquith, Paul, Robert Bruner, and David Mullins, Jr. 1986. Merger returns and the form of financing, photocopy. Boston: Harvard University, October.

Bloch, Farrell E. 1979. *Evaluating manpower training programs.* Greenwich, Conn.: JAI Press.

Connor, Judith, Muriel Converse, Steven Heeringa, and John Jackson. 1984. The Michigan Employment Security Commission longitudinal database of Michigan businesses.'' Ann Arbor: Institute for Social Research, University of Michigan.

Connor, Judith, Steven Heeringa, and John Jackson. 1985. Measuring and understanding economic change in Michigan. Ann Arbor: Institute for Social Research, University of Michigan.

Franks, Julian R., Robert S. Harris, and Colin Mayer. 1988. Means of payment in takeovers: Results for the United States and the United Kingdom. In this volume.

Louis Harris and Associates. 1987. A study of the attitudes of the American people and top business executives toward corporate takeovers, mimeo. Chapel Hill: University of North Carolina Institute for Private Enterprise.

Jensen, Michael C. Takeovers: Folklore and science. *Harvard Business Review* 85 (November–December 1984): 109–21.

Ruback, Richard S. 1988. Do target shareholders lose in unsuccessful control contests? In this volume.

Comment   Geoffrey Carliner

Brown and Medoff have directed their attention to the market for corporate control of very small firms. The other papers in this volume, and all the controversy surrounding mergers and acquisitions in other media, focus on very large and visible corporations with thousands of employees and price tags in nine figures. Brown and Medoff's study is therefore useful in reminding us that a substantial fraction of the work force is employed by small firms, among which the only hostile takeovers are fights among brothers and sisters over who should run the family business.

As the authors note, the market for ownership of small firms is highly turbulent. According to their data for 1978, 129,932 private sector firms in Michigan were included in the unemployment insurance system, with a total employment of 3.029 million workers (see table 1).[1] By 1984 only 86,272 of these firms were still contributing to Michigan's unemployment insurance system. The remaining 43,660 firms had

Geoffrey Carliner is executive director of the National Bureau of Economic Research.

1. Unfortunately, all of Brown and Medoff's tables report data for a 20 percent sample of firms with no change in ownership and for the entire population of firms that changed hands. Thus, it is impossible to know the number of characteristics of all the firms in Michigan directly from their tables.

Table 1

	Number of Firms			Number of Employees (thousands)			
	All Firms		Surviving Firms	All Firms		Surviving Firms	
	1978	1984	1978–84	1978	1984	1978	1984
No predecessor	107,675	115,930	70,025	2,369	2,319	2,031	1,891
Reorganization	12,814	13,194	9,363	115	132	94	103
Transfer in ownership	9,443	8,492	6,884	545	473	512	459
Type 1	6,166	5,376	4,055	105	91	85	81
Type 2	2,815	2,665	2,391	321	264	311	261
Type 3	462	451	438	119	118	116	117
Total	129,932	137,616	86,272	3,029	2,924	2,637	2,453

Source: Brown and Medoff, table 1.3.

presumably gone out of existence. In addition, 6,884 of the surviving firms experienced type 1, 2, or 3 changes in ownership during this period, according to the authors' data.

Although the firms that disappeared tended to be small, the number of workers affected was not small. Total employment in all firms in Michigan in 1978 was 3.029 million. The firms still in existence in 1984 had 2.637 million employees in 1978. Thus 392,000 employees, or 13 percent of Michigan's private sector employees in 1978, worked for firms that had disappeared by 1984, and an additional 545,000 employees, or 18 percent of all 1978 employees, worked for firms that later changed ownership.[2]

In the regression results shown in tables 1.5–1.8, Brown and Medoff restrict their sample to firms with data for all seven years, that is, the surviving firms. They recognize, however, that omitting firms that die within a few years may distort their estimates of the effect of ownership transfers on wages and employment. They therefore also ran their employment regressions for a sample including the firms that subsequently disappeared.

2. On top of this loss of jobs, total employment fell in the firms that did survive, from 2.637 million to 2.453 million. The increased employment among new firms of 471 thousand (2.924 − 2.453) did not offset the declines from these two sources, and so on net total employment in Michigan fell during this period.

Changes in Employment, 1978–84 (in thousands)

Firm deaths	2,637 − 3,029 = −392
Change in firm size	2,453 − 2,637 = −184
Firm births	2,924 − 2,453 = 471
Total change	2,924 − 3,029 = −105

A priori, I would have expected firms that change hands to fail more often than other firms, at least for the small stores and service firms that constitute two-thirds of Brown and Medoff's observations. A firm owned by a new, presumably less experienced, owner seems more likely to disappear than an otherwise similar firm that does not change hands, and so I expected the regressions on the full sample to have a smaller coefficient for type 1 firms (simple change in ownership). Brown and Medoff's finding of a 3 percent to 15 percent increase in employment for type 1 firms, even when corporate deaths are included in the regression, is quite surprising.

I also question their estimate that workers in type 3 firms (mergers) experienced wage declines of up to 5 percent. Their calculations of the number of firms and workers involved in transfers of ownership is seriously understated, and it may bias their regression results. As Brown and Medoff recognize, they observe only transfers that occurred between firms in Michigan, since their data source has no information on mergers or acquisitions between Michigan firms and out-of-state firms. For instance, General Motors' acquisition of EDS and Hughes Aircraft would probably not be recorded in their data. Since most Fortune 500 firms are continually buying and selling small firms, Brown and Medoff fail to include a large number of employees who should be counted as working for type 3 firms.

One indication of the size of this problem is the estimate of average firm size. As calculated from their table 1.3, the average number of employees per firm in Michigan in 1984 was 21. In contrast, national data from the Current Population Survey indicate that 56 percent of private sector employees work for firms with 100 or more employees, and 42 percent are with firms that have 500 or more employees.[3] It is very unlikely that firms in Michigan are so much smaller than firms in other states. The likely explanation of this difference is that the Michigan data exclude out-of-state employment. Only the Michigan employees of large firms show up in the data used by Brown and Medoff.

The effect of omitting firms with out-of-state mergers is probably to overstate the effect of mergers on the wages and employment of the acquiring firm. When GM buys a small auto parts maker in Illinois, the effect on the number and wages of its employees in Michigan is likely to be negligible. By Brown and Medoff's definitions, however, GM and its Michigan employees should be counted as a type 3 change in ownership in this case.

---

3. The U.S. Small Business Administration (1986, 229). The U.S. data are for private sector wage and salary employees excluding agricultural and private household workers. About 2 percent of the Michigan firms were agricultural.

In conclusion, I think that the type of analysis presented by Brown and Medoff will lead to a deeper understanding of an ignored aspect of labor market dynamics. Economists have examined longitudinal data on individuals for many years now, and as a result we know a great deal more about the effects of individual characteristics on labor force participation, retirement, and unemployment. Until recently we have had panel data only for the largest corporations, and so we have not been able to study the behavior of small firms over time. Studies like this one will offer important insights into the ways in which industries grow and contract. They have little to do, however, with the hostile takeovers and other ownership changes among large firms that are the subject of the other chapters in this volume.

Reference

U.S. Small Business Administration. 1986. *The state of small business*. Washington, D.C.: GPO.

Comment   Henry S. Farber

Given the public and professional perception of mergers and acquisitions as involving one Goliath joining or swallowing another, the analysis presented by Brown and Medoff serves as a refreshing reminder that the modal merger or acquisition actually involves two Davids rather than two Goliaths. When viewed in this context, the popular image of a corporate raider taking over a large and probably unionized company, abrogating or renegotiating existing implicit or explicit labor contracts, and reducing both wages and employment seems to be less applicable than one might have thought.

Brown and Medoff conclude from their analysis of data from the Michigan unemployment insurance system administrative records that there are only small and sometimes positive changes in wages and employment on average following a merger or acquisition. Although the analysis is straightforward and the authors are candid about its limitations, a few points bear closer examination.

The central limitation of the data is that it deals exclusively with employment in Michigan. The implications of this go substantially beyond the usual caveat that Michigan may be different from other states. In particular, many firms have business operations that span state

Henry S. Farber is professor of economics at the Massachusetts Institute of Technology and a research associate of the National Bureau of Economic Research.

boundaries, so that looking strictly at Michigan employment is likely to give a misleading picture of both the employment size distribution of firms involved in mergers and acquisitions and the employment effects of mergers and acquisitions. This point is obviously more important for larger firms because they are more likely to have operations that cross state boundaries.

This limitation of the data interacts in a serious way with the central classification scheme used by Brown and Medoff. They break mergers and acquisitions into three categories that are potentially affected by examining only Michigan employment. For example, simple sales (type 1 events) are said to occur when the successor firm has no prior *Michigan* employment. But an out-of-state firm with substantial employment could acquire a Michigan firm in what is really a merger with or acquisition by a previously existing firm.

More generally, the authors' classification scheme is not entirely satisfactory, as they recognize. Aside from the caveat noted in the previous paragraph, the classification of simple sales seems straightforward. Nevertheless, the distinction between "assets-only" acquisitions and mergers that retain the workers is less convincing. Since an important part of what Brown and Medoff are interested in is the employment effect of a merger or acquisition, using employment changes to classify the event does not seem appropriate. This classification scheme leads to problems later when the authors investigate the employment effects of the three types of acquisitions. It is not surprising that they find type 2 (assets-only) mergers and acquisitions have small negative employment effects. The effects were defined not to have positive employment changes. Similarly, it is not surprising that type 3 (assets and work forces) mergers and acquisitions have positive employment effects. The effects here were defined not to have negative employment changes.

The method of analysis is quite straightforward. Both the wage and the employment level equations are estimated conditional on past wage and employment levels, and dummy variables are included for each of the three types of events. The coefficients of these dummy variables are interpreted as the effects of each of the events on wages and employment. With regard to wage changes, this analysis is not bad. The finding that average wages drop by 3 to 5 percent after simple sales is interesting, and it would be considered by some to be substantial. The finding that wages seem to be 3 to 5 percent higher after type 2 mergers and acquisitions is interesting, but it cannot get at what happens to the wages of the acquired workers precisely because type 2 mergers and acquisitions are defined as cases in which there are no acquired workers. The mixed results, though with predominantly negative point estimates obtained for the type 3 mergers and acquisitions, when combined with the consistently significantly negative wage effects found for simple sales, serve as evidence that *acquired* workers receive lower wages after a merger or acquisition. Whether the magnitudes involved are large or small is a matter of judgment.

With regard to employment levels, the analysis is less convincing. This is largely because the classification system obscures the true effect of mergers and acquisitions. The interesting question is how prevalent the negative employment effects are relative to the positive employment effects. The method of constructing the data almost guarantees that type 2 mergers and acquisitions will have nonpositive employment changes, while type 3 mergers and acquisitions will have nonnegative employment changes. Econometrically, the dummy variables are defined in a way that ensures their correlation with the dependent variable and hence with the error term in the regression. It might be more useful *not* to make a distinction between type 2 and type 3 mergers and acquisitions.

If no distinction were made between the two types, the coefficient of the "non–simple sale" dummy variable might be a useful summary statistic for the employment effects of these events. On the basis of the numbers presented, a very crude estimate of the overall employment effect can be derived as a weighted average of the estimated effects for each type of event. By the data in table 1.3, type 2 mergers and acquisitions account for approximately 70 percent of the employment in the two types of mergers and acquisitions in total. Using the results in table 1.7, I assume an average employment effect of type 2 mergers and acquisitions of $-.04$ and an average employment effect of type 3 mergers and acquisitions of $+.04$. Weighting these by .7 and .3, respectively, yields an admittedly crude overall effect of $.7(-.04) + .3(.04) = -0.016$. Of course, this calculation does not account for any systematic bias in the estimates in table 1.7 induced by the endogenous categorization scheme, but it does suggest that the average employment effects are close to zero.

One useful modification of the analysis would be to estimate the wage and employment equations as straightforward differences, rather than as levels equations with lagged dependent variables. This alteration would make interpreting the results very easy, and an additional column in table 1.4 with average proportional changes in employment between $T - 3$ and $T + 1$ would serve as a useful summary of the employment effects. A table similar to table 1.4 for wages could also be constructed.

Overall, Brown and Medoff present some fascinating facts, although I wish they had presented simpler summary statistics and frequency distributions for their data. I find the analysis of wage changes to be fairly convincing, and we have the interesting finding that wages do indeed drop on average after mergers or acquisitions. The analysis of employment changes is less convincing. The distinction between type 2 and type 3 events is artificial, and it serves only to confuse the empirical analysis. In addition, the exclusion of non-Michigan employment must add considerable noise to the employment change analysis.

A final comment concerns the relevance of the authors' analysis to the general debate on the causes and effects of mergers and acquisitions. Obviously, the debate has focused on the very large events. Brown and Medoff's sample is very heavily weighted toward much smaller events. On this basis their analysis and the general debate are on different planes. Nonetheless, although the authors may have little to say about Carl Icahn and compatriots directly, the phenomenon they do address is important, and their study is a useful contribution to our limited stock of knowledge of the smaller acquisitions.

2 Breach of Trust in Hostile Takeovers

Andrei Shleifer and Lawrence H. Summers

2.1 Introduction

Corporate restructurings through hostile takeover, merger, or management buyout are wealth enhancing in the sense that the combined market value of the acquiring and the acquired companies usually rises. Many economists, notably Jensen (1984), have argued that the large premia received by corporate shareholders derive from the improved management and increased efficiency brought about by restructurings. These economists point to the increase in market value created by takeovers as evidence of the magnitude of these efficiency gains. And they suggest that the effect on market value serve as a touchstone for evaluating the social desirability of various tactics for launching and defending against hostile takeovers. Jensen (1984) captured this view by stating:

> Positive stock price changes indicate a rise in the profitability of the merged companies. Furthermore, because evidence indicates it does not come from the acquisition of market power, this increased profitability must come from the company's improved productivity.

Many business leaders and some academic commentators (Drucker 1986; Lowenstein 1985; Law 1986) have dissented sharply from this

Andrei Shleifer is assistant professor of finance and business economics at the Graduate School of Business, University of Chicago, and a faculty research fellow at the National Bureau of Economic Research. Lawrence H. Summers is professor of economics at Harvard University and a research associate of the NBER.

The authors are indebted to Oliver Hart, Benjamin Hermalin, James Hines, Barry Nalebuff, Robert W. Vishny, Oliver E. Williamson, and especially Bengt Holmstrom and Michael C. Jensen for helpful comments, and to the Seaver Institute for financial support. Their help does not constitute an endorsement of the views expressed in this paper.

view, arguing that takeovers create private value by capturing rents but create little or no social value. Their argument is that shareholder gains come from the exploitation of financial market misvaluations, from the use of tax benefits, and from rent expropriation from workers, suppliers, and other corporate stakeholders. The dissenters suggest that the disruption costs of at least some hostile takeovers may well exceed their social benefits.

This chapter examines theoretically and empirically the elements of truth in the claims that improved management and redistributed wealth are the sources of takeover premia. We show how hostile takeovers can be privately beneficial and take place even when they are not socially desirable. Our argument does not invoke tax, financial markets, or monopoly power considerations.

Instead, we start with the insight of Coase (1937) and Fama and Jensen (1983) that corporations represent a nexus of contracts, some implicit, between shareholders and stakeholders. As argued by Williamson (1985), many institutions are designed to minimize the problems associated with opportunistic behavior where contracts are implicit. We argue that hostile takeovers facilitate opportunistic behavior at the expense of stakeholders. In this way hostile takeovers enable shareholders to transfer wealth from stakeholders to themselves more so than to create wealth. The available empirical evidence suggests that the redistributions associated with takeovers can be large and that perhaps some inefficiencies result as well. It is then incorrect to gauge the efficiency gains from takeovers by looking at event study measures of increases in shareholder wealth.

The chapter is organized as follows. Section 2.2 distinguishes between the value-creating and value-redistributing effects of hostile takeovers and argues that the latter are likely to be of dominant importance. The succeeding three sections treat three questions central to the argument that takeover gains come largely from breaching implicit contracts. First, what is the value to shareholders of being able to enter into implicit contracts with stakeholders? Second, how does trust support these implicit contracts? Third, how can hostile takeovers breach this trust and thus enable shareholders to realize the gains from default on stakeholder claims? Having described the role of breach of trust and wealth redistributions in hostile takeovers, we turn to a more systematic examination of their welfare properties in section 2.6. Section 2.7 then examines some empirical evidence shedding light on this theory of takeovers, and section 2.8 presents our conclusions.

2.2 Value Creation and Value Redistribution

Consider three scenarios. In scenario A, T. Boone Pickens takes over Plateau Petroleum and immediately lays off 10,000 workers, who immediately find work elsewhere at the same wage. Pickens also stops purchasing from numerous suppliers, who find that they can sell their output without any price reduction to other customers. The stock of Plateau Petroleum rises by 25 percent.

In scenario B Frank Lorenzo takes over Direction Airlines and immediately stares down the union so that the wages of the existing workers are reduced by 30 percent and 10 percent of the work force is laid off and unable to find subsequent employment at more than 50 percent of their previous wage. Lorenzo does not change the airline's route structure or flight frequency. The stock of Direction Airlines rises by 25 percent.

In scenario C Carl Icahn takes over USZ. He closes down the corporate headquarters and lays off thousands of highly paid, senior employees, who had previously been promised lifetime employment by the now-displaced managers. Icahn also shuts down factories that dominate the economies of several small towns. As a consequence numerous local stores, restaurants, and bars go bankrupt. The stock of USZ goes up by 25 percent.

All three takeovers yield equal private benefits to the shareholders of the target firms. Yet their social consequences are very different. In scenario A society is better off because resources are diverted from less productive to more productive uses. The increased value of Plateau Petroleum approximately reflects the value of this gain. In Scenario B society is about equally well off. The gains to Direction shareholders are approximately offset by the losses to the human wealth of Direction employees. The redistribution is probably antiegalitarian. On the other hand, it may ultimately lead to advantages for customers of the airline. In Scenario C society is worse off. The gains to USZ shareholders are offset by the losses incurred by the laid-off employees and by the firms with immobile capital whose viability depended on the factories' remaining open. And other firms find that once their workers see what happened at USZ, they become less loyal and require higher wages to compensate them for a reduction in their perceived security. These firms also have a harder time inducing their suppliers to make fixed investments on their behalf.

These three examples make it clear that increases in share values in hostile takeovers in no way measure or demonstrate their social benefits. Scenario A is the only one in which share price increases capture the elimination of waste and the gains in social welfare. In contrast, shareholder gains in scenarios B and C to a large extent come from losses of the value of employees' human capital. Even if some efficiency is realized from wages' coming more into line with marginal products, the efficiency is only a second order effect relative to the transfer from employees to shareholders. Scenario C has additional external effects of the acquisition which, while not resulting in gains to the acquirer, should enter the social calculation. The claim that the 25 percent take-over premium in scenarios B and C measures social gains is simply incorrect.

In the remainder of the chapter we develop issues raised by scenarios B and C. Why are there implicit contracts it pays to breach? Why are raiders willing but incumbents unwilling to breach implicit contracts? What are the transfers accompanying such a breach? What are the social costs of the breach of implicit contracts? Before taking up these questions, however, we must stress an a priori consideration suggesting that scenarios B and C have much more to do with observed takeover premia than does scenario A.

Consider a rather stylized firm that has a capital stock worth $100, hires 14 workers at $5 a year, purchases $20 worth of materials, and has sales of $100 a year. Its profits are $10 a year and its cost of capital is .10, and so its market value will be $100. The ratios of market value, earnings, and payroll are roughly accurate as representations of typical firms in the U.S. economy. Imagine that the firm is in steady state. Suppose the firm, because of an excess of free cash flow, starts to invest excessively rather than keeping its capital stock constant, to the point that it invests half its profits in projects with a present value of .5. If the market expects this practice to continue indefinitely, the firm's value will fall by 25 percent. Eliminating this rather disastrous policy of excessive reinvestment in terrible projects could presumably pro-duce a takeover gain of about 25 percent.

Now suppose that the firm invests rationally but, because of agency problems involving management's greater loyalty to the employees than to the shareholders, overpays the work force by 5 percent. To put this figure in perspective, note that unions typically raise labor costs by about 15 percent and that firms in the same industry in the same city typically pay wages to workers in the same detailed occupational category that differ by 50 percent or more (Krueger and Summers 1987). This overpayment to labor, if expected to endure, will reduce profits by $3.50 a year, leading to a reduction in market value of 35 percent. To the extent that the cash flows obtainable by cutting wages are safer than the firm's profit stream, this figure is an underestimate.

The point of these examples is simple. Since firms' labor costs far exceed their profits and since even poor capital investments yield some returns, very small differences in firms' success in extracting rents from workers and other corporate stakeholders are likely to be much more important in determining market value than the differences in corporate waste associated with differences in firms' volume of rein-vestment. An intermediate case is provided by changes in the level of employment. Here the reduction in payroll is likely to be offset by some loss of product, so that it is more difficult to raise value by increasing efficiency in this way. Moreover, some rent extraction is involved since the appropriate opportunity cost for laid-off labor is likely to be less than its wage.

These considerations suggest that takeovers that limit managerial discretion increase the acquired firm's market value primarily by redistributing wealth from corporate stakeholders to share owners. To this extent, the existence and magnitude of takeover premia is not probative regarding the social costs and benefits of takeovers. Rather, the social valuation of hostile takeovers must turn on the impact of these redistributions on economic efficiency, which will obviously vary from case to case.

In this chapter we focus on one particular efficiency aspect of hostile takeovers that captures the concerns of many observers, namely, their impact on the ability of firms to contract efficiently. Our motivation is twofold. First, we show that the arguments of those who see hostile takeovers as destructions of valuable "corporate cultures" are coherent. Second, and much more tentatively, we suggest that the reputational externalities associated with hostile takeovers may in fact have extremely serious allocative consequences.

2.3   The Value of Implicit Contracts

A corporation is a nexus of long-term contracts between shareholders and stakeholders. Because the future contingencies are hard to describe, complete contracting is costly. As a result, many of these contracts are implicit, and the corporation must be trusted to deliver on the implicit contracts even without enforcement by courts. To the extent that long-term contracts reduce costs, such trustworthiness is a valuable asset of the corporation. Shareholders own this asset and are therefore able to hire stakeholders using implicit long-term contracts.

The principal reason why long-term contracts between shareholders and stakeholders are needed is to promote relationship-specific capital investments by the stakeholders (Williamson 1985). An employee will spend time and effort to learn how to do his job well only if he knows that his increased productivity will be subsequently rewarded. A subcontractor exploring for oil will buy site-specific new equipment only if he believes that the contracting oil firm will not try to squeeze his profits once he sinks the cost. A sales representative will service past customers only if she is assured she will continue to benefit from their loyalty. In these and other cases it is important to the shareholders that the stakeholders do a good job, but shareholders may be unable to describe what specific actions this calls for, let alone to contract for them.

The necessary arrangement to ensure appropriate investment by stakeholders is a long-term contract, which allows them to collect some of the rewards of doing good work over time.[1] The expense of writing a complete contingent contract ensures that these long-term contracts are implicit. Examples of such contracts are hiring an oil exploration company for the long haul, so that it acquires the equipment best suited for the long-term customer; lifetime employment for workers who then learn how to do the job efficiently; and surrender of customer lists to sales representatives who can then profit from repeated purchases (Grossman and Hart 1986).

Even when no capital investments are required, long-term contracts can be used to elicit effort (Lazear 1979) or risk sharing (Harris and Holmstrom 1982) on the part of the contractor. Although these long-term contracts are usually thought of as covering managers or employees, they also commonly apply to customers and suppliers. The contracts are beneficial both to stakeholders and to shareholders, as they split the ex ante gains from trade. Shareholders in particular benefit because no easy alternative arrangements would ensure that stakeholders do a good job.

2.4   The Importance of Trust

Although both shareholders and stakeholders benefit ex ante from implicit long-term contracts, ex post it might pay shareholders to renege. For example, it will pay shareholders to fire old workers whose wage exceeds their marginal product in a contract that, for incentive reasons, underpaid them when they were young. Or shareholders might profit from getting rid of workers whom they insured against uncertain ability and who turned out to be inept. Or shareholders might gain from refusing to compensate a supplier for investing in the buyer-specific plant, after this plant is built. Or an insurance company can repossess its sales representative's customer list. In all these cases implicit contracts specify actions that ex post reduce the firm's value, even though agreeing to these actions is ex ante value maximizing. Breach of contract can therefore raise shareholder wealth, and the more so the greater is the burden of fulfilling past implicit contracts. Conversely, the value of workers' human capital or of suppliers' relationship-specific capital stock suffers a loss.

To take advantage of implicit contracts, shareholders must be trusted by potential stakeholders. Otherwise, stakeholders would expect breach whenever it raises the firm's value and would never enter into implicit contracts. To convince stakeholders that implicit contracts are good, shareholders must be trusted not to breach contracts even when it is value maximizing to do so.

A standard solution to the problem of how implicit contracts are maintained is the theory of rational reputation formation, described most notably by Kreps (1984). In this theory managers adhere to implicit contracts because their adherence enables them to develop a reputation for trustworthiness, and thus to benefit from future implicit contracts. If violating an implicit contract today would make the managers untrustworthy in the future, they will uphold the contract as long as the option of entering into future contracts is valuable enough. Conversely, if it is not important for the managers to be trusted in the future, that is, if a reputation is not valuable, they will violate the implicit contract. Formally, a rational reputation is modeled as a small probability that the manager is irrationally honest, sustained by honest behavior on the part of the manager.

The position that the sole reason to trust a manager (or anyone else for that matter) is his reputation is not plausible. People commonly trust other people even when no long-term reputations are at stake. Most people do not steal not only because they fear punishment, but because they are simply honest. Those who leave their cars unlocked do so relying more on other people's integrity than on police powers. Waiters rely on their expectation that most people tip in restaurants even when they expect never to come back. In fact, evidence shows that travellers' tips are no smaller than those of patrons (Kahneman, Knetch, and Thaler 1986). Even more striking is the fact that people believe a garage mechanic is as likely to cheat a tourist as a regular customer, thus defying the importance of reputation (Kahneman, Knetch, and Thaler 1986).

As do the rest of us, managers often fail to take advantage of others they deal with simply because it would violate an implicit trust. One example in which such trust appears to us more germane to managerial behavior than pursuit of a rational reputation is pensions. First, a large part of the retirees' benefits often takes the form of medical and insurance benefits that are not explicitly contracted for and are not protected by the Employee Retirement Income Security Act (ERISA; Congressional Information Service 1985). Pensioners obviously count on the employer to provide them with these benefits without explicit contracts. In the case of pension benefits themselves, most defined benefit pension plans raised the payments to their beneficiaries after the inflation of the late 1970s even though they were *not* under contract to do so (Allen, Clark, and Sumner 1984).[2] Moreover, the stock market recognizes that such increases are forthcoming and does not regard excess pension fund assets to be the property of shareholders. When firms remove excess assets from their pension funds, the market greets the news with a share price increase (Alderson and Chen 1986). The market expects that managers do what employees trust them to do.

To dispel the fear of breach on the part of stakeholders, shareholders find it value maximizing to *seek out* or *train* individuals who are capable of commitment to stakeholders, *elevate* them to management, and *entrench* them. To such managers, stakeholder claims, once agreed to, are prior to shareholder claims. Even when a rational reputation is not of high enough value to shareholders to uphold the implicit contracts with stakeholders, as would be the case if the company suffered a large permanent decline in demand, trustworthy managers will still respect stakeholder claims. From the ex ante viewpoint, such dedication to stakeholders might be a value-maximizing managerial *attribute* (not choice!). In a world without takeovers, potential stakeholders counting on such managers to respect their claims will enter into contracts with the firm.

How, then, can shareholders appoint as managers individuals whom stakeholders can trust? It is probably most likely that prospective managers are trained or brought up to be committed to stakeholders. In a family enterprise, for example, offspring could be raised to believe in the company's paternalism toward all the parties involved in its operation. Alternatively, a person who spends 20 or 30 years with a company before becoming a CEO will have spent all that time being helped by the stakeholders in his ascent, and he therefore becomes committed to them. These are examples in which managers pass through a "loyalty filter," using Akerlof's (1983) phrase, before reaching the top. Having done so, they find stakeholder welfare has now entered their preferences, thus making them credible upholders of implicit contracts.[3] Whatever the exact mechanism, it is essential to see that shareholders *deliberately choose* as managers individuals for whom value maximization is subordinate to satisfaction of stakeholder claims, and then surrender to them control over the firm's contracts.

This characterization of managers has an interesting connection with Kreps's (1984) theory of rational reputation. In that theory the world is inhabited by a minor fraction of randomly located trustworthy individuals, and stakeholders start out with the view that there is a small chance that the manager of the firm is of this irrational type. This small chance nonetheless suffices to entice the stakeholders to enter into the implicit contract. By mimicking the behavior of the irrationally trustworthy individual, the rational manager maintains the stakeholders' anticipation that he might be trustworthy, thereby ensuring their agreement to the implicit contract. In contrast to this theory our argument says that shareholders actually locate (or train) the truly trustworthy people and install them as managers because it is ex ante value maximizing to do so.

It is natural to ask why shareholders appoint these truly trustworthy people, rather than the deceptive ones who just pretend to be trustworthy (as in Kreps 1984), but then maximize value when push comes to shove. The primary answer is that trustworthiness is correlated with other personal characteristics and actions, ones that shareholders and stakeholders can learn about. With the wealth of information at hand, genuinely trustworthy people can be selected. Managers who are trusted per se can enter into more efficient contracts than those who must rely on their reputation. Alternatively, Akerlof (1983) argues that it is so costly to learn to be deceptive that one might as well not be. Lastly, CEOs by the time they come to power have a long public record of conduct vis-à-vis commitments. There are no lifetime moles.

2.5   Breach of Trust in Hostile Takeovers

In some circumstances upholding the implicit contracts with stakeholders becomes a liability to shareholders. The incumbent managers are nonetheless committed to upholding stakeholder claims. In these cases ousting the managers is a prerequisite to realizing the gains from the breach. This is precisely what hostile takeovers can accomplish. As the incumbent managers are removed after the takeover, control reverts to the bidder, who is not committed to upholding the implicit contracts with stakeholders. Shareholders can then renege on the contracts and expropriate rents from the stakeholders. The resulting wealth gains show up as the takeover premia. Hostile takeovers thus enable shareholders to redistribute wealth from stakeholders to themselves.

Managers committed to upholding stakeholder claims will not concede to the redistribution. They will resist it, even though the shareholders at this point will withdraw their support from the managers to realize the ex post gain.[4] Not surprisingly, then, takeovers that transfer wealth from stakeholders to shareholders must be hostile.

The importance of transfers in justifying the takeover premium does not imply that breach of implicit contracts is always the actual takeover motive. Breach can be the motive, as for example is the case in some takeovers explicitly aiming to cut wages. At other times the acquisition is motivated by the overinvestment or other free cash flows of the targeted firm. Even in these takeovers much of the gain must come from reducing the wealth of stakeholders, who did not count on changes in operations when agreeing to work for the firm. Take, for example, a railroad whose management invests in upgrading and extending the tracks when this investment has a negative net present value. The management's goal is to provide jobs for railroad employees and other stakeholders who count on continuation of the business. When a hostile acquisitor cuts off these investments, the shareholders gain. To a large extent, however, the gains come at the expense of the employees' employment and wage losses.

For breach to be an important source of gains, hostile takeovers must come as a surprise to stakeholders, who entered into implicit contracts expecting the firm to be run by trustworthy managers. For if the stakeholders anticipate a hostile takeover, they will realize the trustworthiness of the incumbent managers is worthless, since they will be duly removed when shareholder interest so demands. Implicit contracts based on trust are feasible only insofar as the managers upholding them are entrenched enough to retain their jobs in the face of a hostile threat.

The elements of the story now fall into place. In a world without takeovers, shareholders hire or train trustworthy managers, who on their behalf enter into implicit contracts with the stakeholders. Subsequently, some or many of these contracts become a liability to shareholders, who cannot default on them without replacing the incumbent managers. Managers are hard to replace internally because to a large extent they control the board of directors, their own compensation scheme, and the proxy voting mechanism (Shleifer and Vishny 1988b). This failure of internal controls may in fact be in shareholders' ex ante interest, since it may be the only way to assure commitment by shareholders to stakeholders in the absence of takeovers.

Hostile takeovers are external means of removing managers who uphold stakeholder claims. Takeovers then allow shareholders to appropriate stakeholders' ex post rents in the implicit contracts. The gains are split between the shareholders of the acquired and the acquiring firms. At least in part, therefore, the gains are wealth redistributing and not wealth creating.

2.6 Welfare Analysis

As described in section 2.2, contract breach accompanying takeovers allows for a redistribution of rents from stakeholders to shareholders. To some extent takeovers in this case are rent-seeking and not value-creating exercises, with investment bankers' fees and management time representing wasted resources. If this is the scenario capturing reality, then shareholder wealth gains in takeovers are not an appropriate measure of value gains. Even if the combined value of the acquired and the acquiring firms rises as a result of a merger, at least part of value increase is offset by stakeholder wealth losses.

Thus, even if there are some efficiency gains from a takeover, they may pale by comparison with the transfers of wealth. Consider the case of disciplinary takeovers, in which target managers who are failing to run their firm to maximize its value are forcibly removed. Following an acquisition of this type, the buyer usually cuts wages, lays off many employees, raises leverage, eliminates executive perquisites, and in general significantly tightens operations. Because these changes increase profitability, hostile takeovers designed to eliminate a firm's free cash flows are taken as paradigmatic cases of efficiency-improving transactions.

Although there probably are some efficiency gains in such takeovers, it is also the case that employees and suppliers lose a great deal of their previous rents with the firm. Much of the shareholder gains in this case are stakeholder losses. The argument is similar to that for eliminating monopoly in a market. Although there is an efficiency gain equal to the Harberger triangle, by far the biggest impact of going from monopoly to competition is a transfer of rents from profit owners to consumers. Just as it is inappropriate to measure the efficiency gains from eliminating monopoly by the trapezoid under the demand curve, it is incorrect to measure efficiency gains from removing incompetent managers by shareholder wealth gains. And just as it would be inappropriate to gauge the benefit of banning monopoly by the willingness of consumers to pay for the ban, it is wrong to measure efficiency gains from takeovers by share price increases on the announcement of the deal.

In some disciplinary takeovers the transfers from stakeholders can also lead to significant welfare losses that mediate against welfare gains. As we show below, the transfers can lead to ex post inefficient resource allocation if efficient contracting is impaired in the postbreach environment. In addition, by limiting the scope for contracting, takeovers can reduce ex ante welfare.

2.6.1 Ex Post Efficiency

So far we have shown only that the transfer component of a shareholder wealth increase should not be counted as value creating (scenario B) and that such transfers can be large relative to the total shareholder gain. Breach can in addition entail efficiency losses. In some cases, when the acquirer and the stakeholders renegotiate after the breach, they are unable to do so efficiently. As the following examples show, the magnitude of the efficiency losses depends on whether the conditions needed for the Coase theorem to hold obtain in the postbreach environment. If they do hold, breach is just a transfer; if they do not, it entails some ex post inefficiencies.

Consider, first, an example of asymmetric information between the buyer and the employees of the acquired firm. To be specific, suppose Carl Icahn takes over Trans World Airlines and breaches the agreement that its flight attendants be paid $15 per hour. Let the marginal product of these experienced flight attendants, who have made an investment in their TWA jobs, be $10, but let this be known to Icahn only. Let these flight attendants' opportunity wage at the outside be $5, which is also the cost and the marginal product of their replacements at TWA. As long as Icahn pays the existing flight attendants below $10, he can make money. Unfortunately, the flight attendants do not know that their productivity is $10, and they might insist on a higher wage. If no agreement is reached in this situation of asymmetric information, the flight attendants quit and go to work elsewhere at $5, and gains from trade are not realized.

Note that the Icahn takeover has two implications. First, shareholders regain the extra $5 they were overpaying flight attendants under the old regime, which is just a transfer. Second, however, because of asymmetric information in the ex post contracting environment, the takeover entailed a misallocation of resources as the TWA-specific capital of flight attendants went to waste. The second problem is not unique to takeovers; it occurs in many environments with asymmetric information. But takeovers can exacerbate this inefficiency by moving negotiations into the environment of less trust and greater informational asymmetries.

The second reason for the failure of the Coase theorem that can lead to the inefficiency in the ex post contracting environment is the free rider problem. Suppose that in Bartersville, Oklahoma, the residents earn some rents from the presence of Phillips Petroleum in their town, perhaps because it distributes charity there or indirectly subsidizes some businesses. If Boone Pickens takes Phillips over, he will recapture those rents, perhaps by moving out. It is possible that Bartersville residents would choose to pay him to stay, but doing so would require a collective action they might not be able to mount. This again leads to an ex post efficiency loss in addition to a transfer from Bartersville residents—who are Phillips stakeholders—to the shareholders.

Both of these examples are manifestations of ex post inefficiencies accompanying takeovers. The source of these inefficiencies is the failure of the Coase theorem in the ex post environment, that is, gains from trade are not realized. Although takeovers are not responsible for this failure of the Coase theorem, they are responsible for creating the environment in which it is likely to fail.

The implications of these welfare losses for share price behavior are ambiguous, since the price depends on how much is lost by shareholders and how much by stakeholders. What is unambiguous, however, is that, in general, these welfare losses will not be taken into account by looking at the change in value of the acquirer and the target. We already see, therefore, two sources of miscalculation: Transfers from stakeholders cannot be counted as value creating; and the combined value changes do not reflect the part of efficiency losses not borne by shareholders.

2.6.2   Ex Ante Efficiency

The discussion has so far been concerned solely with the ex post consequences of unanticipated takeovers. To this end, we assumed that people contracted as if takeovers never took place, and then we traced the distributional and efficiency consequences of breach. In fact, it seems quite plausible that hostile takeovers and the attendant opportunities for breach of implicit contracts came as a surprise to many U.S. workers and managers.

Although the ex post analysis is the one that sheds light on the interpretation of event studies, it leaves open the question of contracting in the environment where takeovers do occur. This is the question of the ex ante welfare implications of breach of trust through takeovers, which we take up next.

If potential stakeholders believe that their contracts will surely be violated whenever they collect more from the firm than they put in, they will not agree to implicit contracts. Potential suppliers will not invest in relationship-specific capital, the young will shirk if they expect no raise in the future, and firms will be unable to reduce labor costs by offering insurance against uncertain ability to their workers. Even if breach via takeover is not a certainty but only a possibility, the opportunities for long-term contracting will be limited. To the extent that realizing gains from trade requires such contracting, these gains will remain unrealized and ex ante welfare will be reduced.

A common example of a postacquisition change is the consolidation of headquarters, which usually results in dismissal of a number of highly paid employees of the acquired firm. This change can be viewed as a reduction in the acquired firm's corporate slack, since large corporate headquarters represent on-the-job consumption of top executives. But the closing of headquarters can also be viewed as a breach of contract with the long-term employees who work there, even when those employees do not produce much. An idle employee at corporate headquarters could be there to get his career-end reward for previous service to the company or his consolation payment for having lost the tournament for the top job. In either case the employee is costing the company more than he is contributing at the moment, and therefore his dismissal is a gain to the shareholders. It nonetheless might have been in the shareholders' interest to use an implicit long-term contract to attract this employee ex ante and to entice him to work hard or to participate in the tournament. In line with this interpretation, those fired after an acquisition often talk about broken promises (Owen 1986) and claim they will never again trust a large corporation.

These considerations raise the important issue of the scope of fear of breach. That is, if some firms are taken over, how severely will this limit contracting opportunities at other firms? The spread of fear that implicit contracts are worthless is an example of reputational externalities (Zeckhauser 1986) in that it concerns the extent to which events in some firms affect expectations in others. The larger the fear of takeovers spreading through the economy, the more severe are the limitations on contracting, and the larger is the welfare loss.

As we said at the start of this section, the ability to enter into implicit contracts and to be trusted to abide by them may be one of the most valuable assets owned by shareholders. Takeovers may substantially reduce the value of these assets. In the popular literature this phenomenon has been called the decline of corporate loyalty, which is widely cited as a cost to firms. This cost can show up in explicit costly contracts with stakeholders (such as labor protection provisions, or LPPs), or in the need to pay them more now in return for their accepting uncertainty about future payments, or simply as forgone profitable trade. Whatever form this cost takes, it should *ultimately* show in the declining value of corporate equity.

In summary, this section attempted to describe how shareholders can benefit in takeovers by defaulting on their implicit obligations to the stakeholders. In the situation of incomplete contracts or incomplete markets, it is incorrect to equate changes in shareholder wealth with value created in takeovers. Even taking ex post efficiency as the welfare index, a change in shareholders' wealth includes redistributions from stakeholders and ignores efficiency losses that are not paid for by the shareholders. Looking at shareholder wealth also completely ignores the ex ante welfare costs of ex post opportunism, which could be very large.[5]

2.7 Empirical Evidence

In evaluating the importance of transfers from stakeholders to shareholders, we always compare them to efficiency gains, whose significance has been emphasized in much of the literature (for example, Jensen and Ruback 1983). We proceed in four steps. First, we show that the presence of large redistributions is consistent with established statistical generalizations about takeovers. Second, we study a special case—Carl Icahn's takeover of TWA—to determine how much of the takeover premium can be accounted for by the expropriation of rents from corporate stakeholders. Third, we look at the effects of a takeover of Youngstown Sheet and Tube on the welfare of stakeholders whose losses were not captured by the shareholders, namely, the members of the local community. Last, we present some anecdotal evidence on the consequences of takeovers for employee morale.

2.7.1 Basic Facts

In this section we note that the stylized facts of takeovers are consistent both with the prevalence of efficiency gains and with the prevalence of transfers of wealth. In reviewing the evidence, we return to calling the first case scenario A and the second scenario B or C.

Our theory clearly explains the takeover premia since some portion of stakeholder wealth is transferred to shareholders. More subtly, it explains why most of the wealth gains accrue to the acquired firm's shareholders. If it takes little skill to break implicit contracts, the market for corporate control is essentially a common values auction. In such a competitive auction all the gains accrue to the seller, namely, the target's shareholders.

Managers would resist takeovers both if the gains come purely from eliminating their incompetence, as in scenario A, and if they come from transfers from stakeholders, as in scenarios B and C. In the former case poor managers are reluctant to be exposed and lose control. In the case of breach managers are reluctant to let stakeholders' claims be ignored. This is confirmed especially by the common incidence of managers negotiating severance provisions for employees even after they know that the takeover will occur (Commons 1985). The existence of golden parachutes suggests that the managers do not forget themselves, as stakeholders, either.

Patterns of reorganization following a takeover can also be understood using either scenario A or scenarios B and C. Either efficient cost cutting or breach can justify employee dismissals, plant closings, project curtailment, divestments, and subcontractor removals. To see whether the parties that lose association with the acquired firm suffer wealth losses, one must trace their subsequent employment. This is necessary, but not sufficient, to establish breach, and it is hard to do empirically. Otherwise such separations could be efficient, as in scenario A (Jensen 1984).

One striking fact militating in favor of the importance of wealth transfers as opposed to pure efficiency gains is that a significant fraction of hostile acquisitions are initiated and executed by only a few raiders. It is hard to believe that Carl Icahn has a comparative advantage in running simultaneously a railcar leasing company (ACF), an airline (TWA) and a textile mill (Dan River). It is more plausible that his comparative advantage is tough bargaining and a willingness to transfer value away from those who expect to have it. In fact, those who describe him (including he himself) point to this as his special skill. The industrial diversity of many raiders' holdings suggests that their particular skill is value redistribution rather than value creation.[6] It is not at all surprising, in this context, that many of these raiders have hardly any employees of their own.

It is important to emphasize at this point that our discussion of efficiency gains and of transfers concerns *hostile* takeovers. As stressed by Mørck, Shleifer, and Vishny in this volume, these are disciplinary acquisitions designed to change the operations of the firm. They should be contrasted with synergistic acquisitions, which are usually friendly and motivated by market power, diversification, or tax considerations. Mørck, Shleifer, and Vishny show that the two types of deals are targeted at very different companies and hence should not be treated as examples of the same economic process.

The study by Brown and Medoff in this volume reveals how important this distinction can be. The authors look at a sample of several hundred acquisitions of small Michigan companies and find that employment and wages rise after the sale of a firm. Because the companies in their sample are so small, it seems plain that the sample is one of friendly mergers, ones that presumably serve as a means of expansion by the buyer. In fact, we doubt that they have any hostile deals in their sample at all. Our arguments for breach do not then apply to their results and vice versa. In this and other instances it would be a serious conceptual mistake to use the data on friendly acquisitions to interpret theories of hostile takeovers.

A significant problem for virtually any theory of hostile takeovers that we know is posed by acquisitions by "white knights." These are companies that top the hostile offer and merge with the target in a friendly combination, often retaining the management. How can white knights pay more and at the same time forgo management improvement or contract breach? We suspect that white knights are not as friendly as they appear. For example, after a "friendly" rescue of CBS by Lawrence Tisch (who did not even buy the company to gain control), he dismissed hundreds of employees, sold several divisions, and instituted many cost-containment reforms. Even white knights have a shade of grey.

2.7.2 Case Study: Carl Icahn and TWA

Carl Icahn's takeover of TWA in 1985 has attracted enough attention and commentary to provide us with sufficient data to assess stakeholder losses. In particular, Icahn's gain of control was accompanied by changes in compensation for members of the three major unions at TWA. By looking at changes in the wages and benefits of TWA's workers, we can gauge stakeholder losses. At the same time, we acknowledge from the start that the case of TWA does not strictly fit our model. Wages for union members at TWA were determined under governmental regulation. The pre-Icahn management had not been successful (or competent) in renegotiating wages; for a variety of reasons TWA had bad labor relations. It is, therefore, not the case that TWA management resisted the acquisition to avoid a breach of contract. All the evidence suggests that the managers wanted to keep their jobs and resisted acquisition for that reason. Nonetheless, the main observation of this paper—that takeover premia are often paid for by stakeholders—is much more general than the particular model of managerial behavior we develop.

Before Icahn began investing in TWA on the open market, its 33 million shares traded at $8. Icahn eventually bought 40 percent of the airline through open market purchases and the rest through a (hotly contested) tender offer. Although his cost per share on the open market varied from $8 to $24, the offer was completed at $24 per share. At most, then, Icahn's premium was $500 million. There is evidence, however, that he bought 20 percent of the stock at an average price of $12 and another 20 percent at the average price of $16 to $18. Icahn's overall average price therefore was $20, putting the premium in the range between $300 million and $400 million. This figure is consistent with estimates made in the popular press (*Fortune, Business Week, "Takeover"*).

TWA's three major unions represented its pilots, flight attendants, and machinists. Contracts signed between the pilots and Icahn basically prohibited significant trimming down of TWA operations and, in particular, pilot layoffs or significant airplane sales. In fact, leases on three Boeing 747s were not renewed, and one was sold. There were also some, though not major, layoffs at TWA's St. Louis headquarters. Most of the action by far came from wage reductions for the "production" workers, calculated below.

Before Icahn took control TWA paid its 3,000 pilots an average salary of $90,000 per year, including benefits. The agreement with Icahn cut this around 30 percent, for an annual savings of approximately $100 million (Fortune, *"Takeover"*). The company employed about 9,000 machinists at an average cost of $38,000. They agreed to a 15 percent cut, saving TWA around $50 million per year. The story with flight attendants is more complicated, since no agreement was reached. On average, a TWA flight attendant made $35,000 a year. Some of the attendants (around 2,500 out of 6,000 within 3 months) were replaced by rookies paid an average of $18,000 per year. This is essentially a transfer of wealth from the existing flight attendants, who could presumably take entry-level jobs, to Icahn. In fact, some of them accepted wage cuts, and it appears that, over time, most who did not were replaced. Assuming conservatively that the average saving was $10,000 per flight attendant, the total annual saving adds up to $60 million. Since TWA's operating losses assured it a tax free status, these labor cost savings should be counted before tax.

This brief analysis indicates that the average annual transfer from TWA's unionized employees amounted to at least $200 million under Icahn.[7] Since TWA was a very risky investment (and Icahn was not diversified), the appropriate discount rate for these savings could be as high as 25 percent. This yields a present value for the transfer of $800 million. In return for these wage concessions, employees received a profit share and an ownership stake in TWA, which together amounted to about one-third of the company. Immediately after the takeover, market value of these shares was under $200 million, which reduces the value of the transfer from unions to $600 million. By these very conservative estimates, then, the transfer from members of the three unions to Icahn amounted to one and a half times the takeover premium.

It is hard to gauge the efficiency consequences of Icahn's acquisition. There appears to be a consensus that the previous TWA management was awful. If the airline went bankrupt, some of the valuable assets of TWA (such as its name and goodwill) might have lost value, which is a social cost. Moreover, TWA can probably make better investment decisions now than in the past, since its labor costs more accurately reflect shadow prices. On the other hand, some inefficiencies might have resulted from the replacement of well-trained flight attendants by rookies. In addition, large time costs of Icahn and others as well as large transaction costs were incurred. Overall, we suspect efficiency has been gained. This is not the main point, though. The point is that at least one and a half times the premium can be explained by transfers, which in this case were an *explicit* part of the justification for the acquisition. Shareholders gained primarily because stakeholders lost.

2.7.3 Case Study: Youngstown Sheet and Tube

Not all of the stakeholder losses in hostile takeovers are gains to shareholders. Losses in stakeholder wealth can also lead to numerous externalities and losses by third parties that are not captured by shareholders. Consider, for example, a company town in which spending by the employees of the company is a large source of demand in local stores. Those stores might simply be unable to cover their fixed costs if employees of the company are laid off and dramatically reduce their spending. The specific investments these merchants have made in their businesses yield no payoff in this case, and as a result potentially productive capital becomes worthless. This is a case of a social loss and not of a redistribution, since merchants' losses are not captured by shareholders.

An example of community distress following a takeover is the case of the acquisition of Youngstown Sheet and Tube (YST) by Lykes Steamship Company in 1970, and the subsequent acquisition of the latter by LTV Steel in 1979. Between 1977 and 1979 over 6,000 YST employees were layed off. One result of those layoffs, reported by the Youngstown Area Chamber of Commerce (1983), has been a second tier increase in unemployment from businesses' losing their sales to YST employees. Perhaps even more telling are statistics on bankruptcies in Youngstown, which rose from 769 in 1977 to 1,000 in 1979 and 1,948 in 1981. Although YST was only one of two or three Youngstown area steel mills laying off employees, the effect of the layoffs on other businesses in the area has been large and protracted. Interestingly, when by 1982 other firms had begun moving into the Youngstown area and hiring the unemployed local labor, they did so at much lower wages, contrary to scenario A (Youngstown Area Chamber of Commerce 1983).

Perhaps the most telling evidence on the social loss borne by the Youngstown community after the layoffs at YST and other steel mills comes from sale prices of used homes (U.S. Department of Housing and Urban Development 1968–85). Between 1968 and 1980 sale prices of used homes in the Youngstown-Warren area rose at roughly the same rate as those in the rest of Ohio and the nation. In 1980 the median sale price of a used home was $43,324 in the United States as a whole, $37,604 in Ohio, and $32,400 in the Youngstown-Warren area. In 1981 when the effects of the layoffs really hit Youngstown, the median sale price of a used home rose slightly in the United States to $45,676, declined somewhat to $35,168 in Ohio, and plummeted to $25,000 in the Youngstown-Warren area. The last number reflects a decline of 23 percent in a single year! Arguably, that decline might reflect composition effects if the selling steelworkers owned less than average houses. It should also be counterbalanced by house price increases in areas to which the departing Youngstown residents might move and buy houses.

With these caveats in mind, we note that the Youngstown-Warren area had 148,000 single-family housing units at that time, and hence if the median sold house is representative of the housing stock as a whole, the housing stock could have declined in value by over $1 billion. These wealth losses are not transfers to shareholders and therefore, modulo the above caveats, represent the social costs of the layoffs, some of which resulted from the takeover.

It is quite possible that, from the point of view of steel production, the takeovers have increased the efficiency of YST operations. Nevertheless, it is obvious that the YST employees suffered substantial wealth losses, as in scenario B. Furthermore, the losses of wealth of other members of Youngstown community should also be counted in any social appraisal of the deals.

2.7.4   Reactions to Takeovers

We do not have information to verify the predictions of our theory for the ability of firms to contract ex ante. For to do this, we must analyze a world in which people trust each other less, workers are not loyal to firms, and spot market transitions are more common than they are at this time. (One can try to think of other cultures, although the comparisons are in many ways suspect. Banfield and Banfield (1958) described a village in southern Italy where trust was absent, hardly any trade took place, especially intertemporally, and people voted for whichever party bribed them most and last, which led to alternating elections of communists and fascists. Nor surprisingly, the village was very poor.) We offer instead a brief survey of opinions expressed by employees of Trans Union Corporation subsequent to its merger with Pritzkers' Marmon group. The comments we present below are based on William M. Owen's privately printed *Autopsy of a Merger,* whose title assures us of the book's impartiality.

Many of the former employees of Trans Union complained that the company violated an implicit understanding that adequate job performance guaranteed continued employment. The virtually universal lesson that interviewees claimed to have learned from their takeover experience was never again to trust a large corporation. One employee remarked that previously he had believed that if he did a good job, he would be appreciated. Now he thinks, "You have to look out for yourself. You really can't hold any loyalty to a corporation." Another offered his view of long-term contracts: "To the average Joe, life in the business world can be compared to walking a tightrope across the Red Sea. It might break at any time, so don't get too comfortable." Many said their loyalty had been killed, and that they developed a more cynical and cautious view of corporate America. As a result, some reversed their prior belief that continued loyalty to a corporation would be rewarded.

What are the tangible results of this change of attitude? In the earlier discussion we suggested that contracting can eventually become more costly and that, in some cases, inferior outcomes can result. There is a bit of quotable evidence on each of these two points. One ex-employee of Trans Union was looking "for an employer where I can participate in ownership." Evidently, she sought equity because "employees got nothing out of the merger," and she wanted her contract to be *explicit.* Other people denied the feasibility of an employment relationship. Of the many who sought self-employment, one thought he could no longer have a sense of security without his own business. Less dramatically, another asked, "How can you go to another company now and give 100 percent of your effort?" While it is premature to interpret these comments as foreshadowing the decline of the corporation, they do suggest a fairly pervasive skepticism about what in the United States is the most common form of the employment contract.

To acknowledge the merits of the alternative hypothesis, we also quote an employee who was doubtless familiar with a working paper by Jensen: "I think Trans Union was fat, dumb and happy and deserved to be acquired."

2.8 Concluding Comments

In this chapter we have stressed the role played by transfers of wealth in hostile takeovers. Breach of trust through corporate takeover enables shareholders to capture the ex post rents from contracts with stakeholders, such as suppliers and employees. Two points made in the foregoing analysis should be sharply distinguished.

First, transfers from stakeholders to shareholders could make for a large part of the takeover premium. Although redistributions from the parties to implicit contracts are important, other transfers are also potentially significant. Tax savings that accompany some takeovers can be viewed as redistributions from the government. At least for some transactions, such as leveraged buyouts, tax savings can account for up to 80 percent of the takeover premium (Kaplan 1987; also Shleifer and Vishny 1988a). If takeovers are motivated by stock market undervaluations of assets, these transactions are rent redistributions from the old shareholders to the buyer. Although evidence of the importance of such undervaluations is lacking, arguments that they are important are not (Drucker 1986). If, as appears to be the case, rent transfers form a significant part of the takeover gains, the combined share price change of the target and the buyer vastly overstates the efficiency gains from takeovers.

It is also argued above, though with much less empirical support, that rent-seeking takeovers may entail large efficiency losses in the long run. The breach of trust accompanying such deals might spread enough fear of further breach through the economy to either vastly complicate or even prevent profitable trade. Managers worried that their stakeholders' claims will not be respected engage in defensive tactics such as restructurings or leveraged buyouts, which themselves take away from the stakeholders. This reorganization of the corporation into more of a spot market system can be socially very costly. To gauge this cost, however, would require an understanding of how trust facilitates contracting, which at this moment we do not have.

Previous academic work has tended to maintain that hostile takeovers are accompanied by increases in efficiency, but it has rarely been successful in isolating the sources of such gains. Undoubtedly, efficiency gains might justify a large part of the takeover premium in some takeovers, such as those in the oil industry. Redistributions, in contrast, seem extremely important in the case of airlines. Unfortunately, to evaluate which of the two sources of gains is the more important, one needs to look at stakeholder losses, which are much harder to measure than shareholder gains.

One promising strategy for testing the role of wealth transfers is to look at cancellation of overfunded defined benefit pension plans, where horror stories abound. We have already mentioned that many benefits that retirees receive are not part of the formal pension contract protected by ERISA, and that even the actual pension benefits are to a large extent set by the company without compulsion. Looking at pension plans after hostile takeovers might be a fruitful way of measuring transfers from stakeholders.

Notes

1. Shareholders' ownership of relationship-specific assets could promote efficient investment in these assets to some extent. If ownership entitles shareholders to residual rights of control of relationship-specific assets, then in some cases where the contract is silent the right thing will be done (Grossman and Hart 1986). But limits of shareholder knowledge and limits of the firm bound the applicability of ownership.

2. This of course could be part of managers' trying to maintain a rational reputation for being "nice guys."

3. In a similar vein we can say that managers become "addicted" to stakeholders who form such an important part of their life (in contrast to constantly changing shareholders). For an illuminating discussion of how such addiction could be rational, see Becker and Murphy (forthcoming).

4. The reason for this is that shareholders are anonymous, and even if they were not, the free rider problem absolves individual shareholders from collective responsibility for the breach.

5. Arrow (1974) stressed the role of trust in the successful functioning of a market economy.

6. The most famous undiversified raider is T. Boone Pickens, who specializes in prompting hostile acquisitions of oil companies. It is interesting that the case for efficiency gains in takeovers is probably the most compelling in the oil industry, where an acquisition is often accompanied by cancellation of a wasteful exploration program.

7. Some estimates in newspapers of total cost decreases after Icahn's acquisition give $600 million, a figure we cannot explain. In part, this includes an annual saving of $100 million from lower fuel costs and probably $50 million from eliminating four 747s. The point is that $200 million is a very conservative lower bound on transfers from the union members.

References

Akerlof, George A. 1983. Loyalty filters. *American Economic Review* 73 (March): 54–63.

Alderson, Michael J., and K. C. Chen. 1986. Excess asset reversions and shareholder wealth. *Journal of Finance* 41 (March): 225–42.

Allen, Steven G., Robert L. Clark, and Daniel A. Sumner. 1984. Post-retirement adjustments of pension benefits, NBER working paper 1364. Cambridge, Mass.: National Bureau of Economic Research.

Arrow, Kenneth J. 1974. *The limits of organization.* New York: W. W. Norton.

Banfield. Edward C., and L. F. Banfield, 1958. *Moral basis of a backward society.* New York: Free Press.

Becker, Gary, and Kevin Murphy. Forthcoming. A theory of rational addiction. *Journal of Political Economy.*

Brown, Charles, and James L. Medoff, 1988. The impact of firm acquisitions on labor. In this volume.

Coase, Ronald L. 1937. The nature of the firm. *Economica 4:* 386–405.

Commons, John L. 1985. *Tender offer.* Berkeley: University of California Press.

Congressional Information Service. 1985. Employee benefits revisions following corporate mergers, H 341–38.1.

Drucker, Peter F. 1986. Corporate takeovers—What is to be done? *The Public Interest* 82 (Winter): 3–24.

Fama, E. F., and M. C. Jensen. 1983. Separation of ownership and control. *Journal of Law and Economics* 26 (June): 301–24.

Grossman, S. J., and O. D. Hart. 1986. The costs and benefits of ownership: A theory of vertical and lateral integration. *Journal of Political Economy* 94 (August): 691–719.

Harris, M., and B. Holmstrom. 1982. Theory of wage dynamics. *Review of Economic Studies* 49 (July): 315–33.

Jensen, M. C. 1984. Takeovers: Folklore and science. *Harvard Business Review* (November-December): 109–21.

Jensen, M. C., and R. S. Ruback. 1983. The market for corporate control: The scientific evidence. *Journal of Financial Economics* 11 (April): 5–50.

Johnston, Moira. 1986. *Takeover.* New York: Arbor House.

Kahneman, Daniel, Jack Knetch, and Richard Thaler. 1986. Fairness as a constraint on profit seeking. *American Economic Review* 76 (September): 728–41.

Kaplan, Steven. 1987. Management buyouts: Thoughts and evidence, photocopy. Boston: Harvard University.

Kreps, D. M. 1984. Corporate culture and economic theory, photocopy. Stanford: Graduate School of Business, Stanford University.

Krueger, Alan, and Lawrence H. Summers. 1987. Interindustry wage differentials. *Econometrica,* forthcoming.

Law, Warren A. 1986. A corporation is more than its stock. *Harvard Business Review* (May-June): 80–3.

Lazear, Edward P. 1979. Why is there mandatory retirement? *Journal of Political Economy* 87 (December): 1261–84.

Lowenstein, Louis. 1985. Management buyouts. *Columbia Law Review* 85 (May): 730–84.

Mørck, Randall, Andrei Shleifer, and Robert W. Vishny. 1988. Characteristics of targets in hostile and friendly takeovers. In this volume.

Owen, William M. 1986. *The autopsy of a merger.* Deerfield, Ill.: William M. Owen.

Shleifer, Andrei, and Robert W. Vishny. 1988a. Management buyouts as a response to market pressure. In *Mergers and acquisitions,* ed. Alan J. Auerbach. Chicago: University of Chicago Press.

———. 1988b. Value maximization and the acquisition process. *Journal of Economic Perspectives,* forthcoming.

U.S. Department of Housing and Urban Development. 1968–85. *Federal Housing Administration homes,* various volumes. Washington, D.C.: GPO.

Williamson, Oliver E. 1985. *The institutions of American capitalism.* New York: Basic Books.

Youngstown Area Chamber of Commerce. 1983. *Steel industry—Narrative of change.* Youngstown, Ohio: YACC.

Zeckhauser, Richard. 1986. Reputational externalities. In *American society: Public and private responsibilities,* ed. Winthrop Knowlton and Richard Zeckhauser. Cambridge, Mass.: Ballinger.

Comment   Bengt Holmstrom

Shleifer and Summers's general point—that changes in the combined market value of stock of an acquired and an acquiring firm can be a biased measure of the efficiency of a takeover—is certainly a valid and valuable one. A major restructuring of the corporation will inevitably imply transfers of wealth between shareholders and stakeholders, and these transfers should obviously be accounted for in assessing efficiency. The authors seem furthermore convinced that changes in stock market value often exaggerate the true benefits from takeovers, because stakeholders will lose some of their rents in the process. In principle (and not implausibly), the bias could go the other way. Stakeholders could benefit from a takeover by capturing some of the efficiency gains. For instance, wages could rise or jobs (with attached rents) could be saved in a takeover that improves the operation of the firm. Or the raider could gain privately by transferring some of the benefits to a company of his that is not directly involved with the merger. In either case these gains would not show up in a market value calculation. Which way market estimates bias the efficiency calculations is therefore an empirical question. To the extent that the authors' work will invite more careful empirical work measuring the benefits and costs of takeovers, it is a very welcome contribution. The TWA case study in particular provides compelling evidence that market value changes overestimated the benefits, but that is thin evidence from which to generalize.

Shleifer and Summers pursue a second efficiency theme that is more controversial and rather independent of the ex post measurements discussed above. They argue that takeovers will interfere with efficient long-term contracting. The hypothesis is that the rents that raiders capture in a takeover are part of an efficient implicit contract between

Bengt Holmstrom is the Edwin J. Beinecke Professor of Management Studies and professor of economics at the School of Organization and Management, Yale University.

This work was supported by funds from the National Science Foundation and the Alfred P. Sloan Foundation.

the firm and its stakeholders. Once it becomes known that those rents will not be possible to appropriate, because of the threat of takeovers, enforcement costs will go up. Thus, even if the above ex post welfare calculation comes out even, the takeover should be deemed socially undesirable on grounds of ex ante efficiency losses. Needless to say, the increased costs of contracting are very hard to assess empirically, but as I will argue later they may be of less concern as well.

I do not find entirely convincing the authors' particular theory of takeovers' being motivated by gains from breaching implicit contracts, nor do I agree with all the welfare implications their logic suggests. In response, I will offer some alternative views. Since we do not have any good models of the takeover process as yet, my own ideas are as speculative as the authors'. I feel a bit diffident about the exercise, however, since in the near future our understanding may improve substantially through theoretical work. I am thinking of the recent interesting papers by Harris and Raviv (1987) and Grossman and Hart (1987), which seem to provide the proper setting for analyzing the motives for takeovers as well as their welfare implications.

The authors correctly recognize that for their breach theory to hold up logically, there must be an asymmetry between the raider and the incumbent management. If not, both would breach under the same circumstances, and no takeover would be necessary. What I find less plausible is the particular asymmetry that the paper focuses on. The claim is that shareholders choose trustworthy managers and entrench them in their positions to facilitate efficient long-term contracting. The choice of a trustworthy manager acts as a commitment device. The authors are led to this logic because the reputation arguments, which would typically be used to explain implicit contracting, are forward looking and would therefore seem to put raiders and management in a symmetric position. In fact, this need not be the case. If the trustworthiness of a manager is unknown, a breach of promise by the manager would be costly. By contrast, the raider need not lose any reputation from a breach because he never made any promise. But I do not place much faith in this logic either. I think that reputations are involved, but in a different manner.

My main problem with the entrenchment logic is that it does not explain why present shareholders could not capture the rents themselves. Since shareholders are assumed to be able to select managers, they should also be able to replace those managers when interests so dictate. In the authors' theory the decision to breach a contract is merely moved one step up (to shareholders) without altering the basic symmetry problem that the authors were careful to address in dismissing the standard reputation argument. While entrenchment implies the added costs of capturing rents, these costs (as well as the increased costs of contracting) have to be borne equally by the raider and the shareholders. Moreover, it would seem that shareholders would gain more from ousting their trustworthy managers because the rents they can thereby capture will not be shared with anybody else. (Raiders have to share a substantial portion of the gains with shareholders—not because this is a common values auction, but rather because shareholders can free-ride). My conclusion is that if one takes seriously the notion that management is selected by shareholders, takeovers should not occur, at least not because of the breach motive suggested in the paper.

Besides this logical problem the evidence in the paper that managers resist takeovers because they are trustworthy and concerned about stakeholders seems thin. In the TWA case, for instance, management had a bad relationship with workers (who subsequently were deprived of some rents). And the comments made about white knights, who "have a shade of grey" and proceed to capture rents themselves, speak against the authors' theory. On a more casual level I think one could collect plenty of evidence indicating that managers are quite capable of ignoring broader social concerns and breaching trust when doing so in their own interest.

Thus, I would prefer a theory of takeovers that does not rely on the selection of trustworthy managers. It is possible to construct a theory within the standard rational framework that assumes managers are as self-interested as everyone else. I have in mind the following story. Managers' behavior is dictated by career concerns. They value their job because of the rents they can enjoy in their managerial position. Their rent-seeking is constrained only by the interests of constituent groups and threats from raiders. Much like politicians, managers need to enjoy the support of their constituents—shareholders, employees, and other stakeholders. Among those constituents, shareholders may be a relatively weak group because of the familiar problems with coordinating the actions of a widely dispersed ownership. Their weakness may in turn lead management to cater more to the interests of employees, for instance, particularly if the latter are organized and strong. It is much more comfortable to have a good relationship than a bad one with employees, as long as the shareholders do not object too strongly. This story, rather than that of implicit contracting, explains the rents that workers enjoy.

But why are the raiders in a better position to capture rents than either management or shareholders? For shareholders my answer is that coordination problems make it difficult for them to act in unison and capture rents. On the other hand, and this is a central ingredient, raiders enjoy an advantage over managers in enacting changes because they typically come in with a reputation for toughness. Managers who have previously given in to labor demands in order to enjoy a more comfortable life will not be able to shift their negotiation position in mid-course. As recent reputation theories would indicate, any such shift would not be credible in the eyes of workers. By contrast, raiders are not burdened by a reputation for weakness.[1]

This reputation theory is quite consistent with the authors' observation that raiders tend to go after firms in industries very distinct from their own (an observation that plays no role in the authors' theory). The returns to raiders come from general bargaining advantages and not from specific knowledge of an industry (witness that their staff is small as well). The theory also accords with the particulars of the TWA case, including the fact that Carl Icahn is known as a hard-nosed bargainer and more than willing to promote an unpleasant image of himself. That unionized labor receives premium salaries (around 15 percent) supports the notion that managers are willing to give away rents if pressed hard enough. Finally, my logic is not inconsistent with the emergence of white knights, who presumably are called in by the managers to save their jobs and help with capturing rents before the raider can get to them.

Having sketched an alternative theory of why there are rents to be captured and why a raider rather than shareholders or management can go after them successfully, let me turn to the efficiency questions raised in the paper. To the extent that my story is correct, it suggests that one should be much more concerned about the potential inefficiencies that might accompany concessions by management to various constituent groups. For instance, excess wages could seriously distort employment decisions. More generally, one is led back to the traditional concern that management may not operate the firm efficiently because of agency problems. Of course, this in no way invalidates the general point that measuring efficiency gains from changes in stock price is inappropriate.

On the other hand, even if one believes that takeovers increase contracting costs (which I do to some extent, as the proposition is not inconsistent with my reputation story), it should be emphasized that these costs, as far as the targeted firm is concerned, are not ones to be added into an efficiency calculation. (The paper may give the misleading impression that they should.) It is important to note that these costs are already accounted for in the evaluation of the post-takeover market value of the firms and the raider's rational decision to buy.

1. One might ask why managers do not bargain hard given the expectation of takeovers. I think the answer is that the recent boom in hostile takeovers came as a surprise. The innovation that was not expected was the emergence of an inexpensive and expedient way to raise substantial amounts of capital for the takeover. Given the low probability of such an event, the managers would not care to push on the bargaining side. Presumably they will try ex post, but they cannot do that as effectively as the raider, given their past reputation.

Consequently, the estimation of cost increases in the acquired firm is of no concern in assessing welfare.

The only issue is what externalities a contract breach can have. The authors mention that a spreading fear of takeovers can jeopardize other firms' contracting opportunities. This is possible, but the paper does not provide much supporting evidence. It is not relevant that the workers in firms that have been taken over feel a lost loyalty, as I argued above. (The anecdotal evidence at the end of the paper appears to be of this kind). Instead, one should focus on those firms that might be future targets. Are the workers there worried? Do they respond to the new reality by demanding higher initial wages, as the implicit contract logic would suggest? I do not know what the facts are here. On the other hand, casual observation indicates that managers will spend substantial energy on defensive activities, including the inefficient restructuring of firms. My guess is that these costs are in the end more significant than the problems with contracting.[2]

Evidently, the factors to consider in any policy decision about takeovers are many and difficult to evaluate. I do not deny that implicit contracting could be an important element, but I think the chapter jumps too quickly to welfare conclusions based on a theory I find somewhat implausible. In asking whether society should intervene and how, one must appreciate the fact that laws cannot be written in a very idiosyncratic fashion. It is hard to discriminate between cases in which welfare is enhanced and cases in which welfare is reduced by takeovers. Many takeovers are of social value, as discussed for instance in Brown and Medoff's chapter in this volume. One should also wait for natural responses to takeovers (resistance measures by management and revisions in corporate charters). Our capitalist economy has proved quite inventive before. For instance, if firms find ways to alter their charters so that they can choose any likelihood of takeover that they desire at a low cost, there is no reason for the government to intervene with the purpose of limiting takeovers. In this case the externality costs from fear would disappear. To this hotly debated issue the best response may therefore be to stay cool and watch from the sidelines until further evidence accumulates and until we find some firmer theoretical ground for assessing the motives and implications of takeovers.

2. Incidentally, there is a reverse externality that tends to reduce the number of takeovers. Potential raiders are presumably uncertain about success. Every time a takeover is attempted, it provides information about success rates, including the costs of raising the required capital and the resistance methods that management might use. Thus, the takeover is an experiment of social value (if takeovers are desirable), but only a small fraction of that value accrues to the raider because of the public goods nature of information. The recent boom in (hostile) takeover activity is indicative of such an externality.

References

Grossman, Sanford, and Oliver Hart. 1987. One share/one vote and the market for corporate control,   photocopy. Cambridge: Massachusetts Institute of Technology.

Harris, Milton, and Arthur Raviv. 1987. Corporate governance: Voting rights and majority rules,   photocopy. Evanston, Ill.: Northwestern University.

Comment   Oliver E. Williamson

The increased valuation of the combined equity securities of firms involved in a takeover is often attributed to prospective improvements in managerial efficiency. Shleifer and Summers argue that this explanation is too simple. They observe that many takeovers bring about an expropriation of rents. To a first approximation, these takeovers are redistributional rather than efficiency enhancing. Indeed, social losses will obtain if, as a secondary or systems consequence, confidence (trust) in the contracting process is lost.

Expropriation is not, however, the only interpretation for the wage cuts that attend the takeovers to which Shleifer and Summers refer. An alternative and, I submit, more plausible interpretation is that a reduction in the scope of managerial discretion is responsible for the wage cuts in question. Before sketching these rival wage cut scenarios—expropriation and managerial discretion—and their welfare ramifications, I will briefly raise a question of theoretical perspective.

The study of economic organization is both very complex and relatively undeveloped. Under these circumstances there are advantages in adopting a "main case" perspective. Rival main case candidates—which include economizing, monopoly, and issues of power—should then be required to show their hand. What are the implications of each, and what do the data support?

I have argued elsewhere that the economizing approach to economic organization, with special reference to economizing on transaction costs, qualifies (comparatively) for main case standing (Williamson 1985, 1987). This fact does not, however, preclude the possibility that other ancillary or auxiliary purposes are also served. How do we evaluate these?

Whereas the main case presumably applies in general, auxiliary purposes are apt to be associated with special preconditions. Strategic behavior by established firms that is designed to discipline rivals or deter market entry, for example, is viable only if supported by preexisting

Oliver E. Williamson is the Gordon B. Tweedy Professor of Economics of Law and Organization at Yale University.

market power. One useful way of discriminating among alternative auxiliary purposes, therefore, is to ask whether the requisite preconditions are satisfied. I suggest that this course be followed in attempting to choose among alternative explanations for the takeover-induced wage cuts that are of concern to Shleifer and Summers.

The condition of asset specificity plays a key role in the study of contract (Williamson 1975, 1985; Klein, Crawford, and Alchian 1978) and features prominently in the Shleifer and Summers expropriation scenario. The basic argument is this: Constituencies that make durable firm-specific investments are exposed to the hazard of expropriation unless special efforts are made to safeguard these investments. Long-term contracts supported by protective governance structures are thus favored wherever asset specificity is great. Selecting managers who exhibit integrity and exude trust helps to supply this contractual glue.

An equilibrium set of contracts with managers operating as trustees can be upset, however, by the appearance of a takeover. The would-be takeover agent offers a bribe to one of the constituencies, namely, the shareholders, to sell out. The successful takeover agent then dismisses the incumbent (trustee) managers and abrogates the contractual understanding that had hitherto prevailed. Workers with firm-specific skills are advised that wages will be slashed by 20 or 30 percent. Because their skills are imperfectly redeployable, the workers accept this deal.

Inasmuch as the wage bill in most firms is very large in relation to profits, a 20 or 30 percent wage cut can have huge consequences for profitability. The existence of firm-specific labor (and other firm-specific factors, such as specialized suppliers) thus represents an enormous inducement to a raider.

As Shleifer and Summers point out, the expropriation from labor has immediate redistributional effects. It also has continuing contractual effects, as employees find their confidence (trust) in the contracting process shaken. Future workers will contract much more carefully, refuse to tailor their human assets to the firm, or both. A pervasive erosion of trust would have adverse systems effects as well, whence both local and global allocative efficiency losses could result.

The managerial discretion models maintain that managers operate the firm with reference to their own interests, subject to the condition that their jobs not be jeopardized by sales, growth, or other management-favored goals.[1] The refutable implications of these models turn critically

---

1. Baumol's (1958) sales maximization hypothesis was the first of the managerial discretion models. Marris (1964) subsequently argued that managers were given to growth maximization, and I (1964) postulated a managerial utility function that featured an "expense preference."

on the proposition that the scope of managerial discretion varies systematically with circumstances. The scope of discretion is assumed to be greater in the degree to which (1) firms are relieved from competition in the product market, (2) competition in capital market forces is weak, and (3) the organization of the firm supports the pursuit of ancillary goals.

This Comment focuses on *changes* in the condition of competition in the product market as these relate to wage behavior. The general argument is this: Firms that operate in highly concentrated industries that are difficult to enter or in regulated industries that allow the pass-through of costs and prohibit entry are especially given to managerial discretion (Williamson 1964; Alchian 1965).

What has been referred to as the agency theory approach to economic organization expressly takes exception to the proposition that the scope of managerial discretion varies with competition in the product market. Thus, Jensen and Meckling (1976, 317) have observed that "it is frequently argued that the existence of competition in the product . . . markets will constrain the behavior of managers . . . , i.e., that monopoly in product markets will permit larger divergences from value maximization. Our analysis does not support this hypothesis." Shleifer and Summers rely on the Jensen and Meckling nexus of a contract conception of the firm and, as set out above, appeal to breaches of trust (breakdowns in the contractual relationship), rather than to changes in the condition of product market competition, in explaining the wage cuts that attend the takeovers in question.[2]

To examine the alternative explanation—managerial discretion—suppose at the outset that the firms in question are operating in highly concentrated industries where entry is difficult, perhaps even where entry is prohibited by regulation. Suppose further that managers have Hicksian preferences for a "quiet life." And suppose finally that the contractual relationship between the firm and each constituency with which management must deal has an influence on managerial tranquility.

Granting wage concessions, especially in the face of a strong labor union, is an obvious way by which to promote labor peace. Assume, for the sake of argument, that the managements of firms in monopolistic and regulated industries do make such wage concessions. Although shareholders will be temporarily disadvantaged as wages intrude on

---

2. Jensen has more recently embraced the managerial discretion view (which he characterizes, however, as the "free cash flow" hypothesis). Thus, he now maintains that "product and factor market disciplinary forces are often weaker in new activities and activities that involve substantial economic rents or quasirents. In these cases, monitoring by the firm's internal control system and the market for corporate control are more important" (1986, 323). In effect, free cash flow is a specialization of managerial discretion theory. It usefully focuses attention on financial issues akin to those addressed by Grossman and Hart (1982).

profits, share prices will thereafter adjust to reflect the reduced profitability. Partial profit recoupment may be effected, moreover, by raising product prices without inviting entry. A stable, easy life equilibrium in which labor is bribed to cooperate thereby results.

Suppose now that a disturbance appears. One possible disturbance is that the government removes the protective mantle of regulation. Another is that import barriers come down so that foreign producers become more viable alternative sources of supply. Entry by new firms that are not subject to the modus vivendi regarding wages now threatens. What to do?

One possibility is for the incumbent managements to roll back the earlier wage concessions, thereby to meet any new competition on parity wage terms. By assumption, however, the incumbent managers still value the quiet life, and labor can be expected to greet the proposal with a storm of protest. Another possibility is for a new management team to form that is better suited to deal with (indeed, may value) turbulence. But how to effect the change?

Since the incumbent managers like their jobs, their voluntarily quitting is not in prospect. And since they will rebuff the offer of a new management team to supplant the incumbents, an involuntary means of displacement will need to be employed. Suppose that the new management team turns to the shareholders and proposes a takeover by paying a premium over the (now reduced) share prices. Assume that the shareholders approve. The takeover and subsequent renegotiation of wages that Shleifer and Summers describe follows.

Whereas the Shleifer and Summers scenario assumes that managers are trustees and focuses on firms in which labor has made significant firm-specific investments, the scenario I describe instead assumes that managers are given to managerial discretion and focuses on industries where the *condition of competition has changed*. Specifically, the managerial discretion scenario focuses on those industries that once were difficult to enter but where now entry impediments have been relieved. (The U.S. automobile industry exhibits some of this attribute. Industries that have recently been deregulated and whose principal durable investments are mobile—such as airlines and trucking—are even better examples.)

Thus, whereas all firms in which labor has made significant firm-specific investments are potential expropriation candidates under the neutral nexus-of-contract hypothesis, the managerial nexus hypothesis looks to conditions that would support managerial discretion[3] and asks if entry restrictions have significantly eased.

3. The argument can be refined with reference to organizational form. The basic argument here follows the M-form hypothesis (Williamson 1975, 150–51), to wit: U-form firms are more given to excesses of managerial discretion than are M-form firms, *ceteris paribus*.

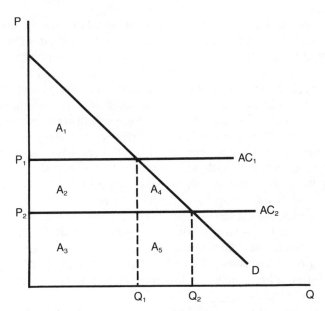

Fig. 1   A geometry of the welfare consequences of takeovers

I now turn to the welfare geometry of the two scenarios. Whether managers behave as trustees (the Shleifer and Summers scenario) or tilt the enterprise in favor of the quiet life (as sketched above), the welfare ramifications can, to a first approximation, be assessed in standard terms of partial equilibrium welfare economics.

Figure 1 sets out the basic geometry. AC_1 in the figure refers to average costs in the pretakeover era. To keep things simple, assume that price (P_1) is equal to AC_1. AC_2 is the level to which pecuniary costs fall as a result of the forced renegotiation of labor contracts that attends the takeover.

Shleifer and Summers treat the workers as locked in to the firm, by reason of firm-specific human capital, and thus the area A_2 is transformed from wages to profits under this scenario. The real productivity of the workers is nonetheless reflected by AC_1, however. Accordingly, new entrants cannot come in and sell at less than P_1 simply by paying a low wage—because the incumbent workers who have built up their firm-specific capital in the established firms will outperform the inexperienced, new workers. Until the incumbent workers retire, therefore, the area A_2 is the initial and continuing profit gain that is realized by the takeover–wage cut scenario described by Shleifer and Summers.[4] This is a redistribution.

4. This geometry assumes that (1) the incumbent workers' productivity does not drop and (2) the existing rivals maintain the price P_1 despite reduced pecuniary costs.

The scenario that I describe also involves an initial shift in amount A_2 from wages to profits. Assuming, however, that AC_1 does not reflect a payment for productivity but is an "easy life" premium instead, the price P_1 will be subject to competitive erosion. New rivalry appears, something akin to a Schumpeterian "handing on" process ensues, and the prices (P_2) will be bid down to the level AC_2. The profit gains are thus transitional. The area A_2 in the final equilibrium becomes consumer surplus. The triangle A_4 is an allocative efficiency gain.

Shleifer and Summers aver that the workers who experience the expropriation will be loath to contract with firms in the same trust-worthy manner as they did in the post-takeover era. Either they will contract much more carefully, thereby to protect their firm-specific human capital against any further expropriation, or they will refuse to specialize their human assets (or some combination thereof). Pervasive systems effects may also obtain, as interested observers thereafter negotiate more cautiously as well. The allocative efficiency losses of moving from a high-trust to a low-trust culture must be counted as a social cost of takeovers.

The managerial discretion hypothesis treats the high wages in the pretakeover era as a bribe. The lucky beneficiaries realize a windfall that evaporates upon takeover. But possibly the situation is more complicated than this. The beneficiaries are workers who have made special efforts to qualify for high-paying jobs through pre-positioning. They have incurred special costs of obtaining credentials (see the rent transformation literature: Krueger 1974; Posner 1975; Tullock 1967), and they may be overqualified as a consequence.

The welfare ramifications of takeovers are therefore complicated under the managerial discretion hypothesis as well. Workers here may also feel a justifiable sense of expropriation. They likewise may attempt to contract more carefully thereafter. But these workers may also be deterred from rent transformation once they realize that wage premia invite takeovers. This is a mixed picture.

In conclusion, although most takeovers are not attended by large wage cuts, some are, and therefore we must ask what factors are associated with wage cut outcomes. The two alternative scenarios discussed here have somewhat different foci of attention. Whereas the expropriation scenario assumes that pretakeover managers are trust-ees, the managerial discretion scenario assumes that pretakeover managers sacrifice profits in favor of the quiet life. Labor, under the expropriation scenario, is highly firm-specific, whereas labor can be either specific or nonspecific under the managerial discretion hypothesis. Probably the most telling difference between these two scenarios is the importance each attaches to competition in the product market.

The managerial discretion hypothesis assumes that wage cuts are attended by (indeed, induced by) increased product market competition (greater import competition, deregulation, or the like), while the expropriation scenario is silent in this respect. Finally, whereas both product prices and wages fall under the managerialist explanation, only wages are reduced under expropriation.[5]

Which hypothesis is most powerful awaits a systematic development of the data. The specific examples to which Shleifer and Summers refer are nonetheless congruent with the managerialist interpretation.

References

Alchian, Armen. 1965. The basis of some recent advances in the theory of management of the firm. *Journal of Industrial Economics* 14 (December): 30–41.

Baumol, William. 1958. *Business behavior, value and growth.* New York: Macmillan.

Grossman, Sanford, and Oliver Hart. 1982. Corporate financial structure and managerial incentives. In *The economics of information and uncertainty,* ed. J. McCall, 109–37. Chicago: University of Chicago Press.

Jensen, Michael. 1986. Agency costs of free cash flows, corporate finance, and takeovers. *American Economic Review* 76 (May): 323–29.

Jensen, Michael, and William Meckling. 1976. Theory of the firm: Managerial behavior, agency costs, and ownership structure. *Journal of Financial Economics* 3: 305–60.

Klein, Benjamin, Robert Crawford, and Armen Alchian. 1978. Vertical integration, appropriable rents, and the competitive contracting process. *Journal of Law and Economics* 21 (October): 297–326.

Krueger, Anne O. 1974. The political economy of the rent-seeking society. *American Economic Review* 64 (June): 291–303.

Marris, Robin. 1964. *The economic theory of managerial capitalism.* New York: Free Press.

Posner, Richard. 1975. The social costs of monopoly and regulation. *Journal of Political Economy* 83 (August): 807–27.

Tullock, Gordon. 1967. *The politics of bureaucracy.* Washington, D.C.: Public Affairs Press.

———. 1967. The welfare costs of tariffs, monopolies, and thefts. *Western Economic Journal* 5 (June): 224–32.

Williamson, Oliver E. 1964. *The economics of discretionary behavior.* Englewood Cliffs, N.J.: Prentice-Hall.

———. 1975. *Markets and hierarchies.* New York: Free Press.

———. 1985. *The economic institutions of capitalism.* New York: Free Press.

———. 1987. Mergers, acquisitions, and leveraged buy-outs: An efficiency perspective, photocopy. New Haven: Yale Law School, January.

---

5. That prices remain unchanged under the expropriation scenario is an oversimplification. A more accurate statement is that prices fall *more* under the managerialist explanation.

3 The Effect of Takeover Activity on Corporate Research and Development

Bronwyn H. Hall

3.1 Introduction

Economists generally agree that research and development activity is an important factor in the long-term growth of the economy. The purpose of this paper is to explore the effects on corporate research and development of the recent increase in takeovers in the United States. R&D is interesting in this context because the firm's decision to invest in these activities is viewed as a long-term commitment. If a wave of mergers distracts managers from all but decisions for the near term, we might expect that R&D performance would cease to be optimal.

To shed some light on this question, this paper uses evidence on the characteristics of mergers that actually take place. To quantify the role of R&D in acquiring and acquired firms, I explore the factors that determine the probability of an acquisition as well as the valuation of these factors at the time of the takeover. The model of acquisition choice I have built for this purpose is tractable for estimation and allows for heterogeneity across firms and therefore unique synergies to a merger. In particular, different targets are worth different amounts to acquiring

Bronwyn H. Hall is assistant professor of economics at the University of California, Berkeley, and a research economist at the National Bureau of Economic Research.

The author is grateful to Zvi Griliches and Timothy Bresnahan for ongoing discussions, to Alan Auerbach, Charles Brown, Lawrence Lau, Tom Macurdy, Ariel Pakes, and John Shoven for comments at various times during this research, and to Chris Hall for help with the data collection. Comments by seminar participants at Stanford University, the University of Santa Clara, Boston University, Harvard University, MIT, the University of Chicago, and the University of California, Berkeley, were also helpful in preparing this chapter. Some of this work was done while the author was a Sloan Dissertation Fellow and a John M. Olin graduate research fellow, and she thanks these foundations for their support. The data preparation was partially supported by a National Science Foundation Grant and by the National Bureau of Economic Research.

firms, and the highest valuer is the one most likely to make the acquisition.

The question whether increased merger activity is a good thing for the economy in general remains unresolved and unlikely to be resolved by focusing solely on the experience of the firms involved. Jensen (1986) and others have argued that mergers represent an unambiguously positive shifting of assets into their best use and provides the best mechanism for ensuring that managers act in the shareholders' interest. A more neutral view would be that the level of merger activity is just a by-product of this asset shuffling and has no particular externality; it fluctuates from time to time in just the same way as the number of shares traded on the stock market fluctuates from day to day. The negative view, associated with Scherer (Ravenscraft and Scherer 1986), sees acquired entities ("lines of business" in his empirical work) as almost always suffering declining profitability after merging, and Scherer inferred from this result the conclusion that increased acquisition activity is likely to be a wasteful thing for the economy as a whole.

Roll (1986) provided what is essentially an efficient financial markets explanation of the phenomenon observed by Scherer, although that was not his specific aim. He claimed that we see the transactions only where the managers of acquiring firms misperceive the value of the target firm as too low. Hence, according to Roll, even under efficient markets we find more negative surprises than positive ones. This picture of acquisitions implies that an increase in mergers is associated with an increase in corporate "hubris" (Roll's term), which is not good for the economy as a whole. But for this view to hold in the presence of efficient markets, the offer made by an acquiring firm should be associated with a drop in its share price, since shareholders should be capable of divining that the decision to buy is likely to be a bad one. The existing evidence on returns to the bidding firm does not seem consistent with this.

Is merger activity likely to have a negative effect on R&D performance? One reason it might is substitution. If firms with large amounts of cash would rather spend it than return it to shareholders in the form of dividends, we would expect R&D and acquisition to be substitutes for these firms. An increase in the attractiveness of acquisition opportunities would depress spending on internal investment, including R&D. Takeovers and R&D may be substitutes on the real side as well. There are two ways to acquire knowledge capital: either by investing within the firm (an R&D program), or by purchasing another firm after its R&D program has yielded successful results. The latter strategy has the advantage that more information is available about the output of the R&D, activities that tend to be highly uncertain. Under the two assumptions of no scale economies or diseconomies in R&D over the relevant range *and* perfect capital markets, the two strategies should, in fact, be perfect substitutes for the firm.

Alternatively, the view that some acquisitions are used as "cash cows" to service the debt incurred to finance them also implies a negative effect on R&D activity. An easy way to increase short-term cash flows at the expense of long-term profits is to cut spending on such things as R&D. Evidence that this indeed takes place is not, however, evidence that it is the wrong thing to do. The long-run profit rate may not have been high enough to justify the premerger R&D level of the acquired firm, and cutting back on R&D may be precisely what a now presumably better management should do.

Some evidence exists on a few of these questions. Using roughly the same data as mine, Addanki (1985) found no support for the hypothesis that firms with larger R&D programs were more attractive acquisition prospects. If anything, innovators were less likely to be acquired than other firms. A Securities and Exchange Commission study (1985) found that firms that were taken over invested less in R&D than other firms in their industry. The authors of the study did not control for size, however, which could account for some of the result. The same study produced a related piece of evidence on the market valuation of long-term investments such as R&D: The 20-day excess return for an announcement of an increased level of R&D was 1.8 percent, suggesting that the market placed a positive value on such announcements.

On the other hand, for a sample of 1,337 Industrial File firms in 1976, of which 301 were acquired by 1983, I found that once I had controlled for Tobin's q at the beginning of the period, the R&D-to-assets ratio was positively related to the probability of being acquired. The coefficient was consistent with a shadow price for the R&D capital stock of around 0.6 times that for the physical capital stock of the firm. In other words, firms for which the measured ratio of market value to book value was high because they also had intangible assets, such as a large R&D program, were more likely to exit from the sample by merger, *ceteris paribus*. In this version of the probability model I did control for size, so that the R&D effects would not be confounded by the negative correlation between the size of the firm and its R&D intensity. Nonetheless, the coefficient was rather imprecisely measured, and the results tended to be sensitive to the exact choice of sample (whether or not the sample included firms traded over the counter, for example).

In this chapter, I investigate these somewhat inconsistent results on the attractiveness of R&D-intensive firms as takeover candidates further, as well as some of the other issues related to R&D performance and takeover activity. To this end I have assembled a data set on all the publicly traded U.S. manufacturing firms that were acquired between the years 1976 and 1986 in order to examine the pattern of the acquisitions and mergers. In particular, were the acquired firms more or less R&D intensive than others in their industry? What were the characteristics of the acquiring firms, and what kinds of synergy favored the merger? What happened to R&D at the new, larger firm, and is there any evidence that the acquisitions took place partly to reduce R&D expenditures because of scale economies or other reasons? Finally, is there any evidence that R&D winners (successful innovators) were being singled out by the mergers and acquisitions process, suggesting that this is how successful innovators capture the appropriate rate of return?

3.2   Modeling the Acquisition Decision

In modeling takeover activity, I view it as a response to changes in states of the world (such as technology shocks) that make some assets less productive in their current use than they would be in some alternative use. Because of information lags, transaction costs, or whatever, these assets do not move continuously into their optimal use, and so the shocks induce a disequilibrium that is resolved by other firms' purchasing discrete bundles of the assets. In other words, merger activity is the result of a rearrangement of productive assets in response to changes in the available technology, or, in the case of the domestic manufacturing sector, to changes in the nature and level of competition from the rest of the world.[1]

I begin by denoting the value of the assets of a particular firm as $V(X) = V(X_1, X_2, \ldots)$, where X is a vector of the characteristics of the firm, such as its capital stock, R&D stock, industry, tax characteristics, and so forth. The value function V can be thought of as the present discounted value of the revenue streams that could be generated from these assets either alone or in combination with other assets. For the moment I do not necessarily identify $V(X_i)$ with the current stock market value of the firm, although in a world with fully informed, rational shareholders and efficient markets, $V(X_i)$ would of necessity be the price at which this bundle of assets traded. The reason I do not make this assumption here is the well-known fact that acquisitions take place at a significant positive premium over the preannouncement stock market value (Jensen and Ruback 1983, and the references therein). This fact implies that some agents place a higher value on X_i than the market does. Thus, it would be a mistake to impose at the outset a constraint that the market for corporate assets is in a fully informed equilibrium, since it is the disequilibria that drive the acquisition process. The implications of this assumption for the estimation strategy will be clarified after I present the model.

I assume that in each period (a year, in my data) the optimal configuration of corporate assets changes because of shocks to the economic environment. The acquiring firms are subscripted j, and the possible targets, which consist of my entire sample of firms, are subscripted i. Each firm in my sample can acquire any other firm; if it does so, the increment to the value of the acquiring firm j attributable to the new configuration of assets is denoted $V_j(X_i)$. If we assume for the moment that only one acquisition is possible in each period, firm j will buy firm i (that is, j and i will find it beneficial to combine) if

$$
(1) \qquad V_j(X_i) - P_i > V_j(X_k) - P_k \qquad \forall \, k \in \text{Sample}
$$

$$
V_j(X_i) - P_i \geq 0
$$

where P_i is the price j will have to pay for i's assets. The last conditions ensures that there is a positive gain from the acquisition; many potential acquirers will find that it holds for none of the targets and hence will acquire no firms during the period.

Equation (1) is similar to the equations that define product choice by a consumer in a random utility choice model (McFadden 1973; Manski and McFadden 1981; Train 1986; and references therein). To see this, think of the asset aggregation function (Vs) in this model as analogous to consumer utility expressed as a function of the underlying (Lancastrian) characteristics of the good. Thus, the market for acquisitions resembles the market for differentiated products, with one important difference. In the consumer demand literature, price enters the indirect utility function directly, since the consumers are assumed to be price-takers. In this market one cannot assume that the price firm j will pay for the assets is independent of j's attempt to purchase them. The empirical evidence is that by making a bid, firm j reveals something about the value of the assets that was not previously known and hence finds it necessary to bid above the current trading price. In a companion piece (Hall 1987b) I derive the equilibrium price in a market with a large finite number of unique, differentiated buyers and sellers and show that it will lie somewhere between the value of the good to the highest valuer and the value to the next highest valuer. In the econometric work here I assume that the price at which the potential acquirers will evaluate the purchase is not P_i, the current trading price of firm i's stock, but an unobservable $V(X_i)$, which is a function of the assets X_i.

The advantage of viewing the acquisition decision in this way is that there exists a large body of literature on which we can build to describe the types of mergers that take place and how the characteristics of targets are valued by different buyers. That is the literature on the econometric estimation of models of the demand for differentiated products. Although I frequently use the language of consumer demand to describe the acquisition decision throughout this paper, the reader should bear in mind that because price is not exogenous, what is actually being estimated can be interpreted as an equation determining the gains from particular mergers, ones in which the buyers and sellers are treated symmetrically, rather than as an equation describing the demand of an acquiring firm for a target.

An estimating equation is derived from the conditions in equation (1) by partitioning the gain to firm j from the acquisition into observable and unobservable components:

$$(2) \qquad V_j(X_i) \ - \ P_i = f(X_i, X_j) + \epsilon_{ij}$$

and by letting ϵ_{ij} have an extreme value distribution. If the ϵ_{ij} terms are independently distributed across the alternatives, one obtains the usual multinominal logit probability that an acquisition will take place:

$$(3) \qquad P(j \text{ buys } i | C) \ = \ \frac{exp[f(X_j, X_i)]}{\sum_{k \in} exp[f(X_j, X_k)]} \, ,$$

where C is the entire pool of firms. The likelihood function is formed by multiplying these probabilities and conditioning on the observed characteristics of the acquirers and the potential targets.[2]

At this point the alert reader will notice that the choice set C is very large; it potentially includes any firm in or outside the United States. Even if I confine the choice set to my data set, it consists of more than 2,000 firms, which raises questions as to the feasibility of econometric estimation and the validity of the IIA assumption. Fortunately, McFadden (1978) has examined the large choice set problem and suggested two approaches for dealing with it. The first solution is to construct a nested logit model, which describes the choice from 2,000 alternatives as a hierarchical sequence of choices each of which considers vastly fewer alternatives. For example, I might hypothesize that firms first choose the industry in which they wish to make an acquisition and then choose among the firms in that industry. This solution requires more a priori information, but it has the advantage that it gets around the IIA problem somewhat. I have not chosen to use this model in my initial exploration of the data, however, because I wished to avoid imposing too much structure on the choice problem at the outset.

The second solution suggested by McFadden for the problem of very large choice sets is simpler to implement, though possibly not the most powerful or realistic in terms of its assumptions. One randomly samples from the unchosen alternatives and includes only a subset for each observation. McFadden showed that as long as the sampling algorithm has what he called the "uniform conditioning property," and the choice probabilities satisfy the IIA assumption, the estimates obtained using the subset of alternatives and a conventional multinomial logit program are consistent. The uniform conditioning property is defined as:

(4)   If $i,j \in D \subset C$, then $\pi(D|i,z) = \pi(D|j,z)$,

where D is the subset of alternatives used, π is the probability distribution used to draw D from C, and the z terms are the exogenous variables of the model. The algorithm I used to generate my subsets D has this property, since my D consists of the chosen (numerator) alternative augmented by a random sample selected from the other alternatives. The size of the D I used was seven, but this is obviously an operation in which more experience and experimentation would be desirable.

For the econometric estimation of the model in equation (3) I need to specify a functional form for $f(X_i,X_j)$. The difficulty with this function as written is that the gains from different acquisitions are likely to have extremely heteroskedastic and possibly non-normal disturbances ϵ_{ij} because of the large size range of the firms in the data set.[3] I would like to choose a specification that mitigates this problem as much as possible, since the multinomial logit estimates will be biased in this case. My solution to the problem is to specify the acquisition choice problem in terms of rates of return to acquisitions rather than total gains. This specification implies a condition of the form:

(5) $V_j(X_i)\,/P_i > V_j(X_k)/P_k$

rather than equation (1). By using a multiplicative disturbance for the value functions and then taking logarithms, I arrive at the following estimating equation for the econometric model:

(6) $P(j \text{ buys } i|C) = \dfrac{exp[v_j(X_i) \; - \; v(X_i)]}{\sum\limits_{k\in} exp[v_j(X_k) \; - \; v(X_k)]}$,

where the lowercase v denotes the measurable component of the logarithm of the valuation function. The subscripted v denotes the valuation from the perspective of the acquiring firm, whereas v without a subscript is the function describing the equilibrium price at which the firm's assets will trade.

For the econometric estimation I model the logarithm of V as a function of firm characteristics, including the logarithm of the capital stock, R&D intensity, and the two-digit industry. The exact functional form I use is motivated partly by a simple intertemporal optimizing model of a firm with a given stock of assets A and partly by a desire for the tractability and interpretability of the estimating equation. A Cobb-Douglas price-taking firm with one type of capital for which there are adjustment costs, and with all other inputs freely variable, has a value function

$$(7) \qquad\qquad V(A) = a_0 A^\sigma$$

as a result of maximizing the present discounted cash flow, where σ is a scale parameter equal to unity in the constant returns case (Lucas and Prescott 1971; Mussa 1974; Abel 1983,1985). In the absence of a good model for the value function of more than one kind of capital (see Wildasin 1984; Griliches 1981), I incorporate a second capital, knowledge capital K, by the simple expedient of aggregating it with A, but with a freely varying coefficient:

$$(8) \qquad V(A,K) = a_0 (A + \gamma K)^\sigma = a_0 A^\sigma [1 + \gamma(K/A)]^\sigma.$$

Taking logarithms,

$$(9) \qquad \begin{aligned} v(A,K) &\approx \sigma \log A + \sigma \log [1 + \gamma(K/A)] \\ &\approx \sigma \log A + \sigma\gamma \ (K/A). \end{aligned}$$

Thus, the coefficient of size in my estimating equation can be interpreted as a scale coefficient, and that of R&D intensity as representing a premium (or discount) the R&D capital receives in the market over that of ordinary capital. Of course, to interpret the R&D coefficient in this way, one must be careful to measure K and A in comparable stock units.

Using the basic underlying model for the valuation of the assets of the firms, I capture the synergy of combining the two firms in two different ways. The first models the gain from the acquisition $v_j(X_i) - v(X_i)$ as a linear function of the assets of the two firms and the distance between them in asset space, such that:

$$(10) \qquad v_j(X_i) - v(X_i) = X_j\beta_1 + X_i\beta_2 + |X_j - X_i|\beta_3,$$

where the X variables are the vector of variables describing the assets of the firm in question (for example, $\log A_i$ and $[K/A]_i$). Because of the form of the multinominal logit probability, the coefficients of the acquiring firm's characteristics, β_1, will not be estimable since they cancel from the numerator and denominator, so that only X_i and $|X_jX_i|$ will enter the logit equation in this case. In any case these coefficients will contain both terms from $v(X_i)$ and the linear terms from $v_j(X_i)$.

The second method for modeling the synergistic relationship between the two firms starts from the notion that each acquiring firm has a value $v_j(X_i)$ for the target firm i that is a different function of firm i's characteristics, so that:

$$(11) \qquad\qquad v_j(X_i) = \gamma_j X_i + \eta_{ij}.$$

I then model the "shadow prices" γ_j as linear functions of the characteristics of firm j. This will imply that cross-products of the variables for firm j and firm i enter the equation for the probability of a choice. The advantage of this formulation is that it allows us to place a valuation interpretation on the estimated coefficients; in other words, the γ_j estimates are hedonic prices of the characteristics X_i.

3.3   The Data and Sample Statistics

The data from which I draw my sample consist of 2,519 manufacturing firms that appeared at some time on the Industrial and Over-the-Counter Compustat tapes over the years 1976–85. The basic features of the 1976-based subset of this sample were described in Bound et al. (1984) and Cummins et al. (1986), and the construction of the whole sample is described in Hall (1987a; 1987c). The sample consists of a rolling panel of firms, with annual data available as far back as 1959 for some firms; all firms are followed as long as they remain publicly traded and therefore in the Compustat files, with the last year of coverage being 1985. The number of firms actually in the sample in any one year declined from a high of about 2,000 in 1976 to around 1,500 in 1985.

I used four sources of information to identify the reasons why 875 firms had exited the file as of 1985, as well as the name of the acquiring firm for all acquisitions: the Federal Trade Commission Merger Reports of 1977 through 1980; a list of around 400 acquisitions involving Compustat firms supplied to me by Auerbach and Reishus (for more detail see Auerbach and Reishus 1985; 1987); the 1986 Directory of Obsolete Securities; and Standard and Poors' Corporate Records, which provide news reports indexed by firm name every year for the entire period in question. This research yielded a nearly complete breakdown of the reasons for exit. Of the 875 firms that had left the sample by 1985, 601 had been acquired, 94 had gone bankrupt or had been liquidated, 115 had changed their name (and should have data for the new entity restored to the file), 45 had been reorganized (the capital structure was changed enough so that it was reported in the Directory of Obsolete Securities), and 20 exits remained unexplained.

After splicing in records for those firms whose names had changed (for example, U. S. Steel became USX Corp.), and also for those firms whose CUSIP numbers and symbols had changed because of reorganization, I updated this distribution of exits and searched out the remaining unexplained exits. The final tabulation is shown in table 3.1 by year of exit. The most striking fact in this table is the well-known one that the rate of acquisition rose between the late 1970s and the

Table 3.1   The Number and Employment of Firms Exiting from the Publicly Traded Manufacturing Sector, by Reason for Exit, 1976–86

| | Number of Firms (N) and Employment (E, in thousands) | | | | | | | | | |
| | Total Exits | | Acquisition by Public, Domestic Firm | | Acquisition by Private, Domestic Firm | | Acquisition by Foreign Firm | | Liquidated or Bankrupt | |
Year	N	E	N	E	N	E	N	E	N	E
1976	28	92	24	89	1	0	2	2	2	0
1977	55	256	35	165	5	6	11	81	2	2
1978	42	243	20	204	13	22	8	16	1	0
1979	33	131	23	80	5	14	2	7	1	14
1980	59	353	31	270	5	15	8	21	9	17
1981	81	323	35	220	22	58	6	18	11	16
1982	67	190	23	72	23	47	7	36	11	30
1983	71	249	27	102	21	66	3	1	10	16
1984	115	596	44	290	38	161	10	74	11	10
1985	111	823	43	552	36	138	7	78	19	11
1986	58	466	23	153	15	86	8	52	5	14
Total	704	3,721	332	2,195	199	615	72	385	101	132

Note: The employment columns (E) show the total employment, in thousands, in the firms during the year prior to their exit. The columns and rows do not sum because a few exits remain unidentified as to reason for or year of exit.

1980s (note that my numbers for 1986 are undoubtedly incomplete). In addition, a large part of the increase in the acquisition rate between the 1976–81 period and the 1982–86 period is due to the increase in acquisition activity by privately held and foreign firms. Weighted by employment, those acquisitions tripled, while the acquisitions by publicly traded firms increased by one-third. In this case acquisition by a "privately held" firm means acquisition by a firm that does not file 10-K forms with the Securities and Exchange Commission on a regular basis and therefore is not in the sample; some of these firms are leveraged buyouts by management or other investors (known as "taking the firm private").

Because the privately traded acquisitors perform roughly half the acquisitions, and these acquisitions are likely to be a nonrandom sample (for example, they are on average about 50 to 60 percent smaller), throughout the paper I will try to compare results for my subsample of acquisitions with those for the whole sample. Unfortunately, it is not in general possible to obtain data on the pre- and postacquisition experience of these buyers, which is a limitation of this study.

Some simple statistics on all the acquisitions are presented in table 3.2a, where I show the industrial breakdown for the firms in the manufacturing sector in 1976 and 1981 and for the subset of firms that were acquired between the two periods 1977–81 and 1982–86. To give an idea of the relative importance of acquisition activity by industry, I also report the total employment in these firms. Judging by the percentage of an industry's employees who were affected by acquisition during both periods, the industries with the greatest activity were food, textiles, and machinery. In fact, over a third of the employees in the manufacturing sector subject to takeover were in these three industries. The other industries with a substantial number of employees involved in acquisitions were rubber and plastics, fabricated metals, and machinery. There does not seem to be much of a pattern, except when we look at the second period. There, the industries with the largest acquisition share seem to be the older, somewhat technologically backward industries that are in the process of upgrading to meet foreign competition. Is the acquisition activity in these industries primarily oriented toward consolidation and shrinkage of the industry, or is there also an attempt to buy smaller firms in the industry that have been successful innovators? I will defer this question until we examine the R&D-to-sales ratios of the stayers and exiters.

Of the approximately 600 firms that were acquired, I was able to identify 342 that were acquired by firms in the Industrial or OTC Compustat files; of these, there are about 320 for which I have good data on both the buyer and the seller. This set excludes any firms that were acquired by foreign firms, as well as those acquired by privately held firms. It *does* include nonmanufacturing firms that acquired firms in the manufacturing sector. The characteristics of the subset for which I have data on the buyer are given in Table 3.2b. Although these data account for only half the acquisitions made during this period, they cover two-thirds of the employees involved in acquisitions (two million out of three million). The table also shows the industrial distribution of the firms doing the acquiring. There are fewer firms in this column since some made more than one acquisition during the period.

Table 3.2b demonstrates that there is no overwhelming pattern to the merger and acquisition activity; the distribution of buyers and sellers is quite different from industry to industry but not in a particularly meaningful way. The largest share of firms were taken over in the aircraft, machinery, and electrical machinery industries, while the aircraft, electrical machinery, and petroleum industries had the largest share of firms performing acquisitions. This last fact is a consequence of the fact that these industries are also the ones with the largest number of employees per firm on average.

In tables 3.3a and 3.3b, I investigate the differences in R&D intensity between exiting firms and those remaining in the industry, and then between acquiring firms and those they acquired. Among those firms acquired by other firms in the publicly traded manufacturing sector,

Table 3.2a   The Number and Employment of Manufacturing Firms Acquired, 1977–86

Industry	1976		1977–81		1981		1982–86	
	N of Firms	E (000)	% Firms	% E	N of Firms	E (000)	% Firms	% E
Food	158	1,753	19.0%	18.6%	120	1,771	25.0%	17.0%
Textiles	153	996	7.2	6.1	117	831	26.5	24.3
Chemicals	103	1,378	19.4	4.6	87	1,382	10.3	9.0
Pharmaceuticals	92	739	10.9	4.4	99	793	14.1	15.3
Petroleum	66	1,456	9.1	5.2	58	1,681	8.6	8.1
Rubber, plastics	76	708	9.2	1.0	61	545	23.0	22.3
Stone, clay, glass	58	373	17.2	8.2	47	342	23.4	13.4
Primary metals	87	771	11.5	8.0	76	796	15.8	18.0
Fabricated metals	136	565	13.2	5.2	115	576	21.7	18.9
Engines	59	592	10.2	9.6	53	570	5.7	1.5
Computers	113	1,107	12.4	3.0	130	1,566	3.8	0.6
Machinery	157	657	21.0	17.3	122	557	14.8	11.2
Electrical machinery	82	1,492	14.6	7.1	84	1,447	22.6	8.5
Electronics	192	2,000	8.3	2.6	198	2,376	7.6	5.6
Autos	77	1,357	14.3	4.6	62	1,041	19.4	10.3
Aircraft	40	823	12.5	1.7	37	984	21.6	9.4
Instruments	87	232	8.0	5.3	88	265	8.0	2.6
Lumber and wood	154	916	9.7	6.1	127	824	16.5	7.2
Misc. mfg.	166	957	11.4	5.0	150	1,091	18.0	10.0
Total Mfg.	2,056	18,874	12.8	6.6	1,831	19,436	15.6	10.4

Note: All employment figures include part-time and seasonal workers and exclude any contract employees or consultants. The first four columns refer to acquisitions made between 1977 and 1981 as a share of the industry as it existed in 1976. The next four columns show acquisitions made between 1982 and 1986 as a share of the industry in 1981. The number (N) of firms acquired and the employment (E) in those firms are shown as a percentage of the base-period number of firms and employment.

Table 3.2b   Characteristics of the Buyers and Sellers in 314 Manufacturing Acquisitions, 1977–86

Industry	1976		Firms Aquired, 1977–86				Acquiring Firms, 1977–86	
	N of Firms	E (000)	N	%	E (000)	% E	N	%
Food	158	1,753	26	16.5%	541.5	30.9%	23	14.6%
Textiles	153	996	11	7.2	50.0	5.0	14	9.2
Chemicals	103	1,378	19	18.4	182.1	13.2	12	11.7
Pharmaceuticals	92	739	17	18.5	110.7	1.5	12	13.0
Petroleum	66	1,456	8	12.1	164.6	11.3	14	21.2
Rubber, plastics	76	708	11	14.5	8.2	1.1	9	11.5
Stone, clay, glass	58	373	10	17.2	31.3	8.3	8	13.8
Primary metals	87	771	12	13.8	161.3	20.9	5	5.7
Fabricated metals	136	566	25	18.4	45.7	8.1	16	11.8
Engines	59	592	6	10.2	44.3	7.4	3	5.1
Computers	113	1,107	18	15.9	53.4	4.8	10	8.8
Machinery	157	657	31	19.7	143.9	21.9	14	8.9
Electrical machinery	82	1,492	18	22.0	131.9	8.8	13	15.8
Electronics	192	2,000	27	14.1	173.0	8.9	16	8.3
Autos	77	1,357	6	7.8	21.0	1.5	11	14.3
Aircraft	40	823	10	25.0	89.3	10.8	6	15.0
Instruments	87	232	11	12.6	18.1	7.8	9	10.3
Lumber and wood	154	916	23	14.9	71.3	7.8	10	6.5
Misc. mfg.	166	957	25	15.1	47.1	4.9	11	6.6
Total Mfg.	2,056	18,874	314	15.3	2,088.7	11.1	216	10.5

Note: The sample consists of manufacturing acquisitions in which both the buyer and the seller appeared on the Compustat Files.

All employment figures include part-time and seasonal workers and exclude any contract employees or consultants. The first two columns are totals for the manufacturing sector in 1976. The next four columns are totals for the firms acquired between 1977 and 1986. The columns labeled % show those firms' share of the industry in 1976, both in number of firms and in employment. The last two columns tally the firms in the industry that made acquisitions of publicly traded manufacturing firms between 1977 and 1986.

the difference in R&D intensity between the acquiring firms and the acquired was insignificantly different from zero both in the entire manufacturing sector and in each industry taken separately. Only in primary and fabricated metals is there a suggestion that the acquired firms were doing slightly more R&D than those that remained. There is no evidence that the *dominant* pattern is either a weeding out of firms that are technologically backward or a culling of successful R&D projects.

The firms acquired by private companies or by foreign firms did, however, have significantly lower R&D intensity than those acquired by the manufacturing sector: 1 percent on average rather than 2 percent. This pattern persisted throughout the period; it was not a result of the rise in private buyouts in the latter part. It occurred partly because these acquisitions tend to take place in the less R&D-intensive, more slowly growing industries such as textiles. With only one exception, the petroleum industry, the industries with less than average R&D intensity were those in which private and foreign acquisitions were a larger than average share of all acquisitions. These industries, which contain half the firms in the sample, accounted for 70 percent of the acquisitions by private or foreign companies. This suggests that the recent increase in acquisition activity due to leveraged buyouts or other such private purchases is more or less orthogonal to the R&D activity in manufacturing. Even if all such purchases resulted in the complete cessation of R&D activity by the firm, this would amount to only around 500 million 1982 dollars annually compared to expenditures on R&D by the manufacturing sector of approximately 40 billion 1982 dollars annually.

R&D intensity does appear to have been lower in the acquiring firms than in the acquired ones; the firms sold had on average a higher R&D-to-sales ratio than those that bought them. But this finding is primarily due to the 38 takeovers of manufacturing firms by nonmanufacturing firms: here the firms were combined with an entity that probably did considerably less R&D in its nonmanufacturing lines of business. At the industrial level, it is difficult to draw any strong conclusions because of the relatively small samples.

The data in the columns labeled $\triangle R/S$ in tables 3.3a and 3.3b help answer the question of what happens to the R&D program of the combined firm after an acquisition has taken place. In table 3.3a the $\triangle R/S$ for nonacquired firms is the average two-year change in R&D intensity over the period for the firms in the industry. The $\triangle R/S$ for acquired firms is the two-year change in R&D intensity around the time of acquisition for the firms involved in the acquisition, classified by the acquired firm's industry. In table 3.3b the same quantity appears, classified by the acquiring firm's industry. The preacquisition R&D intensity is computed in the following way:

$$(12) \qquad (R/S)_{pre} = (R_j + R_i)/(S_j + S_i),$$

where i and j index the two firms involved. The conclusions are not changed by restricting attention to those acquisitions in which both R_j and R_i are nonzero, so that the numbers presented are for all firms.

The individual industry data are difficult to interpret because of the imprecision with which they are estimated, but there did seem to be some significant increases in R&D around the time of acquisition, particularly in textiles, machinery, computers, and electronics. Viewed in the context of differing patterns of industry growth, this finding may have different meanings for different industries. In the textiles and machinery industries for example, two-thirds of the acquirers were outside the publicly traded manufacturing sector. The acquisitions here are therefore a special group and perhaps reflected the improved prospects for the remaining firms after the industry had shrunk. (See Schary 1986 for a more detailed study of the long-run reaction of firms in the textile industry to its declining profitability.) In computers and electronics, however, almost all the acquisitions were in the manufacturing sector, specifically in closely related industries, and the growth in R&D is perhaps another indicator that the firms engaged in acquisition activity need to invest more rather than less in R&D to exploit the value of their acquisitions.

Overall, however, there is little evidence of a significant difference in the mean growth rates of R&D intensity between firms involved in acquisitions and nonacquiring firms. Comparing the means is only part of the story, however. It is possible that R&D intensities change in different ways for different types of acquisitions in such a way as to leave the mean growth rate unchanged. Figure 3.1 plots the distribution of these changes for all firms in the manufacturing sector and for the acquisitions only. Figure 3.2 plots the same distribution but also includes the firms not engaging in R&D. These plots show some evidence that the variance of the changes in R&D intensities was somewhat higher for the acquisitions and that more of them experience a decline than the overall sample. Nonetheless, nonparametric tests[4] for the difference in the overall means of the $\triangle R/S$ data in tables 3.3a and 3.3b accept equality in almost all cases (whether or not publicly traded nonmanufacturing acquisitions are excluded and whether or not those firms doing no R&D are excluded). In only one case did a significant positive difference exist, that which included all publicly traded firms and firms that engaged in no R&D, and here that difference resulted

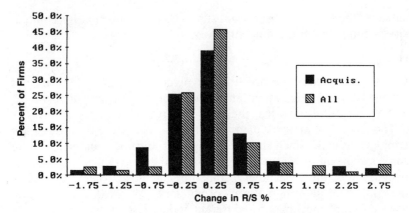

Fig. 3.1   Two-year change in R&D intensity at acquiring and nonacquiring firms in manufacturing, 1976–86

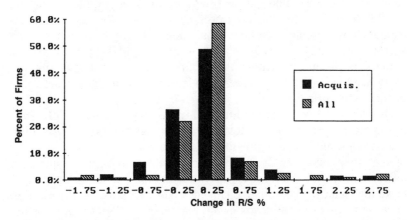

Fig. 3.2   Two-year change in R&D intensity, with data including firms
not engaging in R&D, 1976–86

in only two of the four nonparametric tests. The same conclusion holds
looking at three-year changes around the time of acquisition (not reported here). The conclusion is that there is no overwhelming evidence
that acquiring firms experience a change in R&D behavior around the
time of acquisition.

Because firm size is systematically related to both R&D intensity
and the probability of being acquired, the data in the preceding tables

are difficult to interpret in detail. In the next section I therefore attempt to quantify the determinants of acquisition further by estimating probability models with more than one explanatory variable.

3.4 Estimating the Probability of Entering the Acquisition Market

Before I present results for the full-blown multinomial logit model of acquisition matches, I present estimates of the "marginals" of such a model. These estimates are not marginals of the distribution of the multinomial logit model in the statistical sense, since they cannot be obtained by aggregating over the choice set,[5] but they summarize the data from the perspective of the acquiring and the acquired firms separately. They also provide an indication of the change in the sample when I restrict the data to the approximately 300 acquisitions for which I can observe both partners.

Assume that the reduced form for the probability of being acquired in any one year can be written as a logit function of various firm characteristics:

(13) $P(i$ acq. in year $t|X_{it},t)$
$$= exp(\beta X_{it} + \alpha_t)/[1 + exp(\beta X_{it} + \alpha_t)],$$

where X_{it} represents the characteristics of the firm. The estimates of β and α_t can then be obtained with a conventional maximum likelihood logit estimation. The same type of model can also be used to estimate the probability that firm j will make an acquisition in year t, conditional on the firm's characteristics X_{jt}.

The model of acquisition sketched in section 3.2 uses the assets of the firms to predict their valuation and, hence, the gain from merger. To keep things simple, I focus on two assets: capital stock (including all plant and equipment, inventories, and other investments), and the stock of knowledge capital. These two assets tend to be the most significant ones in a simple stock market value equation. For the buyers and sellers in 311 transactions that took place between 1977 and 1986, I have constructed estimates of the book value of the physical assets in current dollars and the R&D capital held by those firms one year before the acquisition, using the methodology described in Cummins et al. (1985). Adjustments for the effects of inflation on the book value of the physical assets have been applied, and R&D capital has been depreciated at a rate of 15 percent per year (see Griliches and Mairesse 1981, 1983). I then deflated these variables to be in 1982 dollars, using a fixed investment deflator and an R&D deflator (Cummins et al. 1985), respectively, since I would be pooling across years.

Table 3.3a   Comparison of R&D-to-Sales Ratios for Acquired and Nonacquired Firms, by the Acquired Firm's Industry, 1977–86

Industry	N of Firms	Acquired Firms		Nonacquired Firms		R/S Difference	
		R/S	Δ R/S	R/S	Δ R/S	Avg.	t-Statistic
Food	26	.253%	.06%	.160%	.01%	−.093%	−1.5
Textiles	11	.158	.41	.169	.02	.012	0.1
Chemicals	19	1.79	−.21	1.80	−.35	.015	0.0
Pharmaceuticals	17	7.21	.23	4.87	.59	−2.34	−0.6
Petroleum	8	.322	.14	.337	.01	.016	0.1
Rubber, plastics	11	.573	−.04	.915	.06	.342	0.8
Stone, clay, glass	10	.411	.01	.372	.03	−.039	−0.2
Primary metals	12	.623	−.10	.269	−.01	−.354	−2.1
Fabricated metals	25	.986	.16	.563	.02	−.422	−2.3
Engines	6	.826	−.07	1.37	.11	.547	1.1
Computers	18	5.64	.48	5.32	.26	−.319	−0.1
Machinery	31	1.12	.40	1.58	.20	.455	0.7
Electrical machinery	18	3.51	−.13	4.40	.40	.893	0.3
Electronics	27	4.07	.88	3.44	.44	−.631	−0.3
Autos	6	.782	−.12	.766	−.18	−.016	−0.0
Aircraft	10	2.12	.09	2.02	.26	−.107	−0.1
Instruments	11	4.56	.35	4.10	.43	−.455	−0.2
Lumber and wood	23	.345	.03	.342	.32	−.004	−0.0
Misc. mfg.	25	.620	.04	.340	.02	−.028	−1.6
Total mfg.	314	1.97	.18	1.82	.16	−.154	−0.4
Acquisitions outside the sample	254	0.92		1.82		−0.90	−3.0

Note: R/S is the deflated R&D-to-sales ratio. The deflator for sales is the producer price index for finished goods (U.S. Bureau of Labor Statistics) and that for R&D is according to Griliches method, following Jaffe (see Cummins et al. 1985 for details). The columns labeled "acquired firms" show the average R&D-to-sales ratio for the 314 firms that were acquired by other firms in my sample, measured one year before the acquisition (R/S) and, for the combined firm, measured from one year before acquisition until one year later ($\Delta R/S$). The columns labeled "nonacquired firms" show the average R&D-to-sales ratio and the change in that ratio for the firms that were not acquired, averaged over the 1977 to 1986 period. These data are based on several hundred observations per industry. The last two columns show the difference in R/S between the two groups of firms and the t-statistic for the hypothesis that the difference is zero.

Table 3.3b Comparison of R&D-to-Sales Ratios for Acquired and Acquiring Firms, by the Acquiring Firm's Industry, 1977–86

	N of Firms Acquired	Acquired Firms R/S	Acquiring Firms R/S	Acquiring Firms Δ R/S	R/S Difference Avg.	R/S Difference t-statistic
Food	30	.320%	.209%	.07%	−.111%	−1.1
Textiles	15	.276	.467	.49	.191	0.6
Chemicals	18	3.22	2.69	.18	−.532	−0.7
Pharmaceuticals	14	7.33	4.77	.31	−2.56	−0.9
Petroleum	11	.864	.383	−.06	−.481	−1.5
Rubber, plastics	11	.841	.921	.11	.080	0.2
Stone, clay, glass	9	1.11	1.10	.12	−.017	0.0
Primary metals	7	.084	.204	−.02	.120	1.0
Fabricated metals	28	.849	.649	−.12	−.199	−0.6
Engines	3	1.18	2.11	.06	.935	1.1
Computers	10	6.61	5.76	.46	−.854	−0.6
Machinery	21	1.08	1.24	.52	.161	0.4
Electrical machinery	23	3.34	2.00	.02	−1.34	−1.4
Electronics	17	3.92	4.07	1.88	.145	0.2
Autos	14	2.59	1.12	−.05	−1.47	−1.1
Aircraft	9	3.97	3.61	−.26	−.361	−0.3
Instruments	11	1.79	3.33	.12	1.54	1.9
Lumber and wood	10	.520	.304	.01	−.215	−0.6
Misc. mfg.	18	.656	.179	−.06	−.477	−1.3
Total mfg.	279	2.05	1.68	.22	−.369	−0.9
Nonmfg.	38	1.38	.168		−1.21	−3.4
Total	317	1.97 %	1.50 %		−.472%	−1.5

Note: The two columns labeled R/S give the average R&D-to-sales ratio for the acquiring firms and the firms they acquired. R/S is defined the same way as in table 3.3a. The column labeled Δ R/S is the average implied change in R/S around the time of acquisition for acquisitions by firms in that industry. The last two columns again test the difference between the two R/S ratios.

I estimated equation (14) using, as regressors, size (the log of capital stock), the ratio of R&D stock to capital stock, and a trend variable. I also included a dummy variable for the more technologically oriented industries (those with R/S greater than 1 percent in table 3.3a) to check whether the R&D effects were in reality industry effects. Table 3.4 shows these estimates. The first column pertains to the complete sample of acquisitions for which data existed; the other columns are for two subsets: those firms acquired by private or foreign firms, and those firms acquired by the firms in my sample (mostly manufacturing, with a few nonmanufacturing firms).

The estimates for the two groups are quite different, confirming the findings in the simple statistics of table 3.3a. The privately traded acquisitions show a much steeper positive trend than the others, and all the other variables have predictive power. Size, R&D intensity, and whether the firm is in a science-based industry have a significant negative effect on the probability of its being acquired by a privately held or foreign firm. On the other hand, these variables have no effect on the probability of its being acquired by a publicly traded manufacturing

Table 3.4   **Maximum Likelihood Logit Estimates of the Probability of Acquisition (21,900 observations; heteroskedastic-consistent standard errors in parentheses)**

	Probability of Being Acquired		
	by All Firms	by Private or Foreign Firms	by Manufacturing Firms
N of Acquisitions	557	229	328
log A	−.042(.022)	−.166(.030)	.036(.028)
K/A	−.139(.144)	−.514(.314)	.058(.167)
$D(Tech)$	−.232(.097)	−.830(.175)	.146(.122)
Trend†	.125(.016)	.239(.028)	.054(.020)
$\chi^2(3)$ for A, K, $Tech$	12.0	60.2	3.4

	Probability of Making an Acquisition		
	1976–86	1976–81	1982–86
N of Acquisitions	319	167	152
log A	.432(.025)	.546(.036)	.320(.034)
K/A	−.314(.266)	.218(.340)	−.994(.385)
Trend†	.027(.023)	−.015(.049)	.264(.079)

log K = Log of deflated capital stock of the firm in the year before it acquired another firm or was itself acquired

K/A = ratio of R&D stock to assets in the same year

$D(Tech)$ = dummy variable for the chemical, pharmaceutical, engine, computer, machinery, electrical machinery, electronics, aircraft, and instruments industries

†Includes a dummy variable for 1986 because the data for that year are incomplete

firm. Thus, it is likely that the private acquisition activity is targeted toward those industries and firms where the current management has already been perceived the growth opportunities as unprofitable. This could be construed as evidence that management has cut R&D spending in an effort to avert takeovers, but if so, they have not been successful. It seems more likely that this activity facilitates a needed shrinkage in the assets devoted to these particular activities. Without knowledge of subsequent events in these firms, it is difficult to be more precise about the reason for this finding. What can be said is that, in manufacturing, the acquisitions seem indistinguishable from the non-acquired firms.

The bottom part of table 3.4 shows the probability of making an acquisition for three different samples: acquisitions made during the full sample period, those made from 1976 to 1981, those made from 1982 to 1986. The results are unsurprising: Size is positively related to the probability of making an acquisition; that probability rose toward the end of the period; and R&D intensity is not important. When I focus on the two subperiods, a difference does emerge. In the 1980s the firms making the large acquisitions had a somewhat lower R&D intensity than the other manufacturing firms, suggesting some substitution between R&D performance and acquisition activity. I also included the *Tech* variable in these equations, but it was completely insignificant in all periods. This result is therefore not the result of a shift of acquisition activity toward low-technology industries.

3.5   Results for the Matching Model of Mergers

I now turn to estimates of the multinomial logit model of the match between the acquiring and the acquired firms. Here I confine my sample to the firms that made acquisitions; that is, the estimates are conditional on a firm having chosen to enter the takeover market, and they describe the choice made once the firm is in the market. A reasonable way to augment this model so that it also describes the decision to enter the market would be to build a nested logit model where the decision to make an acquisition is logically prior to the choice of target. The estimates obtained here are consistent for the lower branch of such a nested logit model (McFadden 1978,1984), although the interpretation of the coefficients would change. The upper branch would be somewhat similar to the logit model estimated in table 3.4, since it would describe the choice between making any acquisition or making none, but it would include an additional term corresponding to the "inclusive value" of the set of takeover candidates available. In other words, the characteristics of the available targets would enter in the form of a kind of index function along with the characteristics of the acquirer.

With this caveat in mind, I now describe the application of the random utility choice model to this problem. It is well known that when the unobserved part of the utility function has an extreme value distribution, the probability a particular choice will be made from a set of alternatives has the multinomial logit form (again, see McFadden 1973 and Manski and McFadden 1981). It is only slightly less well known that any model for choice probabilities can be written in the multinomial logit form, with the proviso that if the independence of irrelevant alternatives assumption does not hold, characteristics of the other choices may enter into the "utility" function associated with a particular choice. This statement should be kept in mind because it allows us to view the multinomial logit model estimated here as a descriptive summary of the data observed, even if the underlying interpretation of the V functions as determining the acquisition probability is suspect.

The results of estimation conditional on an acquisition's being made are shown in table 3.5.[6] These are estimates of the choice model given in equation (7), with the choice set consisting of the chosen alternative plus six others randomly selected from the firms in the sample that year. Model I, shown in the first two columns, captures the character of the match $v_j(X_i)$ very crudely with the absolute value of the difference in size and the difference in R&D intensity of the two firms. In addition, the size of the target and its R&D intensity enter the logit equation through $v(X_i)$. The second column includes a dummy variable for whether or not the firms are in the same industry; it improves the explanatory power ($\chi^2[1] = 183.$), but it does not affect the other coefficients very much. The estimates imply that mergers between firms of very different sizes are less likely to take place, and that mergers between firms with differing R&D intensities are also less likely to happen. Thus, the evidence is fairly strong that mergers within the manufacturing sector tend to be between firms of like size and like R&D intensity.

The next set of estimates in table 3.5 are for the model (model II) suggested in equation (12). These provide a richer description of the matching taking place in the merger market. If the estimates in the last column are representative, they imply an equation for the incremental value of an acquisition to a firm of the following form:

$$(14) \qquad v_j(X_i) = \gamma_{0j} + \gamma_{1j} \log A_i + \gamma_{2j}(K/A)_i.$$

The term γ_{0j} is not identified in the conditional logit model because it cancels from the numerator and denominator of equation (6), but the other coefficients are the following:

$$(15) \qquad \gamma_{1j} = \gamma_{10} + 0.17 \log A_j - 0.18\ (K/A)_j$$

$$\gamma_{2j} = \gamma_{20} + 0.32 \log A_j + 4.1\ (K/A)_j.$$

In other words, the bidding firms value the size of the target at an increasing rate with respect to their own size, and at a decreasing rate

Table 3.5   **Conditional Logit Estimates of Acquisition Choice, 1977–86**
(311 acquisitions; standard errors in parentheses)

Variables	Coefficient Estimates			
	Model I		Model II	
$\Delta \log A$	$-1.04(.15)$	$-1.00(.17)$		
$\Delta(K/A)$	$-4.05(.60)$	$-3.78(.66)$		
$\log A_j \cdot \log A_i$			$.17(.02)$	$.17(.02)$
$(K/A)_j \cdot \log A_i$			$-.31(.16)$	$-.18(.20)$
$\log A_j \cdot (K/A)_i$			$.28(.08)$	$.32(.08)$
$(K/A)_j \cdot (K/A)_i$			$3.82(.98)$	$4.05(1.09)$
D(Same ind.)		$2.34(.21)$		$2.41(.18)$
$\log A_i$	$-.72(.14)$	$-.73(.16)$	$-1.13(.13)$	$-1.21(.15)$
$(K/A)_i$	$3.30(.53)$	$3.09(.58)$	$-2.98(0.72)$	$-3.28(0.82)$
log of likelihood	-502.3	-424.7	-557.8	-467.2

Note: The standard error estimates are robust heteroskedastic-consistent estimates; they differ from the conventional estimates by less than 10 percent in almost all cases.

$\log A$ = log of deflated assets in the year before the acquisition, where assets equal the sum of capital stock, inventories, and other investments

(K/A) = ratio of R&D stock to assets in the year before the acquisition

$\Delta \log A = |\log A_j - \log A_i|$

$\Delta(K/A) = |(K/A)_j - (K/A)_i|$

D(Same ind.) = 1, if the acquiring and the acquired firms are in the same two-digit industry

The subscript j indexes the acquiring firms, and i indexes target firms. The coefficient estimates are for the probability that firm j chooses firm i when it makes an acquisition. Models I and II are described more completely in the text.

with respect to their R&D intensity. More interesting, the shadow price for the R&D intensity of the target is an increasing function of the size and the R&D intensity of the bidding firm. This finding may arise partly because of management's preference to acquire firms similar to those in their own industry. Nevertheless, the simple correction of controlling for the match being in the same industry had very little effect on the magnitude of the estimates, although it did reduce the R&D match coefficient somewhat, as expected. Further investigation of this finding, particularily within and across industries, seems warranted.

What do these estimates tell us about the valuation of the R&D stock of the firm at the time of acquisition? Unfortunately, we cannot say very much about this without making strong assumptions about the way in which $v(X_i)$, the price paid for the acquisition, is determined, since the estimated coefficients of the target firm's characteristics will contain terms from both the $v_j(X_i)$ (for example, γ_{10}) and the $v(X_i)$ equation.[7] This problem limits our ability to interpret equations (15) beyond pointing out that the shadow value placed on R&D capital is steeply rising with the acquiring firms' R&D intensity.

On the other hand, it is possible to know something about the price actually paid for the assets of the firms that were acquired and to compare this amount to the preacquisition value of these assets. I collected such data for 271 of the 311 acquisitions in the sample, namely, the value of debt plus equity in the year before the acquisition serves as the preacquisition market value of the firm (see Cummins et al. 1985 for details). I then collected data on the price paid to each holder of a share of common stock in the acquired firm at the time of acquisition and used the rate of return thus earned by holders of the common stock between the year before acquisition and the time of acquisition to update the value of debt plus equity (assuming that the total value of the firm was increasing along with the value of the common stock). This procedure is necessary because of the difficulty of valuing the claims of all stock and bond holders at the time of acquisition.

Using these numbers, I estimated a valuation equation for the 271 firms in the year before acquisition and at acquisition time. The results were:

$$(16) \qquad \log V(A,K) = \alpha_t + \underset{(0.02)}{0.96} \log A + \underset{(0.12)}{0.49} (K/A)$$

$$(17) \qquad \log V(A,K) = \alpha_t + \underset{(0.03)}{0.95} \log A + \underset{(0.14)}{0.65} (K/A),$$

where α_t denotes a dummy variable for the year in question. These equations suggest that a firm's R&D stock is valued at a slight premium over its value in the stock market when the firm is a candidate for takeover. This finding is strikingly consistent with Addanki's (1985) findings using some of the same data but a different model, and it deserves to be investigated further by integrating these equations into the full multinomial logit model of acquisition choice.

The analysis in this section has yielded two findings that bear on the role of R&D in acquisition activity. First, the takeover premium is positively related to the amount of R&D capital the acquired firm possesses. Second, some sort of matching does seem to be at work in the merger market: Firms prefer to acquire other firms that are similar to themselves, especially with respect to R&D intensity. This result is not one that is easily determined from the aggregate (marginal) patterns of merger estimated in table 3.4, suggesting that the full matching model I tried for the first time here may yield more information about the merger market than we have hitherto been able to obtain. Further research is needed to verify this result with additional information about the other firm characteristics that prompt takeover activity.

3.6 Conclusions

I began this paper with some questions about the costs and benefits of increased merger activity in the United States and suggested that exploring the role of research and development activity might shed some light on whether at least the firms involved have benefited from the increase. I also cited some previous and rather inconsistent evidence on the attractiveness of R&D in the takeover market. With respect to this last point, a richer model of acquisition, one that attempts to match buyers and sellers, seems to provide an explanation for some of the earlier results. Although on average acquired firms invested the same amount or slightly less in R&D as the industry norm, the R&D they engaged in was valued more highly at the margin by the firms that took them over. This result at least hints that successful innovators are being taken over. In addition, the evidence suggests that larger gains are generated by acquisitions where both firms involved have high R&D intensity.

I also found evidence that much of the acquisition activity by private and foreign firms in the domestic market was directed toward firms and industries that were relatively less R&D intensive and had a weaker technological base, so that this kind of acquisition activity cannot be a major factor in causing a shift in focus away from innovation activity, unless we take the view that managers in these industries saw themselves as threatened with takeover far in advance and cut R&D spending in anticipation of a takeover. But given the nature of the industries involved, this view seems somewhat unlikely. Explaining this result will require further investigation into the motives for private acquisitions.

Finally, the existing data (through 1985) provide very little evidence that acquisitions cause a reduction in R&D spending. In the aggregate the firms involved in mergers were in no way different in their pre- and postmerger R&D performance from those not so involved. At the individual industry level the results were too imprecisely measured to draw solid conclusions.

Many questions remain deserving of further attention. First, at the level of econometric specification, what are the optimal regressors and the optimal sampling for the choice set in the model I employed, and how do the results change when a nested logit model is used to estimate the probability of acquisition and the probability of the choice made? Second, can we learn more about the precise valuation of this part of the returns to R&D by incorporating takeover prices directly into the model of acquisition probability? Finally, is there more information about the relative importance of other reasons for merger to be gained from a more complete model of the acquisitions market using this framework? These questions await further research.

Notes

1. An additional reason for changes in merger activity might be changes in the transactions or other costs associated with buying another firm. For example, Jensen (1986) has suggested that the innovation of junk bonds facilitates the takeover of large firms by small ones, which would not have taken place previously. In my investigation here, I am abstracting somewhat from the changes in takeover "technology" that have occurred in recent years because they primarily affect factors in a time-series analysis and my focus is on cross-sectional differences and similarities in takeovers.

2. As was suggested by Ariel Pakes, one of the discussants of this paper, it is possible to reverse this model by viewing the decision from the perspective of the potential target. In this case the coefficients of the gain function are estimated from a comparison of the actual acquirer and those firms that might have acquired the target. If the specification is correct, and the ϵ_{ij} terms are truly independent, both methods should give the same estimates of the structural parameters. A full exploration of the econometric specification of such a model, though interesting, is beyond the scope of this paper. Work now under way on this topic suggests that differential propensities to be acquired or to acquire (that is, a lack of independence of the alternatives) may have a role here.

3. In data of this kind, with a skewed size distribution, the functional form typically having disturbances that are normally distributed is the log-log. For example, consider the form

$$\log V = \beta_0 + \beta_1 \log X + \epsilon, \quad \epsilon \sim (0, \sigma^2).$$

If we choose instead to estimate using V, we obtain

$$V = e^{\beta_0} X^{\beta_1} e^{\epsilon} \approx A_0 X^{\beta_1} (1 + \epsilon e^{\epsilon})$$

by a first order Taylor-series expansion. This disturbance is obviously very heteroskedastic (and skewed).

4. I used the Wilcoxon rank sum test (which is best for the logistic distribution), the median score test (best for double exponential), the Van der Waeden test (best for normal), and the Savage test (best for exponential).

5. In the special case where there are no synergies in acquisition (the gain is additively separable in the characteristics of i and j), these are the true marginal probabilities of acquiring and being acquired, but it seems unlikely that this particular model holds for these data. Simple significance tests on the interaction terms confirm this.

6. All the logit estimates in the table were obtained with the logit procedure TSP Version 4.1 (Hall, Cummins, and Schnake 1986).

7. I am grateful to Charles Brown, one of the commentators, for pointing out that the identifying assumption used in the first version of this paper, $\gamma_{10} \equiv 0$, is not very reasonable.

References

Abel, Andrew B. 1983. Optimal investment under uncertainty. *American Economic Review* 73:228–33.

————. 1985. A stochastic model of investment, marginal q, and the market value of the firm. *International Economic Review* 26:305–22.

Addanki, Sumanth. 1985. Innovation and mergers in U.S. manufacturing firms: A first look, photocopy. Cambridge: Department of Economics, Harvard University.

Auerbach, Alan J., and David Reishus. 1985. Taxes and the merger decision, photocopy. Philadelphia: University of Pennsylvania.

————. 1987. The effects of taxation on the merger decision. In this volume.

Bound, J., C. Cummins, Z. Griliches, B. H. Hall, and A. Jaffe. 1984. Who does R&D and who patents? In *R&D, patents, and productivity,* ed. Z. Griliches. Chicago: University of Chicago Press.

Cummins, Clint, Bronwyn H. Hall, Elizabeth S. Laderman, and Joy Mundy. 1985. The R&D master file: Documentation, photocopy. Cambridge: National Bureau of Economic Research.

Gilson, Ronald J., Myron S. Scholes, and Mark A. Wolfson. 1985. Taxation and the dynamics of corporate control: The uncertain case for tax motivated acquisitions, photocopy. Stanford: Stanford University.

Griliches, Z. 1981. Market value, R&D, and patents. *Economics Letters,* vol. 7.

Griliches, Z., and J. Mairesse. 1981. Productivity and growth at the firm level, NBER working paper 826. Cambridge: National Bureau of Economic Research.

————. 1983. Comparing productivity growth: An exploration of French and U.S. industrial and firm data. *European Economic Review* 21:89–119.

Hall, Bronwyn H. 1987a. The new R&D master file: 1959–1985, photocopy. Stanford: National Bureau of Economic Research.

————. 1987b. Equilibrium in the market for acquisitions, Stanford: Stanford University.

————. 1987c. The relationship between firm size and firm growth in the U.S. manufacturing sector. *Journal of Industrial Economics* 35:583–606.

Hall, Bronwyn H., Clint Cummins, and Rebecca Schnake. 1986. *TSP version 4.1 reference manual.* Stanford, Calif.: TSP International.

Jensen, Michael. 1986. The takeover controversy: Analysis and evidence, Harvard Business School working paper 9-786-001. Boston: Harvard University.

Jensen, Michael, and Richard Ruback. 1983. The market for corporate control. *Journal of Financial Economics* 11:1–53.

Lucas, Robert E., and Edward C. Prescott. 1971. Investment under uncertainty. *Econometrica* 39:659–81.

Manski, Charles F., and Daniel McFadden. 1981. *Structural analysis of discrete data with economic applications.* Cambridge, Mass.: MIT Press.

McFadden, Daniel. 1973. Conditional logit analysis of qualitative choice behavior. In *Frontiers of econometrics,* ed. P. Zarembka. New York: Academic Press.

————. 1978. Modelling the choice of residential location. In *Spatial interaction theory and residential location,* ed. A. Karlqvist. Amsterdam: North Holland.

————. 1984. Qualitative response models. In *Handbook of econometrics,* vol. 2, ed. Z. Griliches and M. D. Intriligator. Amsterdam: North Holland.

Mussa, Michael. 1974. Market value and the investment decision in an adjustment cost model of firm behavior, discussion paper 74-15 (July) Rochester, N.Y.: Department of Economics, University of Rochester.

Ravenscraft, David, and F. M. Scherer. 1986. The profitability of mergers, photocopy. Swarthmore: Swarthmore College.

Roll, Richard. 1986. The hubris hypothesis of corporate takeovers. *Journal of Business* 59:197–216.

Schary, Martha. 1986. Exit, investment and technological diffusion in a declining industry: An empirical study, photocopy. Cambridge: Massachusetts Institute of Technology.

Securities and Exchange Commission, Office of the Chief Economist. 1985. Institutional ownership, tender offers, and long-term investments, SEC study. Washington, D.C.: GPO, April.

Train, Kenneth. 1986. *Qualitative choice analysis*. Cambridge, Mass.: MIT Press.

Wildasin, David E. 1984. The q theory of investment with many capital goods. *American Economic Review* 74:203–10.

Comment   Charles Brown

Hall's paper presents needed evidence on the relationship between corporate takeovers and R&D activity. It actually provides a broader picture than its title promises, since it analyzes both the changes in R&D activity following mergers and the impact of R&D activity on acquisitions.

The introduction of the paper poses several possible relationships between merger activity and R&D spending. These follow from conjectures about discretionary managerial behavior, not derived as the "optimal" behavior of managers with particular objectives and constraints. It is not obvious to me, however, that the picture would be sharpened by such an effort.

For the most part, the managerial behavior discussed has to do with investment in general rather than R&D in particular. It would be interesting to undertake a parallel analysis, for the same firms, of whether investment in physical capital is changed by corporate takeovers.

The model of merger partners allows one to raise interesting questions, but two things are, in a sense, missing. First, j acquires i when it is profitable for j to do so (as Hall emphasizes) but only when it is not more profitable for some other firm k to acquire i. It is true that competition for i among potential suitors would raise the price of i, and when the dust clears the acquisition is profitable for only one firm. Yet the information that it was not profitable in the end for the other firms to acquire i is not explicitly included in the estimation. Second, the price that j will ultimately pay for i is taken as a function of i's characteristics and not identified with the preannouncement value of

Charles Brown is professor of economics, Department of Economics, and program director, Survey Research Center, Institute for Social Research, at the University of Michigan, and a research associate of the National Bureau of Economic Research.

i, because "by making a bid, firm *j* reveals something about the value of the assets that was not previously known and hence finds it necessary to bid above the trading price." If so, the potential acquisition price might depend on *j*'s characteristics, and the distinction between the v_j and v functions is blurred.

Assembling the data for this study (Hall was part of the team that did so) was a sizable task, and it would be bad form to overemphasize the potential for omitted-variable bias in the "lean, mean" empirical specification that data limitations impose. Constructively, a quick survey of the determinants of R&D and the determinants of merger activity found in previous studies might give one a better feel for the direction any such bias is likely to take.

Hall presents several interesting results, whose full explanation will provide a likely topic for future work. Some of the conclusions will benefit if a few years of "merger mania" expand the sample to be studied. There is surely room for disagreement about one's favorites; mine are the very different pattern of acquisitions between manufacturing firms and firms that are not publicly traded (table 3.3) and the premium placed on the stock of R&D by potential acquirers (table 3.6, model II).

Comment   Ariel Pakes

There are two parts to Hall's paper. The first documents the characteristics of an extensive data base on mergers and acquisitions that Bronwyn has put together. The second suggests a framework for the econometric analysis of merger activity and then presents some preliminary estimates. I am going to focus my comments on the second part of the paper (since this is where my own value added is likely to be highest). There is no doubt, however, that the first part of the paper makes a substantive contribution to the literature on mergers and acquisitions. Hall has produced both a valuable data set and an apt characterization of the trends in merger activity over a ten-year period (broken down by industry and type of buyer). This information should prove extremely valuable in considering the possible causes and effects of merger activity.

Finding a sensible framework for a detailed econometric analysis of merger activity is not a simple task. The spectrum of forces that the literature refers to as motivating mergers is large and depends on many

Ariel Pakes is associate professor of economics at the University of Wisconsin and a research associate of the National Bureau of Economic Research.

factors that are difficult to quantify. The best we can do is look for a way to summarize the data that makes some "reduced form" sense, and then be very careful in the way we interpret the estimates.

Hall's framework consists of three main equations. If we let $V_j(X_i)$ be the increment in firm j's value that results from the purchase of firms i's assets (X_i), then Hall assumes firm j purchases firm i if

(a) $V_j(X_i) - P_i \geq V_j(X_k) - P_k$, for all possible firms k, and

(b) $V_j(X_i) - P_i \geq 0$,

with

(c) $P_i = V(X_i)$,

where P_i is the price of firm i. The logic underlying equations (a) and (b) is that if firm j purchases firm i, the increment in firm j's value from this coupling, or "match," must be both greater than the increment from any other possible match j could make and greater than zero. Equation (c) states that the price of firm i depends only on its own assets. Note that P_i is observable so that (with some additional functional form assumptions) equation (c) could be estimated.

I think that this form of a "matching" model is not appropriate for the merger problem. If we take (c) as given, (a) and (b) are likely to be satisfied for a large number of potential acquisitors simultaneously, and only one coupling will actually take place. Moreover, the price of firm i is unlikely to depend only on firms i's own assets. Simple economics tells us that the price firm i sells for must be between the values assigned to firm i by the potential purchasers with the first and second highest evaluations of firm i's assets. Since these evaluations are likely to depend on the characteristics of these two potential buyers, so will P_i. What is lacking in this system of equations is some allowance for the workings of the market as a whole.

An alternative to the matching model is the look for "equilibrium" conditions and estimate from them. We might, for example, consider replacing (a), (b) and (c) with

(a') $V_j(X_i) = max_k V_k(X_i)$

(b') $V_j(X_i) \geq P_i \geq V_r(X_i)$,

with

(c') $V_r(X_i) = max_{(k \neq j)} V_k(X_i)$,

where *max* refers to the operation of taking the maximum. Equation (a') states that if j purchases i, the value of i to j must be at least as great as the value of i to any other potential buyer (or else the other acquiror would make the purchase; note that $V_j[X_i]$ must also be greater than $V_i[X_i]$ which is the value of i as an independent entity). Equations (b') and (c') filter in the price of acquisition by insuring that it lies between the values assigned to i by the two potential buyers with the highest evaluations of i.

There are also problems with the kind of frictionless, complete-information, equilibrium approach embodied in (a'), (b'), and (c'). For example, this model is not complete without an additional rule specifying the set of potential buyers, or the set over which the maximum is taken (this problem also plagues Hall's framework). Still, I think it is useful to begin with a set of equations that have some simple economic justification and then try to build in the appropriate complexities as best we can. Note that the difference between (a) and (a') is in the comparison set. Statement (a) compares $V_j(X_i)$ to other purchases firm j could make; (a') compares it to the values attached to i by other potential buyers. If we were to use the type of logit specification Hall implements, it would be just as easy to estimate one version as the other.

The "equilibrium" strategy can be pushed further than this. Statements (a'), (b'), and (c') use only the equilibrium conditions in the current period. There are also equilibrium conditions in prior periods. Since in period $t - 1$, firm i existed as a separate entity, it should be the case that $max_k V_k^{t-1}(X_i^{t-1}) \leq V_i^{t-1}(X_i^{t-1}) = P_i^{t-1}$, where the subscript $t - 1$ denotes evaluations made in the period prior to the merger, so that P_i^{t-1} is the observed value of the ith firm in period $t - 1$. Thus, if we let t be the merger period, putting together the equilibrium conditions from the period prior to merger with the period after the merger gives us the statements

$$V_j^t(X_i^t) - V_j^{t-1}(X_i^{t-1}) \geq P_i^t - P_i^{t-1}$$

if j actually makes the acquisition, and

$$V_k^t(X_i^t) - V_k^{t-1}(X_i^{t-1}) \leq P_i^t - P_i^{t-1}$$

if k does not.

Although combining information from different periods should provide us with more precise estimators if the assumptions of the model are correct, it also places a heavy burden on the (clearly inappropriate) assumption that every possible buyer evaluates all possible purchases in every period. In fact, evaluating potential acquirees is a costly and time-consuming task. An alternative strategy would be to provide a model of when an evaluation process is initiated. A model of when the costs of acquisition are actually incurred could also provide us with a formal way of determining the set of potential buyers (and this, in turn, would do away with the need to invoke the independence-of-irrelevant-alternatives assumption that is now being used to constrain the number of potential buyers in the estimation algorithm).

Once Hall moves on to her choice of functional forms for $V_j(X_i)$, I am much happier with her assumptions. She assumes $V_j(X_i) = \Sigma \alpha_{jk} X_{ik} + \epsilon_{ij}$, where $\alpha_{jk} = \Sigma z_{jr} \delta_{kr}$. Here firm j's evaluation (α_{jk}) of firm i's assets (X_{ik}) depends on firm j's characteristics (z_{jr}). I think this is an intuitive way of looking at the reduced form relationships between the characteristics of the acquiring firm and those of the acquired firm. My only recommendation would be to try to augment the list of characteristics (the X_k and the z_r) and to allow for a disturbance term in the equation determining the α_{jk} (it is difficult to quantify all the factors that make firm i's assets attractive to firm j). It would be particularly useful if we could find and use variables that might capture the effects of some of the alternative explanations of merger activity. I imagine that all these tasks are in Hall's list of things to do.

4   Characteristics of Targets of Hostile and Friendly Takeovers

Randall Mørck, Andrei Shleifer,
and Robert W. Vishny

4.1   Introduction

Economic analysis has identified two broad classes of takeovers. The first is what we call disciplinary takeovers, the purpose of which seems to be to correct the non-value-maximizing (NVM) practices of managers of the target firms. These practices might include excessive growth and diversification, lavish consumption of perquisites, overpayment to employees and suppliers, or debt avoidance to secure a "quiet life." Disciplinary takeovers thus address the problem of what Williamson (1964) has called discretionary behavior by managers and Jensen (1986a) has christened "the agency cost of free cash flow." Because disciplinary takeovers are designed to replace or change the policies of managers who do not maximize shareholder value, the actual integration of the businesses of the acquirer and the target is not really essential. The takeover is only the most effective way to change control and with it the target's operating strategy.

The second class of takeovers can be loosely called synergistic, since the motivating force behind them is the possibility of benefits from combining the businesses of two firms. Synergy gains can come from increases in market power, from offsetting the profits of one firm with the tax loss carryforwards of the other, from combining R&D labs or

Randall Mørck is assistant professor of finance at the University of Alberta. Andrei Shleifer is assistant professor of finance and business economics at the Graduate School of Business, University of Chicago, and a faculty research fellow of the National Bureau of Economic Research. Robert W. Vishny is assistant professor of finance at the Graduate School of Business, University of Chicago, and a faculty research fellow of the NBER.

The authors thank Oliver Hart, Michael Jensen, Kevin M. Murphy, Edward Rice, and Lawrence Summers for helpful comments and the NBER for financial support.

marketing networks, or from simply eliminating functions that are common to the two firms. Unlike in disciplinary takeovers, the integration of the two businesses is essential for realizing the gains in synergistic takeovers.

It is important to note from the start that the gains in synergistic takeovers could well be gains for the managers as much as for the shareholders. For example, when managers launch diversification programs, they may be creating no value for shareholders but only satisfying their own preferences for growth. The point nonetheless remains that the acquiring firm is seeking a combination of the operations or cash flows of the two firms and not an improvement of the target, as in disciplinary takeovers.

This paper attempts to verify the conjecture that disciplinary takeovers are often hostile and synergistic takeovers are often friendly. We assemble evidence showing that targets of hostile (friendly) bids have the ownership and asset characteristics that one would expect of the targets of disciplinary (synergistic) takeovers. We interpret this evidence as showing that, at least to some extent, the motive for a takeover determines its mood.

The claim that hostility and friendliness typically reflect two different takeover motives is by no means clear-cut. Some diversification-motivated takeovers undoubtedly run into resistance from managers of the targeted firms, who are unhappy either with expected changes in operations or with the compensation they receive for giving up control. Similarly, some takeovers launched to change the target's operating strategy proceed with the consent of the target's managers, who obtain lucrative enough rewards to give up control peacefully, or else simply want to retire. These grey areas suggest the possibility that variation in the monetary incentives of managers across targeted firms can completely account for mood differences from acquisition to acquisition. Walkling and Long (1984) seem to take this view. In contrast, we show that there are numerous characteristics, in addition to measures of the financial incentives offered to the incumbent managers, that differ across hostile and friendly acquisitions. Moreover, these are the differences one would expect to find between the targets of disciplinary takeovers and those of synergistic takeovers.

The analysis of this paper is based on the sample of all publicly traded Fortune 500 firms as of 1980. Of the 454 firms in the sample, 82 were acquired by third parties or underwent a management buyout in the years 1981–85. Based on an examination of the Wall Street Journal Index, 40 of those takeovers appear to have started out hostile and 42 friendly. We call an acquisition hostile of the initial bid for the target (which need not be a bid from the eventual buyer) was neither negotiated with its board prior to being made nor accepted by the board as made. Thus, initial rejection by the target's board is taken as evidence of the bidder's hostility, as is active management resistance to the bid, escape to a "white knight," or a management buyout in response to unsolicited pressure. We sort acquisitions on the basis of the initial mood because we are interested in the source of the takeover gains that sparked the bidding in the first place. Acquisitions that are not classified as hostile are called friendly.

The remaining sections of the paper examine ownership and financial characteristics of the firms in the 1980 Fortune 500 sample. Section 4.2 focuses on the ownership characteristics of targets of friendly and hostile acquisitions. "Friendly targets" appear to have much higher board ownership than either "hostile targets" or the rest of the sample, and in particular much higher ownership by the top officers. Compared to an average firm in the sample, a friendly target is much more likely, and a hostile target much less likely, to be run by a founder or a member of the founder's family. Furthermore, the probability of an acquisition, and particularly of a friendly acquisition, rises with management ownership. In fact, the intentional exit of the founding family or of a CEO with a very large stake in the firm is a frequent impetus for a friendly acquisition in our sample. Although the results on ownership identify some clear differences between hostile and friendly targets, they do not suggest a definite link between the motive for a takeover and its mood.

Section 4.3 examines the asset and performance characteristics of the firms in the sample. The results suggest that the targets of friendly acquisitions have a Tobin's q comparable to that of nontargets, but that hostile targets have a lower q. Hostile targets not only have a low q within their industry but also are concentrated in low-q industries. Friendly targets are younger and faster growing firms than hostile targets and are basically indistinguishable from the sample as a whole in terms of performance variables.

These results are the basic evidence consistent with our conjecture that synergistic takeovers are more likely to be friendly and disciplinary takeovers are more likely to be hostile. Hostile targets appear to be poor performers, as we would expect of candidates for the disciplinary takeovers. In contrast, it seems less likely that the match-specific attractions of synergistic targets would be easily captured by basic performance measures.

Section 4.4 presents probit estimates of the effects of firm characteristics on the probability of a hostile or friendly acquisition. The results confirm that a firm with a low market value relative to the amount of fixed assets it holds is more likely to become a hostile target than the average firm. This appears to be largely accounted for by an industry effect and not just by a particularly low valuation within the industry. Controlling for size, top officer ownership, and Tobin's q, we find that the presence of the founding family reduces the likelihood of hostile bids, but does not raise that of friendly bids. Large management stakes in the target, on the other hand, do more to encourage friendly acquisitions than to discourage hostile ones.

Section 4.5 takes a separate look at management buyouts. These deals deserve special attention because they cannot be motivated by synergistic gains. We define hostile management buyouts as deals done in response to a third party bid or filing of a Schedule 13d with an expression of intent to seek control. Friendly management buyouts, then, are transactions in which such pressure is not apparent. Because our sample of these buyouts is quite small, accurate statistical inference is impossible; all we can do is eyeball the data. Except for the fact that leveraged buyouts are, on average, much smaller transactions than others, the differences between friendly and hostile management buyouts largely mimic the differences between friendly and hostile acquisitions more generally. The external pressure that prompts defensive management buyouts seems likely to be an attempt to discipline the management. Friendly management buyouts, however, seem more likely to be done for tax reasons or possibly to buy undervalued shares.

We interpret this study as furnishing some evidence consistent with the view that hostile targets and friendly targets are very different types of companies. Whereas the targets of friendly bids appear to be a wide range of firms in many industries, the targets of hostile bids are usually older, more slowly growing firms that are valued much below the replacement cost of their tangible assets. Friendly acquisitions could be motivated by corporate diversification, synergies, and, as our results suggest, the life-cycle decisions of a founder or a manager with a dominant stake. Bidders in hostile transactions may be more interested in shutting down, selling off, or redepreciating the physical capital of the target than they are in continuing business as usual. In addition to the possible heterogeneity of financial incentives, managers' resistance to takeovers may be related to their unwillingness to accept the particular changes sought by the bidder, often leading them to seek a white knight or a management buyout. In short, the evidence is consistent with our notion that the source of gains from a takeover can determine its mood.

4.2 Ownership Structure and Acquisitions

In this section we present ownership characteristics of the 1980 Fortune 500 firms that were acquired in the subsequent five years. Recent empirical research (Demsetz and Lehn 1985; Mørck, Shleifer and Vishny, forthcoming) has documented the incidence of substantial managerial ownership of large industrial corporations. These studies have not, however, focused on the ownership structure of acquisition targets, which is the task of this section. Evidence on ownership enables us to see whether the managers of nontargets, hostile targets, and friendly targets have different financial interests in an acquisition.

The relationship between management ownership and takeover mood has been previously examined by Walkling and Long (1984), who found that changes in managers' personal wealth from a successful acquisition are negatively related to the decision to resist. In our analysis we also consider the impact of management ownership on the probability of an acquisition, be it hostile or friendly, as well as the influence of the presence of a founding family and of the chairman of the board's age on the probability of either a hostile or a friendly acquisition. In this way, we hope to obtain a more complete picture of the function of managers' financial incentives in takeovers.

Throughout this analysis we try to avoid sample selection problems, and to this end we begin with all publicly traded 1980 Fortune 500 firms (Walkling and Long might have an unrepresentative sample since they reported abnormally high initial stakes for the acquiring firms: 11 percent for contested offers and 27 percent for uncontested offers). Moreover, because we are interested in differences between firms, we try to avoid the question of cyclical variation and compare all firms as of 1980. In the case of ownership, data come from the 1980 Corporate Data Exchange (CDE) directory, which contains data on the ownership positions of board members as well as large outside shareholders. We do not have data on executive compensation or on the ownership positions taking the form of options; many studies (for example, Murphy 1985) indicate that changes in executive wealth resulting from stock ownership are large relative to those from other sources.

The first measure of ownership we use is the combined percentage stake of the board of directors. Because of the nature of CDE reporting, the stakes are added up over only those board members whose positions exceed 0.2 percent. This may lead to some problems for the largest firms, where even the tiniest percentage ownership positions are worth millions of dollars.

To the extent that the board makes the decision whether to resist an offer, the board's stake may be the appropriate measure of financial incentives. In addition to this measure, we divide the board ownership into that of the top two officers and that of the rest of the board. The first captures the interest of the top officers, whose concern for the outcome of a bid might go well beyond their personal capital gain, and the second captures the interest of important decision makers who might care little about the outcome of a bid except for their personal financial gain. These two measures complement the board's stake as a whole in that they reflect the pecuniary gain of the two constituencies on the board with possibly different attitudes toward the acquisition.

Other personal characteristics of board members might influence their attitude toward the firm's being acquired independent of their ownership stake. First, top officers who are founders or members of the founding family might play a special role in the company, either because they command the loyalty of shareholders and employees or because their attachment to the company is more than just financial. For this reason, it seemed useful to ask what fraction of friendly and hostile takeover targets were run by a member of the founding family. This is of particular interest in the context of executive succession, since sale of the company might be a natural means for a founder's retirement. For a similar reason, we are interested in the age of the board chairman, since his retirement plans might influence his attitude toward the sale of the company.

Recall that we term an acquisition hostile if it was not negotiated prior to the initial bid, was not accepted by the board from the start, or was contested by the target management in any way. This category thus includes acquisitions by white knights. It also includes management buyouts that were precipitated by a bid or a 13d filing expressing the intent to acquire control, since such pressure is clearly hostile (Shleifer and Vishny 1988). Our calling a target hostile whenever there is any evidence of the board's rejection of the initial offer may misclassify as hostile some situations in which the board is only attempting to obtain a higher bid. Because there are only three transactions in our sample where resistance was limited simply to a rejection of the first offer, we proceed using this classification. Our classification records a transaction as friendly either if there is no evidence of resistance from the target management to the first prospective acquirer or if the management implemented a management buyout and we have no evidence of a hostile threat. Again, the classification is far from perfect since the target's management may have been coerced into going along in the face of imminent defeat.

Although section 4.5 below presents some evidence to the effect that it is appropriate to include hostile and friendly management buyouts in the general samples of hostile and friendly transactions, we try to be cautious and present many of the results both including and excluding these buyouts from the samples of targets. Unless noted otherwise, our discussion will concern the results for the case in which management buyouts (MBOs, in the tables) are included.

Table 4.1a presents the means and medians of various ownership variables for different groups of companies, and table 4.1b gives *t*-statistics for tests of the differences of means between these groups.

In the whole sample the board of directors owned on average 10.9 percent of the company; 6.3 percent was the average stake of the top two officers, and 4.5 percent was the average stake of the rest of the board. Not surprisingly, the ownership positions are skewed to the right: the medians for the above three measures were 3.54 percent, 0.61 percent, and 1.09 percent respectively. One way to describe the magnitude of these stakes is that the average value of the top two officers' positions was $40.5 million and the median was $2.26 million. Almost a quarter of the companies in the sample were run by members of the founding family, and the average chairman of the board was a youthful 58 years old.

From the viewpoint of ownership, the friendly targets were very different both from the sample as a whole and from the hostile targets. The boards of the friendly targets owned over 20 percent of the company, on average, which is statistically significantly more than both the 10.9 percent average board ownership in the sample and the 8.3 percent average of the hostile targets. The hostile targets had, on average, less board ownership than the whole sample, though this difference is not statistically significant. The greater board ownership among the friendly targets came from the greater ownership of the top officers. In fact, the stakes of outside board members do not seem to have been much different from either those in the hostile targets or in the whole sample. At the 15 percent confidence level, the hostile targets seem to have had less top officer ownership than did the average firm. The difference in officer positions is even more dramatic if one looks at the dollar values of the stake, where the average for a friendly target was twice that for the sample as a whole, and nine times that for a hostile target. All these results are echoed in the medians as well, although not as dramatically.

The incidence of a member of the founding family on the top management team was also very high in friendly targets, showing up as an impressive 40 percent. This is statistically significantly higher than the 24 percent average for the sample as a whole and the 10 percent average for the hostile targets. The incidence of the founding family's presence in hostile targets was low relative to the sample, with a t-statistic of -2.23. There does not seem to be any significant difference in the age of the chairman or in the outside board ownership between the full sample and friendly and hostile targets. But when the management buyouts are not classified as acquisitions, we find that the chairmen of hostile targets were slightly younger than the average chairman in the sample, perhaps suggesting that the younger managers were more likely to strike a favorable deal with a white knight or fight harder to remain independent, while the older managers were more apt to rely on the management buyout as a takeover defense.

Table 4.1a   Characteristics of Top Management, by Type of Acquisition

Characteristic		Full Sample	Friendly	Hostile	Friendly Non-MBO	Hostile Non-MBO
				Type of Acquisition		
Founding family present on top management team = 1	Mean	.244	.405	.100	.412	.0938
	Median	0	0	0	0	0
Fractional equity ownership by the board of directors	Mean	.109	.208	.0829	.186	.0874
	Median	.0354	.135	.0418	.0894	.0382
Fractional equity ownership by top two officers	Mean	.0635	.145	.0318	.139	.0364
	Median	.0061	.0176	.0049	.0139	.0044
Fractional equity ownership by the rest of the board	Mean	.0455	.0625	.0512	.0464	.0510
	Median	.0109	.0172	.0233	.0152	.0227
Age of board chairman	Mean	58.4	58.7	57.1	58.5	55.3
	Median	59.0	57.0	58.0	57.0	57.5
Dollar value of top officers' stake (in millions)	Mean	40.05	83.75	9.22	60.79	11.23
	Median	2.26	6.02	.795	4.22	1.11

Table 4.1b   T-Statistics for Tests of Equality of Means of Top Management Variables, by Acquisition Type

	Friendly vs. Sample	Hostile vs. Sample	Friendly Non-MBO vs. Sample	Hostile Non-MBO vs. Sample	Friendly vs. Hostile	Friendly Non-MBO vs. Hostile Non-MBO
Founding family present on top management team = 1	2.55	−2.23	2.37	−2.06	3.33	3.12
Fractional equity ownership by the board of directors	4.42	−1.11	3.03	−.811	3.28	2.26
Fractional equity ownership by top two officers	4.20	−1.56	3.45	−1.18	3.33	2.55
Fractional equity ownership by the rest of the board	1.27	.415	.0611	.358	.559	−.23
Age of board chairman	.217	−1.13	.0481	−2.28	.742	1.34
Dollar value of top officers' stake (in millions)	1.55	−1.25	.667	−1.04	2.03	1.60

Before interpreting these results, we should explicitly acknowledge that the means we compute are only intended to be suggestive, since in their calculation we do not control for important differences between firms. For example, firms with very small ownership are larger firms that are less likely to be acquired. Without a multivariate analysis, some of the correlations we describe might be spurious. We deal with these issues in section 4.4 but in the meantime proceed as if the evidence is indicative of the causal relationship between ownership and takeovers.

One interpretation of the results presented so far is that the management teams with strong financial incentives to accept a tender offer at a premium do not resist. This is supported by the fact that the boards of friendly targets had higher stakes and the boards of hostile targets had lower stakes than the sample average. Moreover, the entire difference is basically accounted for by the differential ownership of the top officers. Since officers have more to lose as a result of an acquisition than do other board members, looking at top officers rather than whole boards may be more powerful in explaining the resistance strategy adopted.

An alternative interpretation of the findings on friendly offers is that management teams with very high ownership have close to a veto power over the outcome of the bid, and that therefore the only acquisitions with high management ownership we observe are friendly. This is corroborated by the fact that the firms whose founders were present were more likely to be the targets of friendly bids, since the founders might have had a stronger preference for control as well as a better ability to resist. The two interpretations are not, of course, incompatible. Companies might be targets of friendly offers both because managers have a great incentive to succumb and because if they chose not to, the offer could not succeed.

The latter view suggests that a number of would-be hostile offers end up as friendly offers because of the necessity to bribe the entrenched managers. This view does not, however, explain the higher incidence of total acquisitions among high-ownership firms that we find in the data. Table 4.2a presents the numbers and probabilities of various types of acquisitions for firms with special ownership structures, and table 4.2b provides some hypothesis tests. Table 4.2a shows that, whereas the probability of a non-MBO acquisition within five years was 14.5 percent in the sample as a whole, it was 19.7 percent if the officer stake exceeded 15 percent. If management buyouts are included, the probability that a firm with over 15 percent officer ownership would be acquired exceeds that for a firm with under 15 percent ownership by 11 percent, with a t-statistic of 2.11. That large stakes invite bids suggests that the managers' incentive to sell was probably a factor in the observed pattern of takeover activity.

Table 4.2a   **Acquisition Activity, by Ownership Category**

Ownership	Total Number of Firms	Number of:				Probability of:	
		Friendly	Hostile	Friendly Non-MBO	Hostile Non-MBO	Non-MBO Acquisition	Hostile Non-MBO
Founding family present	111	17	4	14	3	.153	.027
Founding family absent	343	25	36	20	29	.143	.085
Top officers' stake greater than 15 percent	66	15	3	10	3	.197	.045
Full sample	454	42	40	34	32	.145	.070

Table 4.2b   **Differences between Acquisition Probabilities for Various Ownership Categories (*t*-Statistics for tests of equality of acquisition probabilities in parentheses)**

			All Acquisitions	Non-MBO Acquisitions
Probability of hostile acquisition Founder = 1	vs.	Probability of hostile acquisition Founder = 0	−.0690 (−2.23)	−.0575 (−2.06)
Probability of friendly acquisition Founder = 1	vs.	Probability of friendly acquisition Founder = 0	.0803 (2.55)	.0678 (2.37)
Probability of any acquisition Founder = 1	vs.	Probability of any acquisition Founder = 0	.0114 (.270)	.0103 (.27)
Probability of hostile acquisition OFF > .15	vs.	Probability of hostile acquisition OFF ≤ .15	−.0499 (−1.32)	−.0293 (−.858)
Probability of friendly acquisition OFF > .15	vs.	Probability of friendly acquisition OFF ≤ .15	.1577 (4.16)	.0896 (2.57)
Probability of any acquisition OFF > .15	vs.	Probability of any acquisition OFF ≤ .15	.1078 (2.11)	.0604 (1.29)

Note: OFF = percentage ownership stake of the top officer of the firm.

The reason why companies with very high officer ownership have a higher likelihood of being acquired is that they have a much higher likelihood of a friendly bid. The probability that a firm with at least 15 percent top officer ownership was acquired in a friendly non-MBO transaction is 15.2 percent versus 6.2 percent for firms with officer ownership below 15 percent. This difference between high and low officer ownership firms is significant at the 1 percent level ($t = 2.57$). On the other hand, the probability that a non-MBO acquisition would be initiated in a hostile manner is 4.5 percent for high officer ownership firms versus 7.4 percent for firms with less than 15 percent top officer ownership, a difference which is not statistically significant.

These results suggest the possibility that the ownership structure of some firms makes them especially attractive targets of friendly takeovers. For example, if a top officer with a large equity stake wants to retire and simultaneously take some of his wealth out of the firm, he will probably prefer selling out at a premium to a diversification-minded acquirer to selling his shares on the open market. Life-cycle decisions of the officers thus may provide a stimulus for friendly bids.

Further evidence on this point comes from the results on founders. Table 4.2a shows that the probability of any acquisition of a firm run by the founding family is not much different from that of an average company in the sample. The likelihood of a friendly bid, however, is much higher for founders' firms, and that of a hostile bid is much lower. For the entire sample the probability of a hostile non-MBO acquisition is 7.0 percent, and the probability of a friendly non-MBO acquisition is 7.5 percent. For firms run by founding families, in contrast, the likelihood of a friendly bid is 12.6 percent and that of a hostile bid is 2.7 percent. The probability of a friendly bid is statistically significantly higher for firms with founding families than for firms without ($t = 2.37$), and the probability of a hostile bid is significantly lower ($t = -2.06$). If founders can effectively deter hostile bids, and end up selling their firms when they intend to leave the business, such results might be expected.

A final piece of statistical evidence that corroborates the top management exit story concerns the age of the chairman. Although the average chairman in our sample was 58.4 years old, and the average chairman of a firm with a founding family member at the helm was 59.7, the average chairman in firms that were run by the founding family *and* sold to a friendly acquirer was 62.6 years old. These findings are consistent with the notion that founders who sell off their firms before retirement should on average be older.

An examination of the stories of individual companies confirms the statistical evidence. A common story (for example, ABC, Beckman Instruments, Clark Oil, and others) is an elderly founder wishing to sell the business before he retires. In fact, of the 14 founder-run firms that were acquired by another party in a friendly transaction over the period in question, one was the case of bankruptcy, one of a need to get money to pay inheritance taxes, one of a super-manager merging into a larger firm to get a bigger job, and the rest of founders or of their family members wishing to get out.

If an important part of friendly acquisitions is simply a personal life-cycle decision of top management, it is natural to ask how high takeover premia can be paid in such transactions. One possibility is mismanagement under the founder's reign, such as insufficient risk taking, insufficient expansion to maintain high fractional equity ownership, or just poor decision making. In this case the founder's exit is accompanied by a disciplinary takeover. An alternative possibility is that the takeover is synergistic but the desire of managers to run their own show often precludes such combinations. The founder's wish to get out provides the impetus for realizing the already available gains. Some evidence shedding light on these two possibilities is presented in the next section.

4.3 Financial Characteristics of the Targets

The financial motivation of the target's management is unlikely to be the only factor entering into the decision to oppose a tender offer. Some acquisitions might be undertaken for reasons management particularly dislikes, such as its own replacement or the liquidation of the firm. In this section we pursue such possible heterogeneity of acquisition targets.

The starting point of our analysis is Tobin's q. As the ratio of the market value of the firm to the replacement cost of its *tangible* assets, Tobin's q can be viewed as measuring the intangible assets of the firm. These may include future growth opportunities, monopoly power, quality of management, goodwill, rents appropriated away from unions, and so on. Since we are looking at the measured q, this interpretation can be troublesome. The replacement cost of assets could be overstated, for example, if the firm bought its assets a long time ago and their value has depreciated significantly because of technological progress, foreign competition, or other changes. In these cases the inflation-adjusted historical cost is a poor guide to the true replacement cost, but a very low q is probably still a reliable indicator of a declining firm.

Alternatively, q might just capture the mispricing by the stock market of the firm's physical assets in their current use. If, however, a low q genuinely measures the low valuation of the firm's tangible assets in their current use, it may pay to sell off assets when q is low because those assets have a higher value in another firm or sector. Even when the firm's capital is highly firm- or sector-specific, it may pay simply to abandon the unprofitable capacity or insist on a reduction in union wages that were set under more profitable conditions.

A related measure of profitability relative to the value of physical assets is the deviation of a firm's q from the average q of its three-digit (Standard Industrial Classification code) industry, Dq. The market might attach low value to the assets of the whole industry, and it could attach an even lower value to the assets of a particular firm within that industry. If the market does the latter, we must look at the firm's idiosyncratic characteristics, such as its management, as a source of potential acquisition gains.

Tobin's q can shed light on the hypothesis that hostile acquisitions are essentially purchases of old physical assets that can be redeployed more profitably elsewhere either from an efficiency or a tax viewpoint. If a low q reflects a low valuation of physical assets relative to their potential, acquiring the firm might be a cost-effective way to buy and redeploy its physical capital. In the same vein we look at the age of the firm, which might give us an idea of the age of its capital. Apart from serving as an indicator of a declining firm, the age of the capital stock is a proxy for the potential for a step up in the basis from which this capital can be redepreciated. From the tax viewpoint acquiring older assets is more advantageous; Shleifer and Vishny (1988) argue that such tax considerations can be important in management buyouts.

Since Tobin's q might be mismeasured, we are also interested in other potential measures of the firm's performance. In particular, we look at a ten-year growth rate of the firm's work force, GL. If q and GL are simultaneously low, we are more confident in attributing low valuation to past or current troubles rather than to mismeasurement or market mispricing.

In two effective papers, Michael Jensen (1986a, 1986b) has proposed a free cash flow theory of low stock market valuation of targets of hostile takeovers. In his theory, because some firms waste shareholders' wealth on unprofitable investments and managerial perquisites, eliminating this waste can create shareholder value. An example of wasted free cash flow, proposed by Jensen and by Jacobs (1986), is exploration activity in the oil industry that did not slow down in the face of changing economic conditions. Jensen suggested that interest and dividend payments alleviate the problem of free cash flow. In this regard he points to the role of debt as a means to commit future corporate revenues to being paid out.

Strictly speaking, to be properly tested, Jensen's theory requires controlling for a variety of aspects of the firm's opportunity set. We nevertheless check what fraction of their earnings nontargets, hostile targets, and friendly targets allocate to dividends, interest payments, and investment. The question is whether higher payouts and lower investment preclude hostile action.

Another important strand in the discussion of corporate acquisitions argues that capital market imperfections can deter otherwise feasible transactions. A firm with a large market value could be difficult to acquire, especially without the cooperation of its management, because financial markets might be unable to supply the credit necessary for the acquisition. This view attributes the lively hostile takeover activity of the 1980s at least in part to the appearance of junk bond financing. Looking at the market values of acquired firms should thus enable us to appraise the extent to which capital market imperfections matter. Not surprisingly, all types of targets have fewer assets and lower market values than do firms that are not acquired, indicating that capital market imperfections might deter some corporate control transactions. Because market value is correlated with both q and management ownership, we defer further discussion of this issue to the multivariate analysis section.

The means and medians of the variables of interest by the type of firm are presented in table 4.3a, with the *t*-tests of differences of means in table 4.3b. Recall that all the variables are measured at the end of 1980. The average Tobin's *q* of the sample is .848, which is the standard result of the low valuation of corporate assets by the stock market in 1980. The average *q* of a friendly target is .796, which is not significantly below that of the sample. In contrast, the average *q* of a hostile target is only .524, which is significantly below .848 ($t = -2.84$). A similar pattern emerges in the medians.

Unfortunately, a variety of interpretations are consistent with this result. The first possibility is that hostile targets were mismanaged and therefore had a low Tobin's *q*. The result of such mismanagement is the inefficient utilization of the fixed assets of the firm and in turn the low valuation of these assets by the market. Removing the management might justify the takeover premium, although the managers would probably resist because they would not want to lose control or to have their incompetence revealed. Managers of friendly targets, in contrast, are safe; they do not need to worry about being removed.

Mismanagement can come in two forms. It can be a firm-specific or an industrywide phenomenon. In the former case what should matter for hostility is the extent to which the firm underperforms similar firms. To some extent this difference is measured by *Dq*. In fact, the mean of *Dq* is positive for friendly targets and negative for hostile ones, with the difference significant at the 10 percent level ($t = 1.72$). On the other hand, the differences in the medians are much smaller. To ascertain whether the industry effect or the firm effect is more important in predicting hostile activity, the next section presents some probit estimates.

An alternative interpretation of the extremely low Tobin's *q*'s of the hostile firms is that, while the assets may be managed properly, they simply are not particularly valuable. For example, if the hostile targets invested a long time ago when their industry was growing, but now the fortunes of the industry have turned around, they will be stuck with a lot of capital. Under this scenario hostile targets might be in smokestack industries ruined by technological progress and foreign competition.

Consistent with this view is the finding that the hostile targets were older and more slowly growing than the average firm in the sample. The difference in the year of incorporation between hostile targets and other firms was over six years, and it is significant at the 6 percent level. The difference in the growth rates of the work force was 1.4 percent (or almost twofold), which is significant at the 12 percent level. Friendly targets, in contrast, were younger than the average firm and were growing at roughly the same rate.

Although this view suggests why firms with a great deal of old, fixed capital would have a low Tobin's *q*, it does not explain why these firms are attractive candidates for hostile acquisitions. One explanation is the free cash flow theory. If low-q industries are in decline, managers may be too slow to close down or sell off plants, curtail investment, and trim down operations. There is some evidence that the hostile targets were investing a smaller fraction of earnings than the average firm in the sample ($t = -1.86$).

If managers' dedication to the survival of organizations, stressed by Donaldson and Lorsch (1983), keeps them from shrinking their operations sufficiently fast, then acquirers can increase value by speeding up the decline of the target company. Our numbers on the growth of the work force, the incorporation year, investment, and q are all consistent with the version of the free cash flow theory that stresses management's tendency to disinvest too slowly.

Another reason why old tangible assets could attract acquirers has to do with taxes. An important feature of the pre-1986 U.S. tax code was the General Utilities doctrine, according to which if a firm's assets were sold in a liquidation, capital gains taxes could be avoided at the corporate level. After such an acquisition, the target's assets could be redepreciated, presumably using the accelerated schedules of the 1980s. The step-up in basis could have been an important tax motivation for acquiring old capital. In addition, of course, there are tax gains from leverage. Although these apply equally to firms without too much fixed capital, it may be more costly for these firms to obtain debt financing. If managers oppose a loss of control to an acquirer, they can lever up by themselves or lever up and step up the basis by effecting a management buyout or finding a white knight. These, in fact, have been common responses to hostile pressure.

One final explanation for hostile offers that is consistent with our findings is underpricing by the market. If the stock market does not value some firms properly, an acquirer who understands their intrinsic value may be able to buy their assets more cheaply on the stock market than on the new or used capital goods market. Managers reluctant to give up assets at below their intrinsic worth would resist such acquisitions. One problem with this explanation of hostile bids is that it says nothing about why the older, slow-growth companies with mostly tangible assets are the only ones undervalued on the stock market. Moreover, since once a company is in play the corporate control market becomes very competitive and a great deal of information is revealed, acquirers are definitely limited in their ability to profit in this way.

In summary, hostile targets appear to have sharply distinguishable asset characteristics. Relative to the market value of the firm, they appear to have a considerable amount of old tangible capital. They are growing slowly and have heavy debts. Although these characteristics suggest that hostile acquisitions might be related to the desire to purchase these fixed assets, a variety of explanations are just as consistent

Characteristic		Sample	Friendly	Hostile	Friendly Non-MBO	Hostile Non-MBO
q	Mean	.848	.796	.524	.774	.545
	Median	.645	.617	.452	.624	.461
Dq	Mean	0	.0163	−.113	−.0368	−.119
	Median	−.0304	−.0662	−.112	−.0794	−.115
Replacement cost	Mean	2772.6	1372.0	1947.5	1534.6	2237.1
	Median	1055	747.7	791.4	843.1	960.6
Growth rate of work force (GL)	Mean	.0272	.0258	.0137	.0270	.0140
	Median	.0199	.0183	.00948	.0232	.00948
Year of incorporation	Mean	1918.3	1924.6	1911.9	1924.6	1914.9
	Median	1920	1925	1913	1925	1916
Total market value	Mean	2092.6	969.8	1009.1	1028.4	1181.1
	Median	808.2	683.2	384.2	732.0	387.8
Investment/income	Mean	.704	.651	.576	.687	.588
	Median	.640	.522	.579	.629	.609
Dividends/income	Mean	.183	.158	.178	.162	.176
	Median	.175	.151	.176	.151	.172
Interest/income	Mean	.193	.246	.219	.254	.232
	Median	.175	.261	.211	.269	.223
Value of long-term debt/total market value	Mean	.248	.285	.330	.269	.335
	Median	.208	.228	.267	.213	.299

Table 4.3b   T-Statistics for Tests of Equality of Means of Asset and Financial Variables, by Type of Acquisition

	Friendly vs. Sample	Hostile vs. Sample	Friendly Non-MBO vs. Sample	Hostile Non-MBO vs. Sample	Hostile vs. Friendly	Hostile Non-MBO vs. Friendly Non-MBO
q	-.360	-2.84	-.464	-2.36	-2.66	-2.19
Dq	.163	-1.43	-.337	-1.34	-1.72	-1.39
Replacement cost	-1.13	-.840	-.914	-.485	.641	.656
Growth rate of work force (GL)	-.148	-1.54	-.0191	-1.37	-1.02	-.985
Year of incorporation	1.97	-1.92	1.78	-.922	-2.78	-2.02
Total market value	-1.19	-1.46	-1.04	-1.09	.0866	.285
Investment/income	-.701	-1.86	-.204	-1.57	-.818	-.96
Dividends/income	-1.26	-.318	-.938	-.354	.966	.624
Interest/income	2.07	1.14	2.18	1.56	-.804	-.622
Value of long-term debt/total market value	.864	2.45	.460	2.31	.646	.859

with this general story. In particular, incompetent management, asset redeployment, free cash flow, taxes, and underpricing of the firm's assets by the market could all invite takeover bids. At the same time, we think the evidence is consistent with the notion that hostile takeovers are motivated by the need for disciplinary action against the target management.

The analysis of this section has said virtually nothing about the targets of friendly bids. Except for the fact that they are on average smaller and six years younger than the rest of the sample (with t-statistics of -1.13 and -1.97, respectively), friendly targets are very similar to the average firm in the sample. Most notably, their Tobin's q is not statistically or substantively different from that of the average firm in the sample, and it is significantly higher than the q of an average hostile target ($t = 2.66$). In a sense these findings are consistent with the view that friendly targets are just regular firms, and their acquisition derives from some idiosyncratic circumstances such as a life-cycle decision of a top officer with a large stake or a match-specific synergy (such as the desire of the acquiring management to enter a particular new business). One interesting feature of friendly targets is that they appear to have higher interest payouts and lower dividend payouts than the average firm in the sample, perhaps indicating that they are starved for capital. But their total outside payouts are very similar to those of the average firm.

The results of this section provide the basic evidence supporting the notion that disciplinary takeovers are more often hostile than the average takeover, while synergistic takeovers are more often friendly. The evidence indicates that hostile targets are older, poorly performing firms, possibly with many old plants or equipment that should be abandoned or more profitably deployed elsewhere. This is exactly what one would expect of the targets of disciplinary takeovers. In contrast, the financial characteristics of friendly targets do not appear to be very different from those of the average firm in the sample. If what attracts acquirers to these targets are match-specific synergies (as well as the target manager's interest in selling), we would not expect to see any real differences in the basic financial variables. In short, the results suggest that the motive for a takeover might well determine its mood. Treating hostile and friendly acquisitions as reflecting the same underlying fundamentals might be very misleading indeed.

4.4 Probit Estimates

The previous section offered evidence suggesting that the motives for hostile and friendly acquisitions might be different. In this section we present results on some further statistical tests of what makes a firm the target of a friendly takeover and what makes a firm the target of a hostile takeover. This question is different from asking what makes the mood of a takeover of an already selected target hostile or friendly, since the latter question presumes that the characteristics that make firms targets in the first place are the same across moods. If hostile and friendly takeovers typically reflect different motives, it is misleading to think of a firm becoming a general target. Rather, separate considerations are appropriate for predicting which firms are subject to hostile (disciplinary) takeovers and which are subject to friendly (synergistic) ones.

Accordingly, this section presents probit estimates for the whole sample of 1980 Fortune 500 firms, estimates that separately predict hostile and friendly acquisitions. The models are either $prob$(hostile vs. anything else) $= f$(characteristics), or $prob$(friendly vs. anything else) $= g$(characteristics). In short, we separately compared hostile and friendly targets with the rest of the Fortune 500 sample.

We did a multivariate analysis because many of the company characteristics we looked at were correlated with one another. For example, the growth rate of the firm's work force was so closely correlated with Tobin's q that it became dominated by q in the regressions. Although we ran several additional probits to identify the separate sources of influence of firm characteristics on the probability of a friendly acquisition and the probability of a hostile acquisition, the results presented below reflect our main findings.

Table 4.4a presents the two probits estimating the likelihood that a Fortune 500 firm would go through a successful friendly acquisition. Mimicking our earlier finding that the friendly targets were just like the sample as a whole, the probits did not reveal particularly strong correlations. Specifically, the probability of a friendly acquisition is not clearly related to the log of the firm's market value, the presence of the founding family, industry q, or Dq. That high market value does not deter friendly acquisitions is inconsistent with the preliminary indications from table 4.3a. This could be because size is negatively correlated with officer ownership, which is, in turn, positively related to friendly bids. In this case, the finding in table 4.3a is spurious. Since friendly bids are often made by large, cash-rich companies and sometimes for stock, it is not entirely surprising that capital market constraints are not particularly binding.

When friendly management buyouts were included in the set of acquired firms, there was some evidence that high officer ownership promoted friendly acquisitions. This result grew weaker when these buyouts were excluded, since, as we show in the next section, firms going through friendly management buyouts often have dominant management ownership. We should also point out, however, that the

Table 4.4a   Probit Regressions of Friendly Acquisition Dummy Variables on Ownership and Financial Variables

	Dependent Variable	
Independent Variable	Friendly Acquisition $= 1$	Friendly Non-MBO $= 1$ Acquisition
Intercept	−1.29	−1.60
	(−2.00)	(−2.37)
Log of total market value	−.0579	−.0195
	(−.591)	(−.191)
Founding family present $= 1$	−.122	−.162
	(−.387)	(−.477)
Proportion of equity owned by top officers	1.50	1.21
	(1.81)	(1.34)
Industry q	−.0459	−.0199
	(−.176)	(−.749)
Dq	.0531	−.108
	(.202)	(−.348)
Number of firms in regression	371	371

Note: t-statistics in parentheses

Table 4.4b   Probit Regressions of Hostile Acquisition Dummy Variables on Ownership and Financial Variables

	Dependent Variable	
Independent Variable	Hostile Acquisition $= 1$	Hostile Non-MBO $= 1$ Acquisition
Intercept	.563	−.106
	(.960)	(−.177)
Log of total market value	−.184	−.116
	(−2.00)	(−1.24)
Founding family present $= 1$	−.737	−.604
	(−1.81)	(−1.50)
Proportion of equity owned by top officers	−1.33	−.888
	(−1.00)	(−.689)
Industry q	−.872	−.734
	(−2.26)	(−1.92)
Dq	−.701	−.693
	(−1.53)	(−1.51)
Number of firms in regression	371	371

Note: t-statistics in parentheses

ownership results were generally weaker in the probits than in the earlier tables because we lost a substantial number of observations due to missing values for q. We had q values for only 20 friendly targets and 31 hostile targets.

The result that as far as assets and performance go, friendly targets are just like other firms is confirmed using both industry q and Dq. Neither industry q nor Dq mattered for predicting friendly acquisitions. These negative results are consistent with the notion that friendly takeovers are motivated by synergy.

The story is very different with hostile acquisitions, the probits for which are presented in table 4.4b. For the sample including hostile management buyouts, the likelihood of a hostile acquisition was negatively related to the log of value, negatively related to industry q, and negatively related (at the 10 percent confidence level) to the presence of a founder. Surprisingly, the negative effect of officer ownership on the probability of a hostile acquisition was not statistically significant.

The result that, controlling for the q variables, high market value deters hostile acquisitions seems likely to reflect capital market imperfections. It suggests that some firms are too large to be acquired through a hostile bid, even when fundamentals dictate that they should be. This result became substantially weaker when hostile management buyouts were excluded from the sample of hostile targets, since these were very small firms. In fact, these buyouts are probably the best case for the argument that poor capital markets limit large transactions. The results in table 4.4b also confirm our earlier finding that hostile targets had low market valuations relative to tangible assets and that the presence of a founder discouraged hostile action, *holding officer stake and valuation constant*. This suggests that founders or their family members fight hostile bids more effectively than other managers, either because they value control more or because they command shareholders' or directors' support.

One important question we could not answer by simply comparing means is whether industry-specific or firm-specific components of performance are related to hostile activity. In our estimated probits industry q had a significant negative effect on the likelihood of a hostile acquisition, whereas Dq had an insignificant negative effect. It appears that industry performance is a more reliable predictor of hostile bids.

Viewed in the context of the mismanagement story, this finding says that hostile activity is often brought on by non-value-maximizing responses to adverse industrywide shocks and less often by company-specific mismanagement in an otherwise healthy industry. The finding that, in predicting hostile action, industry q is more important than Dq may indicate the existence of entire industries whose assets can be profitably redeployed. For example, many steel and textile firms might be in need of shutdowns and selloffs that do violence to the preferences of existing managers. These managers are not necessarily just trying to shirk or save empires. They may simply be opposed to changes that enrich shareholders at the expense of employees. The point is that hostile acquisitions can be a way to move large quantities of fixed capital into more profitable (and possibly also more productive) uses, as one would expect of disciplinary takeovers.

Although the statistical evidence is fairly weak, it is consistent with our observation that the motive for friendly acquisitions is more likely to be synergistic than disciplinary, and the motive for hostile ones is more likely to be disciplinary than synergistic. Specifically, friendly acquisitions seem to be related to high officer ownership, which suggests that an important impetus for these acquisitions may be a life-cycle decision of a large shareholder. Furthermore, all other basic firm characteristics we have looked at appear to be irrelevant for predicting friendly acquisitions. We might expect this of synergistic or diversification-oriented takeovers. Hostile bids, in contrast, seem to be targeted at firms located in low-q industries. One interpretation of the low q finding is that hostile acquisitions are a way to redeploy tangible assets in a more profitable way. Many of these redeployments can either be unacceptable to managers (such as liquidation and employee dismissals) or can be more painlessly replicated by a white knight or through a management buyout (such as a step-up in depreciable basis and increases in leverage). This, of course, is the story of the disciplinary motive for hostile takeovers.

4.5 Management Buyouts

Management buyouts are an important form of acquisition to think about because we know that the motive behind them cannot be synergistic. Whatever gains realized by management buyout organizers must come either from a more profitable exploitation of the firm's own resources, including its managerial talent, or from the ability of the organizers to buy the firm's assets for less than their intrinsic worth under the existing operating strategy.

Schipper and Smith (1986), Shleifer and Vishny (1988), and Kaplan (1987) have discussed the sources of gains in management buyouts. All of these authors found that tax considerations, especially for leveraging up and stepping up the basis, could justify a large part of the takeover premium. Kaplan estimated that 80 percent of the takeover premium can come from the tax savings. Other prime candidates for the source of gains include buying underpriced assets, improving incentives through higher management ownership and leverage, and the restructuring of declining companies along the lines sought by raiders.

Hence, it is important to distinguish between two types of management buyouts. The first is the buyout that responds to hostile pressure on the target's management. This pressure can take the form either of an outside bid or simply of an acquisition of a beachhead along with a 13d filing to the effect that control might be sought. The fact that managers and their investment banker partners can win the bidding for the firm in such situations suggests that the gains from an acquisition can be realized by them as well as by outside bidders. If these gains come from tax savings or buying underpriced assets, this result is not surprising. But it also seems likely that after a management buyout managers redeploy the target's assets in better uses. Managers may have been unwilling to implement these changes before being forced to make a defensive bid for the firm at a large premium.

The second type of management buyout is the transaction initiated by the managers without any apparent outside threat. We call this a friendly management buyout. One of the motives for these takeovers may be the exit story we developed for friendly deals more generally. In this case the buyout can be a way for a dominant CEO to pass the leadership on to the next generation of managers without dissipating control. Another motive for friendly management buyouts may just be to realize tax gains from leverage and stepping up the depreciable basis of the firm's assets. Although another oft-cited motive for these buyouts is to improve incentives through increased management ownership, this seems less plausible for our sample of friendly management buyouts because that management ownership was already quite high.

A final motive for friendly management buyouts that may be important is for managers to buy the share of the firm's assets they do not already own for less than its true value (either under the existing operating strategy or under a new one). Of course, this story requires that the management have some ability to freeze out minority shareholders once it takes over, so that it can get shareholders to tender for less than the true value of their shares. In addition, the story presumes that competitive bidding from third parties will not drive the profit from this strategy to zero. But both of these requirements seem likely to be met in many cases where managers have much better information than outsiders about the true value of the firm and management already owns a good deal of the stock (as in our sample of friendly management buyouts).

Of the 16 management buyouts in our sample of 82 acquisitions, 8 were hostile in the sense described above and the other 8 were friendly. Table 4.5 presents data on the ownership and financial characteristics of these buyouts. Comparing this table with tables 4.1a and 4.3a we see that hostile management buyouts share many of the features of

Table 4.5   Ownership and Financial Characteristics for Management Buyouts

	Sample	Friendly MBO	Hostile MBO
Founding family present on top management team = 1	.244	.375	.125
Fractional equity ownership by top two officers	.0636	.170	.0135
Fractional equity ownership by the rest of the board	.0454	.131	.0517
Age of board chairman	58.4	59.8	62.5
q	.848	.916	.436
Dq	0	.318	−.0873
Replacement cost	2772.6	450.3	740.5
Growth rate of work force (GL)	.0272	.0205	.0119
Year of Incorporation	1918.3	1924.3	1898.4
Total market value	2092.6	638.1	292.1
Investment/income	.704	.456	.499
Dividends/income	.183	.136	.185
Interest/income	.193	.204	.135
Value of long-term debt/total market value	.248	.373	.310

other hostile transactions. Firms experiencing them have very low Tobin's q's, low growth rates, low investment, large amounts of debt, and relatively low board and officer ownership. The average year of incorporation for a hostile management buyout target is a strikingly low 1898. These companies are much smaller than the run-of-the-mill hostile target, and they have a lower incidence of a founder's presence. Our examination of particular instances of hostile management buyouts confirms the observation that they are often acquisitions of old tangible assets, ones that can be subsequently redeployed more profitably or redepreciated. The picture of hostile management buyouts that emerges is consistent with their being a defensive response to the threat of a disciplinary takeover.

Friendly management buyouts are a very different type of transaction, and it is much less clear how they compare with other friendly deals. These buyouts are management-initiated deals that are not foiled by higher third party bids. Not surprisingly, 37.5 percent of these firms were run by the founding family, and the average board stake before the buyout was over 30 percent.

Since the officers in friendly management buyouts often have virtually complete control of the company, their motives for the transaction may be suspect. Purchasing undervalued shares in the presence of coercion and disadvantaged competitive bidders seems like a distinct possibility. Consider two cases in our sample. One was the buyout of Metromedia at a 100 percent premium, which was followed by the sale of the parts of the company (previously dictatorially run by the same boss for 30 years) for more than double the acquisition price within 18 months. Another was the management buyout of Beatrice foods, followed by the sale of several divisions that paid for the whole acquisition (Beatrice, however, did not have dominant insider ownership). There were other companies where management initiated a buyout when its voting control was already effectively absolute, such as Levi-Strauss and Questor.

In sum, although we do not have a clear idea of how friendly management buyouts relate to other friendly acquisitions, our consolidation of the hostile management buyouts with the other hostile acquisitions does not seem to do too much violence to the data. Firms undergoing a management buyout in response to hostile threats resemble other hostile targets quite closely. In fact, we can use our knowledge of hostile management buyouts to make inferences about hostile takeovers more generally.

4.6 Concluding Comments

The notion developed in this paper is that the motive for a takeover can have a large influence on its mood. Disciplinary takeovers are likely to be hostile, whereas synergistic takeovers are likely to be friendly.

Compared with the universe of Fortune 500 firms in 1980, firms experiencing hostile takeover bids between 1981 and 1985 were smaller, older, and more slowly growing, and they had lower Tobin's q's, more debt, and less investment of their income. The low q seems to be as much an industry-specific as a firm-specific effect. In addition, the hostile targets were less likely to be run by the founding family and had lower officer ownership than the average firm. A low q value, low market value, low growth and investment, and the absence of a founder were the corporate characteristics most likely to make the firm the target of a hostile bid.

Compared with the universe of Fortune 500 firms, the friendly targets were smaller and younger but had comparable Tobin's q values and growth rates. The friendly targets were more likely to be run by a member of the founding family and had higher officer ownership than the average firm. The decision to retire of a CEO with a large stake in the firm or with a relationship to the founder often precipitated a friendly acquisition. High officer ownership was the most important attribute predicting friendly acquisitions.

We conclude that differences between synergistic and disciplinary takeovers, captured in part by differences in their moods, should be recognized in empirical work. Specifically, studies that fail to distinguish adequately between acquisitions with different motives can be guish adequately between acquisitions with different motives can be misleading. First, difficulties can arise when disciplinary and synergistic takeovers are analyzed together, presenting the researcher with a mix that may have few common characteristics. Our results suggest that, as a first cut, separating hostile and friendly takeovers can help address this problem. A second difficulty can occur when facts about one type of acquisition are used to make inferences about another. An example of a good study that could be misread is Brown and Medoff's paper in this volume. The authors found that in a large sample of small Michigan companies, employment and wages rose after they were acquired. Since most of their sample seems to consist of friendly acquisitions of very small firms with high management ownership, one cannot conclude from their work that employment and wages do not fall on average after a firm is acquired in a disciplinary takeover. To get at the latter question, one would have to look at hostile targets. The key implication of our study for future work, therefore, is that research results on friendly bids may have little to say about hostile bids, and vice versa.

References

Brown, Charles and James L. Medoff. 1988. The impact of firm acquisitions on labor. In this volume.

Demsetz, Harold, and Kenneth Lehn. 1985. The structure of corporate ownership: Causes and consequences. *Journal of Political Economy* (December): 1155–77.

Donaldson, Gordon, and Jay W. Lorsch. 1983. *Decision making at the top.* New York: Basic Books.

Jacobs, E. Allen. 1986. The agency costs of corporate control, working paper. Cambridge: Massachusetts Institute of Technology.

Jensen, Michael C. 1986a. Agency costs of free cash flow, corporate finance and takeovers. *American Economic Review* 76 (May): 323–29.

————. 1986b. The takeover controversy: Analysis and evidence. *Midland Corporate Finance Journal* (Summer).

Kaplan, Steven. 1987. Management buyouts: Thoughts and evidence, photocopy. Boston: Harvard Business School

Mørck, Randall, Andrei Shleifer, and Robert W. Vishny. Forthcoming. Managerial ownership and market valuation: An empirical analysis. *Journal of Financial Economics.*

Murphy, Kevin J. 1985. Corporate performance and managerial remuneration: An empirical analysis. *Journal of Accounting and Economics* 7 (April): 11–42.

Palepu, Krishna G. 1986. Predicting takeover targets: A methodological and empirical analysis. *Journal of Accounting and Economics* 8: 3–35.

Schipper, Katharine, and Abbie Smith. 1986. Corporate income tax effects of management buyouts, photocopy. Chicago: University of Chicago, July.

Shleifer, Andrei, and Robert W. Vishny. 1988. Management buyouts as a response to market pressure. In *Mergers and acquisitions,* ed. Alan J. Auerbach. Chicago: University of Chicago Press.

Walkling, Ralph A., and Michael S. Long. 1984. Agency theory, managerial welfare, and takeover bid resistance. *Rand Journal of Economics* (Spring): 54–68.

Williamson, Oliver E. 1964. *The economics of discretionary behaviour: Managerial objectives in a theory of the firm.* Englewood Cliffs: Prentice-Hall.

Comment   Oliver S. D'Arcy Hart

Mørck, Shleifer, and Vishny's paper provides an empirical investigation of the characteristics of Fortune 500 firms that are the target of a takeover bid, with particular emphasis on how those that are subject to a friendly takeover differ from those that are subject to a hostile one. The main results are that, relative to the average Fortune 500 firm, the hostile targets are small, slow growing, in industries with a low Tobin's q, are unlikely to be run by a founding family member, and have low officer ownership. The friendly targets, again relative to the average Fortune 500 firm, are small, have average Tobin's q values and growth rates, are likely to be run by a founding family, and have high officer ownership. The authors argue that these results are by and large reasonable and supportive of the idea that the form or mood of a takeover is largely determined by its motive: In particular, friendly bids are likely to be associated with synergies, while unfriendly bids are likely to be disciplinary in nature.

I found this paper both interesting and instructive. It is one of the first to analyze the differences between friendly and hostile takeovers, and it provides a wealth of useful findings. These should be particularly helpful to researchers who hope to develop a theory of the determinants of different types of takeovers. It is worth noting that we do not now have such a theory. The models on takeovers in the literature focus either on hostile bids or on friendly mergers; they do not consider the choice between the two.[1] Of course, the absence of a theoretical framework makes a detailed interpretation of the authors' results difficult. My attempts in this direction should therefore be regarded as both

Oliver S. D'Arcy Hart is professor of economics at the Massachusetts Institute of Technology.

1. For examples of the former see Blair, Gerard, and Golbe (1986), Grossman and Hart (1988), and Harris and Raviv (1988); and of the latter see Grossman and Hart (1986). I should mention a recent paper that does study the choice between friendly mergers and hostile bids: Berkovitch and Khanna (1986).

provisional and tentative. I should also note that my interpretation does not differ greatly from the authors' own.

A reasonable starting point for the authors' analysis is the idea that a hostile bid is costlier than a friendly one, and hence, *ceteris paribus,* an acquirer would prefer a friendly transaction. There are many reasons for this. To mention a few, hostile bids are likely to be costlier because the acquirer may have to overcome various defences and resistance tactics from incumbent management, such as poison pills and lawsuits; the acquirer may have to pay more for the firm than otherwise if management resists by a recapitalization plan or a restructuring or by encouraging a white knight to make a counter-offer (or by engaging in a management buyout); a hostile bid may alienate incumbent managers and may make it difficult for the acquiring firm to work with them after control has changed hands; and the acquirer may find it more difficult to freeze out minority shareholders in a (two-stage) merger without management's approval of the bid as "fair."

The fact that hostile bids are costlier has an interesting implication. In a world of symmetric information and costless bargaining between the acquirer and the target management, no hostile bids should ever take place! This is simply a consequence of the Coase theorem. The argument is clear for the case in which a hostile bid would succeed with certainty: Management, recognizing that the writing is on the wall, will be prepared to agree to a (cheaper) merger in return for a small sidepayment (for example, a golden parachute). But the argument also applies to the case in which the bid outcome is uncertain. In fact, it is a simple consequence of the Coasian idea that two parties will always negotiate to a point on the efficiency frontier. Here, since a hostile bid is more expensive than a friendly bid, an efficient outcome can only be a friendly merger together with some sidepayment, or no merger at all.

We can learn two lessons from this observation. First, to understand the occurrence of hostile bids, we must introduce imperfections into the bargaining process, such as asymmetric information or limits to managerial sidepayments.[2] Second, a bid can appear friendly without being so. If management agrees to a merger because the alternative is to be the subject of a hostile bid, it seems inappropriate to label this as a friendly transaction. Yet that is the way it will appear in the data. Mørck, Shleifer, and Vishny recognize this problem, but there is little they can do about it. It should be borne in mind, therefore, that a

---

2. These limits may be reasonable. If managers accept a large sidepayment in return for agreeing to a merger, their action might be regarded as a breach of fiduciary responsibility toward the shareholders.

number of the bids the authors have classified as friendly really belong in the hostile category.[3]

As I have noted, a theory that can explain both hostile bids and friendly mergers will have to incorporate such features as asymmetric information and sidepayment limits. Until such a theory is available, one can only guess at the conclusions it will yield. Some plausible predictions, however, are that: the higher the costs of a hostile bid, the less likely it is that such a bid will be attempted; to the extent that hostile bids can be used to coerce management, an increase in the cost of a hostile bid might also be expected to reduce the probability of a friendly bid; and if for some reason managers become less concerned about losing control (because, for instance, they want to retire), the probability of a friendly bid will rise both in absolute terms and relative to a hostile bid (there is no reason to incur the costs of a hostile bid if management will relinquish control voluntarily).

These ideas can help us understand some of the authors' results. Let us accept their point that the motive for a takeover is likely to be either synergistic or disciplinary. A synergistic takeover is more likely to rely on the cooperation of the incumbent managers than a disciplinary takeover. The former is being carried out to take advantage of some externality between the operations of the two firms rather than because the current management is doing a bad job. Replacing the incumbent managers is unlikely to yield significant benefits, and, to the extent that they are good at what they are doing, it may result in significant costs. In contrast, almost by its nature, a disciplinary takeover is unlikely to require the cooperation of the incumbents. A disciplinary takeover is carried out either because the managers are incompetent, in which case getting rid of them will yield a positive benefit, or because they are competent but are enjoying too many managerial perquisites. Although it is true that in the latter case keeping management on with reduced perks might be desirable, when the two cases are taken together, the probability that managerial cooperation is required is likely to be relatively low.

To the extent that a loss of managerial cooperation is one of the disadvantages of a hostile bid (see above), we may conclude that the costs of a hostile bid are higher in a synergistic takeover than in a disciplinary one. Hence, we would expect to see relatively many synergistic takeovers consummated as friendly transactions and relatively many disciplinary bids as hostile ones. The absolute number of friendly

---

3. This problem is lessened by the fact that the authors classify a bid as hostile if it is initially resisted by management, even if management eventually accepts the bid (or a revised version of it). It would be interesting, by the way, to know how many bids change mood in this way.

disciplinary bids may not be insignificant, however, to the extent that some apparently friendly transactions are actually a form of coercion (the iron fist in the velvet glove).

Of course, if we could distinguish between synergistic and disciplinary transactions in the data, we would have a good test of these ideas. Unfortunately, we cannot. What the authors have done, however, is to identify characteristics of targets that make them likely to fall into one of the two categories rather than the other. For example, slowly growing, low-q firms are arguably badly managed and therefore appropriate targets for a disciplinary takeover. We thus might expect relatively many bids for these firms to be hostile, which indeed they are. On the other hand, firms with high officer ownership may be better run because management operates under a good incentive scheme. As a result, to the extent that these firms are taken over, it is likely to be for synergistic reasons, and we might expect relatively many of these transactions to be friendly. To put it another way, the managers of firms with high officer ownership have a direct interest in the market value of their firm as well as in managerial perks. They are therefore likely to welcome a friendly bid at a premium even if it does involve their losing control. Since the effective cost of a friendly bid is lower for them, we would expect the probability of a friendly bid to rise both relatively (to a hostile bid) and absolutely. This is what is observed in the data.

There is another possible explanation for why officer ownership affects the nature of a takeover. If officer ownership is high, management may have sufficient voting strength to block the takeover. In this case a takeover can succeed only with management's permission, which again argues for a friendly transaction. As the authors note, however, this control idea does not explain why high officer ownership is associated with a higher *absolute* probability of a takeover. In contrast, the previous incentive idea is consistent with this finding.

Other of the authors' results can be explained similarly. For example, the presence of a founding family member is likely to make a hostile bid more difficult to the extent that founders have a stronger preference for control as well as a better ability to resist. It is therefore not surprising that the probability of a hostile bid is seen to fall under these conditions. Interestingly, although one might expect the probability of a friendly bid to fall, too, in the presence of a founding family, this turns out not to be the case.

Of all the authors' results one in particular qualifies as a major paradox. Mørck, Shleifer, and Vishny find that what makes the probability of a hostile bid high is not a firm's q but the q of the industry it is in. This find is quite surprising since one would naturally suppose that a good indicator of managerial competence (or slack)—and hence of whether the firm is a likely candidate for a disciplinary takeover—is the firm's q relative to that of its industry. Note that I am not suggesting that the industrywide q should not affect the likelihood of a hostile bid. As the authors note, one can imagine general shocks that lead to slack in a whole industry; they give the example of the decline in oil prices, which should have led to a fall in exploration activity but did not. To the extent that this problem arises because the incumbent managers as a whole find it difficult to adapt to a new environment (to learn new tricks), disciplinary takeovers may be called for to replace them with new, more flexible managers (as Jensen 1986 has argued). Nevertheless, it is still very surprising that *only* industrywide q should be important. That is, one would expect idiosyncratic shocks hitting firms to have the similar implication that a disciplinary takeover may be called for to replace outmoded management. This apparently does not show up in the data, however. It would seem very desirable to examine the robustness of this conclusion in future empirical work.

Let me close with a few other suggestions for future work. First, to obtain further information on whether high officer ownership reduces the probability of a hostile tender offer for incentive reasons or for control reasons, researchers may want to study the small number of companies that have dual classes of shares. In these companies management's profit share and its voting strength can be significantly different from each other. In fact, DeAngelo and DeAngelo (1985) found that management typically has more than 50 percent of the votes but a significantly smaller fraction of the shares. It is possible, therefore, to distinguish between the incentive and the control effects among these firms.

Second, the idea that low-q firms are taken over for disciplinary purposes would receive further support if the firms that acquired them had high q values (showing that they were well run). It would be interesting to know if the data reflect this. Third, to the extent that a friendly merger occurs because cooperation from the incumbent management is important, we would expect the incumbent to continue to play a significant role in the new, merged company. Although obtaining evidence on this is likely to be difficult, it would be useful to know if there is even casual support for this idea.

Finally, as I noted above, the development of a formal theory of the choice between hostile and friendly bids would be very valuable. Those embarking on such a theory will find the results of this paper very instructive. The hope is that the relationship will be a two-way one: A formal theory will improve our understanding of the determinants of the different types of bids and sharpen our ideas about the regularities to look for in the data. Let us hope that it is not too long before such a theory is available.

References

Berkovitch, Elazar, and Naveen Khanna. 1986. A theory of acquisition markets—Mergers vs. tender offers, golden parachutes and greenmail, discussion paper 667. Ann Arbor: University of Michigan.
Blair, Douglas, James Gerard, and Devra Golbe. 1986. Unbundling the voting rights and residual profit claims of common shares, photocopy. New Brunswick, N.J.: Rutgers University.
DeAngelo, Harry, and Linda DeAngelo. 1985. Managerial ownership of voting rights: A study of public corporations with dual classes of common stock. *Journal of Financial Economics* 14 (1): 33–69.
Grossman, Sanford, and Oliver Hart. 1986. The costs and benefits of ownership: A theory of vertical and lateral integration. *Journal of Political Economy* 94 (4): 691–719.
————. 1988. One share/one vote and the market for corporate control. *Journal of Financial Economics,* forthcoming.
Harris, Milton, and Artur Raviv. 1988. Corporate governance: Voting rights and majority rules. *Journal of Financial Economics,* forthcoming.
Jensen, Michael C. 1986. The takeover controversy: Analysis and evidence. *Midland Corporate Finance Journal* 4 (2): 6–32.

Comment   Michael C. Jensen

The paper by Mørck, Shleifer, and Vishny contributes significantly to our knowledge of the takeover process. Analyzing all 454 publicly traded firms in the Fortune 500 in 1980, they find 82 firms, or 18.1 percent, were taken over in the years 1981–85 (including the 16 firms that went private in management buyouts). Of these 82 transactions 40 started out as hostile contests and 42 were friendly.

The authors analyze the differences between the ownership, asset, and performance characteristics of the targets of friendly bids and those of hostile bids to help identify the sources of the takeover gains. They conclude that combinations motivated by gains from the synergies resulting from combining two firms' assets and operations are more likely to occur with friendly mergers, and that takeovers motivated by the gains associated with disciplining poorly performing managers are more likely to be hostile. The hostile targets were poor performers, as measured by their Tobin's q ratios in 1980. The hostile targets had significantly lower q values than the friendly targets, were concentrated in low-q industries, and tended to have lower q values within their industries.

Michael C. Jensen is professor of finance at the Harvard Business School and the LaClare Professor of Finance and Business Administration and director, Managerial Economics Research Center, William E. Simon Graduate School of Business Administration, the University of Rochester.

The evidence indicates friendly targets are younger and faster growing than hostile targets and are indistinguishable from the sample as a whole on the performance dimension. The authors argue we would not expect the synergy gains from merging the target with another firm to be related to any general performance measures, and they therefore conclude that the average performance of the friendly targets means the gains from these mergers come from synergies. This seems to be a weak argument because the alternative hypotheses are not well specified.

The evidence does indicate, however, that the hostile targets tended to be older, more slowly growing firms, whose market values averaged only 52.4 percent of their replacement cost, whereas that of the friendly targets averaged 79.6 percent. The top two managers of the hostile targets owned considerably less stock of their firms than did the managers of the friendly targets, at 3.2 percent versus 14.5 percent, and they were much less likely to be a founder or members of a founding family. Forty percent of the friendly targets were managed by founders or members of the founding family, whereas 10 percent of the hostile targets and 24.4 percent of the sample as a whole were so managed. The intentional exit of the founding family or of a CEO with a very large stake in the firm seems to be a common cause of friendly acquisitions.

The authors conclude that the motive for friendly acquisitions is "more likely to be synergistic, whereas in hostile ones it is more likely to be disciplinary." Hostile targets were older, slow growing firms that were investing a smaller fraction of earnings than the average firm in the sample and whose capital was valued by the market at less than half its replacement cost—all of which is consistent with the theory of the agency costs of free cash, which predicts that managers will generally disinvest too slowly. I agree with the authors' conclusions, but there are a number of things the authors did not examine that would have considerably improved our understanding of the issues.

The authors did not consider takeover attempts that were unsuccessful, that is, attempts in which the target firm remained independent. Their conclusions apply only to friendly or hostile acquisition targets that were eventually taken over. The authors therefore missed an opportunity to tell us something about firms that were more likely to fail at a friendly deal or more likely to successfully fight off a hostile offer.

I also wish the authors had presented data on the total gains generated from the friendly takeovers versus those from the hostile takeovers. Historical evidence indicates the gains in mergers (which tend to be friendly) are lower than the gains in tender offers (which tend to be hostile). But we do not know what the gains to be explained are in these two different samples. Moreover, Grimm (1986) has shown there were only 118 contested tender offers over the years 1981–85, and so the 32 hostile offers (eliminating the 8 hostile management buyouts, which the authors define as preceded by a takeover offer or a 13d filing with control intentions) represent only 27 percent of all the hostile offers during the period. It is interesting that such a high proportion of hostile offers occurs among the largest firms. Indeed, the proportion was undoubtedly higher than this because the authors did not report the number of unsuccessful offers for targets that remained independent.

The authors base their conclusions on the performance of hostile vs. friendly targets solely on the differences in q values in 1980 for the 20 friendly and 31 hostile targets for which they have data on q values. It would be useful to have measured performance by prior earnings and stock price changes as well, to see if these measures of performance add anything to our understanding of the differences in these firms. This calculation would also have increased the effective sample size of the targets for which performance data exist. It appears that the targeted firms had a disproportionately large frequency of cases for which no q values existed; 37.3 percent of the firms with no q values were targets, whereas 13.7 percent of the firms with q values were targets. There may be a systematic reason for this and for the fact that only 25 percent of the hostile firms did not have q values, whereas 47.6 percent of the friendly targets did.

Finally, it would also have been useful if the authors had examined in detail the changes that occurred after takeover in each of the firms, to see if there were systematic differences between the hostile and friendly deals. The authors conjecture that the changes that occur after hostile transactions—for example, liquidation of assets or employee dismissals— are less acceptable to the incumbent managers than those following friendly ones and that this explains their opposition to the takeover. The exact nature of the changes in assets, liabilities, management, employment, and operating strategies would give us a much better understanding of the sources of the gains. But this, of course, would be another paper.

Reference

Grimm, W. T. 1986. *Mergerstat review, 1986*. Chicago: W. T. Grimm and Co.

5   Do Target Shareholders Lose in Unsuccessful Control Contests?

Richard S. Ruback

5.1 Introduction

Empirical studies of takeovers agree that the stock prices of targeted firms rise dramatically at the announcement of a takeover bid. But the studies disagree about the costs of any failure of the takeover bid. Two studies of tender offers suggest that the costs of failure are low. For the three years following the initial offer announcement, Dodd and Ruback (1977) reported abnormal returns of about 1 percent for a sample of 36 targets of unsuccessful tender offers. Similarly, Bradley, Desai, and Kim (1983) found abnormal returns of about −2 percent for the 112 targets of unsuccessful tender offers over the same three-year period. These studies indicate that stock prices do not, on average, return to their pre-offer levels. This evidence implies that the costs of resisting a tender offer, even if all of the competing bidders abandon the contest, are small since the shareholders retain most of the offer-induced increase in stock prices.

In contrast, Pound (1986) found abnormal returns of −30 percent in the three years following 56 unsuccessful takeover contests. Similarly, Easterbrook and Jarrell (1984) reported significant negative returns in the year following 31 unsuccessful takeover contests. These negative, abnormal returns following a tender offer suggest that the costs of failure are indeed high for targeted firms.

Richard S. Ruback is associate professor of finance at the Alfred P. Sloan School of Management, Massachusetts Institute of Technology; a visiting associate professor at the Harvard Business School; and a research associate of the National Bureau of Economic Research.

The author gratefully acknowledges the support of the National Science Foundation and thanks Alan J. Auerbach, Andrei Shleifer, and Robert W. Vishny for comments on a previous version of this paper.

137

A more precise measure of the cost of failure can be obtained from data on the stock price reaction to contest termination announcements. Two studies of mergers, by Dodd (1980) and Asquith (1983), found significant negative abnormal returns to targeted firms at the announcement of a merger termination. These negative abnormal returns completely offset the stock price increases associated with the initial merger announcement. The failure of merger bids, therefore, seems to cost the shareholders of the target firm most, if not all, of the offer-induced increase in stock prices.

This paper attempts to resolve the conflicting evidence on the impact of failed takeover efforts on the value of targeted firms. It examines the stock prices of the targets of unsuccessful contests for control during the contest and in the three-year period following the announcement of its termination. The results indicate that there are large costs to failure for target firms. More specifically, the stock prices of targeted firms fall by about 10 percent at the contest termination announcement. Those losses do not, however, completely reverse the gains made at the initial contest announcement.

The evidence in this paper has potentially important behavioral implications for the managers of targeted firms. The optimal amount of resistance must be related to the costs that would result from the bidder's abandoning the offer; managers should resist less, the greater the cost of failure.

The large stock price declines associated with termination announcements suggest that managerial resistance that results in the abandonment of a takeover bid decreases the wealth of the existing shareholders. Of course, the decision to resist may or may not have been in the target shareholders' interests ex ante. For example, the target managers may have been trying to elicit a higher takeover price from the existing bidder or from a potential competing bidder. For the firms in the sample examined here, no such higher offer was forthcoming, and the existing offers were terminated. Although the stockholders lost ex post, the managers' resistance may have been more than a fair gamble ex ante.[1]

5.2   Data

To identify a sample of unsuccessful tender offers over the years 1962–80, I used a tender offer data base compiled at the Managerial Economics Research Center (MERC) of the University of Rochester. I excluded offers for targeted firms that were not listed on the New York or American stock exchanges, as well as offers that would not result in a change in control of the targeted firm. Offers that could result in a shift in control are defined as those in which the bidder owned less than 40 percent of the target before the offer and would own more than 40 percent after purchasing all of the shares sought.

Following Dodd and Ruback (1977), offers are defined as successful if any of the following three conditions are met:

1. The bidder obtains two-thirds or more of the shares sought in the offer.
2. The bidder's holdings exceed 40 percent of the target's outstanding shares.
3. The tender offer changes to a merger that is completed.

For all offers that did not meet this definition of success, I checked the *Wall Street Journal Index* for competing merger bids that were not recorded in the MERC data base. In 18 cases competing merger bids were successfully completed. Since those bids were outstanding at the same time as the tender offers, these observations are classified as successful takeover contests. Thus, the sampling procedure used in this paper identifies unsuccessful control contests that involved at least one tender offer. The years in which the contests began are presented in table 5.1.

The sample contains 33 targets of unsuccessful control contests. It is about the same size as the sample used in Dodd and Ruback (1977), but it is much smaller than the 112 targets of failed tender offers analyzed in Bradley, Desai, and Kim (1983). The reason for this difference

Table 5.1   **Distribution of Initial Takeover Bids for Unsuccessful Takeover Contests, by Calendar Year, 1962–80**

Year	Number of Initial Bids
1962	0
1963	1
1964	1
1965	0
1966	1
1967	4
1968	1
1969	1
1970	0
1971	0
1972	0
1973	4
1974	2
1975	1
1976	4
1977	0
1978	6
1979	7
1980	0
Total	33

is that the latter set of authors treated each bid separately, whereas I treat bids for the same target that occur at the same time or within one month of each other as competing bids in a single contest for control. Since many contests are resolved within three months, a more appropriate comparison of sample sizes is that with Bradley, Desai, and Kim's sample of 26 targets that did not receive subsequent bids and 21 targets that received subsequent bids after three months.

I also collected control-related announcements made during the contests, which included 56 court filings and decisions, 18 opposition announcements made by the targeted firms, 14 subsequent tender offers or merger bids, 7 bid abandonments, 12 regulation-related announcements, and 15 other announcements.

For each of the 33 unsuccessful control contests in the sample, I examined issues of the *Wall Street Journal* published up to five years after the initial bid to determine if the target was subsequently acquired. Nine targets were so acquired during this time period. I also recorded all control-related announcements made during this five-year period.

5.3   Methodology[2]

The event study method pioneered by Fama, Fisher, Jensen, and Roll (1969) serves to measure the price effects of the initial offer, intermediate events, and termination announcements examined in this paper. Since most stocks tend to move up or down with the market, the realized stock returns are adjusted for marketwide movements to isolate the component of the returns due to the announcements. This adjustment is accomplished using linear regression to estimate the following market model:

$$(1) \qquad \tilde{R}_{jt} = \alpha_j + \beta_j \tilde{R}_{mt} + \tilde{\epsilon}_{jt}.$$

The parameter β_j measures the sensitivity of the jth firm's return ($\tilde{R}_{jt}$) to movements in the market index ($\tilde{R}_{mt}$). The term $\beta_j R_{mt}$ is the portion of the return to security j that is due to marketwide factors. The parameter α_j measures that part of the average return of the stock which is not due to market movements. The term $\tilde{\epsilon}_{jt}$ measures that part of the return to the firm which is not due to movements in the market or the firm's average return.

Two sets of coefficients are estimated for each firm to incorporate potential changes in the market model parameters. Coefficients before the initial contest announcement, α^B and β^B, are estimated using daily returns beginning 260 trading days before the initial offer announcement and ending 61 days before the announcement. Similarly, coefficients after the termination announcement are estimated over the period beginning 61 days after the announcement (if returns are available) through 260 days after the announcement. In those cases in which 100 days of data were not available to estimate either the before or after coefficients, the returns before the initial offer announcement and after the termination announcement are combined to estimate the coefficients. In all cases the returns for the 60 days before the initial offer announcement through 60 days following the termination announcement are excluded from the estimation period.

Prediction errors are calculated for each firm for 60 days before the initial contest announcement through 60 days after the termination announcement, according to the following expression:

$$(2) \quad PE_{jt} = \begin{cases} R_{jt} - (\hat{\alpha}_j^B + \hat{\beta}_j^B R_{mt}) & \text{for time } t \text{ before the initial contest announcement} \\[2ex] R_{jt} - (\alpha_j^A + \beta_j^A R_{mt}) & \text{for time } t \text{ at or after the initial contest announcement.} \end{cases}$$

The abnormal return over an interval of event days is not computed as the sum of the series of two-day prediction errors. Instead, I first compute the abnormal price change from each day. I then divide these abnormal price changes by the firm's share price 10 days before the initial contest announcement to obtain a measure in return form, which is defined as the adjusted prediction error.[3] The abnormal return of an interval or series of events is calculated by summing the relevant adjusted prediction errors for each firm and then averaging across firms.[4] These adjusted prediction errors measure the cumulative dollar effect relative to the value of shares 10 days before the initial contest announcement.

The following t-statistic is used to test the statistical significance of the abnormal returns:

$$(3) \quad t = \frac{1}{\sqrt{J}} \sum_{j=1}^{J} \left[\sum_{\tau=\tau_1}^{\tau_2} PE_{j\tau} \bigg/ \sqrt{Var\left(\sum_{\tau=\tau_1}^{\tau_2} PE_{j\tau}\right)} \right],$$

where τ_1 and τ_2 are the first and last days of the interval, J is the number of observations, and $Var\left(\sum_{\tau=\tau_1}^{\tau_2} PE_{j\tau}\right)$ is the variance of the sum of the prediction errors.

The t-statistic adjusts for heteroskedasticity in the prediction errors by standardizing the cumulative prediction error for each firm by its standard deviation. This standardization gives less weight to those prediction errors with more volatility.[5]

The variance of the sum of the prediction errors is:

$$(4) \quad Var\left(\sum_{\tau=\tau_1}^{\tau_2} PE_{j\tau}\right) = S_j^2\left[T + \frac{T^2}{N} + \frac{\left(T\bar{R}_m - \sum_{\tau=\tau_1}^{\tau_2} R_{m\tau}\right)^2}{(N-1)Var(R_m)}\right].$$

Here S_j^2 is the residual variance from the market model regression, T is the number of days in the cumulation interval, $\bar{R}_m$ is the average market return over the estimation interval, N is the number of days used to estimate the market model, and $Var(R_m)$ is the variance of the market over the estimation interval. This formula for the variance includes the covariance between the prediction errors and differs from previous formulas for the variance of a sum of prediction errors in that the other formulas ignored this covariance (see, for example, Mikkelson and Ruback 1985). To derive this formula, let:

$$R_j^* = \sum_{\tau=\tau_1}^{\tau_2} R_{j\tau},$$

and

$$R_m^* = \sum_{\tau=\tau_1}^{\tau_2} R_{m\tau}.$$

The forecast error is:

$$R_j^* - \hat{R}_j^* = T(\alpha - \hat{\alpha}) + R_m^*(\beta - \hat{\beta}) - \sum_{\tau=\tau_1}^{\tau_2} \epsilon_\tau,$$

where $\hat{R}_j^*$ is the forecasted value and α and β are regression estimates. The variance of the forecast error is:

$$E(R_j^* - \hat{R}_j^*)^2 = T^2 Var(\hat{\alpha}) + R_m^{*2} Var(\hat{\beta}) + T\sigma^2 + 2TR_m^* Cov(\hat{\alpha}, \hat{\beta}).$$

Substituting the values for the variance and covariance of the ordinary least squares coefficients provides equation (4).

5.4 Results

5.4.1 Abnormal Returns before and at the Initial Takeover Bid

Panel A of table 5.2 presents the average adjusted prediction errors for the targets of unsuccessful control contests during selected holding periods before and at the initial contest announcement. The initial bid appears to have increased the stock prices of the target firms. During the two-day announcement period, IB $-$ 1 to IB, the abnormal return for all targets in the sample was 22.21 percent. This is statistically significant, with a *t*-statistic of 30.05, and 94 percent of the 33 individual two-day prediction errors are positive. The two subsamples, targets *not* subsequently acquired and those that were, also had substantial positive, abnormal returns over the two-day announcement period.

Panel A of table 5.2 also indicates that the targeted firms realized significant positive returns over the period before the initial bid announcement. The abnormal returns were 8.76 percent during the nine

Table 5.2   **Percentage Adjusted Prediction Errors for 60 Days before the Initial Bid Announcement (IB) through 60 Days after the Termination Announcement (TD), 1962–80**

Holding Period	All Targets	Targets *not* subsequently acquired	Targets subsequently acquired
Panel A: Before and at the initial takeover bid			
IB − 60 to IB − 41	−3.36	−2.59	−5.42
	(−1.99;24;33)	(−1.60;21;24)	(−1.20;33;9)
IB − 40 to IB − 21	0.97	1.53	−0.53
	(1.10;51;33)	(1.15;50;24)	(0.24;56;9)
IB − 20 to IB − 11	0.90	−0.60	4.89
	(1.43;55;33)	(0.60;42;24)	(1.76;89;9)
IB − 10 to IB − 2	8.76	8.52	9.38
	(7.55;73;33)	(6.30;71;24)	(4.17;78;9)
IB − 1 to IB	22.21	23.49	18.78
	(30.05;94;33)	(28.82;96;24)	(10.49;89;9)
Panel B: Between the initial takeover bid and the termination announcement			
IB + 1 to TD − 1, event days only	−5.48	−6.26	−3.54
	(−2.32;32;28)	(−2.79;30;20)	(0.06;37;9)
IB + 1 to TD − 1, all days	−7.23	−8.59	−3.62
	(−1.18;39;33)	(−1.50;37;24)	(0.18;44;9)
Panel C: At and after the termination announcement			
TD − 1 to TD	−10.69	−8.14	−17.47
	(−13.37;9;33)	(−10.57;8;24)	(−8.34;11;9)
TD + 1 to TD + 10	−1.70	−0.38	−5.22
	(−1.40;45;33)	(−0.49;54;24)	(−1.88;22;9)
TD + 11 to TD + 20	−0.11	−0.14	−0.02
	(0.02;45;33)	(0.08;50;24)	(−0.09;33;9)
TD + 21 to TD + 40	−4.05	−3.05	−6.71
	(−1.07;36;33)	(−0.70;37;24)	(−0.91;33;9)
TD + 41 to TD + 60	−0.94	−0.09	−3.21
	(0.08;52;33)	(0.30;58;24)	(−0.33;33;9)

Note: *t*-statistics; percent positive; and sample sizes are in parentheses.

days immediately before the announcement (IB $-$ 10 to IB $-$ 2). This finding suggests there is some market anticipation or leakage of information before the actual announcement. Including these nine days and the two-day announcement period in the measure of announcement-related performance yields an abnormal return of about 31 percent, which is similar to the results of previous studies (see Jensen and Ruback 1983 for a review).

5.4.2   Abnormal Returns between the Initial Bid and the Termination

Panel B of table 5.2 presents the abnormal returns over the period between the initial takeover announcement and the outcome. Two measures of these abnormal returns are shown. The first, labeled "event days only," includes the day before and the day of each control-related announcement that occurred during this interval. These two-day event-adjusted prediction errors are summed over all such intermediate events for each contest, and these are then averaged across the 28 contests in the sample with intermediate events. The event-days-only abnormal return is -5.48 percent, with a t-statistic of -2.32. Since the sample includes only control contests that failed, this negative abnormal return is consistent with the release of information that reduced the probability that the contest would be completed.

The second measure of abnormal returns in panel B of table 5.2 sums over all days in the intermediate period, both event days and non–event days. This measure of abnormal returns, though statistically insignificant, is similar in magnitude to the event-days-only measure. This comparison shows that the potential advantage of the event-days-only measure is that it increases the signal-to-noise ratio if most new information is published in the *Wall Street Journal*. Of course, the disadvantage to the event-days-only measure is that it excludes information that is not published in the *Journal*.

Table 5.3 presents the average two-day adjusted prediction errors for each type of intermediate announcement. The abnormal return associated with the 14 takeover bids (including both competing tender offers and mergers) announced between the initial and termination announcements was 4.50 percent, with a t-statistic of 6.22. This abnormal return is substantially smaller than the market reaction to takeover bids reported in panel A of table 5.2 and in other studies. A simple explanation for this is that these announcements are all competing bids, which the market might anticipate to a greater degree than initial bids and which may involve lower incremental premiums than initial bids.

The 18 announcements of management opposition to the takeover were associated with positive, but insignificant abnormal returns. This finding should be interpreted with caution, however, because every contest in

Table 5.3   **Percentage Average Two-Day Adjusted Prediction Errors for Control-Related Announcements Made Between the Initial Takeover Bid and the Termination Announcements, 1962–80**

Intermediate Event	Targets of Unsuccessful Control Contests
Takeover bid	4.50
	(6.22;50;14)
Bid abandonment	− 12.31
	(− 5.72;14;7)
Opposition by target managers	1.62
	(− 0.28;39;18)
Litigation	−1.79
	(− 3.43;37;56)
Regulation	− 2.90
	(− 3.20;25;12)
Miscellaneous	− 1.64
	(− 2.84;40;15)

Note: The average two-day adjusted prediction errors are the sum of the adjusted prediction errors for each observation on the day before and day of the announcement. Parentheses enclose t-statistics; percent positive; and sample sizes.

the sample involved some form of opposition by the target management. The 18 announcements classified as opposition include only those events that were not associated with another announcement. Many of the litigation, regulation, and miscellaneous announcements, for example, also had to do with management opposition, and significant negative, abnormal returns were associated with these announcements.

The significant negative return for litigation announcements differs from Jarrell's (1985) finding of no significant negative abnormal returns for litigation announcements. One obvious explanation for the difference is that I limit my sample to contests that ultimately failed. Thus, my sample is more likely than his to include litigation that blocked the bidding firms. Finally, the 7 announcements of bid abandonments had abnormal returns of − 12.31 percent, with a t-statistic of − 5.72.

5.4.3   Abnormal Returns at and after the Termination Announcement

Panel C of table 5.2 presents the abnormal returns at and after the termination announcement. The two-day prediction error associated with the termination, TD − 1 to TD, was − 10.69 percent for all targets in the sample. This is statistically significant, with a t-statistic of − 13.37, and 91 percent of the two-day adjusted prediction errors are negative.

The contest termination announcements consist of 27 tender offer failures, 5 merger cancellations, and 1 unsuccessful proxy fight. A direct comparison of the termination announcements in table 5.2 with prior results is difficult because no study of tender offers has explicitly examined the announcement effects of offer terminations. But some information can be gleaned from the abnormal returns following offer announcements that were unsuccessful. The average time between the initial takeover bid announcement and the termination announcement was about 56 trading days, or about three months. Further, 22 contests concluded within 55 days and only two contests lasted for more than 200 trading days. Thus, the appropriate post-offer comparison period begins immediately after the offer and ends somewhere between three and six months after the offer.

Dodd and Ruback (1977) reported abnormal returns of about -4 percent in the three months immediately following the offer and another -3 percent in the next three months, for a total loss of -7 percent in the six months following the offer. These declines are comparable to, albeit smaller than, the contest termination announcements shown in table 5.2 here. However, 10 of the unsuccessful targets in the Dodd and Ruback study disappeared from the sample in the six months following the offer, suggesting that some takeover announcements and completions also occurred over the interval. Since takeover announcements are generally associated with positive, abnormal returns, the cumulative abnormal return of -7 percent probably underestimates the effect of tender offer terminations for the Dodd and Ruback sample.

The impact of termination announcements on stock prices has been examined in the study of mergers. Dodd (1980) reported a two-day abnormal return of -8.7 percent for the announcements of 80 cancelled merger targets. Asquith (1983) showed abnormal returns of -6.4 percent for 91 unsuccessful merger targets over the same two-day period. These abnormal returns to merger terminations are smaller than the abnormal returns to contest terminations reported in table 5.2. One plausible explanation for the difference is that the expected premiums were higher before the termination announcements in my sample. The higher premiums in hostile tender offers than in mergers, and the higher premiums in offers with competing bidders, are consistent with this explanation.[6]

Panel C of table 5.2 also contains the average adjusted prediction errors for holding periods during the 60 days following the termination announcement. All of the abnormal returns over the holding period were negative and statistically insignificant. The next section examines the post-termination stock price behavior over a longer time period.

5.5   The Post-termination Performance of Targets

Table 5.4 presents the percentage average adjusted prediction errors for 50-day holding periods beginning on the day after the termination announcement and ending three years later. The first column of the table indicates the abnormal returns for all unsuccessful contest targets; the second and third columns show the abnormal returns for the 24 targets *not* subsequently acquired and the 9 targets that were subsequently acquired, respectively. Figure 5.1 plots these cumulative abnormal returns. To reduce measurement error, the market model regressions were reestimated for every 200 trading days.

For the sample of all unsuccessful targets, market efficiency predicts zero abnormal returns following the termination announcement. Investors could adopt a strategy of buying shares on the day after a termination announcement and holding the shares for three years. Such an investment strategy should not, according to the efficient market hypothesis, earn above-average returns. But previous studies of the post-offer performance of takeovers do not uniformly support the efficient market hypothesis. For example, Jensen and Ruback (1983) found negative, abnormal returns for acquiring firms following completed mergers. And Asquith (1983) found significant abnormal returns of −8.7 percent in the 240 days following merger termination announcements.[7]

The average cumulative adjusted prediction error for the sample of all targets of unsuccessful control contests over the three years following the termination announcement is −27.14 percent, with a *t*-statistic of −1.41, and only 27 percent of individual cumulative errors are positive. Though statistically insignificant at standard confidence levels, the total abnormal return over this three-year period is somewhat disturbing to proponents of market efficiency. Nonetheless, two factors should mitigate this concern. First, I imposed some selection bias by including all offers that occurred within a month of each other as part of the same contest. Thus, these firms did not receive any offers in the month following the bid, according to my analysis. Since such bids were possible, this selection bias explains some of the negative, abnormal returns, especially in the first holding period. Second, tests that cumulate prediction errors over long time periods are generally sensitive to specification. In this case the three-year average cumulative return is about 14 percent when estimated using market-adjusted returns instead of a market model. Thus, the negative, total abnormal return reported in table 5.4 may be spurious.

For the 24 targets that were not subsequently acquired, the average cumulative adjusted prediction errors were negative in all but two of the 50-day holding periods. None of the abnormal returns for the holding

Table 5.4   **Percentage Average Adjusted Prediction Errors for Three Years after an Unsuccessful Control Contest, 1962–80**

Holding Period (TD = termination date)	All Targets	Targets *not* Subsequently Acquired	Targets Subsequently Acquired
TD + 1 to TD + 50	−5.23	−2.83	−11.62
	(−1.71;27;33)	(−1.02;37;24)	(−1.61;0;9)
TD + 51 to TD + 100	−4.17	−2.80	−7.80
	(−1.15;36;33)	(−0.61;42;24)	(−1.21;22;9)
TD + 101 to TD + 150	−3.93	−5.76	0.94
	(−1.54;27;33)	(−1.76;25;24)	(−0.07;33;9)
TD + 151 to TD + 200	3.14	1.53	7.97
	(0.36;41;32)	(0.17;42;24)	(0.45;37;8)
TD + 201 to TD + 250	−0.41	−3.04	7.49
	(−0.16;41;32)	(−0.44;37;24)	(0.45;50;8)
TD + 251 to TD + 300	1.70	−2.85	19.91
	(0.33;47;30)	(−0.25;42;24)	(1.24;67;6)
TD + 301 to TD + 350	1.13	−0.13	6.08
	(0.36;60;30)	(0.07;54;24)	(0.67;83;6)
TD + 351 to TD + 400	−0.08	−1.23	5.44
	(0.05;31;29)	(−0.58;29;24)	(1.40;40;5)
TD + 401 to TD + 450	−6.37	−5.29	−11.61
	(−0.58;38;29)	(−0.37;37;24)	(−0.58;40;5)
TD + 451 to TD + 500	−4.09	−2.06	−16.31
	(−0.25;50;28)	(−0.27;50;24)	(−0.01;50;4)
TD + 501 to TD + 550	−3.14	−2.97	−4.48
	(−0.11;41;27)	(−0.30;37;24)	(0.54;67;3)
TD + 551 to TD + 600	−0.80	−1.98	8.60
	(0.43;44;27)	(0.09;42;24)	(1.03;67;3)
TD + 601 to TD + 650	−1.64	−0.48	−10.89
	(−0.57;33;27)	(−0.33;37;24)	(−0.79;0;3)
TD + 651 to TD + 700	−4.88	−3.78	−18.09
	(−0.93;50;26)	(−0.65;54;24)	(−1.09;0;2)
TD + 701 to TD + 750	−3.74	−3.70	−4.26
	(−0.84;42;26)	(−0.87;42;24)	(−0.00;50;2)
TD + 751 to TD + 800	2.21	1.49	9.39
	(0.43;59;22)	(0.08;60;20)	(1.18;50;2)
Total	−27.14	−36.10	−3.23
	(−1.41;27;33)	(−1.79;21;24)	(0.21;44;9)

Note: *t*-statistics; percent positive; and sample sizes in parentheses

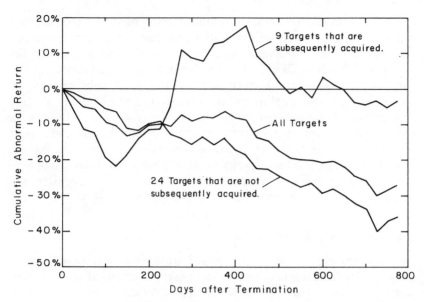

Fig. 5.1   Post-termination performance of 33 targets of unsuccessful control contests. The sample period for the initial contest announcements is 1962–80. The cumulative adjusted prediction errors for the terminations begin on the day following the announcements. The cumulations end on the day of a control change for the 9 observations with control changes and three years after the termination announcement for the 24 targets without subsequent control changes

periods was statistically significant. Overall, the total abnormal return was −36 percent, with a *t*-statistic of −1.79. Though not significant at standard confidence levels, this negative return would be predicted because these firms did not, ex post, receive a takeover bid during this period.

For the 9 targets that were subsequently acquired, the total abnormal return was −3.23 percent, which is not significantly different from zero. This insignificant return is surprising because positive, abnormal returns would be predicted as the market reacted to the takeover bids these firms received. One explanation is that the favorable impact of the takeover bid announcements are being masked by the noise in the data. To test this, I computed the average cumulative adjusted prediction error by using only the day before and the day of *Wall Street Journal* announcements. In other words, I excluded non–event days from the calculations. The event-day-only total abnormal return was 35.16 percent, with a *t*-statistic of 9.19, and all of the cumulative returns were positive.

The post-termination results in table 5.4 and figure 5.1 indicate that the losses that occur at the termination announcement are not reversed on average. The subsample results are broadly consistent with the findings of Bradley, Desai, and Kim (1983). Failed targets are often the subject of subsequent takeover bids. Firms that are subsequently acquired realize additional abnormal returns. The stock prices of firms that do not receive subsequent bids incur further declines in their stock prices. Thus, the stock price response to the termination announcement may be determined, in part, by the anticipation of future bids. Nevertheless, the significant stock price decline at the termination announcement suggests that the expected value of the failure is negative and therefore not in the interests of the existing stockholders.

5.6 Summary and Conclusions

The empirical results in this paper are based on a sample of 33 unsuccessful target firms. Significant abnormal returns of about 31 percent were associated with the initial announcement of the control contest. There were negative, but statistically insignificant, returns during the period between the initial offer announcement and the termination announcement. At the time of the termination announcement, these firms realized statistically significant negative abnormal returns of about − 10 percent. The negative returns at the termination announcement did not completely offset the gains from the initial announcement. In addition, no significant abnormal returns occurred in the three years following the termination of the offer.

The negative returns for termination announcements indicate that the failure of a control contest is costly to the stockholders of targeted firms. Opposition to takeover bids can therefore be harmful: Potential acquirers may choose to abandon the takeover attempt when the target's managers resist. Of course, the potential acquirers may instead choose to raise the offer price, and this response would benefit the target's shareholders. Opposition to tender offers, therefore, is a gamble. The evidence presented in this paper does not indicate whether the gamble is a value-maximizing strategy for the stockholders of targeted firms. Instead, it simply shows that losing the gamble imposes costs on the shareholders.

Notes

1. See Ruback (1986) for an overview of takeover defenses.
2. This section draws heavily on Mikkelson and Ruback (1986).
3. Instead of using the actual stock prices, I used a price index that equals one dollar eleven days before the initial contest announcement. On each suc-

ceeding day the index equals the compound value of the one dollar investment, such that:

$$P_{\tau-1} = \prod_{t=-1}^{\tau-1} (1 + R_{jt}),$$

where $P_{\tau-1}$ is the price index on day τ, and R_{jt} is the stock return to firm j on day t. The adjusted prediction error, $APE_{j\tau}$, each day is calculated as: $APE_{j\tau} = (PE_{j\tau})P_{\tau-1}$, where $PE_{j\tau}$ is the prediction error on day τ. Thus, if the share price is higher after the takeover announcement, the adjusted prediction error after the announcement is greater in absolute value than an unadjusted prediction error.

4. When there are missing stock returns within a holding period, the normal return is cumulated over the days in which there are missing stock returns. This cumulative normal return is subtracted from the next observed stock return to calculate the abnormal return.

5. The average abnormal return and the t-statistic can differ in sign because the former assigns uniform weights to each observation whereas the latter assigns non-uniform weights (equal to the inverse standard deviation) to each observation.

6. See Bradley, Desai, and Kim (1986) for evidence on premiums for offers with and without multiple bidders.

7. Asquith's sample excluded any target that received a subsequent bid in the year after the termination announcement. Asquith argued that the post-outcome negative abnormal return in his data was caused by this selection bias.

References

Asquith, Paul. 1983. Merger bid, uncertainty, and stockholder returns. *Journal of Financial Economics* 11 (April): 51–83.

Bradley, Michael, Anand Desai, and E. Han Kim. 1983. The rationale behind interfirm tender offers. *Journal of Financial Economics* 11 (April): 183–206.

———. 1986. Gains from corporate acquisitions and their division between target and acquiring firms, photocopy. Ann Arbor: University of Michigan.

Dodd, Peter. 1980. Merger proposals, management discretion, and stockholder wealth. *Journal of Financial Economics* 8 (June): 105–38.

Dodd, Peter, and Richard Ruback. 1977. Tender offers and stockholder returns: An empirical analysis. *Journal of Financial Economics* 5 (December): 351–73.

Easterbrook, Frank, and Gregg Jarrell. 1984. Do targets gain from defeating tender offers? *New York University Law Review* 59: 277–97.

Fama, Eugene F., Larry Fisher, Michael Jensen, and Richard Roll. 1969. The adjustment of stock prices to new information. *International Economic Review* 10: 1–21.

Jarrell, Gregg A. 1985. The wealth effects of litigating by targets: Do interests diverge in a merge? *Journal of Law and Economics* (April): 151–77.

Jensen, Michael C., and Richard S. Ruback. 1983. The market for corporate control: The scientific evidence. *Journal of Financial Economics* 11 (April): 5–50.

Mikkelson, Wayne, and Richard S. Ruback. 1985. An empirical analysis of the interfirm equity investment process. *Journal of Financial Economics* 13 (December): 523–53.

———. 1986. Targeted repurchases and common stock returns, working paper 1707-86. Cambridge: Massachusetts Institute of Technology, June.

Pound, John A. 1986. Takeover defeats hurt stockholders: A reply to the Kidder Peabody study. *Midland Corporate Finance Journal* 4 (Summer): 33–38.

Ruback, Richard S. 1986. An overview of takeover defenses, working paper 1836-86. Cambridge: Massachusetts Institute of Technology, September.

Comment   Andrei Shleifer

In his interesting and careful paper Ruback finds that termination of a takeover contest reduces the wealth of the shareholders of the targeted firm. The author takes this finding as evidence that target managers' actions to end the contest are probably not in the interest of target shareholders, although he is careful to note that resistance might have been value maximizing ex ante. This would be the case if, for example, target managers resisted in order to raise the offer price, and in some cases, contrary to their intention, drove the acquirer away. In this scenario, it is unclear why, once the bidder retreats, the target managers do not in fact try to lure him back. If they are acting in the interest of shareholders, this is what they should try to do, given Ruback's evidence.

There are other scenarios in which managers acting in the interest of shareholders will resist takeovers, although none is completely compelling. It might be the case that targeted firms are undervalued and managers are reluctant to sell their firms for less than they are worth to shareholders who will hold the stock until this undervaluation is corrected. Ruback's work suggests, however, that over three to five years, the targeted firms lose all of the premium offered in the original takeover bid. For the undervaluation theory to explain this finding, mispricing must persist for periods longer than three to five years, without being altered by the bid. Furthermore, it needs to be explained how long the horizon of shareholders must be for managers to impose on them the cost of waiting until mispricing disappears.

The more natural, though not necessarily correct, explanation of Ruback's results is, of course, that managers do not act in the interest of shareholders. They may be acting in their own interest or, alternatively, to protect other constituents of the firm. To understand mana-

Andrei Shleifer is assistant professor of finance and business economics at the Graduate School of Business, University of Chicago, and a faculty research fellow of the National Bureau of Economic Research.

gerial motives, one has to know more about the takeover scene before 1980, which is Ruback's sample. In particular, one must ask what menu of defenses was available then, and how they were used. Only by examining the characteristics of various episodes can we hope to come up with clear-cut answers to the questions posed by Ruback.

Comment   Robert W. Vishny

Ruback's paper carefully documents the loss to target shareholders upon termination of a control contest. The methodology of the paper represents a significant improvement over previous attempts to gauge the costs of a failed control contest. I see three main improvements in the author's work. First, Ruback obtains a more precise measure of the cost of failure by focusing on the termination announcement rather than on stock price behavior over a long period following the bid. Second, he adheres to a strict definition of a contest and does not double-count failed bids for the same target that were made around the same time. Finally, Ruback omits unsuccessful tender offers in which the contest failed because of a successful merger bid that was outstanding at the same time as the tender offer.

For his sample of 33 unsuccessful contests for control over the years 1962–80, Ruback finds that the average abnormal return at the time of the initial announcement of the contest is about 31 percent, with abnormal returns of -10.69 percent at the termination announcement and negative but insignificant abnormal returns of about -7 percent between these two events. I want to spend the rest of this discussion making some suggestions about how to use these numbers in conjunction with other information about control contests in order to better understand the effects of management resistance and the sources of gains in takeovers.

There are several issues that immediately arise in interpreting Ruback's results. First, any estimate of the cost of contest failure must include the stock price reactions associated with the gradual learning that the contest would be unsuccessful and not just the reaction at the time of the termination announcement. Ruback finds a -7 percent effect between the time of the initial bid and the termination announcement, with a standard error of about 6 percent. The noisiness of this estimate suggests that the event-date-only estimate may be preferable

Robert W. Vishny is assistant professor of finance at the Graduate School of Business, University of Chicago, and a faculty research fellow of the National Bureau of Economic Research.

even though it will probably underestimate the information leakage effect. This more precise but possibly biased estimate is -5.48 percent, with a standard error of about 2.4 percent. Including an estimate of the total effect of the contest termination and gauging its reliability will be important if we are to know how much of the initial rise in market value is lost when the initial opportunity vanishes. Even though this involves looking at a noisy number, it is not as serious a problem as following an unsuccessful target for three years.

A second issue arises because a nontrivial fraction (9 out of 33) of the unsuccessful targets were subsequently acquired. This means that if we are interested in knowing whether there is some permanent revaluation of targeted firms even when they are not subsequently acquired, we must remove the value contribution of expected future bids from the post-termination stock price. We can at least get a handle on this calculation by looking at the distribution of subsequent acquisitions and premia for the initially unsuccessful targets. Although Ruback does not look specifically at this distribution, he does find that 27 percent of the unsuccessful targets were subsequently acquired and that the event-day-only estimate of abnormal returns for these firms over the three years following the termination date is 35.16 percent. An interesting question is whether these results are consistent with the hypothesis that there is no permanent revaluation of the targets of unsuccessful bids and that any elevation of the post-termination share price above the pre-bid share price can be attributed to the prospect of future bids. If we combine a 31 percent initial rise with a -7 percent termination leakage effect, a -10.7 percent termination announcement effect, and a 27 percent chance of a future acquisition (which on average leads to a 35 percent abnormal return sometime within three years after termination), I think we can probably conclude that the "no permanent revaluation" hypothesis is a viable possibility.

Apart from worrying about what portion of the initial share price rise remaining after termination is due to future bids, we should think about whether our interpretation of Ruback's results would be different depending on the reason the initial contest was terminated. For example, if most of the initial contests are terminated because the target comes up with a foolproof defense against all takeover bids, any revaluation of the target might be attributed to the market's inference that the bidder considered the target to be undervalued even under the existing management. The same interpretation would be much less valid if the initial bid was just dropped even when there was only weak resistance. For in the latter case the market seems more likely to infer that the bidder simply had second thoughts, and consequently the market would be less likely to suspect gross underpricing of the target's shares. To the extent that the resistance techniques used differ across firms or over the time period of Ruback's sample, we might want to make different inferences about the undervaluation hypothesis for different subsamples.

Another interpretation of a permanent upward revaluation of the target following an unsuccessful contest is that management took positive steps to increase the value of the firm in order to thwart the takeover. Since these defensive restructurings seem to have become much more prevalent in recent years, we may not want to extrapolate the finding of "no permanent revaluation beyond expectation of future bids" for Ruback's 1962–80 sample to conclude anything about the valuation effects of defensive restructurings in recent years.

In sum, Ruback's results on the effects of contest termination, supplemented by evidence on the value of future bids implicit in post-termination share prices, can be very useful in helping us determine both the effects of managerial resistance and the extent to which the targets of unsuccessful takeovers are permanently revalued by the market. Finding out whether these targets experienced permanent increases in their market values would shed light on the hypothesis that stock market underpricing is an important source of gains in takeovers. This information could also help in determining the extent to which managers doing defensive restructurings end up replicating the value-increasing changes raiders sought to make.

6 The Effects of Taxation on the Merger Decision

Alan J. Auerbach and David Reishus

6.1 Introduction

The recent merger wave in the United States has left observers attempting to uncover explanations for its strength and persistence. Some have suggested that tax factors have played an important role. Indeed, the Tax Reform Act of 1986 contained several provisions, not effective until the beginning of 1987, that were aimed specifically at reducing the tax advantages available through merger. In two previous papers (Auerbach and Reishus 1988a; 1988b), we estimated the tax benefits generated by 318 mergers and takeovers that took place in this country over the years 1968–83, and we considered whether the level and type of tax benefits available affected the structure of the merger transactions. Our findings suggested that although tax benefits did not appear to be important in the majority of transactions involving large, public corporations, in a significant minority of transactions the benefits appeared significant enough to play a role in the decision to merge.

By focusing exclusively on mergers that occurred, we were able to estimate the size of the tax benefits involved but not the role that these benefits played in the actual merger process. The presence of such benefits is a necessary condition for tax factors to influence merger activity, but not a sufficient one. Because the issues involved in changing the ownership and management of a company are extremely complex, it is entirely possible that tax benefits, even if significant, come

Alan J. Auerbach is professor of economics at the University of Pennsylvania and a research associate of the National Bureau of Economic Research. David Reishus is an economist with the U.S. Joint Committee on Taxation.

The authors are grateful to the National Science Foundation, the NBER, and the Institute for Law and Economics at the University of Pennsylvania for financial support; and to Kevin Hassett, Eric Gonzales, Ki Ingersol, and Wendy Allyn for research assistance.

into play only "at the margin" once other conditions have been satisfied. Thus, it remains unclear whether the tax benefits received by merging firms represent more than simple transfers to the parties involved, or in other words whether the frequency and pattern of takeovers has been significantly influenced by the availability of the tax benefits.

This paper aims to resolve this question by comparing the sample of mergers we previously analyzed with "pseudomergers," ones that did not occur, drawn from random combinations of firms in a broad sample of U.S. corporations. By estimating a "marriage model" based on the differences between mergers that occurred and those that did not, we are able to discern whether the tax benefits observed in the mergers that took place were available with the same size and frequency in the population as a whole (conditional on other factors), or whether the tax benefits were larger than would have occurred by chance, as would be true if tax factors increased the likelihood of a merger.

The paper is organized in the following way. The next section discusses the tax treatment of mergers and acquisitions and what the potential tax benefits of a merger are. Section 6.3 describes our merger sample, the findings we previously reported on the tax benefits from these mergers, and the relationship of such benefits to the structure of the transactions. Section 6.4 outlines the underlying model of merger activity that we use to generate the multinomial logit specification of the merger decision, as well as how we deal with the estimation problem introduced by the large number of alternative mergers in which a firm could engage. Section 6.5 describes the sampling procedure used to create the sample of pseudomergers and the calculation of variables used in the estimation; section 6.6 presents the empirical estimates themselves. The final section offers some brief conclusions concerning the implications of the recent tax law changes for the level of merger activity.

6.2   The Tax Benefits of Merger Activity

There are several different ways that companies may reduce taxes through a merger or acquisition, and tax benefits can accrue at both the corporate and the shareholder level. In some cases the tax benefits from a corporate combination are also available through other means, and these benefits should therefore not necessarily be attributed to the merger process. The following description, except where noted, applies to the law in force before 1987, during the years when the mergers in our sample occurred.

6.2.1   Corporate Taxation

There are three types of potential corporate tax benefits associated with the combination of two public corporations: increased utilization of tax loss and tax credit carryforwards, increased depreciation deductions obtained by stepping up the basis of assets, and increased interest deductions associated with an increase in the debt-equity ratio of the combined enterprise.

Tax Losses and Credits

Under the tax law, both present and past, corporations with negative taxable income may claim tax refunds based on these losses only to the extent of the previous three years' taxable income (net of intervening losses). Any additional losses must be carried forward, without interest, until the firm has taxable income sufficient to offset them or until they expire, now after 15 years and before 1981 after 5 years. Estimates in Auerbach and Poterba (1987) and Altshuler and Auerbach (1987) suggested that for the average large corporation experiencing tax losses, the present value of tax refunds so deferred is on the order of half their face value, because of deferral and expiration. Because both of these studies derived estimates from samples of firms that continued to operate independently, they may have overstated the true population average, since one would expect disappearance from the sample to be negatively correlated with the likelihood of becoming taxable in the near future.

Further restrictions exist on the use of investment tax credits. Until 1977 firms could offset at most half of their taxable income, after deduction of losses carried back and forward, with investment tax credits. (This fraction rose to .85 by 1982.) Altshuler and Auerbach estimated that the number of firms paying taxes but carrying credits forward was even larger than the number of firms carrying losses forward and paying no taxes. The size of these tax benefits can be substantial. Auerbach and Poterba found several cases of firms carrying forward losses with a face value of tax refunds in excess of the firm's equity value, suggesting not only that these firms had very low values as the result of poor performance, but also that the market did not expect them to obtain close to the full face value of the tax benefits.

Combination with a "fully" taxable firm that has no tax losses and the potential to absorb more credits than it is currently claiming can increase the value of such a firm's tax benefits. Under prior law, a taxable firm could offset the losses and credits of an acquired firm against its own current and future income, subject to the usual expiration provisions and a variety of additional limitations that varied with how the transaction was structured. Few such limitations applied when the benefits were those of the larger, or acquiring, firm being used to offset the income of the acquired company, as was true, for example, in several of the acquisitions by Penn Central that appear in our sample.

The size of such benefits may actually be understated by focusing on current tax carryforwards, since many firms with previous tax losses and unused credits may also have "built-in" losses that will occur in the future. For example, a firm with assets consisting of a depreciable capital good that one year after purchase proved to be valueless will still be entitled to depreciation deductions in subsequent years even without any cash flow from the asset. Such losses have already occurred, in economic terms, but not for tax purposes.

It has often been suggested that the presence of unused tax benefits does not constitute an incentive to merge because firms can dispose of them in other ways, including leasing and reducing debt. The premise of the "safe harbor" leasing provisions introduced briefly in 1981 was to facilitate such transfers, in part to reduce the possible incentives to merge (Warren and Auerbach 1982). Nevertheless, the magnitude of unused tax benefits, and the persistence of firms in states that offer such benefits, suggests that the costs to such alternative activities must be large enough to discourage their use in an important number of cases.

Step-Up in Asset Basis

Many companies carry assets on their books with a basis for tax purposes equal to a small fraction of their replacement cost. Such assets, if depreciable, provide a small fraction of the depreciation allowances available on equally productive, newly purchased capital, including used assets that are resold. Hence, resale provides a channel for increasing such allowances. Opposing this potential tax gain is the tax that must be paid when an asset is sold. Under prior law the seller in a normal asset sale had to pay some combination of capital gains and ordinary income taxes on the difference between the sale price and the basis, making such sales by corporations generally unprofitable for tax purposes (Gordon, Hines, and Summers 1987).

Under the "general utilities" doctrine, however, liquidating distributions of assets to shareholders were exempt from the capital gains portion of this tax liability. These distributions occur, for example, when one corporation acquires another and then liquidates it. They can also occur without an acquisition, with the corporation simply distributing its assets to its individual shareholders. This example has led some observers (such as Gilson, Scholes and Wolfson 1988) to argue that the tax advantage to liquidations does not constitute a tax benefit associated with the act of merging. Although we are aware of no empirical evidence on this issue, it seems plausible that there are many cases in which the transaction costs of such liquidations would be prohibitive, particularly when the value of the firm as a continuing operation substantially exceeds the sum of the values of its individual assets.

Increased Interest Deductions

The theory of optimal capital structure offers no easy explanation of the choice of debt-equity ratios in the presence of a substantial tax advantage to debt. Except for Miller's (1977) theory that the individual tax advantages to equity entirely offset the corporate advantage to debt, most hypotheses about optimal capital structure involve individual firms having interior optimal debt-equity ratios determined by the increasing costs to leverage associated, for example, with increased expected bankruptcy costs, increased agency costs, or the increased probability of tax losses. In these models the firm's costs of leverage may increase with the variance of its earnings, since that variance may be associated with a higher probability of bankruptcy and tax losses. Thus, the reduction of idiosyncratic risk, which would produce no value in a perfectly competitive model with efficient securities markets, could increase value directly through a reduction in total bankruptcy costs and in the frequency of tax losses and indirectly through the reduced marginal costs of borrowing. It is therefore possible to derive models without independent managerial motives in which it is optimal for firms to merge to reduce their own risk, with the models also suggesting that these combinations would involve increased leverage.

Another way in which borrowing could encourage takeovers would be if one of the manifestations of the "bad management" leading to takeovers is an overly cautious debt policy. Because of the differing incentives of shareholders and managers, it is plausible that managers would choose to borrow less than a value-maximizing amount since the risks associated with low earnings or bankruptcy might be more costly to managers than to shareholders. If the incumbent managers are too risk averse, for example, new management could increase value because of its decision to borrow more.

In addition, of course, one would expect increases in borrowing to the extent that takeovers increase value by improving management or the utilization of assets, since these activities essentially increase the scale of the firm, presumably lowering the marginal borrowing cost for a given absolute level of debt. But unlike the first two cases, this would not necessarily lead to increased debt-equity ratios, nor would it be associated with a particular type of merger, such as one in which risk is reduced or the target initially has a low debt-equity ratio.

6.2.2   Shareholder Taxation

There are two primary ways in which acquired firms' shareholders receive payment: shares in the parent (or combined) company, or cash. The mode of payment may affect the use of corporate tax benefits. In addition, however, the tax treatment of shareholders depends on the form of payment. If the shareholders receive cash, they are normally taxed on their capital gains. If they receive shares, they may be taxed, but the firms may structure the transaction as a reorganization and thereby defer shareholder taxation until the new shares are sold. Each type of transaction has potential tax benefits beyond the corporate benefits already discussed.

In nontaxable stock transactions, shareholders typically receive shares in a larger, more diversified enterprise in exchange for shares representing a much larger fraction of a smaller company, a process that can result in creating a more balanced portfolio without the capital gains taxes usually attendant upon such a move. In taxable cash transactions the acquiring firm distributes cash out of the corporate form at capital gains tax rates. In models of corporate equity policy that explain the existence of dividends through constraints on such behavior (which also encompasses the repurchase of a company's own shares), this kind of activity may produce value because the values of the firms are depressed by the anticipation that the acquired firm's value can reach shareholders only through fully taxed dividends (see, for example, Auerbach 1979; Bradford 1981; King 1974). A recent paper by King (1986) estimates an aggregate model attempting to explain merger behavior in the United Kingdom as the result of such a process.

6.3   Previous Findings

In our two previous papers we examined a sample of 318 mergers and acquisitions that took place during the years 1968–83.[1] The sample consisted of all mergers and acquisitions in which both firms were on the 1983 Compustat Industrial File or the 1983 Compustat Industrial Research File and for which usable tax data could be obtained from the companies' annual reports and 10-K filings with the Securities and Exchange Commission. Just over three-quarters of these combinations came about between 1976 and 1982. The parent companies had an average value of equity plus long-term debt of $1.957 billion (before the acquisition), while the average targeted firm's value was just over one tenth of this, or $204 million.

Our estimates (in Auerbach and Reishus 1988a) suggested that tax benefits realizable through increased use of tax losses and credits were potentially present in about 20 percent of the mergers, with an average value of just over 10 percent of the target's market value in the year before the merger. We found smaller evident benefits from stepping up the asset basis, but we encountered substantial difficulty in estimating these benefits. Perhaps most surprising, though we found noticeable increases in the absolute combined level of debt, we found negligible increases in combined debt-equity ratios (calculated before the merger by combining the debt and equity values for the separate firms) over the period beginning two years before the merger years and ending two years after.

In our second paper we focused on the relationship between the form of the transaction and the type of tax benefits available. We found that virtually all transactions were either nontaxable stock transactions or taxable cash transactions, the majority being of the first type. This point is significant because in nontaxable transactions the firm has opted for a corporate reorganization, which generally cannot include a liquidation and step-up of asset bases. Under a taxable transaction either a liquidation with a step-up or a transfer of tax attributes may be chosen. This suggests that taxable transactions might be more common when the potential basis step-up benefits are large, but we could identify no such relationship, perhaps in part because of our inability to measure the benefits precisely. Moreover, since the transfer of tax losses and credits is also treated somewhat differently under a taxable transaction than under a tax-free reorganization, there could be cases in which firms opting for a transfer of tax benefits would still prefer the taxable (to the shareholder) transaction. Thus, it is possible that firms would be responsive to taxes in their merger planning without there being any discernable relationship between the type of tax benefits available and the form of the transaction. This leaves the merger decision itself to be evaluated in assessing the importance of tax factors.

6.4 A Model of Mergers and Acquisitions

In this section we describe a simple model of mergers and acquisitions. Though it is particularly well-suited to the questions we seek to answer, it is also applicable more generally. Hall (1988) uses a related model in her study in this volume of the relationship between mergers and research and development.

The model begins with several simplifying assumptions. Although billed as a marriage model, the marriage process is one not now favored by most cultures, namely, polygamy. We assume that targets can be acquired only once within a year and that acquirers can seek as many targets as they wish. This latter assumption leads to a model of the "choice" made by prospective targets among alternative acquirers.

We assume that in each year every potential parent, x, evaluates a function, $M(x,y)$, that indicates the joint gains to be had from acquiring a target, y. The function $M(x,y)$ may take on negative values, since there may be substantial transaction costs involved in a successful acquisition. If $V_0(y)$ is the value of y if it is not taken over, then firm x will pay up to $V_0(y) + M(x,y)$ to acquire y. Thus, in a competitive market for y, the firm with the highest valuation of y, say x^*, will acquire y if $M(x^*,y) > 0$, for a price between $V_0(y) + M(x^*,y)$ and $V_0(y) + \max_{x' \neq x^*} M(x',y)$. Note that the observed merger premium may be less than $M(x',y)$, since the possibility of a merger may have led the prior price to exceed $V_0(y)$.

We assume that the function $M(x,y)$ has the specification

(1) $$M(x,y) = z_{xy}\beta + \epsilon_{xy},$$

where the vector z includes variables that relate only to the target, only to the parent, or to both, and ϵ is a random disturbance representing benefits to the merger not observed by the investigator. Perhaps the most crucial assumption we make is the one that leads to a tractable empirical model. This is that the error term is uncorrelated with the observed variables and takes on the extreme value distribution. Following McFadden (1973), it is then possible to express the probability that x_i will acquire y as

(2) $$p_{x_i y} = e^{z_{x_i y}\beta}/(1 + \sum_{j=1}^{N} e^{z_{x_j y}\beta}),$$

which is a multinominal logit model of dimension $N + 1$, where N is the number of potential parent firms and the extra dimension is added by the possibility that no merger will occur. As is well known, the multinomial logit model has certain strong properties, such as the independence of irrelevant alternatives, which in this case seems justifiable. This property also simplifies the estimation procedure relative to an alternative approach, such as the multinomial probit. Even for a multinomial logit, however, it is impractical to estimate a model of our dimensions.

This estimation problem has been dealt with in the previous literature in two ways. One approach is to include a small sample of the alternatives. In the current model this would mean that each observation would involve a potential target and several, rather than all, potential acquirers. For our model this estimation approach would pose problems. Many of the parent firm characteristics that appear in the vector z, such as industry dummy variables, occur relatively infrequently in the population. Thus, it might be necessary to include a relatively large number of alternative parents to achieve adequate sampling.

The alternative estimation approach is to treat all combinations with a particular target, except one, as an aggregate "all other" state. This aggregation is not straightforward because of the nonlinearity of the logistic specification. Suppose that for the observation of a potential target firm y the "all other" state includes all possible combinations aside from the one with potential parent x_1. To convert the multinomial logit specification (2) into a trinomial logit, one must then define the aggregate state by the function

$$(3) \qquad f(z_{x_2 y}\beta, \ldots, z_{x_N y}\beta) = \ln \sum_{i=2}^{N} e^{z_{x_i y}\beta}.$$

Consider a second order Taylor expansion of the function $f(\cdot)$ around some constant value α for each of its $N - 1$ arguments. After a couple of steps of algebra, one obtains

$$(4) \quad f(z_{x_2 y}\beta, \ldots, z_{x_N y}\beta) \approx \ln(N - 1) + z_y\beta + \frac{1}{N-1}\sum_i (z_{x_i y}\beta - \alpha)^2$$

$$- \left(\frac{1}{N-1}\right)^2 \sum_i (z_{x_i y}\beta - \alpha)\sum_j (z_{x_j y}\beta - \alpha),$$

where z_y is the mean of $z_{x_i y}$, $i = 2, \ldots N$. By choosing $\alpha = z_y\beta$, one can rewrite statement (4) (since the last term on the right-hand side vanishes) as

$$(5) \qquad f(z_{x_2 y}\beta \ldots, z_{x_N y}\beta) \approx \ln(N - 1) + z_y\beta + \tfrac{1}{2}\sigma^2(z_{x_i y}\beta)$$

or, letting Ω be the matrix whose ijth element is the sample covariance between independent variables i and j,

$$(6) \qquad f(z_{x_2 y}\beta, \ldots, z_{x_N y}\beta) \approx \ln(N - 1) + z_y\beta + \tfrac{1}{2}\beta'\Omega\beta.$$

As argued by McFadden (1984), this approximate specification is exact when the elements of the vector z are joint normally distributed, for then the higher moments of the Taylor approximation vanish.

This second approach to estimating a high-dimension multinomial logit is well suited for our problem because the sample means and variances of the independent variables of our model are easily estimated and have an intuitive economic interpretation.

6.5 Sampling and Data Preparation

The literature on mergers and acquisitions contains several attempts to estimate the factors leading to firms' being taken over (for example, Palepu 1986) by examining the differences between firms acquired and firms not acquired. By looking at merger pairs, rather than just targets, and including firms that were not acquired in the estimation procedure, it should, in principle, be possible to distinguish factors that affect the probability of a firm's being acquired from those that determine the actual match that occurs. The acquisition probability should be influenced by target-specific variables that enter both branches of the model just outlined, while the actual match should be influenced by variables that depend on the actual pairing of the potential target and parent. This is quite important in the current context, where the tax benefits available from a merger depend not only on the tax status of the potential target but also on the ability of the potential acquirer to use these benefits. If mergers occur for tax reasons, one would not expect the firms acquired by Penn Central to have the same tax characteristics as those acquired by IBM.

To the 316 observations we had on firms that were acquired, we added a similar number of observations of firms chosen at random from the Compustat universe of firms, according to the following stratified sampling method.[2] For each actual merger, we created a corresponding "pseudomerger" by selecting a "pseudotarget" firm from all firms in the same size class and year as the target, and a "pseudoparent" firm from all firms in the same size class and year as the real acquirer. The sample of pseudomergers therefore looks almost identical to the actual merger sample in terms of size and year, but it may differ with respect to other variables of interest.

For each observation we constructed variables for the target-parent pair and then constructed corresponding variables for the aggregate "all other" pairs according to expression (6). The variables were either taken directly or constructed from raw data provided by the Compustat files or the annual reports and 10-K filings.

We employed this particular sampling method for two reasons. Although the optimal sampling scheme is uncertain, it has been suggested that an equal number of different alternatives is a good rule of thumb for minimizing variance of estimates when the sample size is limited (Cosslett 1981). The need to obtain from microfiche the tax information for each observation served to limit our own ability to expand the sample. The reason for stratifying the sample by size and year is to match closely the mergers and pseudomergers by variables that may be important but not of direct interest. Perhaps more importantly, this stratification serves to limit the unwanted effects of unobserved variables correlated with year and size, as well as the direct effects of time and relative size that we would be unable to specify exactly. What we gain in precision in our variables of interest we lose in determining the effect of time and relative size on merger activity.

6.5.1 Nontax Variables

To test the importance of tax factors, it is necessary to control for the other factors likely to affect mergers. Not doing so would certainly lead to incorrect conclusions. For example, in our previous work we discovered that there were nine cases in the 316 mergers in which both parent and target were tax constrained. Most of these, however, were mergers of two firms within a single industry, where a high correlation of profitability would lead one to expect a positive correlation of the incidence of tax constraints. Thus, if firms in the same industry are more likely to merge than firms in different industries, not controlling for this factor could lead to a downward bias in the estimated impact of tax factors.

Target-Specific Variables

As discussed above, target-specific variables are those which affect the probability of a firm's being taken over, rather than the probability of a specific merger. We include dummy variables for the target firm's one-digit Standard Industrial Classification (SIC) industry, to account for the fact that mergers might relate to overall industry conditions. To pick up growth-related merger motives, we include the target firm's five-year geometric growth rate of sales.

To gauge management competence, we would like a measure of the market value of the firm to the replacement cost value of its assets. Since firm assets include assets beyond those included in capital stock measures, we suppose that each firm's true capital stock takes the form

$$(7) \qquad K = K_f + \Sigma_i a_i S_i,$$

where K_f is the fixed capital stock, a_i is a parameter to be estimated, and S_i is a proxy for intangible assets, such as research and development expenditures or advertising. This statement leads to the inclusion of the variables $K_f - V$ and S_i, where V is the firm's market value, which we approximate by the market value of equity at the close of the previous year plus the book value of the firm's financial liabilities. In some specifications these variables are expressed as ratios with respect to market value.

Pair-Specific Variables

Among the pair-specific variables we include dummy variables if the parent and target are in the same industry. Because it is unclear how close two firms must be for them to be in the "same" industry, we specify three dummy variables, equal to one if the two firms are in the same one-digit, two-digit, and four-digit SIC industries, respectively.

Finally, we specify two dummy variables based on the relative size of the two firms. The "same size" dummy variable equals one if the prospective parent firm is in the same size class as the target or the next higher size class (these classes are defined in section 1 of the appendix). For example, if the target firm had a market value of $200 million, this variable would equal one for a parent with value between

$100 million and $500 million. The second size dummy, for "larger size," equals one if the parent is in one of the next two higher size classes; in the example, this would be a firm with a value between $500 million and $5 billion in assets. Both dummy variables equal zero only if the parent is substantially larger than the target (or much smaller, though this event does not occur in the data set).

6.5.2 Tax Variables

There are several variables we consider to be tax-related. The first is the target firm's debt-equity ratio. As suggested above, this could indicate the presence of a potential for increasing interest deductions. We would have preferred to include other variables potentially related to borrowing, such as the reduction in risk, but data on the covariance of firm earnings were not available or even estimable from the data we had.

The remaining variables are pair-specific. The first is the estimated tax gain available from stepping up the basis of the target's assets. Because equipment sales and liquidations are subject to recapture at ordinary income tax rates, the main gains to be had from avoiding capital gains taxes should be those associated with structures and depletable resources. The appendix describes the algorithm used to estimate these gains. Given the assumptions necessary to make these calculations, the estimates are subject to substantial error and could greatly understate the potential gains in cases where the targeted firm has assets that have been on its books for many years or have appreciated in value at a rate in excess of the inflation rate, or both.

The appendix also describes the method used to estimate the gains from the use of tax credits and tax losses. We assume such gains to be zero unless one of the firms is fully taxable and the other is tax constrained. This is a conservative assumption, since there should be some gains in any case where the taxable income of the two firms is not perfectly correlated. These gains are hard to measure, however, and arguably too small to have an impact on merger decisions. Where the tax gain is positive, it is calculated under the assumption that the firm with tax benefits becomes a shell after the merger, generating neither positive nor negative taxable income, and that the taxable firm uses these benefits to the extent that the law permits. Here, we ignore the additional restrictions that might apply to the full use of benefits in particular cases, because of our inability to identify such cases.

The remaining tax variables have to do with the shareholder tax incentives for cash acquisitions. Here we are limited by the absence of a clear theory about the constraints firms face in avoiding dividend taxes. If share repurchases are costly, then, as discussed above, a firm wishing to distribute cash in excess of dividends will have the incentive to engage in cash acquisitions in addition to repurchasing its own shares. The same incentive would not be present for a firm already issuing new equity, since cash acquisitions could not be financed by internal funds. We therefore would expect constrained firms to be more likely to engage both in share repurchases and cash acquisitions. This suggests that we include dummy variables indicating whether the parent or pseudoparent firm has repurchased its own shares in the past two years and whether it has sold common equity in the past two years (in excess of threshold values of 4 percent of the firm's shares). In an earlier study (Auerbach and Reishus 1988b) we did indeed find that, among firms that acquire, the probability of using cash as a means of payment is (insignificantly) higher for firms that have recently repurchased their own shares and (significantly) lower for those that have recently issued new shares.

6.5.3 Calculation of Variables for the Aggregate Alternative

For each observation it is necessary to calculate the values of each of the above variables that correspond to the state representing a merger with one of "all other" potential parent firms. The only new calculations needed, however, are those for pair-specific variables, since the others have a value that is independent of the characteristics of the potential parent.

For each pair-specific variable the sample mean must be estimated for inclusion in the vector z_y, and the sample covariance matrix Ω is needed as well. For the dummy variables the mean is simply the fraction of the population in that category (defined to be all firms of equal or greater size). For example, the mean corresponding to the "same industry" dummy variable is the fraction of potential parent firms in the target's industry. The covariance term between dummy variables equals the difference between the fraction of the sample satisfying both characteristics and the fraction that would be predicted by multiplying the sample means of each dummy variable.

For the continuous tax variables the aggregate calculations are based on the simplifying assumption that the value is either zero or a constant amount based on the parent firm's tax status not being affected by combining with the target. For example, a firm with tax losses that acquires a profitable firm retains excess losses after offsetting the target's taxable income, and a taxable parent firm uses all the tax benefits of the target. This is quite reasonable given the relative sizes of acquired and acquiring firms. Once this value, say T, is calculated for each potential target firm, the aggregate mean is calculated as the product of this variable and the fraction of firms in the state where the tax benefit can be used (taxable if the target is nontaxable, and tax-constrained if the target is taxable). The covariance term of this variable with the same-industry dummy, for example, equals the fraction of all firms in the same industry and the opposite tax state of the potential target, less the product of the same industry fraction and the opposite tax state fraction, all multiplied by the magnitude of the tax benefit.

6.6 Results

Before turning to the model estimates themselves, it is useful and informative to compare selected statistics for the two samples of firm pairs, those that actually merged and those that did not.

Table 6.1 presents mean changes in debt-value ratios for the two samples, broken down further by the relative sizes of target and parent. For actual mergers the change is measured by subtracting the ratio of the two firms' debt to those firms' debt plus equity two years before the merger year from the same ratio for the surviving firm two years after the merger. Because of data problems, only long-term debt (at book value) is used in the calculation. The four-year period is used to distinguish "long run" leverage changes from those that might occur only temporarily around the merger date. For the pseudomergers the combined ratio is used for both dates in computing the change.

The results in table 6.1 cast doubt on the association of mergers with increases in indebtedness. For only two of the five groups does the difference in means have the "right" (positive) sign, and for neither of these classes (or for the total sample) is the difference significant. Only for the class where the targets are roughly equal in size to the parents is there any discernible change in leverage, and here there are too few observations to draw any conclusions. This does suggest that data from the post-1983 period, which involved many more acquisitions of large firms, would be useful to examine.

Table 6.1	Mean Changes in Debt-Value Ratios, from Two Years before to Two Years after Merger				
	Actual Mergers		Pseudomergers		
Relative Target Size	Number	Average Change	Number	Average Change	t-statistic
< .1	107	0	71	.013	−0.64
.1 −.25	60	−.032	60	−.011	−0.75
.25−.50	40	.018	38	−.015	1.01
.50−.75	14	−.014	21	.028	−0.76
> .75	25	.071	22	−.032	1.59
Total	246	.001	212	−.002	0.21

Note: Relative target size is the ratio of the target's value (debt plus equity) to the parent's value in the year before merger. The total number of firms is somewhat lower than the overall sample size because of missing data. The t-statistics are for a test of equality of means. Means are unweighted within each cell.

Table 6.2   **Potential Gains from the Transfer of Losses and Credits**

Size of Gain	Actual Mergers (N = 316)			Pseudomergers (N = 291)		
	Total	From Target	From Parent	Total	From Target	From Parent
0	255			235		
< .05	26	19	7	23	16	7
.05–.10	11	7	4	10	7	3
.10–.25	14	9	5	17	9	8
> .25	10	3	7	6	4	2
Fraction with gain	.193	.120	.073	.192	.123	.069
Mean gains:						
Unweighted	.170	.126	.242	.112	.108	.113
Weighted	.105	.049	.163	.078	.058	.100

Note: Gains are expressed as a fraction of the target firm's value (long-term debt plus equity). Mean gains are for those pairs with positive gains, with target firm's values used when weighting.

Table 6.2 presents estimates of the potential tax gains from the transfer of tax losses and credits between parent and target. Again, the calculations are done for both actual mergers and pseudomergers. For the real mergers just under one-fifth of the pairs exhibit a tax gain, with a mean weighted gain of 10.5 percent of the target's market value. This mean is larger than the estimate given in our earlier paper, in which a cruder method was used to calculate the gain. There are fewer cases where the gain comes from the parent, but the average gain in these cases is estimated to be much larger. The incidence of tax benefits among the pseudomergers is remarkably similar, a result that suggests the transfer of tax losses and credits may not be an important factor in the merger decision. There is a noticeable difference between the samples, however, in the magnitude of gains coming from cases in which the parent firm has unused tax losses or credits. These gains are on average much lower for the pseudomerger sample than for the actual merger sample. Distinguishing the source of the tax gain may, therefore, be important in the estimation procedure.

The estimated gains from the target's basis step-up are given in table 6.3.[3] Once again the differences between the two samples are negligible. Further, based on our very imperfect measurement technique, the estimated potential tax benefits from basis step-up are quite small, averaging only about 2 percent of the target's value and exceeding 5 percent in only 7.8 percent of both real mergers and pseudomergers.

We turn next to the estimates of the full merger model. Results for a variety of specifications are given in tables 6.4 and 6.5. The estimated equations differ according to whether certain variables are expressed in levels or relative to the market value of the targeted firm.[4]

Table 6.3   Potential Gains from Basis Step-Up

Size of Gain	Actual Mergers (N = 281)	Pseudomergers (N = 245)
< .05	259	226
.05–.10	12	12
.10–.25	9	6
> .25	1	1
Mean gains:		
Unweighted	.019	.020
Weighted	.018	.021

Note: Gains are expressed as a fraction of the target firm's value. The total number of firms is somewhat lower than the overall sample size because of missing data.

Table 6.4 presents estimates based on the level specification, while those in table 6.5 are for the ratio form. The theoretical model introduced in section 6.5 does not allow us to determine in advance which of these specifications is to be preferred.

A number of variables are robust and quite significant in all the specifications. These include the target's debt-value ratio, which has a positive effect on the probability of a firm's being acquired; the target's sales growth rate; and the same-industry dummy variables, especially that for the four-digit SIC industry. The fact that each of the same-industry dummy variables is always positive suggests that firms are more likely to merge the closer their industrial relationship. The increasing magnitude of the same industry coefficients as one moves from the one-digit to the four-digit variable means that the incremental effect is also increasing: Being in the same four-digit industry *relative* to the same two-digit industry has more of an effect on the merger probability than being in the same two-digit industry, as opposed to the same one-digit industry, for example. The results for the industry dummy variables are interesting but not unexpected; nor is the performance of the sales growth term, given a similar finding by Palepu (1986). The influence of the debt-value ratio, however, is quite surprising, given the argument that firms with unused debt-capacity are more likely to be taken over. One possible explanation is that firms with high debt are firms in trouble, though other variables included in the regression are intended to control for this characteristic.

The industry dummy variables for the target suggest that (relative to the omitted industries, those with SIC codes beginning with 8, which include health, education, and engineering) in only two broad industry groups were firms more likely to be acquired during the period in question: transportation, communication, and utilities; and to a lesser extent finance, insurance, and real estate.

Table 6.4   Logit Model Estimation Results

Independent Variable	Level Specification		
	(1)	(2)	(3)
Constant	11.50	11.50	10.62
	(18.35)	(18.33)	(6.29)
Target's debt-value ratio	3.64	3.64	2.72
	(5.04)	(5.03)	(2.80)
Target's sales growth rate	1.99	1.98	2.75
	(2.28)	(2.27)	(2.25)
Same one-digit SIC	1.45	1.45	1.47
	(1.68)	(1.67)	(0.79)
Same two-digit SIC	2.34	2.34	3.38
	(1.98)	(1.96)	(2.29)
Same four-digit SIC	6.60	6.60	6.95
	(7.54)	(7.51)	(9.11)
Same size parent	−.61	−.61	−.55
	(−.92)	(−.91)	(−.66)
Larger size parent	.36	.36	.50
	(.55)	(.55)	(.58)
New shares issued	−.07	−.06	.22
	(−.12)	(−.11)	(.35)
Shares repurchased	−.85	−.85	−.86
	(−1.26)	(−1.26)	(−1.01)
Tax gain*	.20	—	—
	(3.24)		
Tax gain target*	—	−.09	−.60
		(−.13)	(−.54)
Tax gain parent*	—	.22	.22
		(3.40)	(2.04)
Basis step-up*	−3.10	−3.07	−1.13
	(−1.97)	(−1.85)	(−1.34)
Target's book-market value*	−.05	−.05	−.07
	(−.57)	(−.56)	(−.72)
Target's advertising*	.03	.05	.33
	(.03)	(.03)	(.16)
Target's R&D*	−.92	−.97	−1.11
	(−.56)	(−.56)	(−.36)
Target's industry dummy variables (one-digit SIC)			
1. (Mining and resource extraction)	—	—	−1.80
			(.99)
2. (Nondurable goods manufacturing)	—	—	1.49
			(.87)
3. (Durable goods manufacturing)	—	—	1.15
			(.67)

Table 6.4   (continued)

	Level Specification		
Independent Variable	(1)	(2)	(3)
4. (Transportation, communication, and utilities)	—	—	4.31 (2.24)
5. (Retail sales)	—	—	1.00 (.58)
6. (Finance, insurance, and real estate)	—	—	2.82 (1.52)
7. (Services)	—	—	.53 (.27)

Note: Dependent variable = 1 if merger occurs; *t*-statistics are in parentheses. In "ratio" specifications the variables with asterisks are divided by the target firm's market value.

Table 6.5   **Logit Model Estimation Results**

Independent Variable	Ratio Specification		
	(1)	(2)	(3)
Constant	11.59 (19.14)	11.62 (18.57)	10.87 (6.60)
Target's debt-value ratio	3.55 (4.83)	3.44 (4.56)	2.33 (2.25)
Target's sales growth rate	2.33 (2.57)	2.43 (2.56)	3.29 (2.79)
Same one-digit SIC	1.41 (1.59)	1.40 (1.56)	1.47 (0.81)
Same two-digit SIC	2.25 (1.82)	2.23 (1.80)	3.26 (2.21)
Same four-digit SIC	6.76 (7.35)	6.78 (7.31)	6.96 (8.76)
Same size parent	−.69 (−1.11)	−.69 (−1.13)	−.61 (−.79)
Larger size parent	.35 (.56)	.34 (.55)	.49 (.61)
New shares issued	−.11 (−.20)	−.10 (−.18)	.19 (.31)
Shares repurchased	−.87 (−1.26)	−.85 (−1.23)	−.90 (−1.07)

Table 6.5   (continued)

Independent Variable	Ratio Specification		
	(1)	(2)	(3)
Tax gain*	.27 (.69)	—	—
Tax gain target*	—	−.02 (−.05)	−.90 (−.69)
Tax gain parent*	—	1.75 (.34)	1.93 (.38)
Basis step-up*	−6.90 (−.89)	−6.40 (−.82)	10.82 (2.55)
Target's book-market value*	.26 (.81)	.32 (.94)	.44 (.95)
Target's advertising*	−1.88 (−1.18)	−1.94 (−1.22)	−1.59 (−.69)
Target's R&D*	−7.46 (−2.67)	−7.49 (−2.68)	−4.03 (−1.31)
Target's industry dummy variables (one-digit SIC)			
1. (Mining and resource extraction)	—	—	1.76 (1.01)
2. (Nondurable goods manufacturing)	—	—	1.47 (.89)
3. (Durable goods manufacturing)	—	—	1.11 (.68)
4. (Transportation, communication, and utilities)	—	—	4.87 (2.60)
5. (Retail sales)	—	—	.90 (.54)
6. (Finance, insurance, and real estate)	—	—	2.60 (1.43)
7. (Services)	—	—	.45 (.24)

Note: Dependent variable = 1 if merger occurs; t-statistics are in parentheses. In "ratio" specifications the variables with asterisks are divided by the target firm's market value.

Certain other variables are also robust to the choice of specification and always insignificant. These include the new share and repurchase variables and the parent size variables. The pattern of the size variables suggests that a firm is most likely to acquire other firms that are smaller than itself, but not too much smaller. This is consistent with our observation (Auerbach and Reishus 1988a) that parents are typically larger than the targets they acquire but that relative size is correlated. The repurchase variable has the "wrong" sign in that it suggests firms that have repurchased are less likely to acquire other firms. This result does not necessarily constitute evidence against the "trapped equity" inducement for cash mergers. It may simply mean that firms wishing to get excess cash out of the corporate form tend to specialize in their method, either repurchasing or engaging in cash acquisitions. If this specialization were strong enough, the observation of a firm repurchasing would reduce the expectation that it would also engage in a cash merger, even though, *conditional* on its decision to acquire, it would still be more likely to use cash (as suggested by our previous results cited above). This problem of interpretation underscores the need for a more rigorous model of the constraints that cause equity to be "trapped" and the optimal behavior of firms in response to these constraints.

The performance of the remaining variables, including the tax variables, depends on the model specification. The tax gain variable always has the correct sign and is significant in the level specification. But when this variable is broken down into two variables according to the source of the tax gains (target or parent), only the tax gains from the potential parent are significant in the level specification. This is entirely consistent with the results given in table 6.2, where the only noticeable difference between the sample of real mergers and that of pseudo-mergers was for the case of parent-related tax gains. Moreover, it is plausible that the tax benefits of the target firm would present less of an incentive because of the additional restrictions on their use that we have not taken into account.

Despite this statistical significance, however, the tax variable for the parent is of little *economic* importance. Depending on the exact specification, setting the value of the parent's tax gain to zero (which simulates the impact of a policy change making the transfer of such benefits impossible) reduces the predicted number of mergers by between just under 1 percent and just over 1.5 percent. In contrast, the predicted number of mergers would be reduced by well over one-half by setting the same-industry (at the four-digit level) dummy variable equal to zero (which simulates the impact of a policy of prohibiting combinations of firms in the same four-digit industry occurring with a frequency that cannot be explained by other factors).

The basis step-up variable is disturbingly sensitive to whether the ratio or the level specification is used and to whether industry dummy variables are included. In the level specification it always has the wrong sign. In the ratio specification it has the wrong sign in the two specifications without industry dummies but is significant and has the predicted sign with the industry dummies present. If this last model were correct, the predicted decline in mergers associated with a removal of the tax benefits from basis step-up would be over 8 percent, much larger than the predicted impact of removing the ability to transfer losses and credits. Nonetheless, the instability of this variable's performance and the problems in its construction lead us to discount the importance of this result.

The results for the remaining three variables, which are intended to measure the difference between market value and the value of asset, are also sensitive to whether level or ratio form is used. Under the former all three are quite insignificant. Under the latter the gap between book and market value has the correct sign and is significant, while the R&D variable has the wrong sign and is significant. It should be pointed out, however, that this sign for R&D is "wrong" in a very limited sense, if R&D affects the merger probability only through its use in correcting our measure of the firm's asset replacement cost. If R&D spending exerts an independent influence on the probability of a firm's acquisition, it is not clear without further modeling what sign one should expect it to have.

In summary, then, the basic model specification seems good in that the variables one associates with acquisitions, such as industry relationship and growth, are consistently significant. The significance of the debt-value ratio is also quite robust, through we are not certain how this is to be explained. In light of the results in table 6.1, however, it is hard to argue that acquisitions by large corporations were driven during this period by the opportunity to tap unused target debt capacity.[5] The performance of the tax gain variable suggests a mild, positive effect of tax losses and credits experienced by the potential acquirer, but little effect of those experienced by the potential target. Finally, the basis step-up variable, whose accuracy we have questioned, is of the correct sign (but significant) in only one specification. The values of the likelihood function for the ratio and level specifications are virtually identical, making it difficult to decide which model describes the data best.

6.7 Conclusion

The object of this paper has been to consider the impact of taxes on the frequency of mergers and acquisitions in the United States over the years 1968–83. To do this, we have compared the tax characteristics of a sample of merging firms to those of a similar sample of nonmerging firms chosen at random and, using both samples, estimated a "marriage" model of merger activity. Our results suggests that the potential increase in interest deductions could not have been an important factor influencing merger activity during the period in question. The two samples exhibit very insignificant differences in borrowing patterns, and the logit model estimates suggest that a lower debt-equity ratio is associated with a lower probability that a firm will be acquired.

Likewise, the tax benefits associated with acquiring a firm having tax losses or unused tax credits appear to exert an insignificant influence on merger activity. The frequency and size of the tax benefits are virtually the same in the actual merger sample and the pseudomerger sample, and the size of the potential benefit has no explanatory power in the merger model. One reason for this may be the existence of a variety of restrictions on the use of the tax benefits that, because of their complexity, we have ignored in our analysis.

The two potential tax benefits that do appear to have some impact on merger activity are the use of tax losses and credits by *acquiring* companies to offset the taxable income of the firms they acquire and the option to step up the basis of the assets of the acquired firms without paying corporate capital gains taxes. The first of these is significant in some of the model estimates and is more important in the sample of real mergers than in the sample of pseudomergers. Even so, it is of little *economic* importance in explaining the frequency of mergers. The second potential benefit is significant in one of the specifications estimated, but it has the unexpected sign in all others. Given the difficulty we have encountered in measuring this variable accurately, we are somewhat suspicious of this finding of potential significance.

As to the avoidance of individual taxes, we have found that firms that repurchased their own shares in the previous two years are *less* likely to acquire other firms. This result is hard to reconcile with the theory that firms seek cash acquisitions to free "trapped equity" without a rigorous model of the constraints on and determinants of repurchase activity.

The Tax Reform Act of 1986 attempted to discourage tax-driven acquisitions by repealing the "general utilities" doctrine, which permitted the tax-free basis step-up, and by limiting the acquirer's use of the tax losses and credits of the acquired firm. Our findings suggest that the latter restriction is of little importance. Ironically, the use of the *acquirer's* tax benefits, which appears to have some impact on merger activity, was not restricted by the recent legislation. A change that, some have argued, could encourage mergers is the strengthening of the corporate alternative minimum tax. Just as with the asymmetry associated with gains and losses, it will be possible for firms subject to the minimum tax to combine with taxable firms not subject to the minimum tax and reduce combined tax payments. But the potential tax reductions would appear smaller (since the difference between the two firms' marginal tax rates is lower) than for the combination of a taxable and nontaxable firm. Given our findings about mergers between these types of firms, we strongly doubt that the minimum tax provisions will have a significant impact on merger activity.

The results in this paper should be regarded with caution because we had to make many assumptions to estimate the potential tax benefits associated with particular mergers. Without access to the confidential tax returns of the firms involved, these assumptions were unavoidable. Another research limitation that deserves mention is the terminal date of our sample—early 1983. Since then, the character of the acquisition process has changed, with many more "megamergers" occurring in which larger firms were acquired. There is some inconclusive evidence in our table 6.1 that these mergers may, on average, be associated with increases in leverage for the combined enterprise. Recent observations should facilitate a more precise evaluation of this proposition, along with the one that borrowing to finance acquisitions has, in general, become more important in recent years.

Appendix

In this appendix, we describe the methods used for sampling and for calculating the variables.

Sampling

The actual and "pseudo" samples were matched by year and by the assets of both parent and target. The methods for calculating assets are explained below. The size categories were (in millions) 1–10, 10–25, 25–50, 50–100, 100–250, 250–500, 500–1,000, 1,000–5,000, 5,000+, as well as a category for missing values. The missing values were eliminated for the regressions, which left 310 actual mergers and 291 pseudomergers. The difference is due to the inability to collect meaningful tax or asset information on a portion of the pseudo mergers.

Gain from the Use of Tax Losses and Credits

This calculation uses information on the income tax paid, tax loss carryforward, and investment tax credit carryforward obtained from corporate reports. When a firm without carryforwards and positive tax payments combines with a firm that has carryforwards, we calculate the potential benefit. We assume that the unconstrained firms' level of tax payments grows at a 10 percent nominal rate into the future, while the firm with the loss carryforward contributes no new losses but also no new taxable income in the future—it is simply a shell for holding tax loss carryforwards. We then calculate the net present value of the tax payments (discounted at 10 percent), combining the two firms' tax attributes through the period when the carryforward is used up or expires. The net present value of the tax payments of the two firms separately is also calculated using the same assumptions for the same time period. The difference between the combined calculation and the sum of the separate calculations is the tax benefit.

The aggregate calculation is much cruder. If the target is paying positive taxes, we use three times the tax payment as the tax gain from merging with a parent that has a tax loss carryforward as indicated by Compustat. For targets with tax losses we use the value of the actual tax loss as the potential benefit for parents that do not have tax loss carryforwards as indicated by Compustat.

Basis Step-Up

We begin with the firm's book value of fixed assets at the end of the last year before the merger. Using data on the firm's gross investment and the capital stock at the end of the earliest year for which it is available for the firm, we employ the "perpetual inventory" method to estimate the rate of declining balance depreciation that is consistent with the firm's initial and terminal capital stocks. Given this estimate of economic depreciation, we then estimate the current market value of the capital stock by multiplying the capital remaining from different vintages by the ratio of the price (represented by the GNP deflator) in the current year to that for the year in which the capital was purchased. We also assume that the initial capital stock was valued correctly on the firm books. That is, we solve for δ from the equation:

$$(A1) \qquad K_T = (1 - \delta)^T K_0 + (1 - \delta)^{T-1} I_1 + \ldots + I_T,$$

where K_t is the book capital stock at the end of year t and I_t is fixed investment in year t. We then calculate the market value of the capital stock as

$$(A2) \qquad K_T^m = (1 - \delta)^T K_0 P_T / P_0 + \ldots + I_T.$$

We assume that a fraction, θ, of this market value represents structures, where θ is the fraction that structures represent for all firms in the same industry (taken from Auerbach 1983). Note that this operation will understate the market value of assets that have increased in nominal value at a rate in excess of the GNP deflator or were worth more than their book value even at time zero.

Since structures are written off at a different rate from equipment, they will generally represent a different fraction of the book capital stock than of the market value capital stock. Since structures decay more slowly than equipment, the book fraction will be smaller: Inflation has a greater effect on the ratio of the current value to book value as the time since purchase increases.

If one assumes that the structures fraction of the firm's capital stock at time zero was also θ, and that structures are written off at the declining balance rate γ, it follows that the book value of structures at date T is

(A3) $K_T^{\S} = \theta\{K_0(1 - \gamma)^T + [K_T^m - K_0(1 + \pi)^T]$
$\cdot [1 - (1 - g + \pi)(1 - \gamma)]/[1 - (1 - g + \pi)^T(1 - \gamma)^T]$
$\cdot \{[1 - (1 - g)^T(1 - \gamma)^T]/[1 - (1 - g)(1 - \gamma)]\}\}$,

where π is the average inflation rate over the period 0 to T, and g is the nominal growth rate of investment in structures. These rates are easily calculated for each firm. We set $\gamma = .033$, the aggregate value derived in Auerbach and Hines (1987).

Given the market value of the firm's structures capital stock, we estimate the after-tax value of depreciation allowances the firm would receive by multiplying the corporate tax rate by the average present value of depreciation allowances on all structures, estimated by Auerbach and Hines (1987). It is somewhat more difficult to estimate the depreciation allowances the firm would receive if continuing along its previous depreciation schedule, since its capital stock purchase dates are unknown. We simply assume the allowances would have the same present value as is available on new capital per each dollar of remaining basis. Moreover, we assume that recapture will neutralize the additional depreciation allowances received on increases in basis up to the straight-line basis, and that this latter basis equals the actual book value. Thus, the net estimated gain is the present value of the depreciation allowances of new structures, multiplied by the corporate tax rate, multiplied by the difference between the market and book value estimates for structures.

For 35 real targets and 46 hypothetical targets the data were insufficient to perform the basis step-up calculations. For these firms we use an imputed value equal to the sample average. Use of a separate missing-value dummy variable did not substantively alter the results.

Asset Value

Based on Compustat data the value of a firm is calculated as the market (year-end) value of common stock plus the book value of long-term debt, short-term debt, and preferred stock in the year preceding the merger. For an important fraction of targets a closing stock price was unavailable for that year; if the calculation provided a missing value, we took this value from the previous year.

Notes

1. We have since discovered problems with data for two of the mergers and so report on only 316 observations in this paper.
2. There are actually 291 such observations because of data problems encountered after the second sample was chosen.
3. These are given for all targets and pseudotargets, including the relatively small number matched with a nontaxable parent or pseudoparent that could not use the tax benefits. In the estimation procedure below the potential gain is set to zero in such cases.
4. In all versions of the model estimates reported in the paper, we weight each observation based on the sampling frequency of the target firm's size class as well as status (acquired or not acquired). In principle this is the correct approach, although it gives some observations substantial weight. We also tried an alternative weighting scheme that did not distinguish sample weights by size. The coefficients for most variables were nearly identical, although one of the tax variables, the parent's tax gain, had its size reduced somewhat in some specifications.
5. Needless to say, one cannot and should not interpret this finding as applying to the going-private leveraged buyouts that are not included in our sample.

References

Altshuler, Rosanne, and Alan J. Auerbach. 1987. The importance of tax law asymmetries: An empirical analysis. NBER working paper no. 2279. Cambridge: National Bureau of Economic Research.
Auerbach, Alan J. 1979. Wealth maximization and the cost of capital. *Quarterly Journal of Economics* (August): 433–46.
———. 1983. Corporate taxation in the United States. *Brookings Papers on Economic Activity* 2:451–505.
Auerbach, Alan J., and James R. Hines. 1987. Anticipated tax changes and the timing of investment. In *The effects of taxation on capital accumulation,* ed. Martin Feldstein. Chicago: University of Chicago Press.
Auerbach, Alan J., and James M. Poterba. 1987. Tax loss carryforwards and corporate tax incentives. In *The effects of taxation on capital accumulation,* ed. Martin Feldstein. Chicago: University of Chicago Press.
Auerbach, Alan J., and David Reishus. 1988a. Taxes and the merger decision. In *Knights, raiders and targets,* ed. J. Coffee and L. Lowenstein. Oxford: Oxford University Press.
———. 1988b. The impact of taxation on mergers and acquisitions. In *Mergers and acquisitions,* ed. Alan J. Auerbach. Chicago: University of Chicago Press.

Bradford, David F. 1981. The incidence and allocation effects of a tax on corporate distributions. *Journal of Public Economics* (February): 1–22.

Cosslett, S. 1981. Efficient estimates of discrete choice models. In *Structural analysis of discrete data,* ed. C. Manski and D. McFadden. Cambridge: MIT Press.

Gilson, R., M. Scholes, and M. Wolfson. 1988. Taxation and the dynamics of corporate control: The uncertain case for tax motivated acquisitions. In *Knights, raiders and targets,* ed. J. Coffee and L. Lowenstein. Oxford: Oxford University Press.

Gordon, Roger H., James R. Hines, and Lawrence Summers. 1987. Notes on the tax treatment of structures. In *The effects of taxation on capital accumulation,* ed. Martin Feldstein. Chicago: University of Chicago Press.

Hall, Bronwyn. 1988. The effect of takeover activity on corporate research and development. In this volume.

King, Mervyn A. 1974. Taxation and the cost of capital. *Review of Economic Studies* (January): 21–35.

———. 1986. Takeovers, taxes and the stock market, photocopy. London: London School of Economics.

McFadden, Daniel. 1973. Conditional logit analysis of qualitative choice behavior. In *Frontiers in econometrics,* ed. P. Zarembka. New York: Academic Press.

———. 1984. Econometric analysis of qualitative response models. In *Handbook of econometrics,* vol. 2, ed. Z. Griliches and M. Intriligator. Amsterdam: North Holland.

Miller, Merton. 1977. Debt and taxes. *Journal of Finance* (May): 261–75.

Palepu, Krishna. 1986. Predicting takeover targets: A methodological and empirical analysis. *Journal of Accounting and Economics* 8:1.

Warren, Alvin C., and Alan J. Auerbach. 1982. Transferability of tax incentives and the fiction of safe-harbor leasing. *Harvard Law Review* (June): 1752–86.

Comment   James M. Poterba

Auerbach and Reishus's paper is a first-rate empirical study of whether tax synergies are significant determinants of the incidence and pattern of corporate mergers. It is the first careful examination of the impact of tax considerations on merger decisions. The authors find that the probability that an actual merger yields corporate tax benefits is no higher than the probability that a random pairing between two firms will produce tax benefits. In conjunction with their discovery that significant corporate tax benefits obtain in only one merger out of five, these results cast doubt on the claim that taxes have induced a significant fraction of recent mergers.

James M. Poterba is associate professor of economics at the Massachusetts Institute of Technology and a research associate of the National Bureau of Economic Research.

The authors' conclusion that taxes are an insignificant factor in the merger process is consistent with recent discussions outside academia. In evaluating the potential impact of the 1986 Tax Reform Act on merger activity, the head of the merger division at a major accounting firm estimated that no more than 5 percent of all mergers are "tax driven" (*Mergers and Acquisitions* 1986, p. 10). Although this exceeds Auerbach and Reishus's estimate, the similarity between the two values is encouraging.

While I believe the general conclusion that taxes are not a critical factor in explaining the growth of merger activity in the 1980s, I suspect that Auerbach and Reishus may understate the importance of taxes in the most recent mergers. Their sample period ends in early 1983. Three developments since then may have increased the role of tax factors. First, the number of firms with net operating losses and loss carry-forwards rose substantially after 1981 because of the rapid asset write-offs provided by the accelerated cost recovery system (ACRS) and the deep recession of 1982. The sample includes only one year of this new regime, when transactions designed to take advantage of tax losses would be especially likely. The one post-1981 year included in the sample, 1982, may also differ from subsequent years because at that time firms were still permitted to use "safe harbor" leasing to transfer tax benefits from tax loss firms to taxable firms. Second, the advent of the ACRS increased the incentive for selling assets to step up their basis. Again, this effect would be strongest in the years after the authors' sample period. Finally, the "junk bond" market became a much more important part of the takeover process after 1982 (see Taggart 1988). Thus, by focusing on mergers that took place during the late 1960s and the 1970s, the authors may not capture the importance of taxes in recent takeovers.

At the same time, however, some countervailing factors may lead the authors to *overstate* the importance of taxes. I describe three potential problems below and illustrate each by referring to tax loss carry-forwards. Similar arguments could be made with respect to the other tax incentives for merger.

The first potential problem arises in measuring the size of tax benefits. Auerbach and Reishus implicitly assume that the tax benefit from merging equals the face value of the resulting tax savings. They assume, for example, that a firm with a tax loss carryforward (TLCF) that was party to an acquisition would not have utilized it unless it was involved in a takeover. This assumption probably overstates the gain from merging because mergers are only one of the ways a firm can benefit from a loss carryforward. TLCF firms could alternatively issue new shares and use the proceeds to purchase bonds, generating taxable interest income effectively taxed at the capital gains rate for shareholders.

One could argue that many firms with TLCFs face substantial difficulty raising equity capital. This may be true. These firms might also find it difficult to locate merger partners, however. The relevant issue concerns the alternative opportunities for those TLCF firms that are attractive merger partners; these firms may have many other channels for realizing some of their tax benefits. Similar arguments apply to tax gains from basis step-up and increased leverage (see Gilson, Scholes, and Wolfson 1986). By assuming that the nonmerger alternatives yield no tax benefits, the authors overstate the tax incentives to merge. Since they conclude that taxes are unimportant in the merger process, this argument reinforces their results.

The second potential problem is one of measurement errors in estimated tax benefits. The previous argument implies that the merger tax gains for many firms may be overstated. It does not necessarily imply that errors of different magnitudes affect different firms. Such differential errors may, however, be induced by the problems of measuring both TLCFs and potential basis step-ups.

Financial statements provide an imperfect guide to a firm's tax loss carryforwards. Auerbach and Poterba (1987) observed substantial disparities between estimates of loss carryforwards based on Internal Revenue Service data and those based on financial statements. An additional problem in analyzing mergers comes from the idiosyncratic character of tax benefits. The rules for utilizing loss carryforwards are complex and have varied over time. The 1976, 1981, 1982, and 1986 Tax Reform Acts all affected the use of carryforwards in corporate acquisitions. The simple assumption that taxable firms acquiring firms with losses can use these losses may therefore induce substantial measurement error.

Similar problems arise in calculating the potential gains from basis step-up for individual firms. The authors use a sophisticated algorithm based on average asset composition in each industry. Differences across firms in asset decay rates, in the fraction of assets that have been sold or acquired through takeovers, or even in the types of assets that are used can make these estimates an unreliable guide to potential tax benefits.

The real difficulty with the errors of measurement in both TLCFs and potential basis step-ups is that they are likely to be correlated with the dependent variable, an indicator variable for the presence or absence of a merger. Given two firms with identical estimated potential tax benefits in an acquisition, there is a positive correlation between the measurement error (true benefit minus measured benefit) and the probability of observing a merger. This correlation may contaminate the statistical analysis.

The final problem, one of tax status endogeneity, arises because there are no controlled experiments for analyzing how tax policy affects merger probabilities. We cannot endow an otherwise healthy firm with a $100 million tax loss carryforward and study whether or not it is acquired. Rather, we must track how TLCFs generated by previous corporate actions influence takeover probabilities. The difficulty with this approach is not confined to the Auerbach and Reishus paper; it affects virtually all cross-sectional studies of taxes and firm behavior.

The basic problem is that the presence of a TLCF may signal many things. First, it indicates a potential tax benefit for an acquirer. Second, however, it may suggest that the firm has experienced severe business difficulties. While an otherwise healthy firm with TLCFs might make a very attractive acquisition target, the typical TLCF firm may in fact be very unattractive. Finally, however, there is an opposite bias that is stressed in practitioner accounts of the merger process. Firms with TLCFs have typically faced tight cash flow constraints in the recent past, and they may have postponed high-return investment projects because of this. These firms may therefore be attractive takeover targets for reasons other than their tax status. Separating the direct (tax) effects of loss carryforwards from the other real effects correlated with them is extremely difficult. The authors control for the target's sales growth rate, but this variable is unlikely to capture all of the relevant aspects of recent corporate performance that affect takeover probabilities.

In spite of these three difficulties, I am still inclined to believe the authors' basic findings. Their results suggest that certain types of corporate tax benefits are not important explanators of recent merger activity. The results do not imply, however, that taxes play a small role in the takeover process. A casual reader of takeover trade publications, such as *Mergers and Acquisitions,* discovers about one-fifth of the articles are devoted to taxation. Can this be reconciled with the Auerbach and Reishus findings? It could be if there is relatively little money to be *made* from the tax-related aspects of a merger but much to be *lost* from incorrect tax planning. Tax considerations may therefore be defensive, not offensive, aspects of acquisition activity.

Some contests for corporate control may also be driven by tax factors besides the ones considered in the paper. Leveraged buyouts, for example, have received substantial tax subsidies (see Shleifer and Vishny 1988), but they do not feature in Auerbach and Reishus's analysis of mergers between two firms. King (1986) has proposed a "trapped equity" model of takeover activity, by which acquisitions provide a tax-favored channel for transferring resources to shareholders. If King's analysis is correct, the double-taxation of dividend income may partly explain why firms engage in takeovers. In this volume Franks, Harris, and Mayer (1988) provide some evidence against this view by comparing methods of payment in the United States and the United Kingdom, but the argument is still important in explaining how taxes can influence merger activity through channels other than those considered by Auerbach and Reishus.

The results of this study suggest that corporate marriages are made in heaven, not in the tax lawyer's office. Although that may seem like the way it should be, this presumption may be seriously wrong. The optimal tax policy toward corporate acquisitions depends upon a variety of factors. If takeovers tend to promote efficient management, the socially optimal policy may require provision of some tax benefits for merging firms (see Gilson, Scholes, and Wolfson, 1986). Such a policy would generate an additional incentive for merging, potentially offsetting the costs associated with the takeover process. If, however, takeovers are largely conflicts between stake holders and "stake eaters," as in the Shleifer-Summers (1988) analysis earlier in this volume, and if they adversely affect economic performance, it may be appropriate to place a tax penalty on acquisitive firms. Research like that by Auerbach and Reishus provides the empirical groundwork for future analyses of the optimal taxation of corporate combinations.

References

Auerbach, Alan J., and James M. Poterba. 1987. Tax loss carryforwards and corporate tax incentives. In *Taxes and capital formation*, ed. Martin Feldstein, 305–38. Chicago: University of Chicago Press.

Franks, Julian R., Robert S. Harris, and Colin Mayer. 1988. Means of payment in takeovers: Results for the United Kingdom and the United States. In this volume.

Gilson, Ronald J., Myron S. Scholes, and Mark A. Wolfson. 1986. Taxation and the dynamics of corporate control: The uncertain case for tax motivated acquisitions, research paper 873. Stanford: Graduate School of Business, Stanford University.

King, Mervyn A. 1986. Takeovers, taxes, and the stock market, paper presented at 1986 NBER Summer Institute, Cambridge, Mass.

Mergers and Acquisitions. 1986. Adjusting to tax reform. Vol. 21 (November/December): 10.

Shleifer, Andrei, and Lawrence Summers. 1988. Breach of trust in hostile takeovers. In this volume.

Shleifer, Andrei, and Robert Vishny. 1988. Management buyouts as a reaction to market pressure. In *Mergers and acquisitions,* ed. Alan J. Auerbach. Chicago: University of Chicago Press.

Taggart, Robert A., Jr. 1988. The growth of the junk bond market and its role in financing takeovers. In *Mergers and acquisitions,* ed. Alan J. Auerbach. Chicago: University of Chicago Press.

Comment   John B. Shoven

I like the idea for the Auerbach and Reishus paper—an assessment of the importance of taxes in mergers. The authors review several theoretical tax rationales for mergers and then proceed to an empirical examination of their effects. Before commenting on this study, however, I should mention there are aggregate facts about mergers that do not seem to be related to tax factors. One is that merger activity is markedly cyclical. It would be interesting to know whether there are more firms with loss carryforwards or unused investment tax credits when merger activity is high than when it is low. Some relatively aggregate correlations between the tax factors and merger activity would therefore have been interesting in Auerbach and Reishus's paper. I am skeptical that the correlations would be consistent with the tax theories, but I have trouble determining whether I reached this prior before or after peeking at the results of their paper.

The authors discuss three main ways taxes might affect the merger decision. First, either the target or the acquirer may have unused loss carryforwards and credits. Merging is a potential way of accelerating their use and possibly salvaging them before they expire. Although this may provide an incentive to merge in some cases, the authors' earlier work had found that there was no transfer of carryforwards or credits in slightly over 80 percent of the observed mergers between 1968 and 1983. In this paper, with their construction of hypothetical mergers to be compared with actual mergers, they find there is a tax carryover transfer in 19.2 percent of the hypothetical mergers (versus 19.3 percent for the actual mergers). The weighted average gain is higher for the actual mergers, but this is largely because of the seven instances where the gain resulting from offsetting the parent's unused losses and credits exceeds 25 percent of the target's value. Several of these seven instances (there were only two such cases in the hypothetical merger sample) may have resulted from the same parent (for example, Penn Central). Certainly, the difference in the average gain between the real mergers and the hypothetical ones is the result of a very small number of cases with large gains. It is not at all clear that it is statistically significant.

Certainly, the conclusion of this paper, and of the authors' earlier work—namely, the use of tax carryforwards and credits cannot explain most mergers because these factors are not present in over 80 percent of mergers—is an important one. Even before engaging in high-power

John B. Shoven is professor of economics and chairman of the Department of Economics at Stanford University and a research associate of the National Bureau of Economic Research.

econometrics, the authors are left with only a relatively small role for that theory in the merger decision.

The second corporate tax theory regarding mergers is the step-up in basis and the potential redepreciation of assets after a merger. This redepreciation is profitable only if the difference between the market value and book value of acquired assets is not treated as fully taxable income. Until recently, at least for plant, the gain was less than fully taxed and thus there was an incentive for redepreciation.

Several severe problems arise in measuring with publicly available data the size of the potential tax advantage resulting from a step-up in basis. Auerbach and Reishus do not have any information regarding the market value of a firm's assets. Further, they do not know the age structure of the assets or what fraction of them are plant. The variable they construct is presumably measured with considerable error, and this may account for its failure to be significant in their merger regressions.

The third theory, that the merged company can carry more debt than the separate firms is questionable. The authors do not have information on the variance of the target's earnings or on the covariance of those earnings with the parent's earnings. It seems very doubtful that the observed debt-equity ratio of the target gives reliable information about the extra debt-carrying capacity that the merger would permit. The authors' finding that mergers are much more likely between firms in the same narrowly defined industry indicates that earnings-source diversification and hence greater debt-carrying capacity are not important determinants of mergers.

I find the paper quite convincing that the tax theories are not the most important determinants of mergers. But I also believe the early tables comparing the actual and hypothetical mergers convey that message quite adequately. Most researchers would have stopped right there and declared the result. The authors are to be admired for not letting this deter them and proceeding to develop their logit "marriage" model of mergers. The main result, however, is not fundamentally changed by all their efforts. It still appears, much to the dismay of public finance economists, that the tax factors are not of paramount importance in the merger decision.

7 Share Repurchases and Acquisitions: An Analysis of Which Firms Participate

Laurie Simon Bagwell and John B. Shoven

7.1 Introduction

Contrary to the conventional wisdom that dividends are the primary means of transferring cash from the firm to its shareholders, nondividend cash payments surpassed dividends in the two most recent years for which data are available, 1984 and 1985 (Shoven 1986). This development challenges the "trapped-equity" cost of capital models[1] which equate the opportunity cost of retained earnings to the after-tax yield of the alternative considered, namely, dividends. If dividends are the only alternative to retaining earnings, the high taxation of dividends lowers the shadow cost of retained earnings and hence lowers the cost of capital. On the other hand, if cash can be and is paid out in nondividend form, with lower taxes, the economics profession needs to change the way it computes the cost of equity capital.

In this paper we review the theoretical rationale for nondividend cash payments. These payments can take the form of either share repurchase programs or cash mergers. The primary new material of this paper is an econometric investigation into what types of firms engage in these two forms of share acquisition programs: repurchasing own shares or acquiring the shares of other firms. We examine whether the same characteristics of the firm determine both mergers (or acquisitions) and share repurchases. Because these activities are so much more prominent now than in the past, we also examine whether the

Laurie Simon Bagwell is a graduate student in economics at Stanford University. John B. Shoven is professor of economics and chairman of the Department of Economics, Stanford University, and a research associate of the National Bureau of Economic Research.

The authors would like to thank Clint Cummins and Bronwyn Hall for their generous econometric advice on this project.

type of firm involved in these activities has changed since a decade ago.

7.2   Alternative Hypotheses about Nondividend Cash Payments

The literature has spawned numerous hypotheses about why firms make nondividend cash payments. We discuss several in turn.

7.2.1   Taxation and the Preference for Share Repurchases

In the absence of informational asymmetries between stockholders and management, and in the absence of taxes and transactions costs, dividends and repurchasing shares are equivalent. Whether it disburses a given amount of cash in one form or the other, the firm's total value will be the same. It will have the same debt-equity ratio, the same ownership claims, the same real assets, the same opportunities, and therefore the same value. In other words, it is possible to produce exactly the same consequences by either distributional form. After a share repurchase, each shareholder can sell sufficient shares to match the cash flow he would have received from a dividend. After a dividend payment, the shareholder can use the dividend proceeds to buy additional shares in the company and therefore reproduce the percentage interest he would have had if he had declined to sell in a share repurchase program.

Taxes cause a major break in this equivalence, to the disadvantage of dividends and, therefore, to the relative advantage of share repurchase for taxable households or individuals.[2] It is still true, however, that the total equity value of the firm should be the same after the payment of an equivalent amount of cash in either dividend or share repurchase form. This equivalence rests on the idea that the firm has the same assets, capital structure, and future opportunities in either case. If the cash is paid out as a dividend, it is fully taxable. But if it is paid out as a repurchase, the payment results in a capital gain to shareholders of the amount of the purchase.[3] Most of this capital gain, however, is accrued and not realized.

To fully understand the share repurchase strategy, consider the simple example outlined in table 7.1.[4] A hypothetical company is originally financed by the issue of 100 shares at $10 each. The company uses the $1,000 proceeds to purchase productive capital, and after a year it has realized a $100 profit. The competitive market value of the firm is now $1,100 ($11 per share), as the company now consists of a fully restored $1,000 machine and $100 cash.

Consider two strategies of returning the $100 earnings to the shareholders. If the money is paid out as a dividend (strategy A), the personal tax bill will be $28 if the marginal tax rate of the equity holders is 28

Table 7.1   **An Example of a Dividend Payment and a Share Repurchase for a Hypothetical Firm**

			Strategy A $1 dividend payment/share	Strategy B Repurchase $100 worth of shares
Initial financing	100 shares at $10/share	$1,000		
Profit	100 shares at $ 1/share	$ 100		
Value at end of year	100 shares at $11/share	$1,100		
Cash received by shareholders			$100	$100
Value of firm after transaction			$1,000	$1,000
Number of shares			100	90.91
Price per share			$10	$11
Taxes owed[a]			$28	$2.55
Accrued capital gain[b]			$0.00	$90.91

[a]Assumes a personal tax rate of 28 percent.

[b]Accrued capital gains will generate a future tax obligation if realized. A recent estimate of the effective tax rate on accrued capital gains is about 5 percent.

percent. The net-of-tax receipts from the dividend are $72. The value of the company would return to $1,000, or $10 per share, after the dividend payment. On the other hand, if the firm uses its $100 to buy 9.09 of its shares at a price of $11 (strategy B), the total realized gain by those who sell their shares to the firm is $9.09, assuming that the sellers are among those who originally financed the firm at a price of $10 per share. The tax on that $9.09 would be $2.55.

Note that the company's shares will remain at $11 after the repurchase and therefore each of the remaining 90.91 shares has an accrued gain of one dollar. These accrued gains will generate some taxes for the government, although the present value of the taxes depends on average holding periods, as well as any escape from capital gains taxes on assets that pass through estates.

This example demonstrates that share repurchases result in much lower personal taxes than do dividends, under the taxation assumptions stated here. Even so, this case may exaggerate what would actually be paid in a share repurchase. In the real world, investors buy their shares at different times and at different prices, and those most likely to tender their shares back to the company will be those with the lowest reservation price on holding the shares.[5] These will include shareholders who have actually lost money on their investments. The government may therefore receive no immediate revenue from those who receive the corporate cash. The example also illustrates that the advantage of share repurchase over dividends exists even when realized capital gains are taxed at the same rate as dividends (as is the case both in the example and under the new tax law).

The tax advantage of share repurchase relative to dividends may be a powerful explanation of why share repurchases have become more prevalent. But because the explanation hinges on the fact that capital gains are taxed on a realization basis and escape taxation when passed through estates (rather than depending on characteristics of the firm), it is not an argument that can be readily addressed with cross-sectional econometrics. Nonetheless, it does suggest that dividend yield on the common stock and, perhaps, increases in the dividend rate may be predictors of participation in share repurchase activities. The tax advantage implies that share repurchase may be a substitute means of transmitting cash to shareholders, and thus firms with high dividend yields or which have increased dividends may be less likely to repurchase shares.

7.2.2 Repurchase as a Transitional Mechanism for Adjusting the Debt-Equity Ratio

In the absence of transactions costs and taxes at both the personal and corporate level, and with fully informed investors, shareholders will be indifferent about the price offered in a share repurchase plan. In a fundamental way they are buying the shares from themselves, and so their indifference comes from their being both the buyer and the seller. The heterogeneity of shareholders, however, creates a potential transfer between those who sell and those who do not. This possibility is diminished if all shareholders have an equal right to participate, and if shares are offered on a pro rata basis in the event the offer is oversubscribed (as is required by Securities and Exchange Commission rule 13e-4).

With no taxes, as Modigliani and Miller (1958) demonstrated, the value of the firm is also invariant to its financial structure. But in the presence of both personal and corporate taxes, there appears to be a substantial tax advantage of debt, because interest is tax deductible from the corporation income tax, whereas dividends and other equity earnings are not. Miller (1977) argued, however, that although the aggregate amount of debt in the economy is determinate, the capital structure for any individual firm is irrelevant, since the return on debt and equity incorporate taxes (the weak form of the Modigliani-Miller theorem). This proposition received empirical support from Trzcinka (1982). In contrast, Ross (1985), allowing for uncertainty, showed how firms may have an interior optimal debt-equity ratio. The standard model of a firm's optimal debt-equity ratio involves first order conditions trading off the tax advantages of debt against the agency costs of debt, as well as the inflexibility of debt in times of crisis. That is, higher debt ratios increase the likelihood of incurring the real costs associated with bankruptcy.

An adequate model of optimal debt-equity ratios would, of necessity, be very complex and would depend on variables that are unobservable in publicly available information about the firm, variables such as uncertainty and restrictions on the creation of state-contingent claims. Nevertheless, it is possible to predict some changes in the environment facing the firm that might cause its managers to want to adjust its leverage ratio. For instance, a change in the underlying riskiness of the firm (perhaps arising from the maturing of a market or the resolution of some technological uncertainties) may allow the firm to operate with a higher leverage ratio and enjoy more of the tax advantages of debt. This change in risk, or many other factors, may cause higher equity values. When stock market valuations increase dramatically (as they certainly have in the past four years), the leverage ratios of firms are automatically lowered. In many cases it will be optimal for the firm to at least partially offset this change in financial ratios by issuing debt and absorbing equity. When the tax rate applicable to bonds decreases, the optimal aggregate debt level increases, even in a Miller analysis. Both dividends and share repurchases absorb equity. But share repurchases may be a better mechanism for the transitional purpose of changing the debt-equity ratio than an increased dividend (as suggested by the work of Feldstein and Green 1983) because of the penalty that the market imposes on firms that later cut their dividend.

Taxes and transactions costs alter investors' neutrality regarding the price offered in share repurchase programs. Higher prices mean that more of the cash paid out will be taxed as a realized capital gain and less as a return of capital. This effect is probably outweighed, however, by the leverage adjustment effect of higher equity prices just mentioned. The underlying theory suggests, therefore, that higher share prices will encourage share repurchases, rather than discourage them as is the common wisdom. As well, there will be an economywide increase in the debt to equity expected given a decline in the taxation levels applicable to bonds.

One problem with this explanation of share repurchase as a transitional instrument in adjusting debt-equity ratios is that it depends on the difference between actual leverage and optimal leverage, a variable that can be neither observed nor predicted. In the empirical analysis to follow, we include the actual debt-equity ratio as an explanatory variable. The theory does not, however, predict even the sign of its influence on share acquisition activities.

7.2.3 Repurchase as an Anti-Takeover Strategy

Another reason firms may buy back their own shares instead of paying dividends is to fend off a takeover attempt (Bagwell 1986). In paying dividends, a company gives cash to all shareholders in proportion to their shareholdings. However, if the cash is used to make a share repurchase tender offer, only those who tender their shares (or a pro rata proportion of those tendered) will receive cash from the firm. Due to heterogeneous inframarginal rents to holding across shareholders, there exists an upward sloping supply curve representing the prices at which shareholders are willing to sell. The cash dividend does not change the distribution of reservation values, whereas the share repurchase buys out those with the lowest reservation prices, leaving behind those who would sell only when offered a premium above the tender offer price. Moreover, the position of the supply curve endogenizes the distributional choice and its effect on the possibility of takeover. As is shown in Bagwell (1986), the cost to the bidding firm of acquiring control of the target will be larger if the target distributes a fixed amount of cash through share repurchase than if it does so through a cash dividend. This explanation is consistent with the recent spate of repurchases motivated solely as takeover deterrence. We therefore would predict an increase in restructurings, especially repurchases, in response to the threat of takeover.

7.2.4 Free Cash Flow and the Preference for Share Repurchases

Jensen (1986) has analyzed the principal-agent problem that exists when an organization generates a substantial free cash flow. Managers have an incentive to increase the resources under their control, and need to be motivated not to grow beyond wealth maximization. Given this incentive, managers with substantial free cash flow may choose repurchase or dividends instead of investments. This choice gives them control over future cash flow that would be lost if the resources were invested.

Issuing debt to buy back stock creates an incentive for managers to overcome their inefficiencies. The fixed payment pattern of the debt allows them to commit to transferring resources to their financial claimants. Jensen focused on the example of the oil industry in the late 1970s: a case of simultaneous free cash flow and necessary industry shrinkage. He documented that oil firms were purchasing other companies, as well as restructuring themselves, consistent with the agency costs of free cash flow. The theory suggests a positive effect of cash flow on the probability of repurchase and acquisition.

The free cash flow hypothesis also implies that firms with low levels of investment, or poor internal investment opportunities, are more likely to engage in share repurchases. A potentially useful but imperfect measure of internal investment opportunities is the ratio of price to book value. This ratio approximates Tobin's q in our attempt to capture the q theory of investment first developed in Tobin (1969).

An expectation of future cash flow is theorized to be signaled through cash disbursed to shareholders in a tender office. Vermaelen (1981) found the per share earnings of tendering firms were above the predictions of a preannouncement time-series model, a finding he interpreted as evidence that the tender offer serves as an announcement of favorable earnings prospects. Dann (1981) concluded as well that the information signaled by repurchase may be improvements in cash flows. Ofer and Thakor (1986) differentiated the repurchase signal from the signal implied by dividend payments. This hypothesis of a signaling of cash flow reconfirms the free cash flow expectation of a repurchase motivated by high cash flow.

7.2.5 The Equivalence of Share Repurchases and Mergers and Acquisitions

In the absence of informational problems, taxes, and transactions costs, buying shares in another company is nearly equivalent to buying back one's own. Rather than returning cash to the shareholders, the firm instead buys a financial investment. If the market value of the acquired asset is equal to what the firm pays for it,[6] then in the absence of transactions costs the acquisition is as good as cash to the stockholders of the acquiring firm. If there are transactions costs, they would have to be taken into account since some investors might now prefer cash, and some investors may want to rebalance their portfolio after the acquisition.

Although it is certainly true that if we relax the above assumptions share repurchases and acquisitions may serve different purposes, both actions convey similar tax advantages over dividends by transfering value to shareholders in a manner that results in capital gains (both realized and accrued) rather than ordinary income. The actions are dissimilar, however, in that a merger or acquisition does not absorb equity, whereas a repurchase does not a priori increase debt. The two activities, therefore, are not perfect substitutes in attaining optimal debt-equity ratios. This implies that previous appreciation in the firm's stock price may positively predict acquisitions (if the acquisition is done to increase leverage) and similarly may encourage share repurchases (if done to absorb equity).

The equivalence of the two share acquisition policies requires strong sets of assumptions. It is an interesting empirical issue, however. In the analysis below we separate the regressions for the two phenomena, unwilling to accept ex ante the hypothesis that the two are perfect substitutes. We desire to investigate whether the hypothesis appears credible.

7.2.6   Clientele and Management Effects

For many economists, the payment of dividends, appearing to be tax disadvantaged, remains a puzzle despite the multitude of theories offered to explain them.[7] Share acquisition seems to offer too great a tax saving not to be preferred to dividends. But the tax argument is true only for some classes of investors. Nontaxable institutions are indifferent to tax-based arguments, and they are very large market participants. With transactions costs, it can be argued that such organizations as pension funds and private university endowments might find dividends the preferred form of return.

The implication of this argument is that firms may specialize to a clientele. Those firms that pay returns as dividends may be held disproportionately by tax-exempt organizations, whereas those that retain earnings, repurchase shares, or engage in mergers may be predominantly held by taxable owners. Although the necessary taxation information to assess this is not included in our data source, we do know a firm's previous participation history. If the clientele theory is valid, certain firms can be expected to have a propensity to perform these activities year after year.

There are other poorly understood aspects of corporate accounting and financial behavior. One is the choice of inventory accounting techniques, particularly in times of inflation. Firms can choose between first in, first out (FIFO) and last in, first out (LIFO) methods. With inflation FIFO generally leads to larger reported and taxable profits than LIFO. FIFO seems to be a nonoptimizing choice, as if investors cannot "see through" the accounts to ascertain real earnings. We can examine whether some managements are more likely to take advantage of tax-saving opportunities, if they exist, by seeing whether the firms that use the tax-efficient LIFO policy are those that also use nondividend means of transferring value to their shareholders.

7.3   Measurement Model and the Specific Hypotheses

We are interested in modeling the binary choice of whether to do an action of repurchase or acquisition, to study how various explanatory variables affect the probability of participation in such action.

This model is motivated by the definition of an unobserved random variable, the value of the contemplated action, as a linear function of some observed characteristics of the firm and an unknown disturbance:

$$(1) \qquad \text{value (action)} = XB + \epsilon,$$

such that the firm chooses the action if its value exceeds some critical constant (which can be zero). As just noted, this value is not directly observable. Given this limitation, we employ a binary probit to analyze the explanatory variables for the choice between the discrete alternatives of whether or not to undertake the action, representing the choice with a dummy variable. If the disturbance ϵ is normally distributed, the probability that the action will be undertaken is given by the cumulative normal function of XB, and a maximum likelihood estimator of the coefficients B is available that yields consistent and asymptotically normal estimates (see, for example, Amemiya 1985, chap. 9).

7.3.1   Data

The data for this analysis were collected from the 1984 Compustat Industrial, Over the Counter (hereafter OTC), and Industrial Research files, which yielded 2,399, 853, and 1,289 original observations, respectively. We immediately removed 29 observations from the sample because they lacked all data and firm identification information.

Although we are interested in predicting participation in share repurchases, we want to exclude those small repurchases intended to eliminate odd lot holders. We therefore classify a firm as a repurchaser only if it acquires at least one-half of one percent of its outstanding share equity value.

Our use of the computerized data sources gave us a large sample, but it also limited our data selection. We would like to test the hypotheses on the tax advantages of repurchase, but the data source lacked information on the distribution of basis values and on the percentage of holders who escape taxation through death. We thus attempted instead to calculate a marginal tax rate of the firm, although this too proved impossible because of missing data in our source file.

We have posited various relationships between the leverage ratio and cash acquisition. We therefore created the variable *DBEQXY*, the previous year's debt-equity ratio (of book values). (For example, $XY = 75$ for the 1976 regressions, and $XY = 83$ for the 1984 regressions.) We created *DIVINC*, the percentage increase in dividends, to test the substitutability of dividends and acquisitions.

We would also like to test whether repurchase is a response to the threat of takeover, but financial statements do not contain data on whether a threat of takeover, either overt or covert, exists. For the large sample, therefore, we sacrificed such manually gathered information.

To represent the free-cash-flow and signaling-of-cash-flow hypotheses, we created a cash flow ratio, *CASHRAT*, which is operating income before depreciation as scaled by total assets.[8] The cash flow hypothesis also implies the relevance of levels of investment and the potential importance of a measure of internal investment opportunity. We therefore created *INVRAT*, a ratio of the increase in investment to the value of total assets. We created *PRICEBK*, the ratio of the closing price to book value, as an indicator of internal investment opportunities.

If firms are using acquisitions and repurchases to achieve an optimal debt-equity ratio, price appreciation should encourage repurchase. We therefore created *PRICE*, an average of the ratios of one year's to the previous year's high, low, and closing stock prices.

The clientele hypothesis suggests repurchase is done by firms with low dividend yield. We include the previous year's ratio of dividends to share equity value, *DIVRATXY*, to examine this hypothesis. To test the hypothesis further, we are also interested in previous participation history. We therefore included dummy variables for the previous year's participation in repurchase (*REPXYO1*) and acquisition (*ACQXYO1*) as statistics for such habit formation.[9]

The hypothesis that managers who are smart about taxes should use nondividend payments is tested by the inclusion of a dummy variable *IVADUM*, which indicates whether the firm used LIFO or not.

The remaining data sample of 4,512 firms was purged of missing data relevant for respective 1976 or 1984 regressions. This resulted in corresponding samples of 2,366 and 1,820 firms. The appendix analyzes the data and the resultant samples in more detail.

7.3.2 Hypotheses

If the hypotheses of the previous sections are correct, we have certain expectations about the directions and significance of the coefficients.

An increase in general equity levels caused by the stock market growth is hypothesized to encourage firms to increase their relative leverage by absorbing equity. That absorption can be accomplished through repurchase. In addition, the optimal economywide level of debt can increase with a decline in the marginal tax rate applicable to bonds. Acquisition of a firm with higher leverage can assume increased debt in a controlled way. This may suggest a negative relationship between the debt-equity ratio and these actions in 1984, with insignificance in 1976.

The free cash flow hypothesis implies a positive relationship between the cash flow ratio and the probability of both repurchase and acquisition. That repurchase is believed to signal future cash flow may strengthen the implied relationship in the repurchase probit.

The free cash flow hypothesis also suggests that these actions are the result of low levels of investment or poor internal investment opportunities. This would be consistent with negative effects of the investment ratio and our q approximation for both regressions.

If firms use acquisition and repurchase to obtain an optimal debt-equity ratio, we would expect price appreciation consistent with the action, implying a positive effect on the probability of the action of price.

A test of the clientele and habit formation hypotheses would predict significant positive coefficients on previous-action participation dummies. One indication of relative substitutability between actions is whether previous repurchase is correlated with acquisition and vice versa. The clientele effect also predicts a negative relationship between the dividend ratio and repurchase.

We expect a negative relationship between the percentage dividend change and both actions if they are substitutes to dividends. We also expect firms with low dividend yield to repurchase as an alternative to dividend payment. We therefore expect a negative relationship between the dividend ratio and repurchase.

Our test for smart tax managers implies a positive relationship between the use of LIFO and repurchase. Similarly, the tax advantage of acquisitions relative to dividends implies a positive relationship between LIFO and acquisitions.

We are also interested in the "importance" of the explanatory variables, specifically, in what magnitude they alter the probability of the event (the dummy variable equals 1). As well, certain relationships across equations are suggested above. We test between regressions to determine whether a specific action is stable over time. A finding of functional change across periods would reject the null hypothesis that the model has no structural change across time.

7.4   Empirical Results

7.4.1   Estimation of the Model

1976 Probits

Table 7.2 reports the results of estimating the parameters in the 1976 repurchase model, including the estimated intercept and coefficients, (Newton-Raphson) standard errors, and the associated t-statistics. The coefficients on the cash flow ratio and the 1975 repurchase dummy are positive and significant (at the .01 level). The coefficient on the 1975 dividend ratio is significant and negative (at the .025 level). The coefficient on the dividend increase is significant (at the .05 level). The q and the investment ratio coefficients are negative and significant (at the .10 level).

Table 7.3 shows the results of estimating the parameters in the 1976 acquisition model. The 1975 acquisition dummy and the 1975 repurchase dummy are significant (at the .01 level). The price variable is

Table 7.2   Probit Results for the 1976 Repurchase Model

Parameter	Estimate	Standard Error	t-statistic
Constant	-1.4944	0.1329	-11.2430
DBEQ75	-0.0208	0.0190	-1.0958
IVADUM	0.0453	0.0842	0.5384
PRICE	0.0939	0.0779	1.2052
DIVRAT75	-2.8016	1.3843	-2.0238
DIVINC	0.0157	0.0093	1.6805
PRICEBK	-0.1692	0.1248	-1.3555
CASHRAT	1.2997	0.4111	3.1612
INVRAT	-2.1806	1.3688	-1.5931
ACQ7501	0.0950	0.0955	0.9948
REP7501	1.2879	0.0768	16.7790

Table 7.3   Probit Results for the 1976 Acquisition Model

Parameter	Estimate	Standard Error	t-statistic
Constant	-1.6359	0.1339	-12.2210
DBEQ75	-0.0087	0.0153	-0.5692
IVADUM	-0.0427	0.0889	-0.4797
PRICE	0.1775	0.0801	2.2166
DIVRAT75	0.6850	1.2701	0.5393
DIVINC	-0.0113	0.0240	-0.4704
PRICEBK	-0.3394	0.1361	-2.4941
CASHRAT	0.4775	0.4149	1.1510
INVRAT	-1.4709	1.0590	-1.3889
ACQ7501	1.4180	0.0823	17.2200
REP7501	0.2502	0.0894	2.7992

significant (at the 0.25 level). The coefficient on our q approximation is significant and negative (at the .01 level), as is the coefficient on the investment ratio (at the .10 level).

1984 Probits

Table 7.4 reports the results of estimating the parameters in the 1984 repurchase model. The cash flow ratio and the repurchase dummy are significant (at the .01 level). Our estimate of q is significant and negative (at the .01 level). The previous debt-equity ratio and dividend ratios are negative and significant (at the .05 level).

Table 7.5 shows the results of estimating the parameters in the 1984 acquisition model. The 1983 acquisition dummy is significant (at the .01 level), as are the 1983 repurchase dummy (at the .025 level) and price (at the .05 level). Our estimate of q is significant and negative (at the .01 level), as is the 1983 debt-equity ratio (at the .05 level).

Table 7.4   Probit Results for the 1984 Repurchase Model

Parameter	Estimate	Standard Error	t-statistic
Constant	− 0.8676	0.1166	− 7.4408
DBEQ83	− 0.0411	0.0188	− 2.1823
IVADUM	0.0040	0.0756	0.0522
PRICE	− 0.0668	0.1120	− 0.5965
DIVRAT83	− 0.2675	0.1458	− 1.8351
DIVINC	0.0258	0.0201	1.2815
PRICEBK	− 0.4025	0.1035	− 3.8881
CASHRAT	1.2656	0.3452	3.6660
INVRAT	0.3278	0.3955	0.8288
ACQ8301	0.0138	0.0880	0.1569
REP8301	1.2116	0.0806	15.0410

Table 7.5   Probit Results for the 1984 Acquisition Model

Parameter	Estimate	Standard Error	t-statistic
Constant	− 1.0912	0.1073	− 10.1710
DBEQ83	− 0.0340	0.0180	− 1.8902
IVADUM	− 0.0746	0.0798	− 0.9348
PRICE	0.1582	0.0926	1.7094
DIVRAT83	− 0.0386	0.1656	− 0.2329
DIVINC	0.0238	0.0206	1.1553
PRICEBK	− 0.5067	0.1328	− 3.8159
CASHRAT	0.3519	0.3260	1.0793
INVRAT	0.0216	0.4076	0.0530
ACQ8301	1.1762	0.0828	14.2110
REP8301	0.1981	0.0876	2.2615

7.4.2   The Importance of the Variables

We are interested in a notion, beyond significance, of the importance of variables. Estimations of coefficients are not sufficiently informative about the increase in the probability of an event's occuring given a unit increase in the independent variable. Specifically, we look at how the probability of an action changes, given a one-standard-deviation movement in each independent variable, to normalize its impact on the change in probability. Table 7.6 gives the mean probability derivatives from each probit equation and the corresponding standard deviation of each explanatory variable. We create a local approximation of the change in the probability of the event given a one-standard-deviation change in the explanatory variable. We look specifically at those variables found significant in the probit analysis.

Table 7.6   **The Importance of the Explanatory Variables**

Parameter	dp/dx (1)	Standard Deviation (2)	Change in Probability (1) × (2)	dp/dx (1)	Standard Deviation (2)	Change in Probability (1) × (2)
	1976 Repurchase Model			1976 Acquisition Model		
DBEQ75	−0.00428	3.25688	−.0139394	−0.00163	3.25688	−.0053087
IVADUM	0.00933	0.39778	.0037112	−0.00798	0.39778	−.0031742
PRICE	0.01933	0.43843	.0084748	0.03320	0.43843	.0145558
DIVRAT75	−0.57718	0.03149	−.0181753	0.12811	0.03149	.0040341
DIVINC	0.00323	4.05034	.0130825	−0.00211	4.05034	−.0085462
PRICEBK	−0.03485	0.41987	−.0146324	−0.06347	0.41987	−.0266491
CASHRAT	0.26775	0.10373	.0277737	0.08931	0.10373	.0092641
INVRAT	−0.44924	0.06235	−.0280101	−0.27509	0.06235	−.0171518
ACQ7501	0.01958	0.33796	.0066172	0.26519	0.33796	.0896236
REP7501	0.26532	0.36128	.0958548	0.04679	0.36128	.0169042
	1984 Repurchase Model			1984 Acquisition Model		
DBEQ83	−0.01150	3.41099	−.0392263	−0.00856	3.41099	−.0291980
IVADUM	0.00111	0.45003	.0004995	−0.01880	0.45003	−.0084605
PRICE	−0.01869	0.36276	−.0067799	0.03989	0.36276	.0144704
DIVRAT83	−0.07483	0.45437	−.0340005	−0.00972	0.45437	−.0044164
DIVINC	0.00720	1.45608	.0104837	0.00599	1.45608	.0087219
PRICEBK	−0.11259	0.57582	−.0648315	−0.12774	0.57582	−.0735552
CASHRAT	0.35403	0.17869	.0632616	0.08871	0.17869	.0158515
INVRAT	0.09168	0.08341	.0076470	0.00544	0.08341	.0004537
ACQ8301	0.00386	0.37984	.0014661	0.29655	0.37984	.1126415
REP8301	0.33893	0.38720	.1312336	0.04994	0.38720	.0193367

The dummy variable predicting habit formation most drastically affects the probability of all of the outcomes. For instance, in the 1984 repurchase equation a one-standard-deviation move in the dummy variable for 1983 repurchase changes the probability of repurchase by .131. This is an enormous change, particularly relative to the overall sample mean probability of a 1984 repurchase of .2632. The derivative figure indicates that having repurchased in the previous year (the dummy variable equals unity) versus not having done so changes the 1984 repurchase probability by .339, holding other factors constant.

Our estimate of q is also important in all equations. A one-standard-deviation increase in the price-to-book ratio in 1984 decreases the probability of a firm's participating in repurchase by 6.5 percentage points. This finding suggests that firms with low internal investment opportunities seek to spend their money elsewhere.

This analysis of the importance of the explanatory variables indicates that certain factors are more important for particular actions or at particular times. The variables for cash flow and the previous dividend ratio are important in both repurchase equations, consistent with the free-cash-flow hypotheses. The debt-to-equity and dividend ratios are also important in both repurchase equations. Conversely, price appreciation is influential in changing the probability of acquisitions in both 1976 and 1984. Both the price-to-book ratio and the habit variables are consistently important, though more so in 1984.

7.4.3 Model Specification Predictions

The percentage correct of the model prediction is the sum of correctly predicted outcomes scaled by the total number of observations. The percentage-correct values of the 1976 repurchase, 1976 acquisition, 1984 repurchase, and 1984 acquisition models are .849, .866, .783, and .813, respectively. These findings imply that the models have predictive capability. We desire further interpretation of the predictability, however, and so we explicitly compare our models to a "naive" model. For that model we have chosen knowledge of the aggregate ratios of actual one dummies to nonoccurrences and then predicted accordingly. Complete aggregate information is itself a demanding standard of comparison.

Table 7.7 reports matrices of the number of realizations for each model of each of the 4 possible outcomes:

1. Correctly predicting an outcome occurrence (that is, $\hat{Y} = 1/Y = 1$, where $\hat{Y}$ is the predicted value of the dummy variable for the action, and Y is the actual value).
2. Misidentifying a nonoccurrence as an action ($\hat{Y} = 1/Y = 0$). The probability of this outcome gives the size of the type-two error.

Table 7.7   Prediction Realizations

		1976 Repurchase Model $\hat{Y}$					1976 Acquisition Model $\hat{Y}$		
		< .5	≥ .5				< .5	≥ .5	
Y	0	1,892	90	1,982	Y	0	1,928	96	2,024
	1	267	117	384		1	220	122	342
				N = 2,366					N = 2,366

		1984 Repurchase Model $\hat{Y}$					1984 Acquisition Model $\hat{Y}$		
		< .5	≥ .5				< .5	≥ .5	
Y	0	1,227	114	1,341	Y	0	1,305	116	1,421
	1	198	281	479		1	224	175	399
				N = 1,820					N = 1,820

Table 7.8   **"Naive" Predictions**

		$\hat{Y}$	
		$< .5$	$\geq .5$
	0	F_0F_0N	F_1F_0N
Y			
	1	F_1F_0N	F_1F_1N

F_1 = fraction of ones $= \dfrac{\text{number of ones}}{\text{total number}}$

F_0 = fraction of zeros $= \dfrac{\text{number of zeros}}{\text{total number}}$

N = total number

3. Misidentifying an action as a nonoccurrence ($\hat{Y} = 0/Y = 1$). The probability of this outcome is the size of the type-one error.
4. Correctly predicting a nonoccurrence of the event ($\hat{Y} = 0/Y = 0$).

Table 7.8 calculates the realization matrix for our naive model. We assume knowledge of the aggregate ratio of realizations, that is, we know the total number of observations and their true division ratio between zeros and ones. If we predict a one, we are correct by a percentage equal to the fraction of ones. Thus, the number of realizations such that $\hat{Y} = 1/Y = 1$ is equal to the fraction of ones predicted correctly times the number of ones, or $F_1 \cdot F_1 \cdot N$. We similarly calculate the number of realizations in each cell of the matrix for the total number of observations, N. We can therefore calculate the conditional probabilities of the naive model.

The conditional probabilities of the regression models and the naive model are given in table 7.9. Our model excels in improving the size of type-one error, as well as in increasing the power of our predictions.

7.4.4   Structural Change

Across Time

Initial observation of the results may suggest structural change across time.[10] In the repurchase model the investment ratio is significant and negative in 1976 and insignificant and positive in 1984. Whereas the previous year's dividend increase is significant in 1976, it lacks such significance in 1984.

Similarly, the 1975 repurchase dummy is significant in the 1976 acquisition model but not as significant in the 1984 model. The investment ratio is significant and negative in 1976 but insignificant in 1984. Conversely, the previous year's debt-equity ratio is significant and negative in 1984 but insignificant in 1976.

Table 7.9   **Conditional Probabilities of the Regression Models and the Naive Model**

	Regression Models	Naive Model
1976 Repurchase		
prob ($\hat{Y} = 1 / Y = 1$)	.305	.162
prob ($\hat{Y} = 1 / Y = 0$)	.045	.162
prob ($\hat{Y} = 0 / Y = 1$)	.695	.838
prob ($\hat{Y} = 0 / Y = 0$)	.955	.838
1976 Acquisition		
prob ($\hat{Y} = 1 / Y = 1$)	.357	.145
prob ($\hat{Y} = 1 / Y = 0$)	.047	.145
prob ($\hat{Y} = 0 / Y = 1$)	.643	.855
prob ($\hat{Y} = 0 / Y = 0$)	.953	.855
1984 Repurchase		
prob ($\hat{Y} = 1 / Y = 1$)	.587	.263
prob ($\hat{Y} = 1 / Y = 0$)	.085	.263
prob ($\hat{Y} = 0 / Y = 1$)	.413	.737
prob ($\hat{Y} = 0 / Y = 0$)	.915	.737
1984 Acquisition		
prob ($\hat{Y} = 1 / Y = 1$)	.439	.220
prob ($\hat{Y} = 1 / Y = 0$)	.082	.220
prob ($\hat{Y} = 0 / Y = 1$)	.561	.780
prob ($\hat{Y} = 0 / Y = 0$)	.918	.780

We can also expect some structural change across time given how the relative importance of the parameters change over time. The investment ratio alters the probability of repurchase far more in 1976 than in 1984. Our approximation of q alters the probability of acquisition far more in 1984 than 1976. In both habit formation is more important in 1984. In addition to the possibility of changes in the probit coefficients, the increased occurrence of both repurchases and acquisitions suggests that an intercept shift may also have occurred over time.

We test for structural change within an action across time with the likelihood ratio test. The test is computed as $LR = 2(L_2 - L_1)$, where L_2 is the value of the likelihood function for the maximum of the unconstrained model, and L_1 is the value with imposed constraints. This statistic is asymptotically distributed as a chi-squared variable with degrees of freedom equaling the difference in the number of constraints.

We are interested in testing whether the probit coefficients are constant between our sample periods, allowing for the possibility of an intercept shift. We have created two pooled samples: one for share repurchase, and one for acquisition. Each includes a time-specific dummy variable, allowing the intercept to differ for the two subperiods.

Table 7.10   Likelihood Ratio Tests of Structural Change across Time

Unconstrained	Repurchase	Constrained
log L (rep76)		log L (all repurchase)
-886.125		-1799.90
log L (rep84)		
-906.792		

$$2(-886.125 - 906.792 + 1799.90) \sim \chi^2_{10} \text{ (at } p = .05, \text{ critical level} = 18.3)$$
$$LR = 13.96$$

Unconstrained	Acquisition	Constrained
log L (acq76)		log L (all acquisition)
-809.508		-1636.90
log L (acq84)		
-822.448		

$$2(-809.508 - 822.448 + 1636.90) \sim \chi^2_{10} \text{ (at } p = .05, \text{ critical level} = 18.3)$$
$$LR = 9.89$$

Table 7.10 displays our results for the likelihood ratio statistic (LR) for tests of structural change across time. In comparing the figures with the 5 percent critical level for a chi-squared variable with ten degrees of freedom (18.3), we find that the evidence fails to reject the null hypothesis of no structural change in the coefficients for both repurchase and acquisition (as neither 13.96 nor 9.89 exceeds 18.3). Nonetheless, the time-specific dummy variable is large and significant in each pooled probit. In both cases the intercept shift indicates that these actions become more likely for reasons not captured by our explanatory variables. This is consistent with the previous evidence that these activities expanded enormously between the 1970s and mid-1980s.

7.5 Conclusions

The explanatory variables suggested by the hypotheses about non-dividend cash payments collectively have substantial power in predicting participation in share repurchases and acquisitions. For instance, relative to a naive model based on correct aggregate ratios, our probit estimators reduce the occurrence of type-two errors (misidentifying a nonoccurrence of the event) by roughly a factor of three.

Among the hypotheses surveyed, perhaps the free cash flow theory is most consistent with our findings, particularly the share repurchase ones. The cash flow variable and the price-to-book ratio (our q approximation) had the correct sign, were statistically significant, and were quantitatively important in both 1976 and 1984. The coefficient on the price-to-book ratio was consistently negative, significant, and important in both the repurchase and the acquisition probits. This finding suggests, consistent with Tobin's q theory and Jensen's free cash flow hypothesis, that firms that sell at a discount relative to book value are more likely to engage in share repurchases or acquisitions, presumably as an alternative to unprofitable further investments in their primary activity. The investment ratio was marginally significant and consistent with the free cash flow theory for repurchases in 1976, but its coefficient was insignificant in 1984.

Consistently, the variable with the largest t-statistic and the one that most greatly affected the probability of an action was participation the preceeding year. Thus, share repurchases and acquisitions appear to be "habit forming." This trait is consistent with the clientele hypothesis, which asserts that firms specialize in how they transmit cash to their owners.

The tests for structural change across time failed to reject the hypothesis that the determinants of repurchases and acquisitions are unchanged over time. This may be somewhat surprising, given that the aggregate levels of these activities have increased so dramatically in recent years. We do demonstrate that the intercept has time dependence. In subsequent research we hope that by addressing other considerations, including the existence of a takeover threat and tax information, we can explain the effects now captured by the dummy variable. Nonetheless, the failure of this study to find structural change in the determinants of participation does suggest that the theories tested here were consistently operative in both years examined.

In further work we plan to examine how these phenomena are affected by provisions in the 1986 Tax Reform Act. This major realignment of the tax environment may dramatically affect these aspects of corporate financial behavior.

Appendix

The Data

We began with 2,399 Industrial, 853 OTC, and 1,289 Research observations. Of these, 29 lacked all information including CUSIP numbers. Thus, we manipulated the data from 4,512 original observations to achieve the resultant 2,366 points for 1976 and 1,820 points for 1984.

Table 7.11 lists the Compustat definitions of our dependent variables. It should be noted that we included both cash and stock-swap acquisitions. Analysis of data in *Mergers and Acquisitions* indicated the vast

Table 7.11   Compustat Definitions of the Dependent Variables

Acquisition: "The funds for, or the costs relating to, the acquisition of a company in a current or prior year as reported on the statement of changes."

Includes:
1. Cost of the net assets of the business acquired
2. Acquisition of additional ownership (a decrease in minority interest)
3. Additional interest in the company (if the company is consolidated)
4. Retail assets in the business acquired
5. Property, plants, and equipment of the acquired company
6. Long-term debt assumed in acquisition

Repurchase: "Use of funds which decreases common and/or preferred stock."

Includes:
1. Purchase of treasury stock
2. Retirement or redemption of preferred stock
3. Retirement or redemption of redeemable preferred stock
4. Retirement of common stock
5. Conversion of preferred stock into common stock
6. Conversion of Class A, Class B, special stock, etc., into common stock

majority of 1984 acquisitions were cash deals, suggesting that the inclusion of stock-swaps would not strongly affect our analysis for that year.

The 1984 research file consists of companies deleted from other Compustat files because of acquisition or merger, bankruptcy, liquidation, delisting, or inconsistent reporting. Thus, many of those companies may have had observations for 1976 (if they existed before the delisting) but not for 1984. This is one explanation of the disparity between the number of observations for 1976 and 1984.

We then created dummy variables for repurchasing and acquisitions, giving missing values a zero. We did this because Compustat counts insignificant figures as not available. Thus, as missing data are potentially in actuality insignificant, we set them equal to zero to maximize the information obtainable from the dependent variables. (Note, however, that since a firm often has many, or all, points missing, many of these firms were subsequently "relost" by missing another variable.) The repurchase dummy variable was assigned a one only if the firm bought more than one-half of one percent of its outstanding share equity value. We also created the inventory dummy to be one if either the firm chose solely LIFO, or else LIFO was the primary choice of two inventory valuation methods; otherwise it was zero.

TSP probit executes only for complete observations, and we eliminated from the analysis firms missing any of the necessary variables. We then eliminated any debt-equity ratios that were either negative or exceeded 100, as we found ratios outside these parameters implausible, and suggestive of erred data. This procedure therefore resulted in the samples of 2,366 for 1976 and 1,820 for 1984.

Notes

1. See, for example, Auerbach (1983).
2. Gordon and Bradford (1980) argued that the implication of tax rules for the preference for capital gains is not so unambiguously in favor of capital gains. The importance of the differentials between ordinary income and capital gains taxation in dividend policy is still an unsettled issue. See, in addition, Miller and Scholes (1982).
3. The repurchase is treated as a capital gain if, according to Section 302 of the U.S. Internal Revenue Service code, the redemption is "substantially disproportionate." Vermaelen's (1981) sample had only 3 out of 105 tender offers subject to ordinary income taxes.
4. This example is found in Shoven (1986).
5. Recent studies have demonstrated how differing basis values given capital gains taxation result in these choices. The Balcer and Judd (1985) life-cycle model showed the optimal decision rule to be the selling of those shares with the highest basis values first. Bagwell (1986) also demonstrated how the heterogeneous basis values of shareholders result in selling by those with the lowest basis last.
6. There is no evidence that the rate of return on the common stock of the acquiring firm is abnormal, whereas there is an excess return enjoyed by the holders of the securities of the acquired firm (Dennis and McConnell 1986).
7. See, for example, Black (1976).
8. At the suggestion of Jerry Green, we examined an alternative measure of cash flow. It approximated the free cash flow available after replacement investment scaled by total assets. In general, the qualitative results were unchanged.
9. A problem with the one-year lagged participation variables is that some repurchase and share acquisition programs span more than one calendar year. To consider whether this overlap biased the lagged participation coefficient, we ran the probits with a two-year lagged repurchase dummy. Its significance and importance remained.
10. We chose 1976, instead of ten years before 1984, or 1974, because of Nathan and O'Keefe's (1986) finding of a structural change event in 1974. We therefore wanted to separate out this finding from other structural changes and chose two periods on the same side of their shift.

References

Amemiya, Takeshi. 1985. *Advanced econometrics*. Cambridge: Harvard University Press.
Auerbach, Alan J. 1983. Taxation, corporate financial policy and the cost of capital. *Journal of Economic Literature* 21 (September):905–40.

Bagwell, Laurie Simon. 1986. Share repurchase and takeover deterrence. Photocopy. Stanford: Stanford University, September.

Balcer, Yves, and Kenneth L. Judd. 1985. Optimal consumption plans and portfolio management with duration-dependent returns,'' CMSEMS discussion paper 662. Evanston, Ill.: Northwestern University, September.

Black, F. 1976. The dividend puzzle. *Journal of Portfolio Management*, pp. 5–8.

Dann, Larry Y. 1981. Common stock repurchases. *Journal of Financial Economics* 9:113–38.

Dennis, Debra K., and John J. McConnell. 1986. Corporate mergers and security returns. *Journal of Financial Economics* 16 (June):143–87.

Elton, E. J., and M. J. Gruber. 1970. Marginal stockholders' tax rates and the clientele effect. *Review of Economics and Statistics* (February):68–74.

Fama, E., L. Fisher, M. Jensen, and R. Roll. 1969. The adjustment of stock prices to new information. *International Economic Review* (February):1–21.

Feldstein, Martin, and Jerry Green. 1983. Why do companies pay dividends? *American Economic Review* 73 (March):17–30.

Gordon, Roger H. 1982. Interest rates, inflation, and corporate financial policy. *Brookings Papers on Economic Activity* 2:461–91.

Gordon, Roger H., and David F. Bradford. 1980. Taxation and the stock market valuation of capital gains and dividends. *Journal of Public Economics* 14:109–36.

Jensen, Michael C. 1986. The takeover controversy: Analysis and evidence, working paper 86–01. Rochester, N.Y.: Managerial Economics Research Center, University of Rochester, July.

———. 1986. Agency costs of free cash flow, corporate finance and takeovers. *American Economic Review* 76 (May, Papers/Proceedings):323–29.

Jensen, Michael C., and William Meckling. 1976. Theory of the firm: Managerial behavior, agency costs, and ownership structures. *Journal of Financial Economics* 3:305–60.

Judge, George G., W. E. Griffiths, R. C. Hill, H. Lutkepohl and T. C. Lee. 1985. *The theory and practice of econometrics*. New York: Wiley.

Masulis, Ronald W. 1980. Stock repurchase by tender offer: An analysis of the causes of common stock price changes. *Journal of Finance* 35 (May):305–21.

Miller, Merton H. 1977. Debt and taxes. *Journal of Finance* 32 (May): 261–75.

Miller, Merton H., and Myron S. Scholes. 1978. Dividends and taxes. *Journal of Financial Economics* 6:333–64.

———1982. Dividends and taxes: Some empirical evidence. *Journal of Political Economics* 90: 1118–41.

Miller, Merton H., and Kevin Rock. 1984. Dividend policy under asymmetric information, photocopy. Chicago: University of Chicago.

Modigliani, F., and M. H. Miller. 1958. The cost of capital, corporation finance and the theory of investment. *American Economic Review* 48 (June): 261–97.

Modigliani, F., and M. H. Miller. 1963. Corporate income taxes and the cost of capital. *American Economic Review* 53 (June):433–43.

Nathan, Kevin S., and Terrance B. O'Keefe. 1986. The rise in takeover premiums: An explanatory study, photocopy. Rochester, Mich.: Oakland University; Eugene: University of Oregon, July.

Ofer, Aharon R., and Anjan V. Thakor. 1986. A theory of stock price responses to alternative corporate cash disbursement methods: Stock repurchases and dividends, photocopy. Evanston, Ill.: Kellogg Graduate School of Management, Northwestern University, August.

Pettit, R. R. 1977. Taxes, transactions costs and clientele effects of dividends. *Journal of Financial Economics* (December):419–36.

Ross, Stephen A. 1985. Debt and taxes and uncertainty. *Journal of Finance* 40 (July): 637–58.

Schaeffer, S. 1982. Tax-induced clientele effects in the market for British government securities. *Journal of Financial Economics*, 121–59.

Schipper, K., and R. Thompson. 1983. The impact of merger-related regulations on the shareholders of acquiring firms. *Journal of Accounting Research* 184–221.

Shoven, John B. 1986. The tax consequences of share repurchases and other nondividend cash payments to equity owners, paper presented at the "Economics of Tax Policy" conference of the National Bureau of Economic Research, Washington, D.C., November 17.

Summers, Lawrence H. 1981. Taxation and corporate investment: A q-theory approach. *Brookings Papers on Economic Activity* 1:67–140.

Tobin, James. 1969. A general equilibrium approach to monetary theory. *Journal of Money, Credit and Banking,* pp. 15–29.

Trzcinka, Charles. 1982. The pricing of tax-exempt bonds and the Miller hypothesis. *Journal of Finance* 37 (September): 907–23.

Vermaelen, Theo. 1981. Common stock repurchases and market signalling: An empirical study. *Journal of Financial Economics* (June): 139–83.

Comment   David F. Bradford

Bagwell and Shoven's paper investigates a phenomenon that is important in part because of the serious challenge it poses to economic analysis. The problem is this: In an active market populated by agents with very sharp pencils, the participants do not appear to optimize. Year in and year out, which we might interpret as an "equilibrium" state, firms choose to pay out dividends in spite of the availability of other modes of distribution that are significantly better for most shareholders and worse for none. The most obvious alternative is repurchase of the firm's own shares in the market. With apparently minor qualifications, share repurchases are definitely superior to dividend payments. Yet dividends continue to be paid.

Bagwell and Shoven start by reminding us of the superiority argument. They begin with a situation in which the firm has a sum of money it wishes to distribute. The state of the firm after the money has left its hands would seem to be independent of the route by which the money departed. All the state variables describing the firm are

David F. Bradford is professor of economics and public affairs at the Woodrow Wilson School, Princeton University, and a research associate of the National Bureau of Economic Research.

independent of the method by which the funds are distributed. Of the two methods, share repurchase generates lower taxes than dividends. This is true in part because of the rate difference between long-term capital gains and dividends and in part because of the deferral of some income in the hands of shareholders, since they can deduct the basis in shares sold in calculating their income subject to tax. The share repurchase method also offers shareholders an opportunity to choose the cash flow they wish to realize from their ownership in the firm. This sums up the case for share repurchase over dividends.

An only slightly more complicated method—using the firm's cash to purchase the shares of another firm rather than its own shares—may also be superior to dividend payment as a means of routing cash out of the firm and into the hands of the public. All that is required to accept this is to view the pair of firms involved in a consolidated way.

The authors present a statistical analysis of the characteristics of firms that engaged in (more than a negligible amount of) share repurchases or acquisitions of other firms (or both) in 1976 and 1984. (It is not clear from the paper whether the acquisition transactions are for cash from individual shareholders, which they would need to be to accomplish the equivalent of a share repurchase.) There are essentially two parts to the puzzle: which firms distribute cash to shareholders; and, among those, how much do they distribute via each of the possible paths—dividends, share repurchase, and acquisition.

Although the reasoning behind Bagwell and Shoven's empirical work is based partly on the determinants of cash distributions, rather than on the form those distributions take, the authors are especially interested in the latter. Having noted that dividends are inferior to the other forms of distribution from the point of view of their after-tax consequences for shareholders, but noting also that dividends continue to be used, they focus on the factors that make dividends *relatively* more or less costly. Let us then briefly review the weak points in the argument for the superiority of the nondividend forms of transfer. Several might be mentioned.

First, there is the tiny qualification in the argument given above: that the individual tax rate is constant. Because the tax rate may not be constant, the deferral of income associated with share repurchase as a method of distribution may conceivably be disadvantageous; the deferred income may later be subject to a higher tax rate. But if the shareholder anticipates the higher tax rate, the optimal behavior on his part would be to realize the income now in any case, so that this is a very minor problem indeed.

Second, to qualify for capital gains rather than dividend treatment, the net effect of the share repurchase must not look like that of a dividend. That is, the distribution of ownership among shareholders must be changed by the share repurchase, at least in the short run. If not, the tax authorities have the power to require the selling shareholders to report the proceeds as a dividend for tax purposes. Although there is some theoretical reason to expect this sanction, it is in fact very rare and should be easy to avoid.

Third, the share repurchase method may subject the board of directors to some risk. If the firm's shares increase in value, a shareholder who earlier tendered may have a basis for suit against the directors. Again, my impression is that this risk is very small.

Fourth, for some shareholders dividends may in fact be preferable to capital gains. An important class of shareholders for which this is true is corporations. Until recently, a corporation could deduct up to 85 percent of any dividend from its corporate tax base. By contrast, a realized capital gain has been taxed at a flat rate, which, though lower than the tax on ordinary income, is still much higher than 15 percent of the regular rate. Perhaps because of this tax fact, most intercorporate dividends to be found in the statistical series (putting to one side dividends paid to tax-exempt entities) are flows from wholly owned subsidiaries to parents.

Tax-exempt institutions represent another class of shareholders that may prefer dividends to capital gains. One might think that these institutions would be indifferent to the two forms of cash flow, since neither of them has any tax consequences. But for some of these institutions the regulatory restrictions would treat the forms of cash flow differently. Universities, for example, may be allowed to spend cash flowing from dividends, but not cash flowing from share repurchases.

A fifth counterargument to Bagwell and Shoven's analysis is that the two forms of distribution convey different signals to the market. The usual way of putting this is to say that the fact that a firm is able to put cash dividends in the hands of shareholders must indicate that there really are some earnings there. Two comments might be made about this. First, the ability to distribute cash bears no necessary connection to current earnings. Second, it would seem a very simple matter to provide methods for auditing the repurchase of shares by corporations in such a way as to make it entirely equivalent to a dividend as far as any cash distribution can serve as a signal of a firm's underlying conditions. There is no obvious reason one could not make a commitment to future distributions in much the same way that firms appear to have commitments to regular dividend distributions. It should, however, be conceded that one could imagine problems with the tax authorities if the policy looked too much like dividends.

A sixth set of arguments is based on transactions costs. I must say, I find these arguments the most compelling. One can identify significant transactions cost differences at both the firm and the shareholder level.

At the firm level it seems very likely that arranging for share repurchase, which I believe is typically by tender offer at a specified price, is more costly than the routine payment of dividends. At the shareholder level the arguments run in both directions. For the shareholder who wants the cash flow associated with a dividend, the share repurchase route may be more costly, since it is necessary to go to the expense of selling a portion of the portfolio. Furthermore, for small shareholders it will often be impossible to match exactly the tax flow associated with the dividend.

In a world of no transactions costs, the dividend route might be presumed to generate no incentives to change portfolios. The day before the distribution, the shareholder owns a claim to the package of assets represented by the firm, including the firm's bank balance. The day after the distribution, the firm's bank balance is down, but the shareholder's bank balance is up by the same amount. And the shareholder's portfolio is the same in real terms. With transactions costs, however, all bets are off. Shareholders are always in the position of wishing they had different portfolios, but not wishing it enough to incur the cost of rebalancing. A nondividend distribution by the firm, with no offsetting portfolio adjustment, might leave any given shareholder better off or worse off. It is not at all clear that one method of distribution is superior to the other in this respect, that is, in terms either of the shareholder's transactions costs of rebalancing or of his loss of utility resulting from the deviation that might prevail from the portfolio he would have chosen in the absence of transactions costs.

The Bagwell and Shoven discussion of the choice among distribution modes as an element of an anti-takeover strategy depends on this sort of transactions-cost effect. The argument, as I understand it, is that shareholders who would tender their shares in a repurchase transaction are the ones closest to overcoming the transactions-cost impediment to rebalancing their portfolios. By picking those shareholders off, incumbent management can impose higher transactions costs as the price to a would-be takeover bidder.

A final counterargument in favor of dividends is that shareholders are essentially irrational on the subject. That is, they care about the form of the cash flow as well as its substance. They simply like dividends. I regret to say, I'm afraid this explanation may be the leading candidate.

There is a scrap of evidence relating to the nature of this possible irrationality, contained in a paper I wrote with Roger Gordon (1980). The question is whether it is the managers of firms or the shareholders whose behavior is inconsistent with the relevant maximization, which here is presumably maximization of shareholders' after-tax returns. The econometric results in our paper can be interpreted as saying that the market places equal value on returns in the form of dividends and capital gains (appropriately adjusting for risk). If this is true, there would be no reason to fault managers for their choice of policies. Instead, the puzzle is in the behavior of the shareholders.

The problem confronting Bagwell and Shoven is that none of these possible counterweights, except the last, suggests differences that should show up in a cross-section of firms. For the last one implies (a) that firms can do whatever they habitually do and perhaps that (b) shareholders may slowly learn what they are spending on their affection for dividends and gradually come to demand that managements use the more favorable forms of distribution. My reading of the Bagwell and Shoven evidence is that this is the main thing they have found: When firms have a lot of cash, they tend to distribute it. In doing so, they use the mode of distribution they have grown accustomed to. There is some tendency, however, for the nondividend forms to take on the preferred status rather strongly predicted by theory.

Reference

Gordon, Roger H., and David F. Bradford. 1980. Taxation and the stock market valuation of capital gains and dividends. *Journal of Public Economics* 14:109–36.

Comment   Jerry R. Green

The theory of finance has supplied us with no determinate model of the optimal capital structure of the firm. Equally lacking has been a theory of optimal cash flow management. Despite this lack of a theoretical underpinning, Bagwell and Shoven attempt to use evidence on the merger and share repurchase behavior of firms to provide a measure of firms' attempts to adjust toward financial targets and to minimize their owners' tax liabilities. In this respect their paper is openly and unashamedly empirical. By developing data and exploring these issues, the authors have done a great service to future work on this topic. The results of their study, however, with a few exceptions that I will mention below, cannot be regarded as a definitive test of economic hypotheses.

Any model of adjustment toward an optimally determined economic magnitude has two ingredients: a theory of where the target should be; and a theory of the costs of adjustment toward the target level, using

Jerry R. Green is professor of economics and chairman of the Department of Economics, Harvard University, and a research associate of the National Bureau of Economic Research.

one or more instruments. Economic theory is much better at supplying the former ingredient than the latter. Adjustment costs are hard to theorize about—they are just measured.

Their measurement requires knowing where the desired level is. Based on this knowledge one can estimate the speed of adjustment toward it. If we assume the marginal cost being "out of equilibrium," away from the target, increases with the distance from the target, the speed of adjustment is a proper measure of these unknown costs.

In the present context the desired level is itself unknown. It is not something that is parameterized within the model, and the evidence in this paper does not bear upon it. The intensity with which firms use share repurchases and mergers to make financial adjustments cannot be used to identify simultaneously the costs of being away from the target, the costs of adjusting toward the target, and the location of the target itself.

This paper does not claim to be an adjustment cost explanation of firms' financial behavior, although the authors do seem to want to proceed along these lines in their future work. What they do accomplish is twofold. They give a very interesting exploratory data analysis of the incidence of share repurchasing and merger behavior, and they amply document the fact that this behavior, however generated, has not remained the same over the past decade.

As one of the authors has shown in other work, the idea of share repurchases, though not a new one, is being seriously rethought by firms' financial managers. Bagwell and Shoven demonstrate that the two time periods studied are very different indeed. Hence, researchers must be very cautious about pooling time-series evidence on the rate of share repurchases.

Not too many years ago we thought that share repurchases were quasi-legal, or at least somewhat tainted. Up to now, however, we have not become aware of the substantial legal or tax problems that have arisen for firms that have engaged in this activity. Does that mean that the corporate sector is on a learning curve, finding out how much dividend tax avoidance via share repurchases will be tolerated? If it does, the analysis of this paper, though qualitatively interesting, cannot quantify the issue of adjustment costs. How are we to know whether we are just on the beginning of a learning curve, and soon to see share repurchases supplant dividends entirely, or whether the two time periods investigated in the paper represent the beginning and the end of a learning process? One would need more than two points to identify the parameters of any learning curve. One suggestion I have, therefore, is to redo this analysis for other years so that the true rate of acceleration of this behavior can be estimated.

Although the theory of finance has not given us a fully consistent picture of capital structure, it has provided many partial models that would lead us to believe the primary determinants of capital structure are unobservable. Not only are these variables hard to measure, and surely not available in the Compustat data base, but they are fundamentally unobservable. Indeed, the message of these theories of finance is that the very financial practices under investigation in the Bagwell and Shoven paper—dividends, mergers and cash management practices—are used to signal the true unobservables to the financial and product markets. The true determinants of the optimal capital structure may include the costs of bonding between management and shareholders, the ease of monitoring manager's actions, and other informational data. It is not surprising, therefore, that the authors find no evidence at all that the use of share repurchases and mergers is an attempt to alter the capital structure. There is probably just too much heterogeneity in these unobservable dimensions across firms for the few observables to be accurate predictors of cash flow management practices.

Share repurchases are often generated as part and parcel of other financial or other real activities of the firm. In some cases they arise from the sale of a division or a significant contraction in scale. But in other cases they arise in combination with a refinancing unrelated to immediate real operations. They may accompany the issuance of debt or preferred shares.

Bagwell and Shoven look at the cash management side of share repurchases in isolation. It would be interesting to tie the issuance of other securities to the share repurchase question, and the data on this are available in the same sources as those the authors use. One hypothesis that could be tested in this way concerns whether firms are ascertaining the legality of their share repurchases as a dividend tax avoidance action. It seems more likely that share repurchases are defensible when a serious contraction is taking place, rather than as part of a refinancing of a firm operating at constant scale.

This paper also looks at certain aspects of clientele effects: Are firms that repurchase their shares more apt to be held by individuals for whom the tax advantage of such an action is relatively more important? Such a question embodies two hypotheses. First is that the firm, with knowledge of who its owners are, chooses a course of action in their interest. But the second, equally plausible in my opinion, is that the firm chooses what it believes to be a preferable financial strategy, hoping to attract ownership by taxable investors who may benefit from this strategy. I doubt that these two hypotheses can be disentangled by using only data on firms' behavior. Nonetheless, the paper offers an interesting first step in this direction.

Finally, Bagwell and Shoven offer a very interesting discussion of the use of share repurchases as a takeover defense. The evidence accumulated in this paper should be combined with the growing data bases on mergers and takeovers and on the attempt to execute such transactions by tender offers. I have no doubt that the approach taken in this paper will be very useful in such future research efforts.

8 Means of Payment in Takeovers: Results for the United Kingdom and the United States

Julian R. Franks, Robert S. Harris, and Colin Mayer

8.1 Introduction

Many aspects of corporate acquisitions have received extensive investigation, but there has been little analysis of their means of financing. This omission is notable in view of the substantial expenditures involved in takeovers. An earlier paper (Franks and Harris 1986b) records that in 1985 acquisitions represented 6 percent of the capital stock extant in the United Kingdom. By any account these are substantial investments whose method of financing warrants careful scrutiny. This paper provides a detailed empirical assessment of acquisition financing.

Although a descriptive analysis of acquisition finance is interesting in itself, there are more fundamental reasons for pursuing the subject. Over the past few years several theories of acquisition finance have appeared. As in other areas of research on corporate finance, these

Julian R. Franks is National Westminster Bank professor of finance at the London Business School and a visiting professor at the University of California, Los Angeles. Robert S. Harris is professor of finance at the University of North Carolina at Chapel Hill. Colin Mayer is the Price Waterhouse Professor of Corporate Finance at City University Business School, London England.

The authors thank Claude Wolff, Richard Boebel, and Pat Rowan for collecting some of the data, and Nick Grattan and Ed Bachmann for programming assistance. They also acknowledge financial support from the Leverhulme Trust and the Frank Hawkins Kenan Institute for Private Enterprise. Colin Mayer is supported by the Centre for Economic Policy Research project "An International Study of Corporate Financing". In addition to being presented at the NBER conference on which this volume is based, this paper was presented at seminars at UCLA, UNC at Chapel Hill, Oxford University, the London Business School, and the University of Colorado. The authors thank the participants for their comments and suggestions, including Michael Brennan, Elizabeth Callison, Jennifer Conrad, Robert Conroy, Eugene Fama, Michael Fishman, Mark Flannery, Mark Grinblatt, David Hirshleifer, Paul Marsh, Stanley Ornstein, Eduardo Schwartz, Sheridan Titman, Walter Torous, and Fred Weston. The authors are especially grateful for suggestions made by Artur Raviv and Richard Ruback.

theories have emphasized the influence of taxation and information asymmetries. To date, however, little empirical work has examined their validity. An examination of these theories may be of value not only in understanding the acquisition process but also in assessing the relevance of information and tax considerations to more general issues of corporate capital structure.

We have chosen to make international comparisons between the United States and the United Kingdom in the analysis that follows because there are well-documented differences between the two countries in the response of share prices to the announcement of new issues of equity. One interesting question is whether similar differences are observed in equity-financed acquisitions. The two countries also exhibit significant institutional differences in regulations affecting corporate financing activities and taxation, regulations that should affect the preferred means of payment for acquisitions. For example, the U.S. government has demonstrated a much more liberal attitude toward share repurchases than has the U.K. government over most of the period under study here. As a consequence, at least one set of theories would anticipate different financing patterns between the two countries.

Following a preview of this paper's results in the next section, section 8.3 surveys theories of acquisition financing, and section 8.4 summarizes existing empirical studies. The data set and methodology are described in section 8.5. Spanning the period 1955–85, the data include over 2,500 acquisitions in the United Kingdom and the United States, forming probably one of the largest corporate data sets employed in an analysis of acquisitions.

Section 8.6 examines the forms of financing that were used in acquisitions over the 30 years of the study. These financing patterns are related to salient tax and institutional considerations. Section 8.7 describes share price responses around the announcement date of the acquisition and also reports the wealth gains to bidders and targets in cash- and equity-financed acquisitions. Previous studies have recorded performance variations by class of acquisition. For example, bid premia have been observed to be greater in tender offers than in mergers. Here we assess whether these differences can be attributed to the forms of financing or to the type of acquisition. Section 8.8 reports postmerger performance for up to two years after the acquisition. Finally, section 8.9 summarizes the results and discusses how the limitations of the methodology employed here can be avoided in a broader cross-sectional study.

8.2 A Preview of the Results

In view of the length of this paper, we provide a preview of the results to help focus our description of the theory and the hypotheses.

8.2.1 Means of Payment

1. Just over half of the sample of U.K. acquisitions were either "all equity" or "all cash" bids, with an approximately equal distribution between the two. Almost two-thirds of the U.S. acquisitions were either all equity or all cash.

2. The higher proportion of "mixed bids" in the United Kingdom is in part accounted for by the provision of cash alternatives to equity offers. Those cash alternatives are frequently underwritten.

3. In the latter half of the 1960s approximately half of the U.S. acquisitions were effected by an offer of convertibles, although their use dropped significantly by the 1970s.

4. Cash acquisitions in the United States increased from a negligible proportion of all acquisitions during the 1950s to just under 60 percent by number during the 1980s.

5. There has not been a similar discernible upward trend in the use of cash in the United Kingdom.

8.2.2 Returns around the Announcement of a Merger

1. Returns to bidder shareholders were similar in cash- and equity-financed acquisitions in the United Kingdom during the six months before (but not including) the announcement month. U.S. acquirers offering equity slightly outperformed those offering cash in the prebid period.

2. Bid premia to target shareholders in cash acquisitions were significantly in excess of those accruing to shareholders in equity acquisitions in both countries.

3. In the United Kingdom neither cash nor equity acquisitions displayed significant abnormal returns to bidder shareholders in the month of an acquisition. Gains to acquisitions thus accrue to target shareholders.

4. In the United States there are significant positive gains to bidder shareholders in cash acquisitions and significant losses in equity acquisitions.

8.2.3 Postmerger Returns

1. Postmerger returns (measured two years after the merger was finalized) were not significantly different from zero in cash acquisitions in either country.

2. There is evidence that U.S. shareholders sustained abnormal losses in the two years after an equity acquisition.

8.2.4 Results Relating to Capital Gains Tax Theories

1. The larger gains accruing to target shareholders in cash acquisitions than in equity acquisitions may be consistent with the theory that

target shareholders have to be compensated for the capital gains taxes levied on cash but not on equity acquisitions.

2. Nevertheless, differences in bid premia in cash- and equity-financed acquisitions in the United Kingdom existed before 1965, when a capital gains tax was introduced. Bid premia can therefore at best only be partly explained by capital gains tax.

3. Furthermore, this proposition is not supported by other evidence showing the means of payment to be unresponsive to appreciable changes in capital gains tax rates in the United Kingdom.

8.2.5   Results Relating to "Trapped Equity" Theories

1. Theories that treat acquisitions as a tax-efficient method of making distributions to shareholders predict a reduction in cash acquisitions when the costs of alternative forms of distributions (such as dividends) fall (King 1986). The proportion of acquisitions financed with cash was not affected by the 1973 introduction of the imputation tax system in the United Kingdom, which reduced the costs of dividend payments.

2. Despite the fact that repurchases of shares were not feasible in the United Kingdom over the period of the study, the proportion of acquisitions financed with cash in that country was less than in the United States in recent years. Since repurchases are as tax efficient as cash acquisitions, trapped equity theories would predict a greater use of cash in the United Kingdom. The availability of a stepped-up basis on depreciable assets may have provided a tax incentive for the higher use of cash in the United States.

8.2.6   Results Relating to Information and Agency Theories

1. The proposition that cash is used in high-value acquisitions to preempt competing bids (Fishman 1986) is consistent with the finding of larger bid premia paid in cash than in equity acquisitions.

2. Nonetheless, the evidence that cash was more commonly employed in contested bids is not consistent with the view that cash is preemptive.

3. The abnormal losses incurred by shareholders of bidding companies (in the United States, at least) upon announcements of equity acquisitions, and the postmerger abnormal losses associated with equity acquisitions, are consistent with the proposition that asymmetries in information encourage the issue of overvalued equity by acquirers.

8.2.7   Explaining Previous Results

1. A significant proportion of the difference in bid premia between tender and non-tender offers is attributable to the greater use of cash in tender offers.

2. Negative postmerger performance by the firm, which has been observed in some previous studies, appears to be closely associated with the use of equity.

8.2.8   International Comparisons

1. In the U.S., acquirers using equity incur abnormal losses on the bid announcement, whereas those using cash make abnormal gains. In the U.K., in contrast, no significant gains or losses are incurred by bidders using cash or equity. These results are similar to those found in event studies of new (seasoned) equity issues in the United Kingdom and United States, respectively.

2. Underwriters in the United Kingdom played a much more important role in acquisition finance than did their counterparts in the United States. Not only did they play a role in financing acquisitions where the bidder lacked cash, but also where the bidder required external validation of the valuation of its offer.

8.3   Theories of Means of Payment in Acquisitions

In complete markets with symmetric information and in the absence of taxes, shareholders should be indifferent to the means of payment used in acquisitions: share price responses should reflect only the changes in fundamental values induced by the merger. But the tax system and specific features of the capital market do encourage the use of particular forms of finance. This section surveys theories of the choice of acquisition financing. We first discuss the tax-based models and then agency and information theories.

8.3.1   The Influence of Taxation on the Medium of Exchange

The choice of a means of exchange affects the tax liabilities of the acquired firm's shareholders. In an equity acquisition the investor's acceptance of the stock of the acquiring company avoids the realization of any capital gain and does not therefore impose an immediate capital gains tax liability on the investor. These taxes are deferred until the investor sells the shares. In a cash purchase the investor's gain must be realized immediately for tax purposes, thus creating a tax liability at the capital gains tax rate. In the absence of other considerations, we would not expect to observe cash acquisitions. Nonetheless, the payment of capital gains taxes depends on the tax status of the investor, and the full capital gains tax rate may be mitigated by exemptions and allowances. The rate will be smallest for targets with "marginal" investors that are tax exempt or have unused allowances. For these investors personal tax considerations will bear little relation to the desired means of payment.

Where a capital gains tax liability is created, additional considerations must justify the use of cash. For example, under the U.S. tax code a cash acquisition permits the acquiring company to "write up" certain assets of the acquired firm to their fair market value. This write-up produces higher tax deductible depreciation allowances not available in all equity bids. This corporate tax advantage of cash bids is somewhat tempered by the recapture taxes due on the written-up values of tangible assets when the acquisition is consolidated by the acquirer. Thus, the U.S. code can provide an incentive for cash bids in cases in which market values exceed book values of the acquired firms' assets. Such a "stepped up" basis is not available in the United Kingdom. For target shareholders to be indifferent to the use of cash and nontaxable forms of payment, cash purchases must create pretax gains, as measured by bid premia, that are larger than those associated with equity purchases. The net gain to the bidder is then the value of the "write up," less the increment to the bid premium. Thus:

HYPOTHESIS 1. *Bid premia are higher in cash-financed than in equity-financed acquisitions. Other things equal, the use of cash in acquisitions is inversely related to the capital gains tax rate of the acquired firms' shareholders and directly related to the potential for writing up depreciable assets.*

The above-mentioned disincentives to use cash in acquisitions may be offset by considerations of the tax position of the acquiring firm's shareholders. Cash acquisitions may afford tax savings because dividend payments are taxed at shareholders' personal income tax rates. Thus, cash acquisitions may be more tax efficient than dividend payments if capital gains taxes are smaller than personal income taxes on dividend income. According to the models of Auerbach (1979) and King (1977), under conditions in which a firm's marginal valuation ratio (referred to below as q) is less than unity but more than the value of a unit dividend distribution to shareholders, there are disincentives to paying cash dividends. Distributions to shareholders could be achieved at a lower tax cost by share repurchases or voluntary liquidation (see Edwards and Keen 1985). In the United Kingdom share repurchases have been permitted only since 1985. In the United States share repurchases were permitted for the period of our study and have now become widespread (see Shoven and Simon 1987). It is possible, however, that even in the United States restrictions on the tax status of repurchases may favor alternative routes of distributing cash—through, for example, acquisitions. Thus:

HYPOTHESIS 2. *The incentives to use cash in acquisitions are greater in circumstances where share repurchases are prohibited or costly.*

King (1986) has further specified the tax incentive to make cash acquisitions. He argued that, in the absence of share repurchases, cash acquisitions are a tax-efficient way of distributing trapped equity to stockholders. Companies make cash acquisitions because the cost of purchasing assets traded in the corporate sector is less than that of purchasing (equivalent) assets in the unincorporated sector. The difference in cost is accounted for by the tax wedge between income taxed in the corporate and personal sectors.

More formally, let C_a and C_i be the costs of adjustment associated with a unit purchase of capital through acquisition and capital investment, respectively. Equality at the margin of the cost of purchases through cash acquisition and investment requires that:

(1) $$q + C_a = 1 + C_i,$$

if we assume that financial markets place a value of q on an additional unit of capital (which costs \$1 to purchase in the absence of adjustment costs) once it is in the corporate sector. King's model focuses on the implications of having \$1 in the corporate sector (generated from, say, previously profitable investments) that is worth q^* in financial markets; q^* may be less than unity because of the double layers of corporate and personal taxes. As these dollars are used to purchase capital (at a cost of $1 + C_i$), equality at the margin requires that

(2) $$q = q^* (1 + C_i).$$

Substituting (2) into (1) and simplifying yields

(3) $$C_a = q((1/q^*) - 1).$$

If profits in the corporate sector are taxed more heavily than those in the personal sector, q^* is less than unity, and the expression on the righthand side of equation (3) is increasing in q. Thus, under reasonable descriptions of the cost of adjustment function, C_a, acquisitions are increasing in q. For example, letting A represent dollars spent on acquisitions and K the capital stock, the quadratic costs of adjustment are described as $C_a = \beta_0 + \beta_1 (A/qK)$. Substituting this into equation (3) yields

(4) $$A/K = -(\beta_0 q/\beta_1) + (1/\beta_1)q^2[(1 - q^*)/q^*]$$

The driving force behind King's description of acquisitions is the undervaluation at the margin of \$1 in the corporate sector—the so-called trapped equity model of acquisitions. For example, if the corporate tax rate is t and the personal tax rate is m, then under a classical system of taxation, $q^* = (1 - t)$, and under an imputation system with an imputation rate of m, $q^* = (1 - t)/(1 - m)$, which creates an incentive to acquire so long as $t > m$.[1] Thus:

HYPOTHESIS 3. *The tax incentive to make cash acquisitions is increasing in the value of the tax wedge $(1 - q^*)$ and the square of the marginal valuation of capital ratio, q.*

8.3.2   Information and Agency Models

If all parties to an acquisition are not equally well informed about future prospects, the choice of a means of finance may be influenced by considerations other than taxation. In particular, asymmetries in information encourage the pursuit of opportunistic gains. In acquisitions two types of asymmetries in information might be anticipated: either the acquirer has superior information about valuations of its assets, or the acquiree has superior information about its assets. In the former case the acquirer has an incentive to undertake equity acquisitions during periods in which its shares are overvalued—or at least not undervalued. In the latter case the acquiree has an incentive to accept offers during periods in which its equity is perceived to be overvalued.

Myers and Majluf (1984) have examined the influence of misvaluations on the incentives for firms to make new equity issues. They argued that there is a disincentive for firms to use new equity as a means of funding new investments. If managers have superior information about the value of the firm's existing assets and investment opportunities, they will want to restrict sales of shares to periods when current and prospective investments are not undervalued by new investors. New shareholders in turn appreciate this incentive to sell overvalued equity, and as a result they downgrade their valuation of firms that make new equity announcements. Furthermore, since firms have an alternative form of financing available (say, cash or debt) that avoids the adverse selection problem, any new issues of equity must be prompted by overvaluation.[2] Riskless securities will be issued in preference to equity, thereby creating the "pecking order" hypothesis of Myers (1984), according to which retentions are used in preference to debt, which is in turn issued in preference to equity. Smith (1986) reviewed studies demonstrating negative average price effects when a new stock issue is announced.

In the context of acquisitions the Myers and Majluf model has two principal implications. The first is that the use of equity will be discouraged in circumstances in which bidders are better informed about their own asset valuation. The second is that bidders will be discouraged from buying shares in targeted companies if the targets are better informed about their own valuations than are bidders. In sum, asymmetries in information about the value of targets discourage acquisitions, and asymmetries in information about the value of the bidder discourage the use of equity finance. These information asymmetries give rise to the following share price response:

HYPOTHESIS 4. *The announcement of equity as the medium of exchange in an acquisition leads to a fall in the share price of the bidder (the issuer), while the use of cash leads to a rise in share price.*

Changing one's assumptions about the information structure leads to rather different predictions. If information about the quality of the acquirer or acquiree becomes evident only after the bid announcement, revaluations will subsequently occur and managers will have incentives to use particular types of finance. The literature discusses three possibilities.

First, if the acquirer is better informed about the value of its own equity and misvaluations are revealed only after the acquisition, the acquirer has an incentive to use equity during periods of overvaluation. When equity is undervalued, acquirers will offer cash (Myers and Majluf 1984).

Second, if the acquiree is better informed about its own value, and its true valuation is revealed only after the acquisition, equity offers will be preferred to cash when equity is believed to be undervalued (Hansen (1984, 1987)). Acquirees prefer to retain an equity participation in the merged firm in order to capture some of the subsequent gains when the undervaluation is revealed.

Third, if premerger appraisals make the acquirer well informed about the high value of the acquiree, it will offer cash in the acquisition. This follows from the desire of the acquirer to capture the benefits of high value acquisitions and to avoid sharing these gains with the acquiree. Conversely, when it is uncertain about acquiree valuations, the acquirer will wish the acquiree to retain an equity holding. This diminishes the adverse selection problems associated with better informed acquirees (Fishman 1986).

Fishman has also argued that cash will be associated with high offers and high bid premia provided by the acquirer. He assumed some fixed costs for collecting information about the value of the prospective target, which encourage acquirors who establish high-value acquisitions to make preemptive bids.[3] These preemptive bids deter other companies from paying for information and initiating competing offers. Cash offers should therefore be associated with high bid premia for the target, low levels of competition, and positive abnormal performance for the bidder after the bid announcement.

In sum, theories of acquisition finance offer some explicit hypotheses about the means of payment, bid premia, and share price movements after a bid announcement. In the remainder of the paper we examine how well each of the theories explains the empirical results.

8.4 Previous Empirical Work

8.4.1 Means of Payment

Two previous studies have investigated the choice of financing method used in U.S. acquisitions, incorporating, at least to some extent, personal tax considerations. Applying a conditional logit model, Carleton et al. (1983) examined the financial accounts of acquired firms to study the probability of three events: being acquired in a cash offer, being acquired in a securities exchange, and not being acquired. In their sample of companies from the years 1976–77, they found (p. 825) that "lower dividend payout ratios and lower market-to-book ratios increase the probability of being acquired in a cash takeover relative to being acquired in an exchange of securities." The authors concluded that on the assumption that book values measure the basis on which capital gains liabilities are calculated, the finding on market-to-book ratios is consistent with a personal tax disadvantage to cash offers. They also discussed the possibility that a market-to-book ratio may proxy for other effects such as inefficient management of the target. The authors found no satisfactory explanation for their findings on dividend payout.

Niden (1986) has provided an extensive discussion of tax issues in U.S. takeovers. She examined the choice between taxable (essentially all-cash) and nontaxable (mainly equity) forms of payment based on an analysis of variables proxying for the tax position of each of the combining firms. Although her logit models had small explanatory power, Niden found no relationship between the tax paying status of target shareowners and the form of payment.

8.4.2 Bid Premia

A recent study by Asquith, Bruner, and Mullins (1986) focused directly on the impact of the form of financing on merger returns. Using a sample of 343 U.S. mergers over the years 1975–83, the authors found that equity offers were associated with significantly smaller returns to both bidders and targets than were cash offers. For targets they reported bid premia of 27.5 percent for cash bids and 13.9 percent for equity bids. For bidders, those using cash earned 0.2 percent and those using equity earned −2.4 percent, although for relatively large targets the figures were 0.95 percent and − 5.39 percent, respectively. Abnormal losses were positively related to the relative size of the acquisition. The findings suggested that differences in merger returns between alternative forms of financing can completely explain the differences recorded between returns in mergers and those in tender offers.

Controlling for whether a merger was horizontal or conglomerate in nature, Wansley, Lane, and Yang (1983) found acquiree bid premia of 31.5 percent in 102 cash bids and 16.8 percent in 87 securities offers. They concluded that higher bid premia are required in cash acquisitions to compensate for capital gains tax liabilities. Niden (1986) also uncovered higher bid premia to acquirees in taxable acquisitions . Dividing U.S. acquisitions over the years 1963–77 into 230 taxable (largely all-cash) and 318 tax-free (mainly all equity) acquisitions, she reported bid premia of 25.4 percent and 11.9 percent, respectively.

No similar studies of the United Kingdom have been undertaken. Nevertheless, Eckbo and Langohr (1986), in a study of bid premia in French takeovers from 1966 to 1980, found that the average offer premia were significantly higher in the 50 cash offers (53 percent) than in the 49 exchanges of securities (20 percent).

The most consistent result to emerge from these previous studies is that bid premia are significantly higher in cash acquisitions than in equity offers. We provide further evidence on this below.

8.5   Data and Methodology

8.5.1   Sample

Our sample contains data from both the United Kingdom and United States, constructed in parallel fashion. For the U.K. data we started with an exhaustive set of almost 1,900 acquisitions as recorded in the London Share Price Database (LSPD) for the period January 1955 to June 1985 (see Franks and Harris 1986a). The LSPD includes all U.K. companies quoted in London since 1975 and approximately two-thirds of the companies quoted before 1975, with a bias in favor of larger companies. For each acquisition we then gathered data on the means of payment from the Stock Exchange Year Book, which reports information from offer documents only where the acquirer is quoted. Financing data existed for 954 of the acquisitions.

For the U.S. data we extracted information on all firms, recorded in the Chicago Research in Security Prices (CRSP) files, that disappeared through acquisition during the period January 1955 to December 1984. The CRSP files cover all companies on the New York and American Stock Exchanges since 1962 and all firms on the NYSE since 1926. We obtained data on means of payment from *The Capital Changes Reporter*. Our final U.S. sample contains 1,555 acquired firms with financing data, and 850 bidders. Using the *Wall Street Journal Index*, we classified takeovers as tenders or mergers based on when control first passed to the bidder. Thus, if the bidder purchased 60 percent of the target's shares via tender and the remaining shares via merger, the bid would be classified as a tender.

In cases where several acquisitions were made by the same bidder, the bidder was counted separately by each acquisition made.

8.5.2 Merger Dates

For each U.K. acquisition we have up to four key dates. The *first approach date* is the date when the Stock Exchange is first informed that merger talks are under way. The *first bid date* gives the date of the first formal merger offer. This is followed by an *unconditional date* when a sufficient proportion of shares has been pledged to the acquiring company to guarantee legal control. Finally, the *LSPD date* shows the last date for which stock returns data are available for the target, usually the delisting date. The first three dates are taken from records of the EXTEL Company, which collects and records such data. Not all acquisitions had four distinct dates. For example, the first bid date may not be preceded by a formal announcement of talks.

For each U.S. acquisition we obtained three key dates. The first mention of an acquisition in *The Wall Street Journal Index* was taken to be the *announcement date*. This date is often the actual bid date but may also be a positive indication of a forthcoming bid. We record dates of bid revisions, as well as the *final bid date*, the date of the bid that was ultimately successful. Finally, we record the *delisting date* for the acquiree's stock.

8.5.3 Share Price Data

Monthly rates of return are taken from the LSPD and CRSP files. In the United Kingdom these are calculated using jobbers' (market makers') price quotes (the average of the bid and the asking price) at the end of the final trading day of the month. Although traded prices are available, the order of prices during a day is not, thereby prohibiting identification of end-of-day traded prices. Jobbers' quotes may not be available on the last day of the month, either because the company's stock has been suspended or because the shares were not traded that day. If there were no jobbers' quotes on the last day of the month, we calculated the returns using a randomly selected traded price on the day of the month when the stock was last traded. The results were not appreciably affected when we used traded prices only instead of the price quote.

8.5.4   Abnormal Returns and Tests

To assess the effects of mergers on share prices, we use variations of event study methodology. Specifically, for any company j we define an abnormal return (ar_{jt}) as

$$(5) \qquad\qquad ar_{jt} = r_{jt} - c_{jt},$$

where r_{jt} is the continuously compounded realized return (log form) in month t (dividends plus capital gains), and c_{jt} is a control return that estimates shareholder returns in the absence of a merger. Time, t, is defined relative to an event date. For the U.K. mergers we use the first available of either the first approach, first bid, unconditional or LSPD dates; for the U.S. mergers we use the announcement date. Since specification of the control returns is controversial, we define control return in three alternative ways as described later in this section.

Company abnormal returns are then aggregated to form a portfolio abnormal monthly return (AR_t) defined as

$$(6) \qquad\qquad AR_t = \frac{1}{N} \sum_{j=1}^{N} ar_{jt},$$

where N is the number of companies in a particular portfolio, for example, the portfolio of acquirees. The statistical significance of AR_t is assessed with the statistic $TAR_t = AR_t/\sigma$, where σ is the standard deviation of the AR_t terms (assumed to be normally distributed) for a time period assumed to be unaffected by the merger. In the results reported here σ is calculated for the period $t = -71$ to $t = -12$. Given these procedures, TAR_t is distributed according to student's t- (distribution with 59 degrees of freedom. This procedure provides a crude adjustment for cross-sectional dependence, as discussed by Brown and Warner (1980). Alternatively, the statistical significance of AR_t is tested nonparametrically using the percentage of the ar_{jt} terms that are positive. This is accomplished by comparing the positive percentage to a binomial distribution when the probability of a positive return is 0.50.

To measure returns over a number of months, we calculate a cumulative abnormal return, CAR_t, as

$$(7) \qquad\qquad CAR_t = \sum_{i=t_b}^{t} AR_i,$$

where t_b is the month at which the cumulation begins. Under the assumption that the AR_t estimates are independent, the significance of CAR_t can be assessed using the statistic $TCAR_t = CAR_t/\sigma_{CAR}$ where $\sigma_{CAR} = \sigma\sqrt{t - t_b + 1}$ and σ is estimated as described above. $TCAR_t$ is approximately a standard normal variate under the null hypothesis that CAR_t has a zero mean.

Although *CAR* is frequently used for assessing multiperiod returns, it can be unsatisfactory when companies disappear from the analysis because of nontrading or because companies are delisted or suspended close to the bid date. As an alternative to *CAR*, we construct company-specific multiperiod returns. These company "bid premia," bp_{jt}, are aggregated into portfolio bid premia, BP_t, defined as

$$(8) \qquad BP_t = \frac{1}{N} \sum_{j=1}^{N} bp_{jt} = \frac{1}{N} \sum_{j=1}^{N} \sum_{i=t_b}^{t} ar_{ji},$$

where the cumulation process begins at time t_b and includes those monthly abnormal returns which are observed up to and including month t. For example, if in month $+1$ two companies obtain an average residual of 10 percent and in month $+2$ only one survives (or is traded) and obtains a residual of 5 percent, the *CAR* for the two months according to equation (7) is 15 percent, and 12.5 percent according to equation (8). We assess the statistical significance of *BP* using the statistic $TBP = BP/\sigma_{BP}$, where $\sigma_{BP} = \sigma\sqrt{T}$, and T is the average (across companies) number of months for which return data are available to form *BP*. *TBP* is the analogue of $TCAR_t$ shown above.

The calculations of *TBP* and *TCAR* both use σ specified as the standard deviation of abnormal returns for some time period removed from the merger. It can be argued that there are transitory (or permanent) risk shifts associated with mergers that might not be captured by our calculation of σ. As an alternative procedure, we calculated statistics based on the cross-sectional standard error of company-specific bid premia (bp_{jt}). This "cross-sectional" t is calculated as BP/SE, where $SE = SD/\sqrt{N}$, and *SD* is the cross-sectional standard deviation of the bid premia for the N companies averaged to get *BP*. In general, the results using these cross-sectional t-statistics are quite comparable to those using *TBP* and *TCAR* discussed above.

8.5.5 Control Returns

Brown and Warner's (1980, 1985) simulation results on both monthly and daily data suggest that relatively straightforward procedures are as powerful as more elaborate tests in detecting abnormal returns (see also Brown and Weinstein 1985). To see whether the specification of control returns affects our results, we use three alternate models to determine c_{jt} using the following equation:

$$c_{jt} = \alpha_j + \beta_j rm_t.$$

In the first model, the market model, values for α and β are estimated by regressing r_{jt} on rm_t for the 60-month period beginning at $t = -71$. Because of the documented effects of infrequent trading in the United Kingdom on estimated parameters (Dimson and Marsh (1983)), α and β for the United Kingdom companies are adjusted for thin trading using Dimson's (1979) method for the same 60-month period.[4] In the second model we set $\alpha = 0$ and $\beta = 1$ for all firms. The third model is based on the capital asset pricing model and sets $c_{jt} = rf_t + \beta_j (r_{mt} - r_{ft})$, where β is from the market model and rf_t is the yield on a government obligation. For the United Kingdom we use the yield on three-month Treasury obligations converted to a one-month yield basis. For the United States we use yields on one month Treasury bills.

8.6 Forms of Financing in U.K. and U.S. Acquisitions

We first describe the different forms of financing used in our samples of U.S. and U.K. acquisitions, the importance of each form, and the trends over the 30-year period. We then assess whether these patterns of financing are consistent with the predictions of the theories reviewed in section 8.3.

8.6.1 Means of Payment

Table 8.1 shows that all-cash offers and all-equity offers were the two most widely used means of payment in both countries. Together these two types of offers constituted almost one-half of the successful U.K. takeovers and over two-thirds of the U.S. offers. In the United Kingdom an additional one in five acquisitions involved either a combination of cash and equity or the seller's option to receive either all cash or all equity. In the "all cash or all equity" case, each shareholder of the target may elect to receive all cash or all equity. The bidder will provide the cash from its own resources or through an underwriter. In the latter case, shareholders of the target tender their shares to the bidder, which then issues new shares to the underwriter (on the basis of the bid terms); the underwriter then remits the amount prescribed by the cash alternative to the tendering stockholders.

These "all cash or all equity" offers have become increasingly prevalent since 1979. One reason is that they provide shareholders who are liable to pay capital gains taxes on realized gains (if they receive cash) with an equity alternative, and others, who do not want the bidder's paper in their portfolio, with cash. The offer is tax and transaction cost efficient. The role of the underwriter may be twofold: It simply provides a source of cash for a cash-hungry bidder; and it provides a signal to the market of the value of the bidder's equity from an informed (or partially informed) trader. This informed trader must agree to purchase any shares at a predetermined price whenever a target shareholder elects to take the cash alternative. This role may be especially important where the acquisition is relatively large and where there is great uncertainty as to the value of the offer to the bidder.

Table 8.1   Mediums of Exchange in U.K. and U.S. Acquisitions, in Proportions, 1955–85

	U.K.	U.S.
A. *Method of Payment*		
All cash	.253	.306
Cash *or* debt	.016	.003
All debt	.014	.014
All cash or (cash plus equity)	.035	.001
Cash plus equity	.101	.009
Cash *or* equity[a]	.100	.013
Convertibles	—	.118
Equity plus debt	.048	.003
Equity plus convertibles	—	.073
All equity	.246	.371
Other[a]	.189	.090
Total	1.00	1.00
B. *Use of Cash, Equity and Debt*[b]		
At least some equity[c]	.660	.601
At least some cash or some debt	.633	.404
At least some cash	.538	.356

[a]The "*or*" denotes that the seller has the option to receive either form of payment. The option to receive "cash or equity" has become increasingly popular since 1978. Before then the ratio of "all equity" to "all cash or all equity" was 3.27, but during 1978–84 it fell to 1.17. The "other" category includes various mixtures of cash, equity, and debt, as well as other types of payment (such as preference stock). In the U.K. sample the largest single category involves mixtures subsequent to recapitalizations (.083).

[b]Categories are not mutually exclusive so that percentages sum to more than 100. The data include mixture offers after recapitalizations.

[c]For purposes of this tabulation, securities convertible into common equity are treated as equity.

Unlike in the United Kingdom, the cash alternative and cash-equity combinations have not been significant in the United States. All debt offers were rare in both countries, and combination offers involving debt are infrequent, though more common in the United Kingdom. A striking contrast between the two countries is in the use of convertibles securities. In the United States 11.8 percent of takeovers involved full payment with convertibles (such as convertible preferred stock), and an additional 7.3 percent were combinations of equity and convertibles. In the United Kingdom the use of convertibles was negligible.

Panel B shows that a larger proportion of U.K. takeovers than U.S. takeovers involved at least some cash or some debt. In addition, a slightly larger proportion of U.K. offers involved at least some equity. These figures reflect the greater use of combination offers in the United Kingdom.

Table 8.2 divides the entire 30-year period into five-year blocks, and figure 8.1 displays the results by year. In the United States all-cash

Table 8.2   Time-Series of the Forms of Payment in U.K. and U.S. Takeovers,
                   Using an Equally Weighted Basis

| Period | | U.K. | | | U.S. | | |
	N	All Cash	All Equity	N	All Cash	All Equity	Some Use of Convertibles[a]
1955–59	65	.354	.354	69	.000	.768	.072
1960–64	89	.292	.404	121	.008	.669	.248
1965–69	156	.186	.244	386	.013	.381	.500
1970–74	139	.230	.237	177	.192	.599	.107
1975–79	247	.336	.231	373	.491	.247	.070
1980–84	205	.205	.190	429	.585	.228	.054
1985	53	.094	.170	—	—	—	—
Average[b]	954	.253	.246	1,555	.306	.371	.191

Note: Entries are proportions of the sample (N) with a type of offer.
[a]These are offers that are equity plus securities convertible into equity or which are solely convertible.
[b]Averages are weighted by the number of mergers.

takeovers were not observed in our sample until 1965, but after that they became increasingly important.[5] At the same time, all-equity offers fell from three-quarters of U.S. takeovers in the late 1950s to less than one-quarter in the 1980s. This striking increase in the use of cash occurred over a period in which the Williams Act (1968) and its extension (1970) imposed more stringent requirements on cash offers. In contrast, in the United Kingdom financing proportions fluctuated considerably over the 30 years of the study.

Table 8.2 also demonstrates that the heavy use of convertibles in the United States was largely a phenomenon of the 1960s. Over the years 1965–69 fully one-half of United States bids involved convertible securities. By the 1980s the proportion had fallen to only 5.4 percent. The downturn in takeover financing with convertibles was probably due to changes in U.S. tax law and accounting standards. Enactment of Section 279 of the tax code in 1969 eliminated the tax deductibility of interest payments on convertible debt expressly issued for acquisitions. In addition, Accounting Principles Board Opinion 15, issued in 1969, required the reporting of earnings per share on a fully diluted basis. This change may have reduced the incentive to issue convertibles because of the impact of earnings dilution on contractual arrangements, for example, in bond covenants. Also, managers and investment bankers may have been apprehensive about investor reaction to even only cosmetic reductions in earnings per share.

The proportions in both tables 8.1 and 8.2 were calculated on an equally weighted basis. Table 8.3 provides the proportions of all-cash

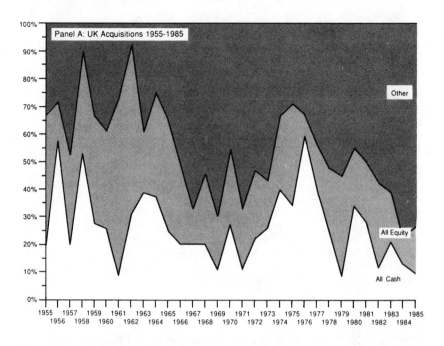

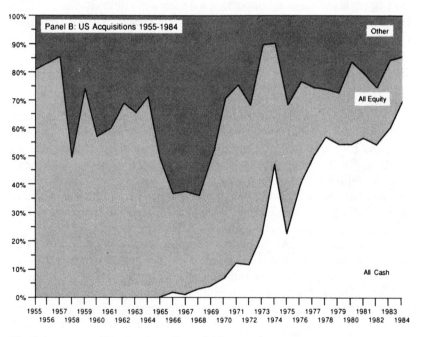

Fig. 8.1   Time-series of acquisition payment type

Table 8.3   **Forms of Payment in UK and US Takeovers, on a Value-Weighted Basis**

	U.K.		U.S.	
	All Cash	All Equity	All Cash	All Equity
1955–59	0.23	0.67	0.0	0.84
1960–64	0.08	0.67	0.0	0.61
1965–69	0.08	0.26	0.01	0.37
1970–74	0.28	0.12	0.21	0.60
1974–79	0.38	0.30	0.38	0.28
1980–84	0.35	0.14	0.39	0.38

Note: Entries are a proportion of the total. Weights are based on market value of the shares of the acquired company.

and all-equity offers based on the market value of the acquisitions. In the United States the proportion of bids that were all cash on a value-weighted basis was almost identical to the equally weighted proportion for the period 1955 to 1974. After 1974 cash offers constituted a smaller proportion on a value-weighted basis than on an equally weighted basis, suggesting that cash offers were used more frequently in smaller acquisitions. For all equity offers the equally weighted and value-weighted results are very close, except for during the years 1980–84.

In the United Kingdom the proportion of all cash offers on a value-weighted basis was appreciably lower than that on an equally weighted over the years 1955–69. The converse was true for the years 1970–84. Over the entire 30-year period the proportion of bids that were all cash was 0.25 on both an equally weighted basis and a value-weighted basis. For the all-equity figures there was no consistent relationship between the value and equal weightings. In aggregate the all-equity proportion on a value-weighted basis was 0.20, whereas it was 0.25 on an equally weighted basis.

8.6.2 Theoretical Predictions and the Evidence

The data shown in tables 8.1 through 8.3 provide some support for the prediction of hypothesis 1 that the use of cash in acquisitions should be inversely related to the capital gains tax rate. The introduction of capital gains taxes in the United Kingdom in 1965 coincided with a decline in the proportion of cash-financed acquisitions from an average of 29.2 percent in 1960–64 to 18.6 percent in 1965–69. This decrease was short-lived, however, and by 1975–79 the proportion had returned to 33.6 percent.

Hypothesis 2—the proposition that cash acquisitions are most prevalent in an environment, such as the United Kingdom, where share repurchases are prohibited—is contradicted by the finding that the proportion of all-cash bids was greater in the United States than in the United Kingdom. But in large part cash acquisitions in the United States began only in the 1970s. Their marked growth may reflect more widespread election of stepped-up basis. Rising inflation in the 1970s increased the benefits of raising the basis for determining depreciation allowances from historic to current prices. Since the stepped-up basis was not available in the United Kingdom, an equivalent trend did not occur there.

The U.K. financing proportions reported here are most informative about the trapped equity hypotheses. Since the trapped equity model is a description of the incentives to make cash distributions through acquisitions, it is worth recalling that a high proportion of acquisitions use "all equity"—in fact, the proportion is as large as that of "all cash". The theory cannot explain the all-equity class of acquisitions. More strikingly, the cycles of merger activity that have been widely observed, and which are an important component of the empirical relationship that King (1986) estimated between the value of acquisitions and stock market prices, do not appear to coincide with peaks in cash-financed acquisitions. According to figure 8.1 the particularly pronounced U.K. merger booms of 1968 and 1972 did not coincide with large upswings in the proportion of cash-financed acquisitions.

Still more troublesome for the trapped equity hypothesis is the poor association between the tax disincentive for dividend distributions and the level of acquisitions using cash. Recall from hypothesis 3 that the incentive for cash acquisitions is increasing in the tax wedge. Over the period under study a number of important tax changes in the United Kingdom should have affected this wedge. Most obviously, the introduction of the corporation tax in 1965 was associated with an increase in the tax price of retaining assets in the corporate sector. The incentive to distribute cash thus rose appreciably in 1965. But figure 8.1 shows that this coincided with a period during which the proportion of cash-financed acquisitions declined. Moreover, the introduction of the imputation tax in the United Kingdom in 1973 should have, in theory, lessened the tax price of retaining assets in the corporate sector. Imputation is a tax credit attributed to shareholders for the payment of corporation tax on the profits underlying a distribution. In 1973, 35 percent of the 52 percent corporation tax was imputed to investors' personal income tax. The corporate tax wedge was therefore only 17 percent, 23 percentage points lower than it was before 1973. Figure 8.1 records, however, that the introduction of imputation was associated with a period in which the proportion of cash acquisitions sharply increased, peaking in 1976.[6]

To summarize, the financing proportions provide little support for the trapped equity model but offer some tentative support for an influence from capital gains tax. The appreciable rise in cash-financed acquisitions in the United States over the period studied can be attributed, at least in part, to tax benefits from stepped-up basis.

8.7   Wealth Effects for Bidder and Target around the Announcement Date

In this section we examine bid premia associated with different means of payment. We discuss, in turn, bid premia around the announcement date in all-cash and all-equity offers; share price changes before the announcement; results for "mixed bids"; the effects of other characteristics of takeover, namely, whether the bids are revised or contested and whether they are tender offers; and finally a cross-sectional regression controlling for these bid characteristics.

8.7.1   Bid Premia in All-Cash and All-Equity Offers

Table 8.4 presents data on bid premia for all-cash and all-equity offers in both countries. Since the results are essentially the same using all three models of control returns, we report only those for the market model. Panel B shows that U.S. acquirers were more than seven times larger than targets in all-cash offers and almost nine times larger in all-equity offers. U.K. acquirers were more than twelve times larger than targets in all-cash offers and more than six times larger in all-equity offers.

Target Shareholders

Panel A in table 8.4 shows that in both countries the bid premia for target shareholders were markedly higher in all-cash offers than in all-equity offers. The month 0 results for the United Kingdom, for example, indicate targets with all-cash offers earned a 30.2 percent bid premium, which was significantly higher than the 15.1 percent premium in all-equity offers. The t-statistic[7] comparing the two figures is 9.49. The differences in the United States are even more dramatic, with the month 0 premium of 11.1 percent in all-equity offers being less than half the all-cash figure of 25.4 percent. We thus find strong evidence that target shareholders receive larger wealth gains in all-cash takeovers than those involving all equity. This observation is consistent with hypothesis 1, the capital gain tax thesis that higher bid premia are required in cash offers to compensate for the capital gains tax liability; with hypothesis 4, the Myers and Majluf argument that there are negative

Table 8.4   **Bid Premia and Market Capitalization in All-Cash and All-Equity Offers**

	A. Bid Premia[a]			
	Month 0		Months −4 to +1	
	U.K.	U.S.	U.K.	U.S.
Acquirees				
All cash	.302	.254	.305	.363
	(28.07)	(42.29)	(11.56)	(24.67)
All equity	.151	.111	.182	.156
	(12.88)	(25.90)	(6.34)	(14.86)
Acquirers				
All cash	.007	.020	.043	.026
	(.75)	(3.56)	(1.98)	(1.89)
All equity	−.011	−.009[b]	.018	.006
	(−.95)	(−2.23)	(.63)	(.61)

	B. Market Value (in millions)[c]			
	U.K.		U.S.	
	All Cash	All Equity	All Cash	All Equity
Acquirees	£ 11.1	£10.6	$ 144.4	$ 134.8
Acquirer	136.1	64.3	1,019.0	1,177.0

Note: Entries are bid premia; *t*-statistics in parentheses.
Cross-sectional *t*-values for bidder wealth gains are:

	Month 0		Months −4 to +1	
	U.K.	U.S.	U.K.	U.S.
All cash	.95	2.99	3.05	2.05
All equity	−1.27	−2.14	.97	.67

where the *t*-value is calculated as BP/SE and where $SE = SD/\sqrt{N}$ and SD is the cross-sectional standard deviation.

[a]Bid premia are calculated using the market model. In the United Kingdom month 0 is the earliest available of the first approach, first bid, unconditional, or LSPD date. In the United States month 0 is the announcement date as defined in the text.

[b]For U.S. acquirers with all-equity offers, where the bid premia are −0.009 for month 0, only 45.7 percent of the 443 acquisitions were positive. The results using a model with $\alpha = 0$ and $\beta = 1$ were virtually identical.

[c]The market value of equity prior to takeover.

signals associated with equity offers; and with the Fishman argument that cash offers coincide with high-value acquisitions.

A comparison of the results for the two countries over the six-month period suggests all-cash bids coincided with slightly higher bid premia in the United States than in the United Kingdom (.363 versus .305), and the differences were statistically significant at better than the .10 level ($t = 1.92$). Comparing the month 0 and month -4 to $+1$ results, we find a greater proportion of the U.S. bid premia in all-cash offers appear to have come prior to month 0. Turning to the all-equity bids, we find the U.K. bid premia were somewhat higher than the U.S. premia (.182 versus .156), though not statistically so when measured over the six-month period ($t = 0.85$).

Bidder Shareholders

Shareholders in the U.K. acquirers earned negligible returns in the bid month for both all-cash and all-equity offers. Over the six-month period, however, small (statistically significant) gains accrued for the all-cash offers. Whether this gain was a result of the bid or of the bidder's timing the offer to correspond to favorable developments in its stock price is uncertain. There is no evidence, however, of significant losses to bidders in U.K. takeovers around the merger announcement date. The results for all-equity offers are similar to those found by Marsh (1979) for the month following the rights issue announcement (results showing small abnormal losses at the time of the announcement).

The difference between the performance of all-cash and all-equity acquisitions in the United States is striking. In all-cash offers the bidders earned significantly positive gains of 2 percent in month 0. In contrast, in all-equity offers they experienced a significant loss of 0.9 percent. These wealth effects were also significantly different from each another ($t = 4.19$).[8]

Taken together, our U.S. results suggest that equity in acquisitions conveys bad news, while cash conveys good news. This role for the medium of exchange is consistent with theoretical predictions (see, for example, Miller and Rock 1985) and with empirical evidence on new equity issue announcements. Smith (1986), surveying an extensive literature on new equity issues, reported a weighted average loss of 1.6 percent. Our results also strongly support Myers and Majluf's predictions described in hypothesis 4.

Our U.K. results indicate the returns to all-equity bidders in the bid month were negative but not statistically different from zero. It is interesting to consider the institutional differences between the two countries. U.K. underwriters play a much more important role in equity issues than do their U.S. counterparts. For example, virtually all new U.K. equity issues have taken the form of rights issues, and virtually all have been underwritten (see Marsh 1979). According to Heinkel and

Schwartz (1985), the underwriter may be able to avoid some of the information problems that would otherwise be associated with equity issues.

Table 8.5 compares U.K. bid premia around the announcement date of acquisitions for the periods 1955–64 and 1965–85. The significance of 1965 is that it was in that year that the government instituted a full capital gains tax. According to hypothesis 1, bid premia in all-cash acquisitions should have differed from those in all-equity acquisitions only in the years after the tax was introduced. The table indicates that although the difference was larger in the later period, bid premia were significantly higher in all-cash offers than in all-equity offers (t = 2.26 in the announcement month) in the earlier period as well. Between 1962 and 1965 there was a short-term capital gains tax on holdings of less than one year. The difference between cash and equity bid premia persists prior to 1962, though the sample is too small to provide meaningful tests of significance. The hypothesis that capital gains taxes can entirely explain differences in the premia of the two kind of offers is therefore rejected.

8.7.2   A Comparison of the Premerger Performance of Bidders Using All Cash and Those Using All Equity

Anecdotal evidence from investment bankers in both the United Kingdom and the United States strongly suggests that they believe the choice of equity or cash is influenced by perceptions of overvaluation of the bidder's shares. We can look to the premerger share price performance of bidders for evidence that the premerger valuation of the acquirer may influence the choice of financing. If overvalued acquirers

Table 8.5   A Comparison of U.K. Bid Premia Before and After 1965

	Month 0		Month −4 to +1	
	1955–64	1965–85	1955–64	1965–85
Acquirees				
All Cash	.185	.327	.260	.317
	(6.28)	(29.26)	(3.60)	(11.60)
All Equity	.108	.166	.194	.177
	(6.39)	(11.17)	(4.67)	(4.86)
Acquirers				
All Cash	.032	.001	.072	.037
	(1.80)	(0.09)	(1.66)	(1.59)
All Equity	.005	−.017	.058	.002
	(0.30)	(1.22)	(1.32)	(0.07)

Note: Entries are bid premia; *t*-statistics in parentheses. Bid premia are calculated using the market model. Month 0 is the earliest available of the first approach, first bid, unconditional, or LSPD date.

choose equity, their premerger performance might be expected to be superior to that of acquirers offering cash.

The table below reports abnormal returns to acquirers for the period beginning six months before the bid and ending one month before the bid. The table shows U.S. bidders offering equity had slightly better performance over the prebid period than did those offering cash. The prebid performance of the two types of bidders was the reverse in the United Kingdom. Only very limited support is thereby provided for the hypothesis that overvaluation can be established from premerger data.

	Bid Premia	N
U.K. Bidders		
All cash	.050	198
	(t = 2.31)	
All equity	.034	150
	(t = 1.28)	
U.S. Bidders		
All cash	−.006	201
	(t = −.45)	
All equity	.024	442
	(t = 2.50)	

8.7.3   Other Types of Offers

In preceding sections the focus was on all-cash and all-equity bids since they are the primary types of bids made in both countries (see table 8.1). Table 8.6 presents additional estimates of the wealth effects of other types of bids.

"Cash or Equity" Offers

Combination offers provide the seller with the opportunity to accept either cash or stock. This option should reduce any detrimental personal tax effects associated with an all-cash offer. As shown in table 8.1, these offers have been made frequently in the United Kingdom but less often in the United States. In the United Kingdom target bid premia in combination offers were quite similar to those found in all-cash offers (table 8.4). For example, the 28.4 percent target bid premium (−4 to +1) in cash-or-equity offers shown in table 8.6 is very close to the 30.5 percent premium shown in table 8.4 for all-cash bids. The small sample size for the U.S. results (N = 20) prevents us from making any definitive statements, although target bid premia appear to be between those for all-cash and all-equity offers (Table 8.4). In neither country did these cash-or-equity offers coincide with significant bidder share price performance.

Table 8.6   The Wealth Effects of Other Types of Offers

Type of Offer	Acquirees		Acquirers	
	0	−4 to +1	0	−4 to +1
1. Cash or equity				
U.K. (N = 95)	.276	.284	.007	.075
	(14.79)	(6.21)	(.49)	(2.26)
U.S. (N = 20)	.180	.266	−.002	−0.010
	(8.41)	(5.07)	(−.09)	(−.18)
2. Cash and equity				
U.K. (N = 100)	.238	.271	.003	.054
	(18.70)	(8.71)	(.23)	(1.63)
U.S. (N = 15)	.099	.212	.057	.015
	(3.24)	(2.83)	(1.88)	(.20)
3. Convertibles only				
U.S. only (N = 184)	.117	.176	.018	.031
	(21.34)	(13.11)	(2.80)	(1.97)
4. Convertibles and equity				
U.S. only (N = 115)	.101	.143	−.004	.009
	(12.50)	(7.23)	(−.42)	(.39)

Note: Entries are bid premia; t-statistics in parentheses. Bid premia are calculated using the market model. The months are defined as in table 8.4.

These results are further evidence that personal tax considerations do not satisfactorily explain the higher target bid premia in cash offers since the equity-or-cash option, though tax efficient, led to bid premia comparable to those in all-cash offers. Thus, the evidence contradicts hypothesis 1.

"Cash and Equity" Offers

"Cash and equity" bids provide the seller with a combination of cash and equity and have been used frequently in the United Kingdom. They appear to offer targets smaller bid premia than do cash-or-equity or all-cash bids, but higher premia than all-equity bids. Furthermore, there are no significant wealth effects to bidders in acquisitions involving cash and equity. The pattern in these bids thus appears to be an average of the results for the all-cash and all-equity offers discussed earlier.

Convertibles

Convertibles were extensively used in the United States in the 1960s (see table 8.2). As shown in table 8.5, target premia for bids involving convertibles (either alone or along with equity) coincided very closely with target premia for all-equity bids. For example, in the United States the month 0 target bid premium was 11.1 percent in all-equity bids (table 8.4), 11.7 percent in all-convertible bids, and 10.1 percent in bids involving both convertibles and equity. A major difference, however, has to do with the bidders. Whereas, as noted earlier, all-equity bids in the United States are associated with a negative wealth effect for acquirers in month 0, all-convertible bids were associated with a significant positive gain (1.8 percent) for acquirers in month 0.

8.7.4 Bid Premia: Further Analysis

Variations over Time

The differences in bid premia between all-cash and all-equity offers shown in table 8.4 may be attributable to variations over calendar years in the performance of acquisitions. This issue is less important in the U.K. data because all-cash and all-equity offers took place over the entire 30-year period in that country.

Table 8.7   **Wealth Effects in U.S. Acquisitions, Partitioned by Time and by Tender Versus Nontender**

A. Time

Time Period	Offer	N	Target BP Month 0	(t-stat)	N	Bidder BP Month 0	(t-stat)
1970–74	All cash	34	.252	(12.35)	21	.066	(3.41)
	All equity	107	.127	(10.88)	80	.006	(.57)
1975–79	All cash	185	.304	(27.84)	85	.012	(1.31)
	All equity	92	.169	(12.45)	75	−.014	(−1.46)
1980–84	All cash	249	.220	(32.39)	90	.018	(1.73)
	All equity	97	.145	(13.79)	64	−.039	(−3.99)

B. Tender vs. Nontender

Offer	N	Target Month 0	Target Month −4 to +1	N	Bidder Month 0	Bidder Month −4 to +1
Tenders all cash	135	.283 (35.20)	.411 (20.87)	78	.014 (1.84)	.025 (1.34)
Tenders all equity	29	.201 (12.50)	.243 (6.17)	23	−.019 (−1.13)	−.060 (−1.46)
Nontender all cash	340	.243 (31.66)	.343 (18.24)	123	.024 (3.00)	.026 (1.33)
Nontender all equity	548	.106 (22.75)	.151 (13.23)	419	−.008 (−2.02)	.009 (.93)

Note: Bid premia (*BP*) are calculated using the market model. Month 0 is the announcement date as defined in the text.

In panel A of table 8.7 we break our U.S. data into three five-year periods beginning with 1970, the onset of significant use of all-cash offers. As the figures show, the month 0 bid premium estimates for the targets was higher in all-cash offers than in all-equity offers in each of the five-year periods. The same patterns hold for the six-month bid premia (not shown here). In addition, in all-equity offers the wealth effects for bidders were consistently lower than in all-cash offers, and they were negative in both the 1975–79 and the 1980–84 period, though significantly so only in the latter. Panel A shows that differences between the wealth effects of all-equity and all-cash bids in the United States cannot be attributed to a particular time period.

Tender and Nontender Offers

Earlier research on acquisitions in the United States has indicated that shareholder wealth effects may be different in tender offers and mergers. For example, surveying a number of studies, Jensen and Ruback (1983) reported acquiree bid premiums of 30 percent in tenders but only 20 percent in mergers; for acquirers the figures are 4 percent and zero percent, respectively. Panel B of table 8.7 shows the data we used to investigate whether the disparity between wealth effects in all-cash and all-equity can be attributed to a greater use of cash in tenders. The data indicate that all-cash bids resulted in higher acquiree bid premia, whether the takeover was a tender or not. Furthermore, panel B suggests that after having controlled for the medium of exchange, a difference in bid premia remains between mergers and tenders. For example, the 28.3 percent premia in all-cash tenders (in month 0) is significantly higher than the 24.3 percent figure in all-cash offers that are not tenders ($t = 3.60$). Panel B also shows that a high proportion of tenders used cash as the form of financing.

Turning to the results for acquirers in Panel B, we find the announcement month wealth effect to acquirers making all-equity bids was negative in both tenders and nontenders, although the sample size is small for all-equity tenders. In contrast, the announcement month wealth effects were positive in all-cash offers whether the bid was a tender or not. Panel B therefore suggests that the medium of exchange and the response of acquirers' share prices are related.[9]

Revised and Unrevised Bids

In table 8.8 we use the U.S. data to test whether the differences in all-cash and all-equity bid premiums (partitioned by tender and merger) are due to the contested nature of the bids. We have evidence from Franks and Harris (1986a) that bid revisions, even when unaccompanied by contestants, show similar wealth effects to contested bids. As a result we partition offers into those that are unrevised and uncontested and those that are revised or contested.

Panel A shows, for unrevised bids, the target bid premia in all-cash tenders were slightly higher than those in all-cash mergers (with six-month bid premia of .384 and .345, respectively). The target bid premia were significantly higher in all-equity tenders (.258) than in all-equity mergers (.154). For bids that were revised or contested a similar pattern emerges, although the difference between tenders and mergers is larger. We can conclude that all-cash bids still provide much larger premia

Table 8.8   **Bid Premia for Multiple Bids (Revised or Contested) versus Single Bids (Unrevised and Uncontested), Partitioned by Tender and Merger, U.S. Data**

	Month 0		Months −4 to +1	
	Unrevised and Uncontested	Revised or Contested	Unrevised and Uncontested	Revised or Contested
A. Targets				
Mergers				
All cash	.247	.240	.345	.328
	(29.80)	(19.77)	(21.62)	(11.95)
	N = 297	N = 85	N = 297	N = 85
All equity	.106	.116	.154	.136
	(19.49)	(10.62)	(11.93)	(4.02)
	N = 505	N = 89	N = 505	N = 89
Tenders				
All cash	.267	.265	.384	.466
	(31.43)	(23.88)	(13.97)	(14.52)
	N = 103	N = 74	N = 103	N = 74
All equity	.242	.192	.258	.293
	(11.22)	(9.52)	(3.85)	(.71)
	N = 18	N = 14	N = 18	N = 14
B. Bidders				
Mergers				
All cash	.026	.016	.029	.023
	(3.13)	(.93)	(1.57)	(.61)
	N = 111	N = 32	N = 111	N = 32
All equity	−.005	−.023	.012	−.024
	(−1.12)	(−2.07)	(1.20)	(.95)
	N = 389	N = 68	N = 389	N = 68
Tenders				
All cash	.016	.011	.026	.045
	(1.96)	(.97)	(1.48)	(1.73)
	N = 67	N = 38	N = 67	N = 38
All equity	−.031	−.021	−.076	−.092
	(−1.19)	(−1.04)	(−1.26)	(−1.18)
	N = 14	N = 12	N = 14	N = 12

Note: Entries are bid premia; *t*-statistics in parentheses. Bid premia are calculated using the market model. Month 0 is the announcement date as defined in the text.

than all-equity bids even after controlling for the form and contested nature of the merger and that tenders still provide larger bid premia than mergers.

Table 8.8 also shows that a larger proportion of all-cash than all-equity bids are revised. If we look at the medium of exchange in the final bid, 28.4 percent of the all-cash bids were contested or revised, whereas only 16.5 percent of the all-equity bids were. From Fishman's model we might have expected the converse: His model predicts that contested bids will occur more frequently in low-value equity bids than in high-value cash bids. In the latter case, the bidder has placed a high value on the target and uses a cash offer to preempt competing bids. In fact, competition appears to be more closely associated with cash than with equity offers. It should be noted, however, that a final cash bid may have evolved from an initial equity bid, although Callison's (1987) data show that of 54 all-cash tenders, only one was preceded by an equity offer.

Panel B of table 8.8 shows the wealth gains for bidders. Gains to bidders appear small, and if anything they were larger in all-cash take-overs than in all-equity bids.

8.7.5   Cross-Sectional Analysis

To investigate further the patterns in acquiree bid premia, we estimate the following cross-sectional regression:

$$BP = a_0 + a_1D_1 + a_2D_2 + a_3D_3 + a_4D_4 + \epsilon,$$

where BP is the estimated bid premium
$\quad D_1$ = 1 if all-cash offer, 0 otherwise
$\quad D_2$ = 1 if tender offer, 0 otherwise
$\quad D_3$ = 1 if contested bid, 0 otherwise
$\quad D_4$ = 1 if revised bid, 0 otherwise
$\quad \epsilon$ = a random error term with zero mean.

Only all-cash and all-equity offers in the United States are included in the regression. Furthermore, since the regression results are qualitatively similar for all three models of forming control returns, we report results for the market model only and bid premiums only for the six-month period around the announcement date. The results are (t-values in parentheses):

$$BP = .163 + .148D_1 + .081D_2 + .038D_3 + .025D_4$$
$$\quad (14.94) \quad (6.43) \quad\quad (3.15) \quad\quad (1.66) \quad\quad (.98)$$

$$R^2 = .08, F = 20.8$$

Although the regression has a low R^2, in part due to the measurement error for individual company bid premia, the F value of 20.8 is statistically significant at better than the .001 level. The results show that acquiree bid premia were larger in contested or revised bids and were significantly larger in tender offers (coefficient of .081). Even having controlled for these effects, however, the all-cash offers appear to coincide with larger acquiree bid premia. The coefficient of .148 (14.8 percent) is significantly different from zero at better than the .001 level. In fact, the medium of exchange has a larger impact than any of the other three effects. The regression results thus suggest that in the United States the medium of exchange is significantly related to bid premia and that this result is not an artifact of other commonly studied characteristics of the data.

We found qualitatively similar regression results for the U.K. data after controlling for schemes of arrangement, contested or revised bids, and time period (a series of dummy variables). The coefficient on D_1 was .104 with a t-statistic of 2.74.

8.8   Postmerger Performance

In their review of studies on U.S. acquisitions, Jensen and Ruback (1983) suggested several possible reasons for the common finding of negative returns following merger. They concluded (p.22) that "explanation of the post-event negative abnormal returns is currently an unsettled issue." Table 8.9 reports estimates of postmerger performance in all-cash and all-equity bids. The results are calculated as the average cumulative return—BP from equation (8)—over the two-year period covering months $+1$ to $+24$. For the purposes of measuring postmerger performance in the United Kingdom, month 0 is the date when the merger was unconditionally accepted; and for the United States, it is the date of the final bid. Four methods of forming control returns are used to test the robustness of the results.

8.8.1   Results for the United States

Panel A of table 8.9 shows that in the United States there is a marked difference between the postmerger performance of all-cash and all-equity bids. Acquirers using all cash did better after merger than did all-equity bidders, no matter what control return is used. The control returns (benchmarks) do, however, give rise to quite different figures for whether postmerger performance is positive, zero, or negative. These results highlight the importance of forming an efficient benchmark (see Grinblatt and Titman 1986).

Table 8.9   Postmerger Performance in All Cash and All Equity Acquisitions

A. *United States*

	Premerger α, β Market Model[a]	$\alpha = 0$ $\beta = 1.0$	CAPM[b]	Postmerger α, β Market Model[c]
All cash	.028 (.70, 55)	−.036 (−1.03, 52)	−.034 (−.95, 51)	.094 (1.59, 53)
All equity	−.184 (−7.73, 36)	−.179 (−9.31, 34)	−.178 (−8.97, 34)	−.018 (−.69, 46)

	α	β	N
All cash			
Premerger	−.003	.99	201
Postmerger	−.007	1.04	127
All equity			
Premerger	.000	.99	442
Postmerger	−.006	.99	392

B. *United Kingdom*

	Premerger α, β Market Model[a]	CAPM[b]
All cash: N = 221 $\alpha = .008$, $\beta = 1.07$	.017 (.50, 53)	.175 (6.09, 65)
All equity: N = 207 $\alpha = .011$, $\beta = 1.07$	−0.094 (−2.31, 51)	.042 (1.23, 64)

Note: Entries are bid premia for months +1 to +24. For the U.K., results month 0 is the unconditional date of the merger. For the U.S., results month 0 is the date of the final bid. The figures in parentheses are *t*-statistics and percent positive. For this table, the *t*-statistic is calculated as BP/SE, where SE is the standard error of the mean.

[a]A market value–weighted average of α and β values for the acquiree and acquirer were also used as parameters in the market model to determine control returns. They showed very similar results as the unweighted parameters.

[b]When β was estimated as the market value–weighted average of betas for the acquiree and acquirer, the results were similar. CAPM is the capital asset pricing model.

[c]The α and β values here are calculated over period $t = +25$ months to +60 months (with a minimum of 24 months of data).

Using either a market model with "premerger" estimated parameters (calculated from six years to one year prior to the bid) or a simple $\alpha = 0$, $\beta = 1.0$ model, we find postmerger abnormal returns were essentially zero in all-cash offers but significantly negative in all-equity offers. It can be argued, however, that these results reflect the use of an inappropriate benchmark, since there may be shifts in a firm's expected returns and risks associated with acquisitions.[10] We therefore estimated α and β values in the market model from a postmerger period producing essentially zero postmerger returns for all-equity offers and positive (though not statistically significant) postmerger returns in all-cash offers. These changes stem from the noticeable reductions in the estimated α values when going from the premerger (six through one years before the bid) to the postmerger (three through five years after the bid) period. The average postmerger α values are negative for both all-cash and all-equity offers.

In summary, acquirers that made all-cash bids on average did not suffer postmerger losses and did better than the bidders that made all-equity offers. Whether all-equity bidders have postmerger losses depends on the benchmark employed. Compared with premerger performance, postmerger returns are negative. But using a benchmark based on postmerger parameters, we find all-equity acquirers did not experience abnormal losses in the two years after an acquisition, but they did have negative α values three to five years after the acquisition.

Given the heavy use of equity in the 1960s, a possible explanation for these different results for cash and equity offers is that they are due to the date of the takeover rather than the medium of exchange.[11] Nonetheless, we found qualitatively similar results (using premerger parameters) when we divided the post-1970 subsample into five-year subperiods (post 1970). The results suggest that the medium of exchange plays an important role in the postmerger performance of acquiring firms in the United States. We can speculate that this role may be related to information asymmetries that may motivate equity rather than cash bids in situations in which the acquirer's equity is overvalued by the market.

8.8.2   Results for the United Kingdom

Panel B of table 8.9 shows that postmerger performance results in the United Kingdom are highly dependent on the formation of control returns. As in the United States, all-equity offers had significantly worse postmerger performance than did all-cash offers. The difference appears to be in the 11 percent to 15 percent range. For example, using the market model, we find postmerger performance in all-equity offers was -9.4 percent, which is 11.1 percentage points lower than the 1.7 percent return in all-cash offers.

The issue that remains unresolved is whether postmerger performance in all-equity takeovers was less than zero. The significant negative figures resulting from use of the market model were essentially the result of the very high premerger α values for the acquirers in all-equity deals ($\alpha = 0.011$ per month, or over 12 percent per year). If one applies the capital asset pricing model, the all-equity takeovers appear to have had small positive bidder returns after merger, and in all-cash offers the bidders had large positive returns of 17.5 percent.

As was the case in the United States, further exploration of these results will be necessary.[12]

8.9 Conclusion

In this paper we have examined the means of payment used in a large set of acquisitions in the United Kingdom and the United States over the years 1955–85. Using data on financing proportions, bid premia, and postmerger performance we tested the validity of several tax and information hypotheses in the literature. Our findings show that it is difficult to explain many of the results in terms of tax effects. The capital gains tax did not appear to be a primary determinant of financing patterns in the United Kingdom during a period in which there were substantial variations in the tax rate. Our data also show that the "trapped equity" model is inconsistent with financing patterns. We could not reject stepped-up basis as an explanation for the substantial increase in cash-financing proportions in the United States, but our data were insufficient to provide a convincing test.

The second set of empirical results we presented concerned wealth gains around the announcement of mergers. In both countries we observed that the bid premia associated with cash bids were much larger than those associated with equity bids. This finding is consistent with Fishman's model that high-valuing bidders make cash offers, and low-valuing bidders make securities offers. After controlling for the form of finance, we found that much of the difference in bid premia between tenders and mergers disappeared. We also examined whether the effects of revised or contested bids could explain the higher bid premia accruing to targets in cash offers than to those in equity offers. After controlling for the form of takeover (tender versus merger) and the contested nature of the bid, we found that cash offers still provided substantially higher wealth gains to shareholders. Moreover, U.S. bidders that offered all equity suffered significant abnormal losses at the time of the bid announcement, consistent with the findings on the wealth effects of seasoned new equity offerings in the United States. Finally, acquirers that made cash offers had better postmerger performance than did those that made all-equity offers. These results support an overvaluation hypothesis, but they are inconsistent with theories of efficient capital markets.

Our findings suggest at least two directions for future work. First, because our results on postmerger performance were sensitive to the benchmark used, further investigation of this topic is warranted (see Loderer and Mauer, 1986). Second, after focusing on the means of payment in takeovers, we believe further insights into the relationships between financing decisions and acquisition performance could be gained by incorporating detailed information on the capital structures of the merging firms.

Notes

1. King's model contains no feature that distinguishes between acquisitions and new investment.

2. It is crucial to Myers and Majluf's argument that all projects have a zero or positive net present value (see idem., 203–4) If projects could have a negative net present value, giving up a new project and not issuing equity may not be good news.

3. Jensen's (1986) theory of free cash flow could also be used to yield the same prediction, since increasing the debt ratio of the bidder (via a cash offer) enables managers to bond their promise to pay future cash flows. See also Grossman and Hart (1982).

4. For the earliest calendar years of our U.K. analysis, prior data were unavailable to calculate α and β. In these cases companies were assigned $\alpha = 0$, $\beta = 1.0$. Our adjustment for thin trading regresses company returns on the market return and one-month leads and lags on the market. The three coefficients in the multiple regression were summed to obtain β.

5. Data from W. T. Grimm show the same upward trend in the use of cash in U.S. acquisitions (and the same decline in the use of stock) beginning around 1970, although the data also reveal that cash was used in the 1960s (the series begins in 1964). Differences in samples probably account for variations in financing proportions. Grimm's data include acquisitions and divestitures of both public and private companies, whereas our data are limited to acquisitions of exchange-listed companies. The latter are, on average, larger concerns.

6. An examination of Department of Trade and Industry (DTI) data on the financing of acquisitions reveals similar changes in financing proportions around the time of the major tax changes discussed here. These data differ from ours primarily in the population from which their samples are drawn. Our data refer to acquisitions by companies that were quoted on the London Stock Exchange. The DTI data are obtained from reports in the British financial press about mergers and acquisitions. We would argue that there is some merit in using data on quoted companies in a study of the financing of acquisitions, on the grounds that the impediments to the choice of financing are less for quoted than unquoted companies. A comparison of the two samples is outlined below.

	Proportion (value-weighted) financed by cash:	
Years	Our sample	DTI sample
1970–74	0.28	0.32
1975–79	0.38	0.59
1980–84	0.47	0.54†

†Up to the third quarter of 1983 only.

7. Significance tests for the difference between two cell means $(M_1 - M_2)$ are based on a t-statistic calculated as $t = (M_1 - M_2)/SD$, where $SD = \sqrt{\sigma_1^2 + \sigma_2^2}$ and σ is the standard deviation used to calculate the bid premia (BP) for the cell mean; in other words, $\sigma_1 = \sigma_{BP}$ for cell 1.

8. As confirming statistical tests, we examined the percentage of companies with positive returns and an alternate method of calculating a t-statistic. For the 200 acquirers making all-cash bids, 59 percent had positive abnormal returns

in month 0, whereas only 46 percent of the 442 acquirers in all-equity bids had positive abnormal returns in that month. We also calculated a t-statistic defined as the mean abnormal return divided by the standard error of the mean. For month 0 this produced $t = 2.99$ in all-cash bids and $t = -2.14$ in all-equity bids.

9. In our U.K. sample over 90 percent of the acquisitions took a form similar to that for the U.S. tenders (see Franks and Harris 1986a), the remaining 10 percent having been schemes of arrangement that required a shareholders' meeting convened under a court's direction. In schemes of arrangement the merger can be consummated if more than 75 percent of the votes cast by those present and voting are in favor of the proposal. Because of the relatively small number of schemes of arrangement, any differences in results for this type of merger are not likely to have a large effect on our U.K. results. Nonetheless, we partitioned our U.K. data into schemes of arrangement that were all-cash bids and those that were all-equity bids. The target bid premia were significantly lower in all-equity bids than in all-cash bids.

10. For example, the merger is combining two firms and hence may change the business mix of the acquirer (but see notes c and d of table 8.9). In addition, a cash offer may be accompanied by an increase in financial leverage, thus increasing risk. Providing some support for this is the fact that in all-cash offers the postmerger β (1.04) exceeded the premerger β (.99).

11. We also examined use of a value-weighted market index in measuring postmerger performance in the United States. Using an $\alpha = 0$, $\beta = 1.0$ model with a value-weighted index, we found all-cash acquirers had positive (.06) abnormal returns over the 24-month period ($t = 1.71$), whereas all-equity acquirers still displayed significant negative postmerger performance (of .111, $t = -5.54$). To further examine the role that firm size may play in postmerger performance in the United States, we subdivided the sample into quintiles and measured the postmerger performance of each portion. The smallest acquirers appeared to outperform the largest acquirers when we used both a market model (with postmerger α and β values) and an $\alpha = 0$ and $\beta = 1$ model. The results were:

Ranking by Market Capitalization	$\alpha = 0$ $\beta = 1$ $N = 195$	Postmerger Market Model	
1 Smallest	$-.078$	.009	$N = 153$
2	$-.102$	.030	$N = 164$
3	$-.135$	.063	$N = 169$
4	$-.194$	$-.104$	$N = 165$
5 Largest	$-.174$	$-.098$	$N = 145$

12. One possible explanation for our postmerger performance results may be related to size effects not captured in our formation of control returns (see Dimson and Marsh 1986). We have some evidence suggesting, however, that such size effects cannot fully explain our results. First, as shown in table 8.4, in the United States the average size of all-equity and all-cash acquirers was quite similar both before and after merger. In the United Kingdom all-cash acquirers were larger than all-equity acquirers. As a result, we cannot explain the poorer postmerger performance of the all-equity acquirers on the basis of

their being larger than the all-cash acquirers. Second, our use of postmerger parameters (α and β) should capture, at least in part, changes in a firm's return-generating process due to an increase in size as of the merger date. (See note 11, above.)

References

Asquith, Paul, R. Bruner, F. Mullins. 1986. Merger returns and the form of financing, photocopy. Boston: Harvard Business School, October.

Auerbach, A. J. 1979. Wealth maximization and the cost of capital. *Quarterly Journal of Economics* 93: 443–46.

Auerbach, A. J., and D. Reishus. 1987. The effect of taxation on the merger decision, photocopy. Cambridge, Mass.: National Bureau of Economic Research.

Brown, S. J., and J. B. Warner. 1980. Measuring security price performance. *Journal of Financial Economics* 8: 205–58.

———. 1985. Using daily stock returns: The case of event studies. *Journal of Financial Economics* 14: 3–31.

Brown, S. J., and M. Weinstein. 1985. Derived factors in event studies. *Journal of Financial Economics* 14: 491–6.

Callison, J. Elizabeth. 1987. An analysis of bid premiums and acquisition offers for *Forbes* 500 firms: 1979–83, Ph. D. dissertation. Philadelphia: University of Pennsylvania.

The Capital Changes Reporter. Chicago: Commerce Clearing House.

Carleton, W., D. Guilkey, R. Harris, and J. Stewart. 1983. An empirical analysis of the role of the medium of exchange in mergers. *Journal of Finance* 38: 813–26.

Dimson, E. 1979. Risk measurement when shares are subject to infrequent trading. *Journal of Financial Economics* 7: 197–226.

Dimson, E., and P. Marsh. 1983. The stability of U.K. risk measures and the problem of thin trading. *Journal of Finance* 38: 735–83.

———. 1986. Event study methodologies and the size effect: The case of U.K. press recommendations. *Journal of Financial Economics* 17: 113–42.

Dodd, P., and R. Ruback. 1977. Tender offers and stockholder returns: An empirical analysis. *Journal of Financial Economics* 5: 351–74.

Eckbo, E., and H. Langohr. 1986. Disclosure regulations and determinants of takeover premiums, working paper. Los Angeles: University of California, May.

Edwards, S. J., and M. J. Keen. 1985. Taxation, investment and marginal Q. *Review of Economic Studies* 52: 665–79.

Fama, E., L. Fisher, M. C. Jensen, and R. Roll. 1969. The adjustment of stock prices to new information. *International Economic Review* 10: 1–21.

Fishman M. J. 1986. Pre-emptive bidding and the role of the medium of exchange in acquisitions, photocopy. Evanston, Ill.: Northwestern University, July.

Franks, J., and R. Harris, 1986a. Shareholder wealth effects of corporate takeovers: The U.K. experience, 1955–85, working paper. London: London Business School; Chapel Hill: University of North Carolina; November.

————. 1986b. The role of the Mergers and Monopolies Commission in merger policy. *Oxford Review of Economic Policy* 2: 58–78.

Grinblatt, M., and S. Titman. 1987. A comparison of measures of abnormal performance on a sample of monthly mutual fund returns, photocopy. Los Angeles: University of California, February.

Grossman, S. J., and O. D. Hart. 1982. Corporate financial structure and managerial incentives. In *The economics of information and uncertainty,* ed. J. McCall, 107–40. Chicago: University of Chicago Press.

Hansen, R. G. 1984. Informational asymmetry and the means of payment in auctions, working paper. Hanover, N.H.: Amos Tuck School, Dartmouth College.

Hansen, R. G. 1987. A theory for the choice of exchange medium in mergers and acquisitions. *Journal of Business* 60: 75–95.

Heinkel, R., and E. Schwartz. 1985. Rights versus underwritten offerings: An asymmetric information approach. *Journal of Finance* 41: 1–18.

Jensen, M. C. 1986. Agency costs of free cash flow, corporate finance and takeovers. *American Economic Review* 75: 323–29.

Jensen, M. C., and R. Ruback. 1983. The market for corporate control: The scientific evidence. *Journal of Financial Economics* 11: 5–50.

King, M. A. 1977. *Public policy and the corporation.* London: Chapman and Hill.

————. 1986. Takeovers, taxes and the stock market, photocopy. London: London School of Economics.

Loderer, C.F., and D. Mauer. 1986. Acquiring firms in corporate mergers: The post merger performance, photocopy. West Lafayette, Ind.: Purdue University.

Marsh, P. 1979. Equity rights issues and the efficiency of the U.K. stock market. *Journal of Finance* 34: 839–62.

————. 1982. The choice between equity and debt: An empirical study. *Journal of Finance* 37: 121–44.

Mikkelson, W., and R. Ruback. 1985. An empirical study of the inter-firm equity investment process. *Journal of Financial Economics* 14: 523–54.

————. 1986. Targeted repurchases and common stock returns, working paper 1707–85. Cambridge: Sloan School of Management, Massachusetts Institute of Technology.

Miller, M., and K. Rock. 1985. Dividend policy under asymmetric information. *Journal of Finance* 40: 1031–51.

Myers, S. C. 1984. The capital structure puzzle. *Journal of Finance* 39: 575–92.

Myers, S. C., and N. S. Majluf. 1984. Corporate financing and investment decisions when firms have information that investors do not have. *Journal of Financial Economics* 13: 187–222.

Niden, C. 1986. The role of taxes in corporate acquisitions: Effects on premium and type of consideration, photocopy. Chicago: University of Chicago.

Roll, R. 1986. The hubris hypothesis of corporate takeovers. *Journal of Business* 59: 197–216.

Shoven, J. B., and L. B. Simon. 1987. Share repurchases and acquisitions: An analysis of which firms participate, working paper. Cambridge, Mass.: National Bureau of Economic Research.

Smith, C., Jr. 1986. Investment banking and capital acquisition process. *Journal of Financial Economics* 15: 3–29.

Wansley, J., W. Lane, and H. Yang. 1983. Abnormal returns to acquiring firms by type of acquisition and method of payment. *Financial Management* 12: 16–22.

Comment   Artur Raviv

Franks, Harris, and Mayer document several very interesting empirical regularities in the means of payment offered in takeovers. The most striking results are:

1. The percentage of all-cash offers in the United States increased over time, from none in 1955–59 to 58 percent in 1980–84. At the same time, all-equity offers declined from 76 percent to 22 percent.
2. The United Kingdom demonstrated the reverse pattern of changes over those years.
3. About one-sixth of the acquisitions in the sample were through a tender offer. Nontender, or "friendly," acquisitions are those obtained by an approving board of directors. The appreciation to the targets of tender offers was higher than to those in nontender acquisitions.

This paper can be best viewed as a fact-finding mission. Although the authors survey several propositions that might explain the empirical regularities, no simple theory can account for all the facts simultaneously. I would find it much easier to evaluate the results if a coherent model had been constructed and then tested by the empirical results. Obviously, this would not be an easy task since the problem attacked by the authors is at the core of the unsolved problems in corporate finance: capital structure, taxation, and corporate control.

In the remainder of my comments I would like to propose an alternative model, which in my view is capable of explaining many of the results given by the authors. This model has been developed by Michael Fishman in a working paper entitled "Preemptive Bidding and the Role of the Medium of Exchange in Acquisitions." Here the key economic difference between a cash offer and an offer of securities is that the value of a cash offer is independent of the future profitability of the acquired target, while the value of a securities offer is not. The willingness to offer or accept a given package of securities may indicate something about the information held by the bidder and the target. In particular, if target managers possess private information regarding the profitability of their firm, they will want to use this information in making their decisions whether to accept a securities offer since the value of this offer depends on the future profitability of the target. Thus, securities offers are a means of making an offer contingent on the target's information. In Fishman's model a bidder learns about the profitability of the target, and if his valuation is high, makes a high, *preemptive* bid in order to eliminate potential competition. This bid is in the form of cash. If the bidder's

Artur Raviv is the Harold L. Stuart Professor of Finance and Managerial Economics at the J. L. Kellogg Graduate School of Management, Northwestern University.

valuation is lower, he will make a securities offer, which will induce an efficient accept/reject decision on the part of the target but may also induce competitors to join the bidding for the target.

The results that can be obtained from such a model are:

1. Cash offers are more frequent in tender offers than in nontender offers. In tender offers target managers do not use their information and therefore there is no need for equity payment. Equity is used in the case of nontender offers.
2. Cash offers are higher on average than equity offers. Equity signals lower value and induces competition.
3. The postmerger performance of the bidder, if the initial offer is for cash, is better than if the initial offer is for equity.
4. The postmerger performance for tender offers (which tend to be for cash) is better than that for nontender offers (which tend to be for equity).

These results are consistent with the Franks, Harris, and Mayer evidence. Additional results implied by Fishman's model and which could be tested by the authors are:

1. Competing bidders appear more frequently in equity offers than in cash offers.
2. Target management will more frequently reject an equity offer than a cash offer.
3. Rejecting an equity offer will result in a reduction in the value of the target's shares, since it indicates that the target's managers believe the target is not as valuable now as it was.

It would be interesting to find out whether these results can be supported by the data the authors have analyzed.

Comment   Richard S. Ruback

Empirical evidence shows that the benefits of takeovers to the target's shareholders are large in mergers and even larger in tender offers. Although mergers and tender offers are substitutes, there are some general differences in the two types of takeover methods:

	Tender Offers	*Mergers*
Process	Through shares	Through management
Perception	Hostile	Negotiated
Payment	Cash	Stock

Richard S. Ruback is associate professor of finance at the Alfred P. Sloan School of Management, Massachusetts Institute of Technology; a visiting associate professor at the Harvard Business School; and a research associate of the National Bureau of Economic Research.

In Jensen and Ruback (1983) we focused on the process difference to explain the larger measured average returns in tender offers than in mergers. Truncation bias could explain the higher *measured* average premiums in tender offers. Low-value merger bids that are rejected by managers do not become hostile tenders because it is more costly to persuade shareholders in hostile deals than in negotiated deals and because hostile deals are more expensive.

Franks, Harris, and Mayer emphasize the payment differences. In particular, they try to use theories of capital structure choice and theories of takeovers simultaneously.

The good part of this approach is that different takeovers do seem to involve different financing schemes, so that the measured effects of takeovers may include factors that are caused purely by the financial restructurings involved.

The bad part of this approach is that it layers ignorance on confusion. As a corporate finance person who works in both areas, I am afraid this is not a pleasant admission. Unfortunately, we have no accepted theory of the choice of takeover method. In contrast, we have many theories about capital structure choice. But none has survived even simple tests. And the interrelations among the many theories are obscure at best. Saying that the state of the art in capital structure choice is confused would be generous.

It is hard to fault the authors of this paper for the confusion of the theory. My complaint is *not* that the authors fail to develop a new theory of capital structure and merger choice. I am mentioning the lack of theory at the outset because it locates and defines what we learn from the authors. Their paper does not really test any particular theory. Instead, it makes perhaps a bigger contribution by providing numerous interesting facts.

The magnitude of the data collection and integration in this paper is huge and competently done. The sample contains merger and tender offer data for both the United States and the United Kindgom over the years 1955–85, including about 2,000 observations.

The facts that I find most interesting are in table 8.7. There, in panel B, the event month abnormal returns are:

Cash tenders	28%	N = 135
Cash nontenders	24%	N = 340
Equity tenders	20%	N = 29
Equity mergers	11%	N = 548

This ranking suggests that both the type of offer and the medium of exchange are important. The regression tests provide an affirmative statistical test of this proposition.

I cannot resist the temptation to explain the rankings. My hypothesis hinges on asymmetric information. Accept the Jensen and Ruback view that the market for corporate control involves competition between management teams for the rights to manage corporate resources. You would then expect most takeovers to be proxy fights.[1] But this is not true. Why? Because these contests require very "management smart" investors—investors that can evaluate the plans of competing management teams. Stockholders are unlikely to have the expertise or incentives to evaluate the plans accurately. Indeed, clever stockholders are efficient risk bearers: They hold a well-diversified portfolio and cannot remember the names of the firms in the portfolio, never mind how they should be managed.

What's a poor potential competing manager to do? Get somebody smarter to make the decision or simplify the decision. If target managers are cooperative, then a merger is more likely. And the range of payment types possible expands because the target managers certify to the shareholders that the takeover is a good deal.

But suppose the target management decides to oppose the merger. Also assume the deal is worthwhile to the bidder even if it becomes hostile. Then the offer has to be simplified. Bidders should use securities that are easy to value—like cash.

In short, the same forces that make some takeovers mergers instead of tender offers also make most tender offers cash transactions and most mergers stock transactions. This means that, as with any set of correlated variables, the attribution of results to particular variables is very risky.

The facts that confuse me the most are in table 8.8. It shows that there were significant negative abnormal returns in the two years following the offer. The returns were about -17.percent in the United States. I have been confused about this issue because we included a table of postmerger performance in Jensen and Ruback (1983) that had similar results. At the time I was convinced the results were due to selection bias or some simple statistical malfunction. Franks, Harris, and Mayer use almost all mergers, and so the selection bias argument now seems less plausible. They also use different specifications and get similar results. Reluctantly, I think we have to accept this result— significant negative returns over the two years following a merger—as a fact.

Accepting the fact does not mean I have to accept the explanation given. I do not believe there is an explanation for this phenomenon that is consistent with market prices, including the information in the *Wall Street Journal*. We finance folks call it semistrong market efficiency. Economists use the label rational expectations. Whatever you call it, this finding can be used to make money. I can tell when a merger

1. This conceptual framework is explained in more detail in Ruback (1984).

is completed. I can sell short. That gives me supernormal returns. And that violates market efficiency.

References

Jensen, Michael C., and Richard S. Ruback. 1983. The market for corporate control: The scientific evidence. *Journal of Financial Economics* 11(1-4): 5–50.

Ruback, Richard S. 1984. An economic view of the market for corporate control. *Delaware Journal of Corporate Law* 9 (3): 613–25.

9 A Time-Series Analysis of Mergers and Acquisitions in the U.S. Economy

Devra L. Golbe and Lawrence J. White

9.1 Introduction

The aggregate numbers and values of mergers and acquisitions in the U.S. economy of the 1980s have attracted a considerable amount of professional, political, and popular attention. Periodic announcements of large mergers or hostile tender offers continue to command media space and time. Something appears to be afoot in the American economy.

Surprisingly (at least to us), the widespread interest in takeovers has spawned relatively little effort to place the current wave in a proper historical context or to perform time-series analysis of the available merger and acquisition data.[1] Moreover, there has been virtually no effort to discuss the limitations of the available mergers and acquisitions data.

In this paper we attempt to help fill these gaps in our understanding of the topic. We first discuss the available time-series data on mergers and acquisitions and their suitability and limitations for time-series analysis; we also offer a historical perspective on the current merger wave. In section 9.3 we review the handful of previous time-series analyses of mergers and acquisitions. Section 9.4 develops a series of hypotheses on mergers that can be tested econometrically. In section 9.5 we discuss the specific methodology of our econometric tests,

Devra L. Golbe is associate professor of economics at Hunter College of the City University of New York. Lawrence J. White is a member of the Federal Home Loan Bank Board and professor of economics at the Graduate School of Business Administration, New York University.

The authors would like to thank Alan Auerbach, Steven Salop, and Robert Taggart for helpful comments on an earlier draft, and Charles Larson for research assistance.

describe our data sources, and provide the results of the tests. We conclude in section 9.6.

9.2   Data Series, Their Limitations, and Some Historical Patterns

9.2.1   Overview

Ideally, a time series on mergers and acquisitions should be comprehensive and consistent and should contain data that cover a long period of time. Unfortunately, none of the available series meets these criteria, and compromises must be made.

One limitation to all of the available series is especially serious and warrants preliminary discussion: No data series includes *every* merger and acquisition in the U.S. economy; all series have a lower limit on the nominal dollar size of the transactions reported. For example, one data series discussed below includes only those mergers in which the acquired firm had assets of $10 million or more. Thus, the purchase of Mabel's Coffee Shop by Sam's Garage—or even the "leveraged buyout" of Mabel's Coffee Shop by Mabel's manager and cashier, Doris—will not be reported in any data series.

This kind of limitation has four consequences. First and most obviously, the smaller transactions are neglected. If these smaller transactions are highly correlated with the larger, reported ones, or if the former are relatively unimportant in the aggregate, then little has been lost. But if otherwise, the series may provide a misleading picture of merger activity over time. (And, since the transactions below the lower limit are not recorded, there is no way to tell.)

Second, if the period covered by the time series was one of significant inflation, the fixed lower limit on dollar size will artificially inflate the number of recorded transactions over time. In essence, the pattern of rising prices over the time period covered by the series will mean that some transactions of a given real size will fall below the fixed cutoff point in the early years and hence not be recorded, whereas in later years inflation will drive the nominal value of identical transactions above the cutoff point and thus cause them to be recorded. The longer the time period covered by a series and the greater the inflation, the more substantial is this problem of a spurious increase in the number of recorded transactions. In addition, this problem is not easily corrected with a simple adjustment for inflation (for example, through the use of a price index or deflator), since one needs to know the shape of the distribution of the real size of merger transactions (and, as a further complication, the shape of that distribution may change over time).[2]

Third, a time series of the aggregate *value* of the reported transactions will be biased upward because of both a pure inflation effect[3] and the cutoff point problem just discussed.

Fourth, many merger announcements (especially those for smaller transactions involving privately held companies) do not provide specific merger terms or values. Consequently, the reporting services may have to guess whether a transaction should be included in their data series. And even if the reporting service is confident that a transaction is large enough to warrant inclusion in its series on the number of mergers and acquisitions, the absence of value information usually causes the service to exclude the transaction from its series on the aggregate value of those mergers and acquisitions. Accordingly, the time series on the aggregate value of the transactions are even less complete than the time series on the number of transactions.

9.2.2 The Available Data Series

Our discussion will first focus on the data available for the period after World War II and then discuss the data for the prewar period.

Post–World War II Data

There are three basic sources of time-series data on mergers and acquisitions for the postwar period: the U.S. Federal Trade Commission (FTC), the periodical *Mergers & Acquisitions,* and the annual reports of W.T. Grimm & Co. We will discuss each of these sources, the nature of the data, and their strengths and drawbacks, in turn.

FTC Data. The FTC collected and published data on mergers in the manufacturing and mining sectors of the U.S. economy for the years 1948–1979.[4] One basic data set covered all mergers in which the acquired firm was in the manufacturing or mining sectors and had at least $10 million in assets (book value) and for which information on the acquisition was publicly available.[5] The FTC published annual figures for both the number of mergers and the book value of the assets acquired. It also provided the relevant information on each transaction, so that quarterly series on numbers of mergers and their value could be constructed.

A second FTC series, which also covered the manufacturing and mining sectors, gave annual numbers of merger transactions extending from 1940 through 1979 and quarterly numbers extending from 1940 through 1954.[6] This second series appears to have been more inclusive than the first, since a far larger number of transactions were registered. But, unfortunately, the FTC did not indicate the inclusion criteria for this series.

The FTC data have a number of shortcomings. First, they cover only the manufacturing and mining sectors, which declined substantially in relative importance in the economy over the 1948–79 period and now constitute only a quarter of U.S. gross national product. Second, the $10 million lower limit obviously created an upward bias, since the general price level (as measured by the GNP deflator) tripled over the 32 years covered by the series. Third, the series excluded acquisitions by an individual or groups of individuals and hence would appear to exclude most leveraged buyouts of divisions or of whole companies. And finally, the FTC ceased collecting and publishing these data in 1981 (with 1979 as the last year for which data were made available), so the series do not cover the merger wave of the 1980s.

Mergers & Acquisitions Data. Quarterly issues of the periodical *Mergers & Acquisitions (M&A)* list the number of mergers and acquisitions consummated in recent quarters for the entire U.S. economy. Before the fourth quarter of 1980 the lower limit for inclusion in the series was a purchase price of at least $700,000; in that quarter the lower limit was raised to $1,000,000. A quarterly series on domestic companies being purchased (by either domestic or foreign companies) extends from the first quarter of 1967 to the present. Another series that also includes domestic companies' purchases of foreign companies extends from the fourth quarter of 1972 to the present. Both series include leveraged buyouts.

The *M&A* series have a number of drawbacks. First, they do not extend as far back in time as the FTC series. Second, the lower limit for inclusion changed abruptly in the middle of the series and, even so, did not properly adjust for the tripling of prices that occurred over the period covered. Third, efforts at integrating or splicing the *M&A* series with the FTC series (to create a longer overall series that would be up-to-date) pose problems of compatibility, since the series cover different universes and have different criteria for inclusion.

The Grimm Data. W.T. Grimm & Co. publishes data on the number of merger and acquisition announcements in the entire U.S. economy. The company's published annual series extends from 1963 through the present; its quarterly series extends from the first quarter of 1974 through the present. The lower limit for inclusion is a transaction involving at least a $500,000 purchase price.

The Grimm data have the same problems as the *M&A* data: a limited historical reach; a fixed lower limit for inclusion; and difficulties of integration with the FTC data. In addition, the Grimm data pertain to announcements rather than consummations.

Pre–World War II Data

The major source of merger data for the years 1895–1920 is the study conducted by Ralph Nelson (1959). Nelson's data appear to cover only the manufacturing and mining sectors. The cutoff limits are not explicit; rather, Nelson relied on financial reporting during the period covered.

Nelson provided annual and quarterly series[7] for the number of transactions and the book value of the acquired firms.[8]

For the years 1919–39 Willard Thorpe compiled a quarterly series
on the number of mergers in the manufacturing and mining sectors, a
series that was reproduced by Nelson (1959, 166–67). The criteria for
inclusion in the series are unclear. The Thorpe series was continued
in 1940 by the broad FTC series discussed above, and the two series
appear to be consistent and compatible.

A Summing Up

Although data series are available that include the merger and acquisition experience of the 1980s, these series do not extend back far
enough to provide an adequate historical perspective. The FTC data
do provide historical reach, but they end in 1979. Furthermore, the
FTC data exclude the services sectors, which are an increasingly important part of the U.S. economy. Finally, the inconsistencies between
the more recent data series and the FTC data complicate any efforts
at statistical inference. These problems will necessarily color the discussion and analysis below.

9.2.3   Some Historical Patterns

Having described the data series (and their drawbacks), we now
present a summary of the historical patterns they suggest. The graphs
below provide some indication of the consistency of the various data
sources as well as a historical perspective on mergers and acquisitions.

The FTC data are a basic source for research on merger activity.
Figure 9.1 shows the annual FTC data for the number of large mining
and manufacturing mergers and for "all" mining and manufacturing
mergers, that is, the broader series. As can be seen, the two series
track each other reasonably well. Both show a rise in the mid-1950s,
a more gradual rise in the late 1950s and early 1960s, and then a sharp
rise in the late 1960s (the "go-go years"[9]), followed by a steep decline
in the early 1970s and another increase in the late 1970s.

It is sometimes suggested that the values of the transactions matter
as much as, if not more than, the number of transactions. In fact, as
figure 9.2 suggests, both sets of FTC data indicate similar patterns.
This figure shows annual data for both the number of mergers and the
real value (in 1982 dollars[10]) of the assets acquired, as measured by the
FTC "large firm" series. Movements in the two series are fairly closely
correlated, and both series clearly show the peak of the "go-go years."

As noted above, a major drawback of the FTC series for our purposes
is their failure to include data on the current merger wave. To place
the recent experience in perspective, we need to splice more recent

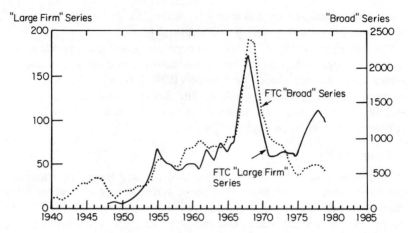

Fig. 9.1   Annual number of mergers and acquisitions: FTC "Large Firm" and "Broad" series for manufacturing and mining

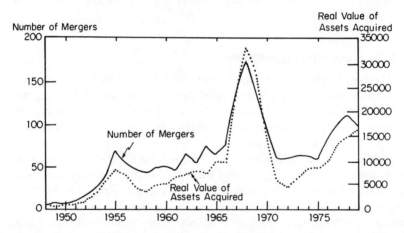

Fig. 9.2   Annual number of mergers and acquisitions and real value of assets acquired (in millions of 1982 dollars): FTC "Large Firm" series for manufacturing and mining

data together with an appropriate FTC series. Figure 9.3 shows the annual number of mergers measured by the "broad" FTC series and by the annual *M&A* series covering purchases of domestic companies. These two series appear to track each other reasonably well, with both showing the peak in the late 1960s. The *M&A* data clearly depict the boom of the 1980s.

Similarly, figure 9.4 presents quarterly data for the number of mergers measured by the FTC "large firm" series and by the *M&A* "domestic" series. These series, too, appear to track each other well.

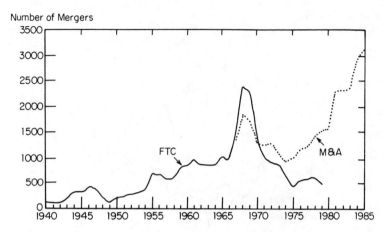

Number of Mergers

Fig. 9.3   Annual number of mergers and acquisitions: FTC "Broad" series and *M&A* "Domestic" series

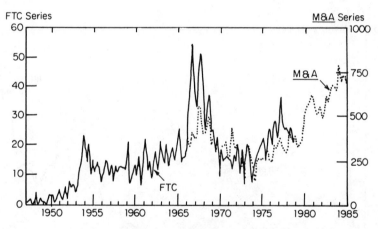

Fig. 9.4   Quarterly number of mergers and acquisitions: FTC "Large Firm" series and *M&A* "Domestic" series

Figure 9.5 allows us to compare the quarterly data in the current sources. It presents the quarterly Grimm data on the number of mergers, along with the "domestic" quarterly series from *M&A* and the more comprehensive quarterly series from *M&A*. The two *M&A* series track each other quite well, but the Grimm data for the 1970s diverge markedly from those in the other two series. The reasons for this divergence are unclear. As was explained above, the Grimm data have a lower cutoff point and pertain to announcements rather than completions. But it seems unlikely that these differences could account for the divergence.

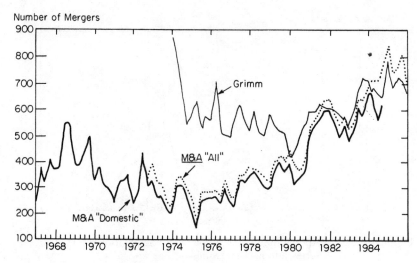

Fig. 9.5   Quarterly number of mergers and acquisitions: *M&A* "Domestic" series, *M&A* "All" series, and Grimm series

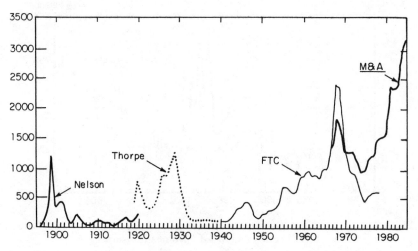

Fig. 9.6   Annual number of mergers and acquisitions: Nelson series, Thorpe series, FTC "Broad" series, and *M&A* "Domestic" series

A longer perspective appears in figure 9.6, which presents annual data on the number of mergers from the Nelson, Thorpe, FTC, and *M&A* "domestic" series. The data show four noticeable peaks or "waves":[11] around the turn of the century, in the late 1920s, in the late 1960s, and in the 1980s. Thus, the merger wave of the 1980s is not an entirely new phenomenon. Merger activity was significant in earlier periods. The previous graphs have provided merger data in terms of absolute numbers and real values. But the real size of the U.S. economy has grown substantially over the period covered. Consequently, the opportunities for mergers may have increased, and the relative importance of any particular merger of a given real size has clearly diminished over time. Accordingly, the merger data should be placed in a suitable historical context.

One possible measure for comparison would be a consistent time series on the number of business enterprises in the United States. This measure might proxy the possible opportunities for mergers among firms. Unfortunately, we were unable to find a satisfactory series that covers the entire period.

Instead, we have used real GNP as our comparison measure. By dividing the absolute number of mergers each year by the real GNP of that year, we achieve a relative measure that is the ratio of two flow measures: the annual number of mergers and acquisitions per billion dollars of real GNP. Figure 9.7 provides the time series for this relative measure (with real GNP measured in terms of billions of 1982 dollars). As can be seen, the peaks of merger activity at the turn of the century and in the late 1920s were much more important relative to the size of the economy at those times than has been true in the 1980s.[12]

The pattern displayed in figure 9.7 does not incorporate information on the size of the pool of companies that were candidates for mergers or the sizes of those firms. As we noted above, a time series covering

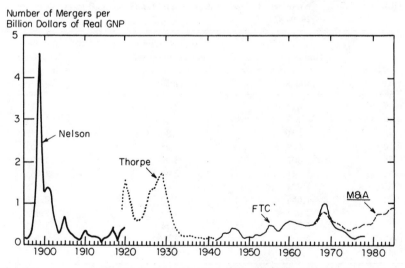

Fig. 9.7   Annual number of mergers and acquisitions per billion dollars of Real GNP (in 1982 dollars): Nelson series, Thorpe series, FTC "Broad" series, and *M&A* "Domestic" series

these characteristics is not available for a suitably long period. But data are available for the period since the late 1930s. As can be seen in table 9.1, the number of registered corporations in the U.S. economy has increased appreciably faster since 1939 than has the level of real GNP.[13] These relative increases held equally true for the period of the 1960s (the previous merger boom) through the early 1980s. Thus, the pattern shown in figure 9.7 *overstates* the relative importance of mergers in the 1980s as compared with the previous four decades if the pool of available merger partners is used as the basis of comparison. Because we do not have comparable data for the period before 1939, we can make no definitive statements about comparisons with the earlier merger peaks. But we strongly suspect that similar conclusions would hold for a longer period of comparison.

Further, the data in table 9.1 indicate that the average real size (as represented by sales expressed in 1982 dollars) of the firms in the available pool has been remarkably stable, except for a temporary increase in the mid-1940s that lasted until the mid-1950s. Thus, the conclusions that we drew with respect to the size of the available pool of merger partners are equally valid with respect to the size of the pool expressed in terms of the real value of sales.

A more direct measure of the relative importance of mergers, as measured by the annual value of merger transactions, is presented in figure 9.8. Here we have used the GNP deflator to achieve a measure

Table 9.1   Numbers of Corporations, Their Real Sizes, and Real GNP, 1939–82

Year	Number of corporations (in thousands)	Average sales per corporation (in millions of 1982 dollars†)	Real GNP (in billions of 1982 dollars)
1939	470	2.23	717
1940	473	2.41	773
1945	421	3.86	1,355
1950	629	3.05	1,204
1955	807	2.92	1,495
1960	1,141	2.40	1,665
1965	1,424	2.48	2,088
1970	1,665	2.50	2,416
1975	2,024	2.66	2,695
1980	2,711	2.74	3,187
1982	2,926	2.40	3,166
1983	2,999	2.23	3,279

Sources: U.S. Department of Commerce (1976); U.S. Department of Commerce, *Statistical Abstract*, various years.
†GNP deflator used, with 1982 = 1.00.

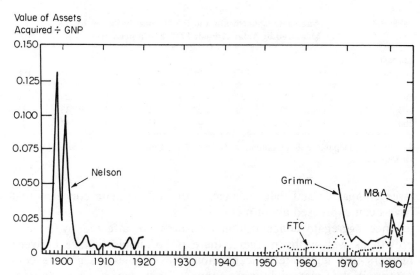

Fig. 9.8   Annual value of assets acquired relative to GNP: Nelson series, FTC "Large Firm" series, Grimm series, and *M&A* series

of the real annual value of mergers and have then divided that by real GNP.[14] The pattern shown in figure 9.8 is consistent with that of figure 9.7: The merger wave at the turn of the century was much larger relative to the size of the economy than was the wave of the late 1960s or the wave, thus far, of the 1980s.

9.2.4   Data on Aggregate Concentration

The time series in figures 9.7 and 9.8, which show that the data on the absolute numbers and values of mergers and acquisitions in the 1980s may give a misleading impression as to their relative importance in the U.S. economy, are echoed by another set of data: recent calculations of the trends in aggregate concentration in the U.S. economy.

Aggregate concentration is a measure of the percentage of some aggregate economic variable (such as assets, employment, sales, value added) accounted for by the largest X (such as 100, 200, . . .) firms in the nation's economy. Comparisons of aggregate concentration over time indicate the rate at which the largest firms in the economy have been growing (including growth through merger) relative to the size of the overall economy. Since the aggregate concentration measure transcends (by far) the boundaries of economic markets, it has no use as an indication of competitiveness. Instead, it may provide some indication of the concentration (and trends in concentration over time) of social and political power that may reside in a comparative handful of

Table 9.2   Aggregate Concentration in the Manufacturing Sector, as
                   Measured by Value Added, 1947–82 (in percent)

Largest companies	1947	1954	1958	1963	1967	1972	1977	1982
50	17	23	23	25	25	25	24	24
100	23	30	30	33	33	33	33	33
200	30	37	38	41	42	43	44	44

Source: U.S. Department of Commerce, Bureau of the Census, *Census of Manufactures*, various years.

large companies and their managers—one of the main concerns that have been expressed about mergers.[15]

Since aggregate concentration measures are affected by internal growth as well as by mergers, there is no simple linkage between mergers and aggregate concentration. Nevertheless, aggregate concentration data may yield some support for the impressions we have gained from the merger data.

Table 9.2 provides data on postwar aggregate concentration (as measured by value added) for the manufacturing sector of the U.S. economy. Aggregate concentration rose through the early 1960s but has remained stable since then, despite the merger wave of the 1960s and the early 1980s. (The increases through the early 1960s were primarily the result of internal growth by large firms in industries that were expanding—for example, motor vehicles, petroleum, tires, chemicals, electrical equipment—rather than of mergers.) This stability, then, is consistent with the relatively modest role that mergers seem to have recently played in the U.S. economy.

The manufacturing sector, however, is only a quarter of U.S. GNP and has been declining in relative importance. Thus, a wider measure of aggregate concentration would be useful.

Table 9.3 provides data on aggregate concentration across the entire private sector of the U.S. economy, as measured by employment and by corporate profits.[16] The data, compiled from the *Fortune* magazine lists of the 1,000 largest manufacturing and mining companies and the 50 largest companies in each of six services areas, indicate that aggregate concentration as measured by employment declined over the period 1972–80. The profits measure shows a general decline through 1979 but then a sharp increase in 1980. It is likely that this last movement was simply a temporary consequence of the increase in oil prices in 1979 and their effects on oil company profits, rather than a reversal of the trend. (The continued downward trend in employment concentration in 1980 supports this interpretation.)

Table 9.3   **Aggregate Concentration in the Entire Private Sector, as Measured by Employment and by Profits, 1972–80 (in percent)**

Largest companies	1972	1973	1974	1975	1976	1977	1978	1979	1980
	Share of nonfarm private sector employment								
100	18.2	—	—	—	—	17.3	—	16.7	16.6
200	23.9	—	—	—	—	22.7	—	22.6	22.1
1,300	37.3	37.4	37.0	36.5	36.1	35.5	34.7	34.2	34.0
	Share of corporate profits after taxes								
100	43.3	—	—	—	—	39.8	—	39.4	44.9
200	55.4	—	—	—	—	50.2	—	49.9	56.5
1,300	76.6	75.1	72.6	71.4	73.8	71.4	70.4	71.1	75.6

Source: White (1981b).

Table 9.4   **Aggregate Concentration in the Entire Private Sector, as Measured by Employment and by Assets, 1970–84 (in percent)**

Largest companies	1970	1975	1980	1984
	Share of nonfarm private sector employment			
25	10.2	9.9	8.9	7.4
100	18.8	17.7	16.6	15.1
200	24.5	23.3	22.1	20.5
	Share of assets of nonfinancial corporations			
25	16.9	17.0	16.0	12.7
100	29.1	29.2	28.0	26.6
200	37.9	37.7	35.9	34.1

Source: Ginsberg (1986); U.S. Department of Justice (1986).

Unfortunately, subsequent changes in the way the *Fortune* lists are compiled make extensions of the 1972–80 data difficult. But the U.S. Department of Justice has recently compiled similar aggregate concentration calculations that yield comparisons through 1984. These data are shown in table 9.4.[17] The data in this table tell a similar story to that told by the data covering the 1970s: Aggregate concentration has not risen, and probably has declined modestly, despite the merger wave of the 1980s.

In sum, aggregate concentration data, both for the manufacturing sector alone and for the entire private business sector, are consistent with the merger data in figures 9.7 and 9.8. Thus, although the absolute numbers and values of mergers in the 1980s are impressive, they are still relatively modest when placed in the context of the size of the U.S. economy of the 1980s.

9.3   Previous Time-Series Studies of Mergers and Acquisitions

As we noted in the introduction, the previous literature that employed time-series analyses of mergers and acquisitions has been sparse. We now offer a brief review of that literature.[18]

9.3.1   Weston

Weston (1953) examined annual merger data for the period between the two World Wars. Employing a multiple regression analysis, he found that mergers were significantly and positively related to securities prices and to wholesale commodity prices but were not significantly related to industrial production levels.

9.3.2   Nelson

Nelson (1959) looked at quarterly merger data stretching from 1895 through 1956, with his primary focus on the years 1895–1920. Much of his book is spent on describing the sources and methodology he used in compiling his 1895–1920 data and the descriptive qualities of those data. Nelson did, however, explore a number of hypotheses concerning the origins and motives underlying the mergers of the period. He rejected the propositions that the mergers were a consequence of a slowdown in growth of the U.S. economy or of decreases in transportation costs. He did find that the achievement of market power and the development of the U.S. securities markets appeared to have played a role in encouraging the mergers. As an "indirect" way of testing this proposition, Nelson calculated and discovered a significant positive correlation between quarterly merger data and the level of securities prices.[19] He also calculated the correlation between mergers and the level of industrial production, but here he found an insignificant relationship between the two. When Nelson extended his analysis to quarterly merger data for the longer period 1895–1954, he uncovered the same quantitative results: Securities prices were significantly and positively related to the mergers, but the relationship between mergers and industrial production was insignificant.

9.3.3   Steiner

Steiner (1975, chap. 8) used multiple regression analysis to try to explain annual merger activity (numbers and value) from 1949 through the early 1970s. For the years 1949–71 he found that GNP and the change in the level of securities prices both had significant positive influences; the prime rate of interest had a positive but insignificant effect.[20] When he added data for 1972 to the analysis, Steiner saw the change in securities prices variable become insignificant, and the prime rate of interest showed a significant positive effect.

9.3.4 Beckenstein

Beckenstein (1979) examined annual data on merger numbers and values for the years 1949–75. Using multiple regression analysis and trying a number of variables, he found that only the nominal level of securities prices and the nominal interest rate had consistently significant effects; but the interest rate effects were consistently positive.

9.3.5 Chung and Weston

Chung and Weston (1982) employed multiple regression analysis to explore the determinants of the annual number of large conglomerate mergers. They found that these mergers were positively and significantly related to the difference between yields on lower and higher grade corporate bonds, the ratio of short- to long-term bond yields, and the rate of growth of GNP; the mergers were negatively related to the rate of return on corporate bonds. When they used Tobin's q instead of the last two variables, the authors found a positive and significant effect.

9.3.6 Melicher, Ledolter, and D'Antonio

Melicher and his colleagues (1983) examined quarterly merger data between 1947 and 1977. Using "prewhitened" logarithmic first difference transformations, they found that mergers were significantly related to lagged stock prices (positively) and to lagged bond yields (negatively) but not to industrial activity or to business failure levels.[21]

9.3.7 Shugart and Tollison

In an analysis of annual merger data for the years 1895–1920 and 1947–79, Shugart and Tollison (1984) concluded that the series could best be described as generated by a "white-noise process with possible drift" or by a "stable first-order autoregressive scheme," and they rejected the characterization of the merger data as occurring in waves. They did not, however, explicitly test a wave hypothesis, nor did they specifically show why their findings were inconsistent with a wave characterization. We will offer a more specific test of a wave hypothesis at the end of section 9.5.

9.3.8 Guerard

Using procedures similar to those of Melicher and his colleagues, Guerard (1985) examined quarterly merger data for the years 1895–1950. He found that mergers were positively related to stock prices but unrelated to the level of industrial production.

9.3.9 Becketti

Becketti (1986) used quarterly data on the number and value of mergers from 1960 through 1985. Using ordinary least squares regressions and emphasizing the lagged values of the explanatory variables, he found that mergers and acquisitions were in general influenced positively by securities prices, negatively by real interest rates, positively by the general level of debt in the economy, positively by the level of capital utilization, and negatively by real GNP; but the statistical significance of his findings was not strong, except for the influence of GNP.

9.3.10 A Summing Up

For a period of more than 30 years, the literature devoted to time-series analysis of mergers and acquisitions has not been large. A few variables have consistently appeared as potential explanatory influences: measures of economic activity (for example, GNP or industrial production), interest rates (or bond yields), and securities prices. The first and third variables have usually been found to be positively related to merger activity, while the second has exhibited both signs. In most instances, however, the theoretical justifications offered for the inclusion of these (and other) variables in the analyses conducted have not been strong.

In the next section we offer a more complete theoretical model of the merger and acquisition process. We will agree that aggregate activity and interest rates should influence merger activity, with a positive effect for the first and a negative effect for the second. But we are suspicious of the role usually assigned to securities prices. We now turn to the development of our hypotheses.

9.4 Developing Hypotheses

9.4.1 The Determinants of Merger and Acquisition Activity

A merger or acquisition usually constitutes an act of investment by the purchasing firm or individuals. But a merger or acquisition is also an *exchange* of *existing* assets (for example, a purchaser pays cash for the plant, equipment, personnel, and goodwill of an existing firm), whereas investment flows (at least, as defined by the GNP accounts) involve the creation of *new* plant and equipment. Consequently, we will focus primarily on the forces that cause individuals or firms to exchange assets among themselves, and we will draw somewhat on the existing literature on asset exchanges.[22]

Bargains

Asset exchanges should occur when potential purchasers believe that the current prices for the assets constitute "bargains." One rough indicator of whether a company can be purchased at a bargain price would be a comparison of the company's purchase price (for instance, market value) with the likely replacement costs of the company's assets—that is, Tobin's q.[23] The lower the ratio of market value to replacement cost (other things being equal), the greater the bargain and hence the greater the likelihood that some potential purchaser will step forward and make the purchase. Equivalently, for a given level of desired aggregate investment, merger activity is likely to be greater when the prices of existing firms are low relative to the prices of new assets, since mergers and acquisitions are alternatives to purchases of new assets. Thus, the level of q for the economy should be an important negative influence on the aggregate level of merger and acquisition activity.[24]

Our approach focuses on the demand side of merger transactions, somewhat neglecting the supply side. For simpler asset exchanges—such as of an office building—this neglect might not be justified. When the prices of office buildings fall below their replacement costs (that is, this q is below 1.0), potential buyers should be looking for bargains; but when their prices rise above their replacement costs, potential sellers should be looking for possibilities to sell out at favorable prices. In the former case, the buyers may be willing to offer prices that are slightly above prevailing levels in order to expedite a sale; in the latter case, the sellers may be willing to shade their prices below prevailing levels to expedite sales. In any event, the volume of transactions and q for these kinds of simple assets are unlikely to be correlated.

For the case of publicly traded firms, the process we have just described should hold when q falls below 1.0. Indeed, to achieve mergers, prospective buyers appear to be willing to offer substantial premiums above preannouncement market prices. By contrast, however, if a company's securities are selling at a q above 1.0 and the company's managers believe that the times are propitious for selling the company (because, for example, they have inside information or strong beliefs that the future prospects of the company are not as rosy as the market believes), they will have trouble expediting the sale by offering to sell the company at a price below the current market value.[25] Accordingly, we believe that focusing on reported mergers as driven largely by the buyers' side of the transaction is justified.

This expectation that q should be an important (and negative) determinant of merger activity is consistent with recent cross-sectional findings on the characteristics of takeover targets.[26] It should be noted that this negative relationship implies that, *ceteris paribus*, there should be a negative relationship between mergers and securities prices. This prediction is in sharp contrast to the expectations expressed in (and empirical findings of) the earlier literature that mergers and securities prices should be positively related. Our examination of that literature has uncovered few valid theoretical arguments for a positive relationship.[27] Melicher, Ledolter, and D'Antonio, for example, posited that securities prices are indicators of "expectations of economic growth" and hence that higher levels of securities prices should be conducive to mergers. Since a merger requires a price that is satisfactory to both buyer and seller, this hypothesis implicitly assumes that buyers are more influenced by the expectations provided by securities prices than are sellers. We see no necessary reason why this should be so.

Our hypothesis that a low value of q should indicate a bargain is at hand and hence encourage mergers implies a simultaneous relationship between q and mergers: A high level of mergers (*ceteris paribus*) should cause q to increase.[28] Consequently, in our estimation procedures below we include simultaneous equations methods that incorporate the determinants of q. We should note here that it is not within the scope of this paper to try to develop and estimate a complete model of q. Rather, the important insight is that when q is relatively low (for whatever reason, including a low level of mergers) bargains will appear; this in turn will encourage mergers, which will tend to increase q; and so on.

Unexpected Changes in Economic Circumstances

As economic circumstances change unexpectedly[29]—for instance, as relative prices among the major sectors of the economy change—different entrepreneurial skills may become valuable and differential profit opportunities may arise.[30] For example, as relative energy prices increase, the skills required to operate an airline, a chemical factory, a petroleum refinery, or a gasoline marketing facility may change. Further, opportunities for greater (or lesser) economies of scale, economies of scope, or economies of vertical integration may arise. Mergers and acquisitions are one way of achieving the changes in ownership and management that can take advantage of these changed opportunities.

Divergences of Opinion

As noted above, mergers require buyers and sellers to agree upon a mutually satisfactory price. If differences of opinion about future profit prospects widen, two effects are possible: First, there is a greater likelihood that a relatively optimistic buyer will find a relatively pessimistic seller and a transaction can be completed. Second, however, there is also a greater likelihood that a buyer-seller pair that previously would have found a merger worthwhile will find that the buyer has become relatively pessimistic or the seller has become relatively optimistic about its own future profit prospects, and the merger is less likely to be completed.[31] Since the two effects offset each other, we cannot offer a precise theoretical prediction as to the net effect of divergences of opinion on mergers. Our prior expectations, however, lead us to predict that the first effect should dominate the second. Accordingly, we expect that periods with increased flows of new information that create divergent opinions[32] or periods of greater changes in relative prices (which could yield differential expectations about the future) should be periods with larger numbers of mergers.

The Real Cost of Capital

The real cost of capital can influence the timing, financing costs, and expected profitability of mergers and acquisitions and hence should have a negative relationship with the volume of these transactions. It might also be the case, however, that in credit crunches small firms that face liquidity problems may become takeover targets by larger firms that have easier access to capital markets;[33] this latter hypothesis would imply a positive relationship between mergers and the cost of capital. Our prior is that the former effect should dominate. A measure of the real rate of interest is likely to be a good proxy for the cost of capital.

The Size of the Economy

A larger economy is likely to have more companies that could merge with each other and hence to have a positive influence on mergers and acquisitions.

Tax Laws

In addition to the effects that *changes* in the tax laws can have in inducing mergers and acquisitions over a short- to medium-run period, alternative tax regimes can make asset exchanges more or less costly and hence have steady-state consequences for the volume of mergers and acquisitions. Tax laws involving inheritances and capital gains are obvious examples.

A Correction Factor for the Fixed Cutoff Point Problem

As we discussed in section 9.2 above, in the presence of inflation a fixed lower cutoff point for the inclusion of a merger or acquisition into a recorded data series creates an upward bias in that series over time. Any empirical testing of the previous hypotheses must include a correction factor for this upward bias.

A Summing Up

The exchange-of-assets view of mergers developed above indicates that the following general factors should influence the observed pattern of mergers and acquisitions:

1. Tobin's q
2. Changes in economic circumstances (including changes in relative prices and changes in tax regimes)
3. Greater divergences of opinions about future economic prospects
4. The real cost of capital
5. The size of the economy
6. The tax regime
7. A corrective factor for the cutoff point bias

9.5   Methodology, Data, and Results

To test the hypotheses advanced in the previous section, we employed standard time-series regression analysis using some of the data series described in section 9.2.

9.5.1   The Dependent Variables

The FTC "large firm" series, reporting the number of mergers in the manufacturing and mining sectors in which the assets of the acquired company were at least $10 million and information concerning the merger was publicly available, was our choice for the dependent variable in our analyses of quarterly data. This is a widely used series, and it offers the maximum number of observations and overlap with potential explanatory variables. These data cover the quarters 1948.1 though 1979.4. For our analyses of annual data we chose the FTC "broad" series. These data cover the years 1940–79. In an effort to extend both these series and include data that cover the merger wave of the 1980s, we spliced each of the FTC series with the "domestic merger" series from *Mergers & Acquisitions*. In each case we isolated the overlapping data of the FTC and *M&A* series and ran least squares regressions (including a first order autoregressive term). These regression equations are shown in table 9.5. We then employed the coefficients from these regressions to extrapolate the FTC series forward through the end of 1985.

9.5.2   Independent Variables

The Ratio of Market Value to Replacement Cost (q)

This variable represents our bargain hypothesis. For the quarterly regressions we tried both unadjusted and tax-adjusted measures of

Table 9.5   **OLS Regressions Used to Splice the FTC and *M&A* Time Series on Mergers**

1. Quarterly data:

   1967.2–1979.4 (51 observations)

   $$FTC = 3.17 + 0.06 \cdot MA + 0.58 \cdot AR(1)$$
   $$\quad\quad (0.6) \quad (4.3) \quad\quad\quad (4.8)$$
   $$D\text{-}W = 2.3$$
   $$\bar{R}^2 = 0.63$$

2. Annual data:

   1969–1979 (11 observations)

   $$FTC = -1349.71 + 1.00 \cdot MA + 0.87 \cdot AR(1)$$
   $$\quad\quad\quad (1.7) \quad\quad (2.2) \quad\quad\quad (4.4)$$
   $$D\text{-}W = 1.9$$
   $$\bar{R}^2 = 0.88$$

Note: *t*-statistics in parentheses.

q.[34] For the annual regressions we used only unadjusted measures of q.[35] We expect this variable to have a negative effect on merger activity.

The Real Rate of Interest

This variable represents our cost-of-capital hypothesis. To construct this variable, we used the interest rate on seasoned, Aaa-rated corporate bonds during a quarter (or a year) and then subtracted the concurrent inflation rate (as measured by the percentage change in the GNP deflator). We expect this variable to have a negative effect on mergers.

Nominal GNP

This variable represents both the size of the real economy and a correction factor for the upward bias in the construction of the merger series. In addition, we decomposed this variable into its separate components—real GNP and the GNP deflator—and entered them separately into the regressions.[36] We expect this variable (and its components) to have a positive effect on mergers.

Tax Regimes

When unadjusted q was included in the regressions, we also included dummy variables to capture the possible effects of different tax regimes on mergers. We believe that the tax laws of 1954, 1963, and 1981 represent the major new regimes in the period covered by our data. Accordingly, we included 0,1 dummy variables separately for 1954 and all subsequent quarters or years, for 1963 and all subsequent periods, and for 1981 and all subsequent periods.

Changes in Relative Prices

This variable represents our hypothesis concerning changed economic circumstances. For each month we computed the variance of the percentage price changes of the major components of the U.S. Bureau of Labor Statistics wholesale price index (and, subsequently, the producer price index).[37] We then averaged these monthly variances into quarterly values.[38] Since larger variances should represent greater changes in economic circumstances, we expect this variable to have a positive effect on mergers.

Divergences of Opinion

This variable represents our effort to capture the effects of new information that creates divergences of opinion. To construct this variable, we used the Livingston data base, which contains a semiannual time series of separate forecasts for a number of macroeconomic variables by a panel of forecasters.[39] We computed the cross-sectional variance of the one-year-out forecasts of the consumer price index[40] for each semiannual period and then computed the coefficient of variation for each semiannual period. For our quarterly estimates we used these semiannual observations or interpolated the in-between quarters by averaging the semiannual observations for the preceding and following quarters. Since a higher value for this variable indicates greater divergences of opinion among forecasters, we expect this variable to have a positive effect on mergers.

9.5.3   The Simultaneity between Mergers and q.

To the extent that the aggregate level of merger and acquisition activity affects the market value of companies (the numerator of q), there is a simultaneous relationship between mergers and q. Accordingly, some discussion of this simultaneity is warranted.

Since q is a ratio of prices at discrete points in time, whereas merger and acquisition activity is measured as a flow over time, it is the *change* in q that should be affected by the flow of mergers. It is easy to show that

$$\Delta q \equiv q_t - q_{t-1} \equiv (\Delta V - q_{t-1} \Delta K)/K_t ,$$

where V is the market value of the capital stock, and K is the replacement cost of that capital stock. Since ΔK is current investment, we can posit a simple accelerator or capital stock adjustment model of investment, in which real GNP and real interest rates are the primary determinants of investment. The change in market value should be related to merger activity and to unexpected changes in future profits and in interest rates.

Since real GNP and real interest rates are already in the model as exogenous variables explaining mergers, we used estimates of the unexpected changes in future profits and in interest rates as our excluded exogenous instruments for the purposes of simultaneous equations estimation of the merger model. To obtain these estimates, we used the residuals from first order ARIMA estimation models involving real GNP and real interest rates.[41]

9.5.4   Regression Results

Table 9.6 provides the list of variables, their symbols, and their average values for the quarterly observations 1948.3 through 1984.1 (For the dependent variables, annual averages are also provided.)

Tables 9.7 and 9.8 present our main regression results for the quarterly data. The first table provides OLS regressions using the FTC merger data for 1948.3–1979.4 and using the spliced FTC–*M&A* merger data for 1948.3–1984.1; the second table presents two-stage least squares

Table 9.6   **A List of the Variables**

Variable symbol	Definition	Mean value, 1948.3–1984.1
NFTC	Quarterly number of mergers, FTC "large firm" series	16.1[a]
NFTCMA	*NFTC* spliced with the quarterly "domestic" series from *M&A*	16.1
BFTC	Annual number of mergers, FTC "broad" series	787.0[b]
BFTCMA	*BFTC* spliced with the annual "domestic" series from *M&A*	733.9[c]
taxadq	Tax-adjusted Tobin's *q*	0.41
unadq	Unadjusted *q*	0.91
ri	Real interest rate	1.88
NGNP	Nominal GNP, in billions of dollars	$1,145
RGNP	Real GNP, in billions of 1982 dollars	$2,184
DEFL	GNP deflator, 1982 = 1.0	0.46
VRPC	Variance of the relative price changes of the industrial components of the wholesale price index	0.79
CVLFC	Coefficient of variation of the Livingston panel forecasts of the consumer price index	0.02
D1954, etc.	Dummy variable taking the value of 1 for all quarters (or years) in 1954 and after; 0 otherwise	

[a]1948.3–1979.4 only.
[b]1948–79 annual data.
[c]1948–85 annual data.

Table 9.7   Quarterly OLS Results, with NFTC and NFTCMA as Dependent Variables

Independent variable	NFTC (1948.3–1979.4)				NFTCMA (1948.3–1984.1)			
	7A	7B	7C	7D	7E	7F	7G	7H
Constant	2.25 (0.6)	2.48 (0.6)	−10.71 (1.5)	−13.81 (1.9)	5.14 (1.3)	5.65 (1.4)	−12.20 (1.8)	−9.32 (1.3)
taxadq	10.32 (3.8)	10.14 (3.8)	7.81 (2.4)	—	10.47 (3.8)	10.10 (3.8)	7.51 (2.8)	—
unadq	—	—	—	23.68 (3.8)	—	—	—	22.71 (3.8)
ri	−0.04 (0.2)	−0.03 (0.1)	−0.06 (0.3)	−0.03 (0.2)	−0.03 (0.4)	−0.08 (0.4)	−0.02 (0.1)	−0.06 (0.3)
NGNP	0.01 (3.2)	0.01 (3.2)	—	0.01 (2.8)	0.01 (2.5)	0.01 (2.6)	—	.005 (1.6)
RGNP	—	—	0.01 (1.4)	—	—	—	0.02 (2.7)	—
DEFL	—	—	−0.11 (0.3)	—	—	—	−0.23 (1.3)	—

VRPC	−0.34 (0.6)	—	—	—	−0.09 (0.2)	—	—	—
CVLFC	23.12 (0.6)	—	—	—	26.44 (0.7)	—	—	—
DI954	—	—	—	−1.54 (0.3)	—	—	—	−1.16 (0.2)
DI963	—	—	—	−2.06 (0.5)	—	—	—	−0.02 (0.01)
DI981	—	—	—	—	—	—	—	2.72 (0.5)
AR(1)	0.45 (5.1)	0.45 (5.2)	0.44 (5.0)	0.46 (5.2)	0.46 (5.6)	0.46 (5.7)	0.43 (5.2)	0.47 (5.7)
AR(2)	0.30 (3.4)	0.31 (3.5)	0.30 (3.4)	0.31 (3.5)	0.33 (4.0)	0.33 (4.0)	0.30 (3.6)	0.33 (3.9)
D-W	2.1	2.1	2.1	2.1	2.1	2.1	2.1	2.1
$\bar{R}^2$	0.73	0.73	0.73	0.74	0.71	0.71	0.72	0.71

Note: *t*-statistics in parentheses

Table 9.8 Quarterly 2SLS Results, with *NFTC* and *NFTCMA* as Dependent Variables

Independent variable	NFTC (1948.3–1979.4)				NFTCMA (1948.3–1984.1)			
	8A	8B	8C	8D	8E	8F	8G	8H
Constant	0.73 (0.2)	0.74 (0.2)	−9.96 (1.2)	−17.18 (1.9)	3.15 (0.7)	3.44 (0.8)	−12.32 (1.7)	−13.78 (1.5)
taxadq	12.27 (3.5)	12.48 (3.5)	13.41 (2.5)	—	12.97 (3.5)	13.23 (3.4)	10.65 (2.6)	—
unadq	—	—	—	27.56 (3.4)	—	—	—	27.56 (3.4)
ri	−0.01 (0.1)	0.003 (0.0)	0.01 (0.0)	−0.01 (0.1)	−0.02 (0.1)	−0.01 (0.0)	0.003 (0.0)	−0.03 (0.2)
NGNP	0.01 (3.3)	0.01 (3.3)	—	0.01 (2.8)	0.01 (2.7)	0.01 (2.7)	—	0.01 (1.8)
RGNP	—	—	0.004 (0.3)	—	—	—	0.01 (2.0)	—
DEFL	—	—	0.27 (0.6)	—	—	—	−0.13 (0.6)	—

	(1)	(2)	(3)	(4)	(5)	(6)	(7)	(8)
VRPC	-0.36	—	—	—	0.10	—	—	—
	(0.7)				(0.2)			
CVLFC	27.20	—	—	—	33.93	—	—	—
	(0.7)				(0.9)			
D1954	—	—	—	-2.43	—	—	—	-1.93
				(0.5)				(0.4)
D1963	—	—	—	-2.95	—	—	—	-0.89
				(0.6)				(0.2)
D1981	—	—	—	—	—	—	—	1.94
								(0.4)
AR(1)	0.45	0.45	0.46	0.46	0.46	0.47	0.44	0.48
	(5.0)	(5.1)	(5.0)	(5.1)	(5.5)	(5.6)	(5.2)	(5.6)
AR(2)	0.30	0.30	0.31	0.30	0.32	0.32	0.31	0.32
	(3.3)	(3.4)	(3.4)	(3.4)	(3.9)	(3.9)	(3.7)	(3.8)
D-W	2.1	2.1	2.1	2.1	2.1	2.1	2.1	2.1

Note: *t*-statistics in parentheses

estimates of the same models. In all cases we included first and second order autoregressive terms.[42]

The OLS results in table 9.7 indicate that the autoregressive terms are the most powerful explanatory factors. Nominal GNP always has a positive effect and is usually significant; when it is broken into its two constituent components, neither has a significant effect (and the price level even has a slight negative effect). Real interest rates always have a negative effect, but are never significant. The q variable, whether in its tax-adjusted or -unadjusted form, always has a positive effect—contrary to our expectations—and is significant. And the relative price variation and Livingston forecast variation variables are never significant, although the forecast variable has the expected sign. The dummy variables constructed to capture the differing tax regimes (when the unadjusted q is used) do not add any explanatory power to the equations.

The two-stage least squares results in table 9.8 yield similar conclusions. Indeed, the coefficients for the 2SLS estimations are quite similar to their OLS counterparts, indicating that the instrumental values for q are quite close to their actual values.[43] Thus, the 2SLS estimations do not appreciably affect or improve the explanatory power of the models.

In table 9.9 we provide results of OLS estimations based on annual data.[44] Again, the same basic conclusions emerge. For the annual data, though, nominal GNP is insignificant as well, but real GNP does have the expected significant positive effect.

When we transform all of the relevant quarterly data series into logarithms and reestimate the models of tables 9.7 and 9.8, we again find the same basic results. When we transform the annual series, however, we find somewhat stronger results. Table 9.10 shows these annual log-log OLS estimations. Nominal GNP now has a strong and significant positive effect, and real interest rates have a significant negative effect for the full 1948–85 period.

We estimated the same models for quarterly and annual data, with the value of mergers as the dependent variable, with the same basic results. We also tried logged values of the independent variables, again with the same basic results.

A number of conclusions can be drawn from the results presented in tables 9.7–9.10. First, the merger series follow a strongly autoregressive pattern. But our efforts to uncover the more fundamental economic forces underlying this pattern have been only moderately successful. The size of the economy has a positive effect on mergers, as expected, and real interest rates appear to have a negative effect, especially when the model is estimated using annual data. But q has a significant positive effect, contrary to our hypotheses. And our efforts to capture the effects of changes in the structure of the economy and of new information that could yield divergences of opinion do not yield satisfactory results.

9.5.5 Are There Merger Waves?

The data we described in section 9.2 suggest to us, and to others, that mergers occur in waves. Indeed, Brealey and Myers (1984) have listed the lack of an explanation for merger waves as one of ten significant unsolved problems in finance. But as we noted in section 9.3, Shugart and Tollison (1984) argued that the merger time-series data are inconsistent with a wave characterization. Their statistical results imply that merger levels follow a random walk or, at most, a first order autoregressive process. From this the authors concluded that mergers do not occur in waves. Implicit in their reasoning is an analogy to stock price data. Although a cursory look suggests that stock prices move in a nonrandom pattern, the statistical evidence indicates that stock prices follow a random walk: Price changes are uncorrelated from one period to the next, so that the best estimate of tomorrow's price is today's price.

Shugart and Tollison appear to have adopted this reasoning in analyzing merger data. They concluded that, since the best estimate of next year's level of mergers is this year's level, the patterns of merger levels are also meaningless.

We believe, however, that the analogy is flawed. The question with respect to stock prices is, can we predict tomorrow's price *change* by knowing today's price *change?* The relevant question with respect to mergers is, instead, if the *number* of mergers this year is high, can we predict that the *number* of mergers next year will also be high? Surely, if stock price changes are uncorrelated over time, the answer to the first question is no. It is not true, however, that if changes in merger levels over time are uncorrelated the answer to the second question is no. Indeed, one could argue that, if the best predictor of the number of mergers in year t is the number in year $t - 1$, mergers do come in waves.

As an alternative test of this hypothesis, we employed a nonparametric "runs" test. Arguably, the pattern of mergers would be consistent with a wave hypothesis if the periods when the numbers of mergers were relatively high and relatively low were not distributed randomly but instead were bunched in adjoining periods of relatively high and relatively low activity. To test this proposition, we regressed each quarterly and annual merger series against a simple time trend. These results are shown in table 9.11. We examined the residuals from

Table 9.9   Annual OLS Results, with *NFTC* and *NFTCMA* as Dependent Variables

Independent variable	*NFTC* (1948–79)				*NFTCMA* (1948–85)			
	9A	9B	9C	9D	9E	9F	9G	9H
Constant	−186.66	−937.81	−112.72	−806.05	−47.59	−1028.06	68.23	−853.73
	(0.6)	(2.6)	(0.3)	(3.4)	(0.1)	(2.5)	(0.2)	(2.5)
umadq	10.47	7.91	10.20	7.09	8.31	8.14	9.61	7.21
	(2.4)	(2.7)	(2.9)	(3.0)	(1.9)	(2.5)	(2.3)	(2.2)
ri	−15.39	−14.34	−15.01	−15.82	−31.19	−3.93	−32.66	−0.56
	(0.6)	(0.8)	(0.6)	(1.0)	(1.0)	(0.2)	(1.2)	(0.0)
NGNP	−0.003	—	0.19	—	−0.27	—	0.06	—
	(0.0)		(1.0)		(1.6)		(0.4)	
RGNP	—	1.64	—	1.54	—	1.57	—	1.13
		(4.7)		(5.5)		(4.6)		(4.2)
DEFL	—	−53.20	—	−52.79	—	−45.93	—	−29.99
		(4.3)		(4.5)		(5.5)		(3.6)

D1954	64.07	−73.97	—	—	246.39	−111.19	—	—
	(0.3)	(0.4)			(1.0)	(0.6)		
D1963	337.33	−79.40	—	—	549.33	−150.39	—	—
	(1.5)	(0.4)			(2.6)	(0.7)		
D1981	—	—	—	—	498.39	754.77	—	—
					(1.6)	(3.3)		
AR(1)	0.97	1.08	1.09	1.09	0.78	0.93	0.84	0.88
	(5.4)	(7.2)	(6.2)	(7.6)	(4.7)	(5.8)	(4.7)	(5.2)
AR(2)	−0.53	−0.69	−0.46	−0.70	−0.46	−0.58	−0.21	−0.45
	(2.9)	(4.5)	(2.5)	(4.8)	(2.7)	(3.5)	(1.2)	(2.6)
D-W	1.9	2.0	1.7	2.0	1.9	1.9	1.8	1.9
R̄²	0.78	0.88	0.79	0.89	0.70	0.83	0.68	0.78

Note: t-statistics in parentheses

Table 9.10   **Annual OLS Results, with All Relevant Variables in Logs**

Independent variable	log *BFTC* (1948 –79)		log *BFTCMA* (1948–85)	
	10A	10B	10C	10D
Constant	−3.01	−3.84	−7.61	−6.29
	(1.3)	(4.0)	(3.2)	(5.7)
log *unadq*	1.46	1.58	2.1	2.1
	(5.1)	(9.3)	(7.2)	(12.2)
ri	−0.02	−0.02	−0.10	−0.15
	(0.6)	(0.5)	(3.5)	(5.5)
log *NGNP*	0.49	0.56	0.86	0.62
	(2.0)	(7.4)	(3.7)	(7.0)
D1954	0.18	—	−0.05	—
	(0.7)		(0.2)	
D1963	0.01	—	−0.30	—
	(0.0)		(1.4)	
D1981	—	—	−0.80	—
			(3.8)	
AR(1)	0.36	0.37	−0.41	−0.09
	(1.7)	(2.0)	(2.6)	(0.6)
AR(2)	−0.31	−0.33	−0.58	−0.31
	(1.6)	(1.8)	(3.4)	(2.0)
D-W	2.1	2.1	2.0	2.0
$\bar{R}^2$	0.86	0.87	0.75	0.69

Note: *t*-statistics in parentheses

each equation and counted any positive deviation as a "plus" and any negative deviation as a "minus." We then counted the number of runs of pluses and minuses and compared the number found to the number that would be expected from a random distribution. For all four cases the number of runs was significantly below the expected number.[45] These results are also shown in table 9.11.

Accordingly, we believe, contrary to Shugart and Tollison, that the merger data are consistent with a wave characterization.

9.6 Conclusions

In this paper we have developed hypotheses concerning the economic factors that should explain the pattern of mergers and acquisitions and subjected those hypotheses to econometric tests on postwar merger data. Along the way we reviewed the previous literature, described the strengths and weaknesses of the various merger series that are available for analysis, and provided a historical perspective on the long-run pattern of mergers in the U.S. economy.

Table 9.11   **Runs Tests of a Merger Wave Hypothesis**

Quarterly data:

1. 1948.1–1979.4 (128 observations)

$$NFTC = 3.12 + 0.19 \cdot TIME$$
$$\quad\quad (2.0)\quad (9.4)$$

$$D\text{-}W = 0.58$$
$$\bar{R}^2 = 0.41$$

Expected number of runs = 61; standard deviation = 5.3
Actual number of runs = 37

2. 1948.1–1985.4 (152 observations)

$$NFTCMA = 6.31 + 0.12 \cdot TIME$$
$$\quad\quad\quad (4.4)\quad (7.8)$$

$$D\text{-}W = 0.54$$
$$\bar{R}^2 = 0.28$$

Expected number of runs = 74; standard deviation = 5.9.
Actual number of runs = 47

Annual data:

3. 1940–79 (40 observations)

$$BFTC = 186.31 + 24.14 \cdot TIME$$
$$\quad\quad\quad (1.3)\quad\quad (4.0)$$

$$D\text{-}W = 0.35$$
$$\bar{R}^2 = 0.28$$

Expected number of runs = 21; standard deviation = 3.1.
Actual number of runs = 7

4. 1940–85 (46 observations)

$$BFTCMA = 359.11 + 12.43 \cdot TIME$$
$$\quad\quad\quad\quad (2.5)\quad\quad (2.4)$$

$$D\text{-}W = 0.36$$
$$\bar{R}^2 = 0.09$$

Expected number of runs = 23; standard deviation = 3.2
Actual number of runs = 5

Note: *t*-statistics in parentheses

Our econometric results are only mildly encouraging. Especially puzzling to us is the apparently strong positive effect of Tobin's q on mergers. Although this result is consistent with the other researchers' empirical findings that securities prices have a positive effect on mergers, we believe it to be inconsistent with the predictions of economic theory. We are thus left with an unresolved puzzle.

We have, however, offered a more specific test of a wave hypothesis for time-series merger activity, and we believe that, contrary to the claims of others, the time-series pattern of mergers is consistent with a wave characterization.

But the task of achieving a better understanding of the economic forces underlying that pattern still lies ahead.

Notes

1. There has been a more extensive cross-section literature. For recent cross-section studies see Harris, Steward, and Carleton (1982); Wansley, Roenfeldt, and Cooley (1983); Hasbrouck (1985); and Knoeber (1986).

2. A simple price index or deflator would work properly only if real merger sizes were distributed uniformly.

3. To the extent that merger values are recorded in terms of historical book value (as is true for the FTC series discussed below), the bias due to the pure inflation effect will not be as severe.

4. The last report, covering 1979 and earlier years, is U.S. FTC (1981).

5. Curiously, the FTC also published information on the value of the acquired assets in mergers for which public information was *not* available, but it did not publish annual data on the numbers of these mergers.

6. The annual data can be found in U.S. Department of Commerce (1976) and in various annual issues of the FTC's *Statistical Report on Mergers and Acquisitions*. The quarterly data can be found in Nelson (1959, 167–69).

7. Unfortunately, the annual and quarterly series are not consistent with each other. The annual series appears to be more complete.

8. Nelson described the transactions as "disappearances" and the book value as "capitalizations".

9. See Brooks (1973).

10. The GNP deflator, with 1982 = 1.0, was used to deflate the nominal dollar series. This procedure is imperfect, for the reasons discussed in the text above.

11. Shugart and Tollison (1984) argue that waves are not a good characterization of the historical pattern of mergers and acquisitions. For our discussion of their article, see Section III below.

12. As Nelson (1959, 25–29) pointed out, the Thorpe data appear to be more inclusive than are Nelson's. Thus, if Nelson's raw data were adjusted upward to correspond roughly with the Thorpe and FTC series, the merger wave at the turn of the century would appear to be even larger in relation to the economy at that time and hence would also be yet larger in comparison with the merger waves later in this century.

13. We chose the number of corporations, rather than the larger number of business enterprises (including sole proprietorships and partnerships), for two reasons. First, the data for the former are more complete. Second, and more important, as we noted in the text the reported merger data include only transactions that are above a given size; since corporations are generally larger than sole proprietorships and partnerships, the former series appeared to be more comparable to the merger data.

14. We can divide the nominal values of mergers in a given year by the nominal GNP of that same year, or, equivalently, we can use the ratio of real values.

15. It is worth noting that the political concerns raised about the merger wave of the 1960s were of the same kind as those being raised in the 1980s. See U.S. Federal Trade Commission (1969) and Mueller (1986).

16. Employment (when multiplied by wages) and profits are the two most important elements of value added. For further details on the computations that underlie table 9.3, see White (1981a, 1982).

17. The data on employment in table 9.4 were collected in a slightly different manner from those in table 9.3 and hence are not strictly comparable.

18. In addition to the studies discussed below, we should also mention the survey article by Markham (1955), the effort by Eis (1969) to compile merger number and value data for the 1920s, and the less quantitative analyses by Nelson (1966), Maule (1968), and Eis (1970).

19. Nelson found this positive relationship for both the number of mergers and the capitalization value of the mergers.

20. Steiner appears to have used nominal values in all instances.

21. Melicher, Ledolter, and D'Antonio appear to have used nominal values for stock prices and bond yields.

22. A merger or acquisition of a firm usually entails one extra element—control over management—that other exchanges of assets (such as purchases of smaller blocks of shares in a company) do not have. For a discussion of the influences on the trading volume of shares of stock, see Epps (1975), Epps and Epps (1976), Verrecchia (1981), Tauchen and Pitts (1983), and Smirlock and Starks (1985).

23. See Tobin (1969). To the extent that replacement costs encompass only physical assets, this type of measure will ignore intangible goodwill.

24. Robert Taggart has pointed out that the bargain hypothesis may explain cross-section results but may not apply to time-series data.

25. The owners and potential sellers of family-owned or closely held companies might be able to shade selling prices so as to expedite mergers.

26. See Hasbrouck (1985). In addition, our expectations about the role of q seem to be consistent with the implications of the "free cash flow theory" of Jensen (1986). To the extent that corporations are heavily laden with cash, financial markets are likely to value them at q levels that either are close to 1.0 (because the replacement cost of a dollar of cash is one dollar) or are below 1.0 (because the market expects that many managers are likely to make foolish purchases with the cash). In the latter case mergers and q will be negatively correlated, either because managers have indeed embarked on foolish mergers that are financed by their free cash flow or because other firms have realized that now is a good time to buy the targeted firms and put the cash to better uses—ones that will yield higher returns for stockholders.

27. The "trapped equity" model—as offered, for example, by King (1986)—may be an exception.

28. This increase in q is a pure price reaction and need not be a reflection of increased market power. If mergers were also to yield increased market power, there might be a yet greater rise in q.

29. This hypothesis and the one that follows it are similar to that advanced by Gort (1969).

30. Note that it is not the changed profit levels for different sectors that are important but rather the new profit opportunities that may arise for different skills.

31. This point was suggested to us by Steven Salop.

32. As an oversimplification, new information that has implications on which everyone agrees should have effects solely on prices, with little or no trading. But as Verrecchia (1981) pointed out, if individuals have different incomes, tastes, or portfolio goals, then even a consensus as to the implications of new information can lead to trading.

33. This point was suggested to us by Alan Auerbach.

34. The tax-adjusted q series come from Bernanke, Bohn, and Reiss (1985); the unadjusted series was provided by the authors of that paper.

35. This series is constructed from the data provided in U.S. Board of Governors (1986).

36. As we noted in section 9.2, the simple use of the deflator is probably an imperfect correction factor.

37. We defined the percentage price changes to be differences in the natural logarithms of the prices in two periods. We then computed a Divisia index of the weighted average of the percentage changes of the individual components. Finally, we computed the weighted variance of the individual rates of change around this average. See Parks (1978).

38. The regressions reported here include a relative price change variable based only on the "industrial commodity" components of the wholesale price index and the producer price index. Including the raw materials components—specifically, the energy sector—produced extremely large spikes in relative price changes in the 1970s, and we were concerned that these observations might be true outliers. When these components were included in the regressions, however, the basic results reported below were unchanged.

39. For further discussion of the Livingston data base, see Carlson (1977), Cukierman and Wachtel (1979) and Cukierman and Wachtel (1982).

40. We also computed the variance of the forecasts for the wholesale price index and for the Federal Reserve Board index of industrial production. When these alternative variables were included in the regressions reported below, the basic results were unchanged.

41. Further details on these equations are available from the authors.

42. As suggested by Fair (1970), in the 2SLS estimations we also included the lagged values of all the exogenous and endogenous variables.

43. We suspect that the use of the lagged variables as instruments, especially lagged q, may have caused this result.

44. Since the OLS and 2SLS results for the quarterly data were so similar, we present only the OLS results for the annual data.

45. The spliced data have an autoregressive structure imposed on the extrapolated observations of the 1980s, which might bias the series toward showing fewer runs. We doubt that this bias explains the strongly significant effects that we find.

References

Becketti, Sean. 1986. Corporate mergers and the business cycle. *Economic Review,* Federal Reserve Bank of Kansas City, pp. 13–26.

Beckenstein, Alan R. 1979. Merger activity and merger theories: An empirical investigation. *Antitrust Bulletin* 24: 105–28.

Bernanke, Ben, Henning Bohn, and Peter C. Reiss. 1985. Alternative nonnested specification tests of time series investment models, photocopy. Stanford: Stanford University.

Brealey, Richard, and Stewart Myers. 1984. *Principles of corporate finance,* 2d ed. New York: McGraw-Hill.

Brooks, John. 1973. *The go-go Years*. New York: Waybright and Talley.

Carlson, John A. 1977. A study of price forecasts. *Annals of Economic and Social Measurement* 6: 27–56.

Chung, Kwang S., and J. Fred Weston. 1982. Diversification and mergers in a strategic long-range-planning framework. In *Mergers and acquisitions: Current problems in perspective*, ed. Michael Keenan and Lawrence J. White, 315–47. Lexington, Mass.: D.C. Heath.

Cukierman, Alex, and Paul Wachtel. 1979. Differential inflationary expectations and the variability of the rate of inflation: Theory and evidence. *American Economic Review* 69: 595–609.

————. 1982. Relative price variability and nonuniform inflationary expectations. *Journal of Political Economy* 90: 146–57.

Eis, Carl. 1969. The 1919–1930 merger movement in American industry. *Journal of Law and Economics* 10: 267–96.

————. 1970. A note on mergers and the business cycle: Comment. *Journal of Industrial Economics* 19: 89–92.

Epps, Thomas W. 1975. Security price changes and transaction volumes: Theory and evidence. *American Economic Review* 65: 586–97.

Epps, Thomas W., and Mary L. Epps. 1976. The stochastic dependence of security price changes and transaction volumes: Implications for the mixture-of-distributions hypothesis. *Econometrica* 44: 305–21.

Fair, Ray C. 1970. The estimation of simultaneous equations models with lagged endogeneous variables and first order serially correlated errors. *Econometrica* 38: 507–16.

Ginsburg, Douglas H. 1986. Statement before the Subcommittee on Monopolies and Commercial Law, Committee on the Judiciary, U.S. House of Representatives, 5 March 1986.

Gort, Michael. 1969. An economic disturbance theory of mergers. *Quarterly Journal of Economics* 83: 624–42.

Guerard, John B., Jr. 1985. Mergers, stock prices, and industrial production: An empirical test of the Nelson hypothesis. In *Time series analysis: Theory and practice,* vol. 7, ed. O. D. Anderson, 239–47. Amsterdam: Elsevier.

Harris, Robert S., John F. Stewart, and Willard T. Carleton. 1982. Financial characteristics of acquired firms. In *Mergers and acquisitions: Current problems in perspective,* ed. Michael Keenan and Lawrence J. White, 223–41. Lexington, Mass.: D.C. Heath.

Hasbrouck, Joel. 1985. The characteristics of takeover targets. *Journal of Banking and Finance* 9: 351–62.

Jensen, Michael C. 1986. Agency costs of free cash flow, corporate finance, and takeovers. *American Economic Review* 76: 323–29.

King, Mervyn. 1986. Take-overs, taxes and the stock market, photocopy. London: London School of Economics.

Knoeber, Charles R. 1986. Golden parachutes, shark repellents, and hostile tender offers. *American Economic Review* 76: 155–67.

Markham, Jesse. 1955. Survey of the evidence and findings on mergers. In *Business concentration and price policy,* National Bureau of Economic Research, 141–82. Princeton: Princeton University Press.

Maule, C. J. 1968. A note on mergers and the business cycle. *Journal of Industrial Economics* 16: 99–105.

Melicher, Ronald W., Johannes Ledolter, and Louis J. D'Antonio. 1983. A time series analysis of aggregate merger activity. *Review of Economics and Statistics* 65: 423–30.

Mueller, Willard F. 1986. Wrong Signals on Antitrust. *New York Times*, 4 August 1986, 17.

Nelson, Ralph L. 1959. *Merger movement in American industry, 1895–1956* Princeton: Princeton University Press.

Nelson, Ralph L. 1966. Business cycle factors in the choice between internal and external growth. In *The corporate merger*, ed. William W. Alperts and Joel E. Segall, 52–66. Chicago: University of Chicago Press.

Parks, Richard W. 1978. Inflation and relative price variability. *Journal of Political Economy* 86: 79–95.

Shugart, William F., II, and Robert D. Tollison. 1984. The random character of merger activity. *Rand Journal of Economics* 15: 500–509.

Smirlock, Michael, and Laura Starks. 1985. A further examination of stock price changes and transaction volume. *Journal of Financial Research* 8: 217–25.

Steiner, Peter O. 1975. *Mergers: Motives, effects, policies*. Ann Arbor: University of Michigan Press.

Tauchen, George E., and Mark Pitts. 1983. The price variability–volume relationship on speculative markets. *Econometrica* 51: 485–505.

Tobin, James. 1969. A general equilibrium approach to monetary theory. *Journal of Money, Credit, and Banking* 1: 15–29.

U.S. Board of Governors of the Federal Reserve System. 1986. Balance sheets for the U.S. economy, 1946–85, photocopies. Washington, D.C.: FRS.

U.S. Department of Commerce. 1976. *Historical statistics of the United States, Colonial times to 1970*. Washington, D.C.: GPO.

U.S. Department of Justice. 1986. Untitled tables and discussion on aggregate concentration, photocopies. Washington, D.C.: USDJ.

U.S. Federal Trade Commission. 1969. *Economic report on corporate mergers*. Washington, D.C.: FTC.

U.S. Federal Trade Commission. Bureau of Economics. 1981. *Statistical report on mergers and acquisitions, 1979*. Washington, D.C.: FTC.

Verrecchia, Robert E. 1981. On the relationship between volume reaction and consensus of investors: Implications for interpreting tests of information content. *Journal of Accounting Research* 19: 271–83.

Wansley, James W., Rodney L. Roenfeldt, and Philip L. Cooley. 1983. Abnormal returns from merger profiles. *Journal of Financial and Quantitative Analysis* 18: 149–62.

Weston, J. Fred. 1953. *The role of mergers in the growth of large firms*. Berkeley: University of California Press.

White, Lawrence J. 1981a. What has been happening to aggregate concentration in the United States? *Journal of Industrial Economics* 29: 223–30.

———. 1981b. The merger wave: Is it a problem? *Wall Street Journal*, 11 December 1981, 26.

———. 1982. Mergers and aggregate concentration. In *Mergers and acquisitions: Current problems in perspective*, ed. Michael Keenan and Lawrence J. White, 97–111. Lexington, Mass.: D.C. Heath.

Comment   Steven C. Salop

The Golbe-White paper is, in a sense, two separate papers. The first presents an overview of the available time-series data on mergers and acquisitions. The second provides an empirical study of the determinants of merger activity over the past 35 years. After a few initial comments on the overview, my main comments will focus on the empirical study.

The time-series overview is a very useful piece of work. Golbe and White set out the various data series and work to splice the data sets together. This was not a trivial task. Their resulting series allows us to see the historical patterns more easily.

I found the most interesting result in this section to be that mergers have not been as significant in the recent economy as they were in the past. The authors compare the number of mergers to real GNP and show that this ratio was larger at the beginning of the century than in the recent past. One can quibble about the proper ratio to calculate here. The number of mergers does not control for the size of the average merger; perhaps a better deflator would be a stock measure (for example, total domestic wealth) rather than a flow measure like real GNP. Nonetheless, the result is striking.

Golbe and White's empirical study focuses on the determinants of aggregate merger activity. In contrast to most of the other papers in this volume that analyze *which* mergers occur, Golbe and White study *how many* mergers occur. Their study is thought provoking, but still very preliminary.

More work is needed before we can draw strong conclusions about the determinants of aggregate merger activity, for two reasons. First, the authors' results are fairly weak. Many of the results were negative; no relationship could be found. Second, the theory underlying the empirical analysis was not fully developed.

This was primarily an empirical paper. The theory section consisted of a list of independent variables and their expected signs. No model was developed beyond this list. In particular, the hypotheses did not flow from a general equilibrium model of financial markets with imperfect information about a stochastic economy, although that apparently is the model underlying the analysis.

This problem can be illustrated with two of the variables. According to Golbe and White, asset exchanges occur when potential purchasers perceive that current asset prices represent "bargains" in the market. They measure this phenomenon by the economywide value of Tobin's

Steven C. Salop is professor of economics at the Georgetown University Law Center.

q, the ratio of market value to replacement cost. Second, because buyers and sellers must agree on a price, substantial divergence of opinion in the economy should affect the likelihood of finding a mutually acceptable price. More divergence of opinion probably leads to more mergers. The authors measure divergence of opinion by the variance among macroeconomic forecasts. These two variables should not be treated as separate ones, discussed independently. They both should flow out of an equilibrium model of expectation formation, where expectations are endogenous and depend on public as well as private information.

An asset is a bargain if its price is low relative to its expected price in the future, not relative to its replacement cost. Thus, the Tobin q is the correct variable for measuring bargains only if one believes that buyers and sellers expect q to equal one in the near future. Instead, at the least, a proxy for expected q in the near future should have been formulated. That should come out of a model of expectation formation. An assumption of perfect foresight and thus the measurement of the ratio of the current value of q relative to its actual future value would have been a superior variable to examine.

Of course, this approach creates two additional simultaneity problems in expectation formation, even beyond the simultaneity problem raised by the authors: that current merger activity raises future prices. First, expected future asset prices will determine current prices. Second, buyers' and sellers' expectations are not independent.

The theory of assets as bargains is incomplete without an analysis of these issues. Consider for example, the implications of the fact that sellers also have expectations. If the ratio of current to future q implies bargains, then it is true that purchasers would desire to buy assets. Yet if these same expectations were held by potential sellers as well, the transactions might not take place.

This possibility raises, of course, the issue of divergence of opinion. First, I think divergence of opinion is not measured with the best variable. Because the real issue is differences of opinion regarding the future value of the assets, divergence in macroeconomic forecasts is not the best proxy. Better proxies might be divergence in stock market forecasts. One simple variable might be the price of "straddle" options. In a market where volatility is expected, straddles are more expensive.

Second, Golbe and White treat that variable independently, rather than fundamentally connected to the "bargains" variable. Yet the two are intimately connected. A "bargain" means that the purchaser thinks the asset is undervalued at the price at which it is offered by the seller. The seller does not think it is a bargain, but a ripoff. In short, the two parties have a divergence of opinion.

The relationship between these variables can be seen in a model of asset exchanges with imperfect information. Golbe and White suggest that, though divergence could in principle reduce the number of exchanges, they expect greater divergence of opinion to lead to more mergers. Although I may agree with their empirical intuition, it still would be useful to set out a model to see the conditions under which the effect could go the other way.

Consider the following simple static model of exchange.[1] Suppose that there are n potential buyer-seller "transactional pairs," indexed by $i = 1, 2, \ldots, n$.[2] A transactional pair will consummate an exchange if the buyer's value b_i exceeds the seller's reservation price s_i—that is, if net surplus $z_i = b_i - s_i > 0$. Even if there are no differences of opinion about the prospects for firms, b_i and s_i still could diverge, and some exchanges will occur, if the buyer has a comparative advantage in managing the assets. Indeed, Golbe and White capture this idea with a variable that measures structural changes in the economy that might lead to shifting comparative advantages.

Consider first an economy with shifting comparative advantages but no differences of opinion, and suppose that in this economy, $m < n$ exchanges would occur, which we denote as the first m transactional pairs, that is, $z_i > 0$ for $i = 1, 2, \ldots, m$.

Now compare this to a more stochastic economy where the buyer's value is given by $b_{ii} = b_i + \beta e_i$ and the seller's value is given by $s_{ii} = s_i + \beta u_i$, where e_i and u_i are random variables, each with a mean of zero, and β is a non-negative multiplier. (The initial economy is given for $\beta = 0$.) Consider the effect of increasing β to a positive number. In this new $\beta > 0$ economy, exchanges occur only if $z_{ii} = b_{ii} - s_{ii} > 0$. As a result, some of the m exchanges would no longer occur and some of the $n - m$ transactional pairs that failed to reach agreement now would succeed. Whether the aggregate number of exchanges rises or falls depends on the relative sizes of n and m and the underlying distribution of z_i, locally and globally.

Golbe and White's intuition is based on the idea that if m is small, the number of disrupted exchanges will be small; in contrast, the pool of potential new exchanges is large. In fact, for a small β, what is relevant is the relative numbers of *marginally* successful and marginally unsuccessful transactional pairs, not the aggregate numbers. For example, if the initial density of z_i were symmetric with a local maximum

1. This model draws heavily on the model of litigation settlement behavior devised by Klein and Priest (1984). See also Perloff and Rubinfeld (1988).

2. For simplicity, assume that each buyer and each seller are involved in only one transactional pair, that is, buyer i is interested *only* in the asset of seller i. He places no value on any other asset. This assumption simplifies the discussion by eliminating all competition among buyers and sellers.

at zero, the number of new exchanges created would just equal the number of old exchanges disrupted, irrespective of the global success rate. Only if the initial number of marginally unsuccessful transactional pairs exceeds the number of marginally successful pairs will increases in β raise the number of successes. Formally, denoting by $f(z)$ the density of z, this means $f'(z) < 0$.

Because the number of asset exchanges in the economy is quite small relative to the potential number of transactions, Golbe and White probably also are correct that the density of z is downward sloping at the margin. As a result, greater differences in opinion would increase the number of successful deals. But this need not be so. Locally, the number of marginally successful pairs may exceed the number of marginally unsuccessful ones.

This formal model also suggests that the relationship is nonlinear. Even under the standard intuition, when the other determinants of merger activity lead to a high number of transactions, an increase in opinion divergence will lead to a smaller increase in the number of exchanges.

Finally, the paper could be improved by recognizing the interaction between the stock market and physical asset markets. I earlier identified one interaction, the fact that options prices may provide a gauge of opinion divergence. But other, more fundamental interactions occur. Acquisition of physical assets in a merger involves two elements— purchasing the existing profit stream of the acquired firm and purchasing the right to manage the acquired firm. A potential purchaser can acquire only the first right by purchasing a block of common stock. Thus, a more complete model would view stock purchases as a substitute for asset acquisition and estimate a general equilibrium model in which both are possible.

In this regard the Golbe and White paper would be improved if it simultaneously studied the determinants of stock market activity. That study would examine the same set of variables and raise the same set of questions. For example, is it true that stock market activity is positively correlated with stock prices? Is it true that stock market activity is positively correlated with divergence of opinion, say, as measured by the price of straddles?

In sum, I learned something from the paper. I also expect the paper to provoke additional research into time-series analysis of merger activity. My only wish is that the additional research had been carried out in the current paper.

References

Klein, Benjamin, and George L. Priest. 1984. The selection of disputes for litigation. *Journal of Legal Studies* 13: 1–55.

Perloff, Jeffrey, and Daniel Rubinfeld. 1988. Settlements in private antitrust litigation. In Lawrence White, ed., *Private antitrust litigation: New evidence, new learning*. Cambridge: MIT Press.

Comment   Robert A. Taggart, Jr.

There is a natural tendency to focus on the dramatic aspects of current events. Thus, the highly publicized takeover battles of the past few years have led many observers to conclude that recent merger activity is more hostile, on a grander scale, and of more far-reaching significance for the economy than ever before.

Because of this tendency, the study by Golbe and White is an integral part of any comprehensive examination of mergers. If we are to understand mergers and their impact on the economy, we need to know if the current merger activity is, in fact, unusual.

An immediate contribution of this paper, therefore, is its finding that the current activity does not appear unusual when viewed in a historical context. The absolute number of mergers during the 1980s has been large, but once allowance is made for the size of the overall economy, the current merger wave does not stand out from the previous episodes, particularly that occurring around the turn of the century. In addition, the data suggest that recent mergers have not led to any significant increase in aggregate industrial concentration for the U.S. economy.

In reaching these conclusions, Golbe and White also perform a valuable ancillary service. They provide an excellent summary of the available data on aggregate merger activity in the U.S. economy since 1895. In particular, they carefully review various noncomparabilities and gaps in the data. This discussion should prove very useful to future students of long-run merger patterns.

Despite the problems with the data, the conclusion that current merger activity is less impressive in relative than in absolute terms seems well founded. That in turn leads to curiosity about the factors that determine the aggregate volume of mergers and how these factors are related to broad economic trends. It is to this issue that Golbe and White turn next.

Unfortunately, this effort is hampered by the fact that most available theory pertains to mergers as a micro phenomenon, whereas it is the aggregate level of mergers the authors seek to explain. What is needed is a theory of mergers at the macro level.

In the absence of such a theory Golbe and White have assembled a number of explanatory variables, which I will place in several categories.

Robert A. Taggart, Jr., is professor of finance at the School of Management, Boston University, and a research associate of the National Bureau of Economic Research.

Certain macro-level variables, for example, can be guessed at relatively easily, even without an explicit theory. We would expect, for instance, that the volume of mergers is positively related to the overall level of economic activity.

The available micro-level theory does suggest certain other variables that should be related to the aggregate merger level. That theory implies simply that mergers take place when they are perceived to have positive net present values. Since those values are in turn a function of cash flows and discount rates, some measure of the cost of capital immediately arises as a potential explanatory variable.

Certain other variables are clearly implied by the theory, but they are very difficult to measure at the aggregate level. Changes in the tax code, for example, should significantly affect the perceived values of mergers. But tax considerations differ enough from one merger to the next that it is hard to recommend much except dummy variables to capture the aggregate effects of these tax changes. In a similar vein, it seems clear that periods in which market participants have sharp differences in expectations or in which industries are in a state of upheaval should be ripe for mergers, but exactly how such periods should be identified is far less clear.

Tobin's q falls into still another explanatory variable category, and it is here, I believe, that the problem of applying a micro theory at the macro level emerges most sharply. At the micro level it makes perfect sense that low values of q should stimulate merger activity. If a firm wishes to acquire a specific set of assets, and if several target firms possess those assets then, other things being equal, it will choose the target with the lowest q. Moreover, the low values of q should make mergers more attractive relative to the alternative of buying the same set of assets in the market for real capital. And indeed, q has exactly this predicted effect in cross-sectional regression studies by Hasbrouck (1985) and Bartley and Boardman (1986).

At the macro level, however, I am not sure what an aggregate measure of q implies for the aggregate level of mergers. Golbe and White argue that unusually low values of q are likely to be associated with larger numbers of undervalued firms and hence more attractive merger candidates. That proposition strikes me as quite plausible as long as the aggregate q primarily reflects these potential targets. Suppose, however that unusually high values of q reflect greater numbers of overvalued firms. For an acquiring firm this type of valuation error might actually encourage mergers, particularly if acquired firms' shareholders are willing to accept shares of the acquiring firm's stock.

Another possibility is that valuation errors are made primarily by acquiring firms' executives rather than by investors in the securities markets. Under Roll's (1986) "hubris hypothesis" of corporate takeovers, for instance, capital markets are presumed efficient in the strong form, and hence acquisition bids at premium prices simply reflect over-valuations on the part of the bidders. Moreover, if the buoyant economic climate associated with high values of q is also conducive to greater bidder hubris, Golbe and White's finding of a positive relationship between q and merger activity may not seem so anomalous.

I do not claim that either of the possible linkages between q and merger activity that I have described above is inherently more plausible than the one described by Golbe and White. Nonetheless, I am not convinced they are less plausible, either, and so I do not find Golbe and White's empirical results necessarily puzzling.

The general difficulty that these remarks are intended to illustrate is that the available theory simply does not give us much guidance in seeking out the determinants of aggregate merger activity. The most appropriate variables and the expected direction to their effects are not very sharply delineated. When this problem is combined with some difficult measurement problems, we should perhaps not be too disappointed that we do not come away from a study of this type with a clear vision of the driving forces behind merger activity.

In the final analysis it may turn out that the volume of mergers does not reflect macroeconomic factors as much as it does industry or sectoral factors. Popular generalizations tend to associate the various merger "waves" with particular industry groups. Thus, the spurt in merger activity at the turn of the century is thought to reflect the consolidation of the steel, oil, and other mining and manufacturing industries; the rise in mergers in the 1920s is commonly linked to the public utility holding company movement; and the most recent increase in mergers is thought to reflect the restructuring of such diverse industries as oil, airlines, broadcasting, and food and consumer products. If there is some truth to these generalizations, it may be that further understanding of merger determinants must come from a more disaggregated analysis.

References

Bartley, Jon W., and Calvin M. Boardman. 1986. Replacement-cost-adjusted valuation ratio as a discriminator among takeover target and nontarget firms. *Journal of Economics and Business* 38: 44–55.

Hasbrouck, Joel. 1985. The characteristics of takeover targets. *Journal of Banking and Finance* 9: 351–62.

Roll, Richard. 1986. The hubris hypothesis of corporate takeovers. *Journal of Business* 59: 197–216.

10 Panel Discussion: Corporate Takeovers and Public Policy

Joseph A. Grundfest, Gregg Jarrell, Steven C. Salop, and Lawrence J. White

Remarks   Joseph A. Grundfest

November of 1986 marked a turning point in the politics of the takeover debate. In the space of ten days, the Securities and Exchange Commission announced settlement of the Ivan Boesky insider trading case[1] and the Democrats gained control of the U.S. Senate. Either event alone would have altered the context of the takeover debate. The combination of the two in such a short period of time, however, added a sense of urgency to the legislative desire to "do something—do anything" about takeovers.

In these remarks I will first discuss the relationship between takeovers and insider trading and explain the illogic of the argument that hostile takeovers should be curbed in order to stop insider trading. I then criticize recently introduced antitakeover legislation that does nothing to prevent allegedly egregious defensive tactics, while at the same time imposing overbroad burdens on stock acquisitions that could adversely affect many transactions wholly unrelated to hostile takeovers.

The Link between Insider Trading and Takeovers

Many takeover critics have tried to link insider trading with hostile takeovers. They argue that hostile takeovers should be curbed so that insider trading can be stopped. This argument is, however, seriously misguided.

Insider trading occurs when someone misappropriates or, through breach of a duty, converts valuable nonpublic information about a pending transaction or disclosure.[2] Thus, insider trading can occur

Joseph A. Grundfest is a commissioner at the Securities and Exchange Commission.

when a friendly merger is pending,[3] when a company has found a substantial mineral deposit,[4] or when unfavorable earnings have not as yet been announced.[5] Hostile takeovers are not uniquely susceptible to insider trading, nor do hostile takeovers cause insider trading in any meaningful sense—just as mineral finds, earnings reports, and friendly takeovers in and of themselves do not cause insider trading. Indeed, efforts to prohibit hostile takeovers in order to deter insider trading make as little sense as efforts to stop vote fraud by cancelling all elections, or efforts to stop bank robbery by shutting down all banks.

Unfortunately, the recently introduced antitakeover legislation falls prey to easy but illogical arguments that seek to prevent insider trading by stopping takeovers. For example, a statement accompanying S. 1323, the "Tender Offer Disclosure and Fairness Act," attacks the "market manipulating corporate raider" and cites trading by Dennis Levine, Martin Siegel, and Ivan Boesky as examples of the abuses engendered by "manipulative raids."[6] The problem with this attack on insider trading, which makes a great deal of sense as an introduction to a legislative definition of insider trading, is that it makes no sense as a rationale for legislation targeting takeover activity.[7]

Insider trading is not caused by hostile takeovers, nor is it uniquely associated with hostile takeovers. To make this point crystal clear, consider the Nestle-Carnation deal, a notorious example of insider trading that involved Messrs. Boesky and Siegel and netted Boesky profits of $28.3 million.[8] In the Carnation trade, Siegel was Carnation's investment banker and participated in extensive friendly negotiations that both Carnation and Nestle sought to keep secret.[9] There were no hostile bids involved, and no raiders were trying to impose their will on Carnation's management. Nonetheless, Siegel tipped Boesky about the friendly deal, and the transaction gave rise to a stunning volume of insider trading.

The Carnation trade demonstrates that friendly deals are every bit as susceptible to insider trading as hostile ones. In fact, a recent study by the Securities and Exchange Commission's Office of the Chief Economist found substantial evidence of stock price runups before the announcement of friendly transactions.[10] It also found that runups before friendly deals were more pronounced than runups before hostile transactions.[11] This finding suggests—but certainly does not establish—that insider trading may be more pronounced in friendly deals than in hostile deals. Friendly deals may be more susceptible to insider trading because more people on both sides of the negotiations are likely to know of the pending deal for a longer period of time. In contrast, a hostile bidder wants to avoid tipping a target that a bid is forthcoming. The hostile bidder is therefore likely to move faster with fewer people knowing of the bid, and is more likely to be able to maintain secrecy.

If friendly deals are more susceptible to insider trading, should Congress stop friendly deals in order to stop insider trading? Of course not. Similarly, Congress should not constrain hostile takeovers on the misguided rationale that those deals are particularly susceptible to insider trading.

In fact, even in cases where insider trading is discovered in connection with a hostile takeover, the trading does not necessarily emanate from the bidder's camp, nor does it necessarily occur with the bidder's approval. For example, the U.S. Attorney's Office has alleged that during Mesa's hostile bid for Unocal one of Unocal's investment bankers tipped Mr. Siegel about Unocal's planned defensive maneuvers.[12] Unocal's defensive tactic caused the value of its shares to decline, and Siegel caused his employer to buy put options that increased in value as a result of the Unocal price decrease. But to blame this insider trading on the raider's conduct is obviously wrong and makes about as much sense as blaming pass interference on the quarterback who throws the football.

Strong rules against theft of information in the form of insider trading are sound public policy, and I support vigorous efforts to protect corporations' and stockholders' property rights in confidential market information.[13] The link between hostile takeovers and insider trading, however, is largely a public relations device used by opponents of takeovers with little regard to the logic of their arguments. Insider trading cannot and should not serve as a rationale for imposing restraints on takeover activity. Insider trading and takeovers are two different issues that call for distinct analyses and distinct legislative approaches.

Takeover Legislation

On the legislative front the Senate Democrats' antitakeover proposals introduced in the first six months of 1987 have suffered from a disappointing gap between rhetoric and reality. The rhetoric speaks of a need to control both coercive bidder tactics and abusive defensive techniques without forgoing the benefits that result from an active takeover market. The legislative reality, however, is that some of these bills would do essentially nothing to control the allegedly abusive defensive techniques they claim to address. They would also impose substantial burdens on anyone seeking to acquire a significant stockholding position in a publicly traded corporation, even if the share acquisition was wholly unrelated to a hostile takeover.

Whatever the rhetoric the message of much of the legislative language is clear: The legislation is designed to stifle takeover activity with little regard to the costs imposed on a broad range of nontakeover transactions. The legislation also seeks to tilt the balance in takeover contests strongly in favor of the incumbent management because the bills contain no meaningful effort to control abusive defensive tactics. Accordingly, even if one is opposed to egregious and abusive takeover tactics and believes federal legislation is appropriate, it would be easy to oppose much of the legislation pending before the Senate in 1987.

Take the example of S. 1323, the "Tender Offer Disclosure and Fairness Act," sponsored by Senator William Proxmire and cosponsored by all eight Democrats on the Securities Subcommittee of the Banking Committee. The statement accompanying S. 1323 explains that "tender offers themselves should be neither encouraged nor discouraged by law; egregious defenses as well as coercive takeover tactics should be limited."[14] Bravo! As a guide for responsible takeover legislation, this formula could hardly be crafted in a more workable and evenhanded way.

Nevertheless, by oversight or calculation, somewhere between the fine rhetoric and the serious work of legislative drafting, something has gone wrong because the bill does essentially nothing to limit "egregious defenses"; restricts a broad range of market transactions that have nothing to do with "coercive takeover tactics"; and seeks to discourage by law the very transactions toward which the statement proclaims neutrality.

Toothless controls on "egregious defenses?"

The authors of the bill have identified greenmail, golden parachutes, and poison pills as defensive practices that they consider egregious. Assuming for the moment that these practices warrant federal regulation—a conclusion I do not embrace—it would make sense to draft legislation that effectively addresses the problems caused by such "egregious defenses." The proposed legislation is, however, toothless when it comes to regulating greenmail, golden parachutes, and poison pills. Indeed, the remarkably ineffective nature of the provisions intended to regulate these three practices unfortunately calls into question the willingness of the bill's authors to control takeover defenses that are purportedly egregious.

Greenmail. In particular, S. 1323 does not prohibit greenmail.[15] Instead, it attempts to control the price at which greenmail can be paid. It does so by establishing a maximum repurchase price equal to the average price over the 30 days preceding the greenmail transaction. This price control provision will be ineffective whenever the average price over a trailing 30-day period is greater than the prevailing market price because, under those circumstances, greenmail can be paid at a price higher than the price prevailing at the time of the repurchase.[16] Thus, the antigreenmail provision of S. 1323 may paradoxically lead to higher greenmail payments. Moreover, because some individuals may have an interest in creating a higher 30-day average price in order to support a larger greenmail payment, the danger exists that some individuals may attempt to manipulate stock prices to take advantage of such a greenmail price control rule. Under no circumstances would the rule prevent a large stockholder from selling his shares back to the corporation for a premium price unavailable to other, typically smaller stockholders.

The proposed legislation would therefore do little to deter greenmail. Instead, if enactment of the bill is construed as federal approval of transactions that comply with its toothless price control rule, passage of the legislation could actually increase the incidence of greenmail transactions. A similar pattern has, in the past, been observed in connection with the tax treatment of golden parachutes: Once Congress established a special tax applicable only to golden parachutes that more than trebled an executive's compensation,[17] a rule of thumb emerged that parachutes that no more than trebled compensation were acceptable.

Golden parachutes. The golden parachute provision in S. 1323 would prohibit a company from adopting a golden parachute only while a tender offer is pending.[18] But at least 198 of the *Fortune* 500 firms already have such plans in place,[19] and the legislation would do nothing to control these existing parachutes. The proposed legislation would also do nothing to deter corporations from adopting parachutes at any point in the future—provided the paperwork is signed before the tender offer begins. Thus, the bill would again be toothless, this time regarding the hundreds of parachutes that have already been strapped on in anticipation of takeover battles.

Poison pills. The poison pill provision of S. 1323 would prohibit only poison pills adopted while a tender offer is pending.[20] More than 400 publicly traded corporations have already adopted poison pills.[21] The pending legislation would not affect the existing pills and would do nothing to prevent the adoption of future poison pills before a tender offer is announced. Thus, this legislative proposal is toothless with respect to the hundreds of poison pill plans that have already been put in place.

Leading takeover counsel have advised clients to adopt poison pills now, so that they will be prepared in the event the bill becomes law.[22] Paradoxically, if companies accept this advice, the simple introduction of S. 1323 will have increased the number of "egregious" poison pills in place.

Antitakeover provisions. The provisions targeting "egregious defenses" are all bark and no bite. Are the provisions aimed at potential hostile bids equally inept? Hardly. The antibidder provisions are so broad and overinclusive that I have neither the time nor space to describe even a fraction of them. Instead, I will describe only one set of provisions with potential consequences that are particularly overbroad. If enacted, these provisions could radically change the structure of the entire stock market and influence thousands of transactions that have nothing to do with hostile takeovers.

S. 1323 would prohibit anyone from acquiring more than 15 percent of a company's shares unless the acquisition is made through a tender offer.[23] Combined with a provision in S. 1324 that prohibits partial tenders by requiring that tender offers for more than 20 percent of a company's shares be for all the company's shares,[24] the legislation would effectively prevent anyone from acquiring more than 20 percent of a company unless he tendered for the entire company.[25]

The consequences of this legislation could radically restructure large portions of the securities market that are unrelated to hostile takeovers. As an example of the reach of these provisions, consider the following illustrations of transactions that would be forbidden.

Suppose a large pharmaceutical company wants to acquire 30 percent of a smaller, biotechnology firm's shares in conjunction with a license or joint venture. The bidder will be prohibited from making that investment unless it tenders for all of the biotech company's shares. Thus, the legislation could force the smaller company out of existence as part of the price of obtaining equity capital.

Suppose a company's founder wants to bequeath his 60 percent holding to an only child. The founder could not do so unless the child tendered for the entire company.

If an investor wants to provide additional equity capital to a company in which she already owns 20 percent, she would be forbidden from doing so unless she offered to buy the entire firm. Indeed, any investor already holding a 20 percent position who simply wants to increase an existing position would be forbidden from doing so unless the investor makes a tender offer for the entire company.

Viewed from the seller's perspective, the situation is potentially even more far-reaching because any seller who owns 20 percent or more of a company's shares would be unable to dispose of those shares in a single block unless the purchaser agreed to conduct a tender offer for all the company's shares. The block would therefore have to be broken into smaller positions before it could be sold outside an any-or-all tender.

The reach of these provisions obviously stretches far beyond any rational concern over hostile takeovers. Because the legislation would seriously deter any share acquisition that creates a holding in excess of 20 percent, the legislation would, over time, cause the gradual extinction of stockholder positions above 20 percent. Strong minority shareholders are a valuable monitoring device in corporate governance, even if the minority shareholders never threaten a takeover or proxy contest. The gradual extinction of these minority positions could therefore change the balance of power between stockholders and managers in ways entirely unrelated to hostile takeovers.

In addition, it is no defense of the provisions to observe that the SEC could craft exemptions "consistent with the purposes and policy fairly intended" by the legislation.[26] It is a foolish bill, so overbroad that its authors would require an administrative agency to construct an armada of exemptions merely to allow garden-variety transactions to continue undeterred.

These constraints should be evaluated in conjunction with efforts to introduce an unworkable extension of the "conscious parallelism" doctrine from antitrust law to the takeover arena; impose on shareholders onerous disclosure requirements unrelated to takeover activity; and create sweeping extensions of private rights of action and theories of liability that invite for extensive litigation and strike suits. In this context it quickly becomes clear that the proposed legislation places far greater burdens on bidders, who may be doing nothing unfair or coercive, than on targeted companies responding to takeover attempts with allegedly "egregious" defenses.[27]

Is the Legislation Balanced?

By no stretch of the imagination does the proposed legislation live up to its promise neither to encourage nor discourage tender offers. Nor does the legislation live up to its promise to limit egregious defenses as well as coercive takeover tactics. Instead, the proposed legislation would seriously deter takeovers without regard to whether the takeover is fair and noncoercive; place impediments in the path of innocent transactions wholly unrelated to hostile deals; and do essentially nothing to deter "egregious defenses."

Obviously, even if one believes that something should be done about takeover activity, legislation of the sort supported by many Senate Democrats is not a reasonable approach to the takeover problem.

Notes

1. *SEC v. Boesky,* No. 86 Civ. 8767 (S.D.N.Y. Nov. 14, 1986).

2. Generally, there must be a purchase or sale of securities in breach of a fiduciary duty or a relationship of trust or confidence while in possession of material, nonpublic information about an issuer or the trading market for an issuer's securities. See, for example, *Dirks v. SEC,* 463 U.S. 646 (1983); *Chiarella*

v. United States, 445 U.S. 222 (1980); *United States v. Carpenter,* 612 F. Supp. 827 (S.D.N.Y. 1985), *aff'd* 701 F.2d 1024 (2d Cir. 1986), *cert. granted,* 55 U.S.L.W. 3424 (U.S. Dec. 15, 1986) (No. 86-422).

3. See, for example, *SEC v. Siegel,* 87 Civ. 0963 (S.D.N.Y. Feb. 13, 1987).

4. *SEC v. Texas Gulf Sulphur Co.,* 401 F.2d 833 (2d Cir. 1968), *cert.denied,* 394 U.S. 976 (1969).

5. See, for example, *SEC v. DePalma,* 86 Civ. 3541 (D.D.C. Dec. 30, 1986); *SEC v. Wahl,* 86 Civ. 0568 (D. Neb. Aug. 20, 1986); *SEC v. Weksel et al.,* 86 Civ. 6063 (CSH) (S.D.N.Y. Aug. 6, 1986); *SEC v. Moorhead,* 85 Civ. 2007 (D. Colo. Dec. 2, 1985).

6. 133 Cong. Rec. S7594 (daily ed. June 4, 1987) (statement of Senator Proxmire).

7. Not all members of Congress make this error. As Congressman Markey, Chairman of the House Subcommittee on Telecommunications and Finance observed, the incidence of insider trading "does not, of course, mean that we should halt all corporate takeovers in order to root out the insider trading problem. But it does mean that those responsible for these transactions have not developed appropriate mechanisms to contain the flow of information relating to takeovers." Subcommittee on Telecommunications and Finance of the Committee on Energy and Commerce, "Congressional Study Finds Persistent Run Ups in Target Company Stock, Indicating Possible Pervasive Insider Trading," at 2 (July 15, 1987) (news release quoting Representative Markey, Subcommittee Chairman).

8. *SEC v. Siegel,* 87 Civ. 0963 (Complaint, ¶ 23).

9. For a description of these negotiations and Nestle's interest in maintaining confidentiality, see *In re Carnation Corp.,* Exchange Act Release No. 22,214, 33 S.E.C. Dkt. 1025, [1984–1985 Transfer Binder] Fed. Sec. L. Rep. ¶ 83,801 (July 8, 1985).

10. Office of the Chief Economist, Securities and Exchange Commission, *Stock trading before the announcement of tender offers: Insider trading or market anticipation?* (Feb. 24, 1987).

11. "Friendly, negotiated takeovers have more pre-bid runup than hostile takeovers (47.1 percent versus 35.3 percent one day before the bid) when foothold acquisitions of the bidder are held constant at zero." Ibid at 3.

12. *United States v. Siegel,* 87 Cr. 118 (RJW) (filed Feb. 13, 1987) (Complaint).

13. J. Grundfest, *To catch a thief: Recent developments in insider trading and enforcement,* address to the National Investor Relations Institute, New York Chapter (June 20, 1986).

14. 133 Cong. Rec. S7594, 7596 (daily ed. June 4, 1987) (statement of Senator Proxmire).

15. S. 1323, 100th Cong. 1st sess. § 8 (1987) (amending Section 14 of the Securities Exchange Act of 1934, 15 U.S.C. 78n).

16. This scenario can occur if there is an intervening bid that is withdrawn or if expectations of such a bid arise and then disappear.

17. *See* I.R.C. § 280G, Golden Parachute Payments (West Supp. 1987).

18. S. 1323, § 8 (amending Section 14 of the Securities Exchange Act of 1934, 15 U.S.C. 78n).

19. V. Rosenbaum, Takeover defenses—Profiles of the *Fortune* 500 (Investor Responsibility Research Center, Jan. 1987).

20. S. 1323, § 8 (amending Section 14 of the Securities Exchange Act of 1934, 15 U.S.C. 79n).

21. S. Labaton, More potency for poison pills, *New York Times*, July 20, 1987, at D2, col. 1.

22. M. Lipton, The Proxmire bill and the pill, memorandum to clients of Wachtell, Lipton, Rosen & Katz, New York, NY (June 6, 1987).

23. S. 1323, § 7 (amending Section 14d of the Securities Exchange Act of 1934, 15 U.S.C. 78n[d]).

24. S. 1324, 100th Cong., 1st sess. § 9 (1987) (amending Section 14d of the Securities Exchange Act of 1934, 15 U.S.C.78n[d]).

25. There are two reasons I analyze these provisions in unison although they are not contained in the same bill. First, proponents of each provision are likely to believe they need the other one to make their provision "effective"; in other words, the mandatory tender offer provision will have a far stronger impact if combined with a mandatory "any or all" rule, and vice versa. Thus, the sentiment is there to combine these two provisions in a single piece of legislation, and they have earlier been considered as elements of a common bill. Second, the adverse consequences of each provision are most far-reaching if the two provisions are combined, and I wish to emphasize the perhaps unforeseen consequences of legislation that mandates tender offers for acquisitions above a certain size threshold while simultaneously prohibiting partial tender offers.

This is not to suggest that these provisions are harmless if uncoupled. To the contrary, the mandatory tender offer provision of S. 1323 and the mandatory "any or all" provision of S. 1324 are objectionable standing on their own. The mandatory tender offer provision would substantially increase the cost of acquiring more than 15 percent of a publicly traded corporation's shares, and it could also substantially and unnecessarily increase the incidence of partial tender offers by investors seeking to establish large equity positions. In addition, the provision would prohibit many large block transactions because the purchaser would have to tender for the large block and, pursuant to SEC rules, would have to accept tendered shares on a pro rata basis from all stockholders, not just the seller of the block. All this would occur without adding any meaningful efficiency or investor protection to the market.

The mandatory "any or all" provision of S. 1324 would prohibit partial tenders and either inefficiently deter valuable partial acquisitions that facilitate technology sharing, venture capital investments, and legitimate "toehold" investments made by investors who want a careful look at a company before deciding to acquire full control; or inefficiently provide an incentive for investors to purchase substantial blocks in transactions that are carefully structured so as to fall outside the SEC's tender offer rules. This latter consequence could stimulate the very "street sweeping" activity that Congress and the SEC seek to deter (that is, efforts to cause the rapid accumulation of blocks that can be "swept up" on the "street" through large, negotiated, private transactions).

26. S. 1323 § 7(b)(3), (amending Section 14d of the Securities Exchange Act of 1934, 15 U.S.C. 78n[d]).

27. See Statement of Charles C. Cox, acting chairman of the Securities and Exchange Commission, before the Senate Committee on Banking, Housing, and Urban Affairs, concerning Corporate Takeover Legislation (June 23, 1987).

Remarks   Gregg Jarrell

John Shad, the outgoing chairman of the Securities and Exchange Commission, and his enforcement chief, Gary Lynch, have engineered a remarkable crackdown on insider trading on Wall Street. Dennis Levine pleaded guilty and agreed to pay a $12 million penalty; Ivan Boesky turned over $100 million and continues to cooperate with the SEC's investigation; and several other major Wall Street figures have since been arrested. Recently, John Shad promised several more major indictments would be forthcoming in the near future. These earth-shattering scandals have precipitated numerous Congressional hearings on insider trading and other abuses stemming from the record mergers and acquisitions activity of recent years. It seems these cases will provide the political momentum necessary for antitakeover lobbyists to accomplish what the Reagan administration has thwarted until now: major new legislation designed to deter hostile takeover attempts.

The new legislative proposals contain major changes in tender offer rules, such as increasing the "cooling off" period for offers from the existing rule of 20 business days to 60 business days. This proposal vividly exposes that the true legislative motivation is to chill takeovers, not to reduce the incidence of insider trading. After all, does anyone seriously believe that tripling the minimum offer period to three months will reduce the opportunities for insider trading?

Before the Wall Street scandals, which can be dated with the 14 November 1986 announcement of Boesky's settlement, the intensive lobbying efforts by big business to achieve legislation conferring "veto power" over hostile offers had yielded few results. These lobbyists (including the Business Roundtable and other spokespersons for top management of large public firms) have been alarmed by the changes in the takeover market that have made America's once untouchable, large public firms vulnerable to hostile takeover bids. These changes include the pro-merger attitude taken by President Reagan's antitrust enforcers; the 1982 Supreme Court ruling striking down first-generation state antitakeover laws; the deregulation of oil and gas, transportation, securities and banking, and other industries; and the neutral stance toward takeover combatants taken by the SEC under Reagan. These developments together have fueled a surge in merger and acquisition activity, and financial innovations have made hostile bids for large firms quite feasible for those willing to pay the requisite premiums over market price.

Gregg Jarrell is senior vice president, director of research for The Alcar Group Inc., Skokie, Illinois.

Although state courts have provided some rulings favorable to the antitakeover forces—such as the Unocal decision upholding the exclusionary self-tender offer and the Household decision upholding management's unilateral adoption of the poison pill defense without obtaining shareholder voting approval—these decisions have been qualified to limit their usefulness as devices for deterrence. The SEC recently passed a rule making exclusionary tender offers illegal, and the Delaware supreme court, while legalizing poison pills, prescribed strict standards to prevent pills from being used to entrench incumbent managements.

But the Wall Street scandals, together with the Democrats' takeover of Congress in 1986 and the corrosive effects of the Iran-contra scandal on the resolve of the Reagan administration, create a recipe for regulatory reform. It is truly open season on corporate raiders. Even Boone Pickens, through his United Shareholders Association, has adopted an "if you can't beat them join them" attitude and proposed a long list of regulatory initiatives, although they are decidedly less hostile to takeover specialists than the Congressional version. Although these new laws will prove costly to the mass of individual shareholders and mutual fund holders, the narrow but powerful political interests of top corporate management and various lobbyists will be the primary voices helping to craft the new laws.

Remarks   Steven C. Salop

I have been charged with discussing the implications for competition policy of the papers in this volume, in particular, their implications for antitrust policy governing mergers and acquisitions. I will briefly set out the regulatory environment governing mergers and acquisitions and then discuss the possible influence of the findings in this volume on merger policy.

Merger policy in the United States is carried out mainly by the Department of Justice (DOJ) and Federal Trade Commission (FTC). Under the Hart-Scott-Rodino Pre-Merger Notification Act of 1976, all proposed acquisitions of assets valued in excess of $15 million by an acquiring firm with assets or sales in excess of $100 million must be reported to the agencies. A merger cannot be consummated until one of the agencies has evaluated its likely effects on competition. If the agency finds a problem of competition, the merging parties can either withdraw the proposal, negotiate a method of alleviating the agency's

Steven C. Salop is professor of economics at the Georgetown University Law Center.

concern (for example, by selling off a plant or an entire division), or litigate the issue. Very few cases are litigated. Over the years 1982–86 the FTC and DOJ brought enforcement actions against only 56 of the more than 7,700 mergers reported.[1]

Mergers are evaluated under Section 7 of the Clayton Act. A merger is illegal if it "substantially decreases competition or tends to create a monopoly." Three concepts of competition may be relevant for merger policy.

First, to economists, this language concerns market power, the ability of firms in a market to restrain output and thereby raise price above the competitive level, as defined by marginal cost. Mergers, especially mergers among competitors, may reduce competition in this regard by facilitating the exercise of market power.

Second, to economists, competition may concern the production efficiency of firms in the economy. Mergers and acquisitions, whether by competitors or by firms in separate markets, may help the merging firms reduce costs.

Third, to some noneconomists (possibly including the Congressmen who drafted and amended Section 7), competition concerns more than economists' definition of market power. Competition also concerns the social and political implications of concentration of assets or production among the largest firms in the economy as well as the ability of small businesses to remain viable in the economy. According to this concept of competition, acquisitions by large corporations can increase aggregate concentration, as measured by the share of assets held by the 200 or 500 largest corporations.[2]

These three concepts of competition have different implications for merger policy. The first definition would suggest that merger policy should focus primarily on "horizontal" mergers (mergers among competitors), and to a lesser extent on "vertical" mergers (mergers between suppliers and customers), where the former raise credible allegations of anticompetitive exclusion. In contrast to the third definition, this view of competition would not be concerned at all with "conglomerate" mergers (mergers among firms that are neither actual nor potential competitors and that do not stand in a vertical relationship to each other). The third definition also may conflict with the second, as in the case of an acquisition by a large competitor. Whereas the second definition would applaud such a merger, this acquisition also may reduce the ability of smaller, less efficient firms to compete, thereby offending the third definition.[3]

The current antitrust authorities focus on the first and second definitions of competition. They are not at all concerned with aggregate concentration. All conglomerate mergers are permitted. Merger policy is concerned only with market power and, as a result, focuses almost exclusively on horizontal mergers. Throughout the Reagan administration years only one or two vertical mergers have been blocked. Cost savings and other increases in production efficiency flowing from mergers now are viewed as reasons to allow the mergers, not the opposite. Formally, these arguments serve as defenses to allegations that a merger will increase market power.

This view of efficiency benefits is stated in the 1984 Department of Justice Merger Guidelines, the bible of merger enforcement, as follows:

> Although they sometimes harm competition, mergers generally play an important role in a free enterprise economy. They can penalize ineffective management and facilitate the efficient flow of investment capital and the redeployment of existing productive assets. While challenging competitively harmful mergers, the Department seeks to avoid unnecessary interference with the larger universe of mergers that are either competitively beneficial or competitively neutral.

The Guidelines relate this statement to efficiency as follows:

> Some mergers that the Department otherwise might challenge may be necessary to achieve significant efficiencies. If the parties . . . establish . . . that a merger will achieve such efficiencies, the Department will consider those efficiencies in deciding whether to challenge the merger.

This view of antitrust is important in understanding the relevance for antitrust policy of the papers in this volume. First, the papers will be relevant only if they concern horizontal or vertical mergers. These mergers are a fairly small fraction of the mergers reported each year to the antitrust enforcement agencies. Second, their main relevance will be to gauge either the likely increase in market power or the magnitude of cost savings and other efficiencies that could be expected from the representative mergers and to characterize more precisely the determinants of these variables for any particular merger.

The impact of mergers on market power is not a particular concern of the papers in this volume. Several of the papers do, however, focus on the potential efficiency benefits of mergers. The Hall paper on research and development and the Brown and Medoff paper on labor both study potential efficiency effects. By gauging the likely (average) efficiency benefits of the average merger, these papers can be of assistance to policy makers engaged in balancing efficiency concerns against likely increases in market power.

Unfortunately, these two papers, at least in their present form, have little direct application to antitrust policy. First, because antitrust was not their focus, they do not distinguish between mergers among competitors and other kinds of mergers. We therefore cannot tell whether the effects uncovered would apply to horizontal mergers. Second, because the sample of horizontal mergers is so small, efficiency effects for this subsample may be statistically insignificant.

Other papers that examined the motives for merger may have more significant implications for antitrust policy, even in their present form. As stated above, antitrust policy presumes that mergers generally are either neutral or motivated by concerns for efficiency. Several of the papers raised questions about this presumption.

For example, the Guidelines quoted above suggest that mergers create efficiency benefits by penalizing ineffective management. In principle, the enforcement thresholds governing market power were set to trade off these benefits optimally against market power concerns. If it were shown that mergers do not have significant managerial control benefits, it would follow that the optimal enforcement thresholds should be tightened.

In this regard, the Shleifer and Summers paper has important implications for merger enforcement. The authors show that the fact that firms are acquired at a premium over current stock market value should *not* create a presumption that the acquisition increases efficiency or social wealth. Instead, the premium may reflect nothing more than the opportunistic transfer of quasi-rents to the acquirer. In acquisitions in which this transfer is significant, there is no efficiency justification for tolerating even small increases in the likelihood of market power.

Shleifer and Summers also raise questions whether antitrust authorities should view attempts to block mergers by incumbent managers and rivals as good signals that the acquisition actually would enhance efficiency and competition. Rivals may legitimately fear that the acquisition would raise their own labor costs by creating a fear in their existing workers that they also will breach their implicit contracts. Incumbent managers may be protecting these contracts in order to minimize long-run costs, not to protect their own jobs.

The Auerbach and Reishus paper raises similar questions with respect to the tax benefits of mergers. The private benefits from reducing taxes exceed the social benefits or may have no social benefits at all. Thus, mergers motivated by tax savings do not create efficiencies that justify increases in market power. This paper finds that tax considerations generally are unimportant, in the sense that they do not explain which mergers take place. Unfortunately, this is not the main issue for antitrust policy. There seldom is a choice of merger partners.

For antitrust analysis, the more salient question would be the effect of tax considerations on the aggregate level of merger activity. This issue is addressed by the Golbe and White paper. Here the authors find no effects from the different tax regimes. To the extent that this finding suggests tax considerations are unimportant, acquisition premiums are more likely to reflect efficiency (or market power) benefits.

In short, the papers in this volume were not geared to antitrust policy considerations and, therefore, have few direct implications. Perhaps the authors might focus in their next round of research on the issues of concern to competition policy planners.

Notes

1. See *Antitrust and Trade Regulation Reporter,* vol. 52, 5 March 1987, 452. Private parties (customers, suppliers, or competitors) and states also can sue to block a proposed merger. Because of the federal government's primary role in the process, however, private and state litigation has generally had little significance. But this is changing now that the government has so relaxed its merger enforcement. More cases are being brought, often successfully.

2. For trends in aggregate concentration, see the Golbe and White paper in this volume.

3. For example, in the *Brown Shoe* case (370 U.S. 294 (1962)), the Supreme Court treated the potential efficiency benefits of the merger as a rationale for blocking it.

Remarks   Lawrence J. White

In this brief set of remarks I will offer two public policy perspectives on the merger and acquisition process: first, that of a former chief economist of the Antitrust Division of the U.S. Department of Justice who was one of the authors of the division's 1982 Merger Guidelines; and, second, that of a current member of the Federal Home Loan Bank Board, which regulates most of the nation's savings and loan associations and savings banks and faces an era of turbulence and change in financial services markets.[1]

Antitrust Policy

Antitrust policy on mergers rests for its legal foundation on Section 7 of the Clayton Act. That act instructs the Department of Justice and the Federal Trade Commission to halt those mergers "where in any line of commerce in any section of the country, the effect of such acquisition may be substantially to lessen competition, or to tend to create a monopoly."[2] It is worth noting that the Clayton Act makes no mention of size or of aggregate concentration across the entire economy.

In 1982 the Antitrust Division issued a set of "Merger Guidelines" that were designed to formalize the paradigm and procedures the division would follow in deciding whether to challenge a merger and also to provide this information to private antitrust attorneys, so that they

Lawrence J. White is a member of the Federal Home Loan Bank Board and professor of economics at the Graduate School of Business Administration, New York University.

could better guide and advise their clients. These Guidelines represented a complete revamping of an earlier (1968) set of merger guidelines. In 1984 the division modified the Guidelines modestly. (Unless otherwise indicated, the discussion below will refer to the 1982 version.)

The conceptual basis underlying the Guidelines is a concern that mergers may create or enhance market power. At the heart of the Guidelines is the belief, in the tradition of Chamberlin (1933), Fellner (1949), and Stigler (1964), that oligopolists in markets where entry is not easy are likely to behave in a noncompetitive fashion.

The Guidelines first provide a paradigm for defining a relevant market for the purposes of judging a given merger.[3] Since the purpose of the antitrust merger limitation is to prevent the significant creation of or increase in market power, markets are defined in terms of the ability of firms, if they act in concert, to exercise significant market power. In essence, the Guidelines define a market as the smallest group of sellers—defined across both product space and geographic space—that, if they acted in concert (that is, as a monopolist), could profitably raise prices by a "small but significant" amount for a "nontransitory" period of time.[4] The Guidelines use a 5 percent increase over a one-year period as the crucial parameters in this paradigm.

Having delineated the market, the Guidelines then ask if any paired set of the merger partners' products are in the same market. If not, the merger immediately passes muster and is unlikely to be challenged.[5] If one or more pairs of products are in the market, however, further examination is needed.

The next focus of the Guidelines is the level of seller concentration in the delineated market. The Guidelines use the Herfindahl-Hirschman index (HHI), according to which each seller's percentage of market share is squared and summed. (The HHI of an atomistic market would approach zero; that of a pure monopolist would be 10,000.) Two HHI cutoff points are specified: If a market's postmerger HHI is below 1,000, a merger will ordinarily not be challenged; if the HHI is above 1,800 (and the increase in the HHI that results from the merger is 100 points or greater), the merger will usually be challenged, unless there are extenuating circumstances, such as easy entry (discussed below). If the HHI falls between these two cutoffs, further investigation is warranted, and a challenge may be forthcoming. (For readers who are more comfortable with the four-firm concentration ratio as a measure of seller concentration, it is worth noting that an HHI level of 1,000 corresponds empirically to a CR4 of approximately 50 percent; an HHI of 1,800 corresponds to a CR4 of approximately 70 percent.)

Because conditions of easy entry would undermine the ability of even an apparent monopolist to act noncompetitively, the Guidelines' primary attention to seller concentration may seem somewhat back-ward in focus. The reason for this primacy, however, is that levels of seller concentration are easily quantified, whereas entry conditions are not easily quantified. The HHI levels do indicate some clear dividing lines (after the market boundaries have been delineated) and thereby provide some "safe harbors" and "clearly treacherous" zones. Still, in their preference for quantification, the Guidelines may be likened somewhat to the drunk who loses his keys in the middle of the road but then spends most of his time searching on the sidewalk under the street lamp "because the light is better there."

After discussing seller concentration, the Guidelines turn to condi-tions of entry. A high likelihood of significant entry into the market within two years (in response to a 5 percent price increase) is the crucial test for whether entry conditions are easy and hence for whether merg-ers between firms in markets with high levels of seller concentration will not be challenged. Unfortunately, no further quantification or pre-cision is offered.

The Guidelines then move on to other market conditions, such as the uniformity of product, level of buyer concentration, and history of prior antitrust violations, that may yield some inferences as to the likelihood of noncompetitive behavior after merger. These conditions should be important in decisions whether to challenge mergers in mar-kets with seller concentrations in the "further examination" range (that is, with an HHI of 1,000–1,800). Again, these are considerations that are solidly within the tradition of oligopoly theory. But, again, the discussion of these elements offers no quantification or greater precision.

Finally, the Guidelines address the question whether the promised economies of scale or other benefits of a merger should count as an offset to the possible creation or enhancement of market power. The 1982 Guidelines took a highly skeptical stance toward these promises; the 1984 Guidelines indicate a greater willingness to accept economies of scale as an offset.

These, then, are the major features of the current set of Merger Guidelines. How have they been used?

Assessments of antitrust policy implementation frequently cite the number of cases brought (the number of mergers challenged) as an indicator of stringency or leniency. This type of measure is largely inappropriate, for two reasons. First, a case is likely to be brought only when each of the litigating parties is sufficiently optimistic about its own chances of success, or about the stakes involved, so as to over-come the expected costs of litigation.[6] Another way of expressing this point is that the "location" of a legal standard (in terms of leniency or stringency) is much less important for the volume of litigation than is the clarity or fuzziness of that standard and the differences of opinion among the litigants that may thereby arise. Second, in circumstances in which a potentially offending merger can be "cured" by one of the merger partners' spinning off a branch plant or a product division to a third party buyer, this cure might be arranged through presuit or postsuit (but prejudgment) negotiations. The difference in method might be more one of litigation style by antitrust enforcers than of substance, but the difference in suits brought could be sizable.

Accordingly, judgments about implementation must instead rest on much more difficult assessments of the nature of those mergers that go unchallenged and of where the border of challenge appears to be. Nevertheless, my horseback judgment, along with that of virtually all other observers, is that merger policy has been more lenient during the Reagan administration than it was before and has become still more lenient in the administration's second term than it was in its first. This greater leniency is probably a product of the somewhat greater leniency that is built into the Guidelines themselves (as compared with the 1968 Guidelines) as well as the apparent tendency of the Reagan appointees to the Antitrust Division and the Federal Trade Commission increasingly to interpret them in a lenient fashion.[7] Even so, it is worth noting that antitrust policy on mergers has not been entirely dormant. In recent years the FTC has successfully challenged the proposed mergers of record producers Warner and Polygram and of soft drink producers Coca-Cola and Dr Pepper, and the DOJ challenged the form of merger initially proposed for the steel producers Republic and LTV. In addition, both agencies have challenged a number of mergers between smaller and lesser known companies and have either stopped them or cured them through appropriate spin-offs.

It has sometimes been claimed that one of the elements contributing to the merger boom of the 1980s has been the perceived leniency in antitrust policy. I am unaware of any quantitative support for this claim, and its validity seems highly dubious since most mergers do not appear to be among horizontal competitors and hence would not be challenged under almost any antitrust standard of competition. Moreover, it is worth invoking here Golbe and White's findings elsewhere in this volume. In their time-series analysis of merger activity, they use a dummy variable to distinguish the time periods before and after January 1981. The authors conceived that variable as one that might measure the effects of the major tax changes of that year, but it might equally well capture the effects of the soon-to-follow changes in antitrust policy. Regardless of interpretation, however, the coefficient on that variable is consistently nonsignificant in a number of alternative model specifications. Perceived antitrust leniency does not appear to be a significant cause of the merger wave of the 1980s.

Mergers in the Banking and Thrift Industries

The commercial banking and thrift (savings and loan and savings bank) industries have been, and are likely to continue to be, ones containing significant numbers of mergers in the 1980s. The reasons for the merger wave in these industries are fairly straightforward: the changed national economic environment in general of the late 1970s and early 1980s; the more specific economic declines of the 1980s in regions of the country that are highly dependent on energy, agriculture, or natural resources; changes in telecommunications and information-processing technologies and innovations in financial services markets, such as the development of the secondary mortgage markets and the general trend toward "securitization" of assets that were previously thought to be unique and nontradable; and the deregulation of depository institutions that has occurred in the 1980s. All four of these reasons are specific examples of the changed economic circumstances hypotheses advanced by Golbe and White in their paper in this volume. I will treat each of the contributing reasons for the merger wave in turn.

General economic conditions. The relatively high inflation rates experienced by the U.S. economy in the late 1970s and early 1980s meant relatively high, and rising, nominal interest rates. For a thrift industry that was accustomed to borrowing short (passbook savings accounts) and lending long (30-year fixed-rate home mortgages), the rise in nominal interest rates was disastrous. Caught with a portfolio of long-lived mortgages that had been made in earlier years at lower interest rates, but forced to pay higher rates on deposits to prevent those deposits from fleeing elsewhere, the thrifts were in a severe bind. The overall industry experienced losses in 1981 and 1982, and hundreds of money-losing thrifts were merged out of existence: With their mortgage portfolios largely "under water," they provided tempting purchase targets for the stronger thrifts (or outside purchasers) that had the staying power and were willing to bet on an eventual decline in nominal interest rates.

Specific regional declines. The economic declines of the 1980s in regions that are highly dependent on energy, agriculture, or natural resources have meant hard times for many of the financial institutions that lent money to businesses located in these areas. Significant numbers of banks and thrifts, not all of them actually located in these areas, have become insolvent from poor loans and investments in these regions, with mergers (frequently with financial assistance from the Federal Deposit Insurance Corporation or the Federal Savings and Loan Insurance Corporation) usually following. It is ironic that a number of thrifts, experiencing losses from the interest rate squeezes, saw investments in the sunbelt region as the means of bailing themselves out—with unfortunate consequences.

Technological change and innovation. Improved telecommunications and data processing have made it easier to operate financial services networks over large geographic areas. And the development of very thick secondary mortgage markets have brought new investors (for example, pension funds and insurance companies) into mortgage funding and encouraged the expansion of mortgage bankers that originate and sell mortgages in the secondary markets rather than holding them in a portfolio funded by deposits. These changed opportunities have certainly encouraged some of the mergers in the banking and thrift industries.

Deregulation. In response to the plight of the thrifts in the late 1970s and early 1980s and in partial response to the changed circumstances of financial markets generally, the Congress passed the Depository Institutions Deregulation and Monetary Control Act of 1980 and the Garn-St. Germain Act of 1982.[8] These acts called for the phasing-out of the Federal Reserve's Regulation Q (which had mandated the interest rate ceilings that banks and thrifts could pay on most of their deposits); authorized all thrifts to offer consumers interest-bearing checking accounts (negotiated order of withdrawal, or NOW, accounts); authorized banks and thrifts to offer adjustable rate mortgages; expanded the authority of thrifts to engage in lending and investment outside of home mortgages, including consumer, commercial, and agricultural loans and direct equity investments; and eased restrictions on banks' and thrifts' ability to purchase other depository institutions across state lines, if the purchased institutions were in financial difficulties. Simultaneously, some states (notably California, Texas, and Florida) were expanding the investment powers of thrifts; and more recently, many states have entered into regional or reciprocal compacts that have permitted interstate purchases and branching of banks and thrifts. Again, these changes have contributed to the merger wave in these industries.

Summary. It seems clear that, at least for the next few years, these changed and still-changing conditions will mean a continuing high level of mergers. The thrift industry has shrunk from almost 4,800 institutions (as members of the Federal Home Loan Bank System) in 1970 to approximately 3,500 today. As of this writing, the FSLIC has a problem list of approximately 400 insolvent thrifts that are unlikely to survive by themselves. Merger, in one form or another, is the likely outcome for most of them. And increased opportunities for interstate purchases and branching will likely mean the merger of many more. This will be true for the approximately 14,000 commercial banks as well.

In sum, flux and changing opportunities are likely to continue in the financial services markets, at least for the next few years. And these conditions will surely be conducive to a continuing wave of mergers in this sector.

Notes

1. Further discussion of merger policy and procedures can be found in White (1985) and Salop et al. (1987).

2. As noted earlier in this panel discussion, the DOJ and the FTC share responsibility for enforcing the Clayton Act. The division of responsibility for investigating potential cases is largely arbitrary, with historical expertise in the industrial or commercial area as the major guiding principle. The DOJ, though, does have sole responsibility for reviewing mergers in most regulated areas, such as transportation and financial services.

3. In my opinion this was the major conceptual advance achieved by the 1982 Guidelines.

4. It is worth noting that the market definition paradigm focuses primarily on a group of sellers, since it is sellers that may exercise market power. If a group could practice price discrimination toward one group of buyers—say, buyers in one geographic region—then the paradigm calls for a focus on those buyers as well.

5. If one of the merger partners is a likely entrant into one or more of the product markets of the other, where entry is difficult and potential entrants are scarce, a challenge to the merger might still be forthcoming.

6. For further discussion of this point see Salop and White (1986).

7. Although the FTC is not formally bound by the Guidelines, informal agency practice has been to follow their broad outlines.

8. Further discussion of the regulation and deregulation of depository institutions can be found in White (1986).

References

Chamberlin, Edward H. 1933. *The theory of monopolistic competition.* Cambridge: Harvard University Press.

Fellner, William H. 1949. *Competition among the few.* New York: Knopf.

Salop, Steven C., et al. 1987. Symposium on merger policy. *Journal of Economic Perspectives* 1 (Fall): 3–54.

Salop, Steven C., and Lawrence J. White. 1986. Private antitrust litigation: An economic analysis. *Georgetown Law Journal* 74 (April): 201–63.

Stigler, George C. 1964. A theory of oligopoly. *Journal of Political Economy* 72 (February): 55–69.

White, Lawrence J. 1985. Antitrust and video markets: The merger of Showtime and the Movie Channel as a case study. In *Video media competition:*

Regulation, economics, and technology, ed. Eli M. Noam, 338–63. New York: Columbia University Press.

White, Lawrence J. 1986. The partial deregulation of commercial banks and other depository institutions. In *Regulatory reform: What actually happened?* ed. Leonard W. Weiss and Michael Klass, case 6, 169–209. Boston: Little, Brown.

Contributors

Alan J. Auerbach
Department of Economics
University of Pennsylvania
3718 Locust Walk
Philadelphia, PA 19104

Laurie Simon Bagwell
Department of Economics
Stanford University
Stanford, CA 94305

David F. Bradford
Woodrow Wilson School
Princeton University
Princeton, NJ 08544

Charles Brown
Survey Research Center
Institute for Social Research
University of Michigan
Ann Arbor, MI 48109

Geoffrey Carliner
National Bureau of Economic
 Research
1050 Massachusetts Avenue
Cambridge, MA 02138

Henry S. Farber
Department of Economics
Massachusetts Institute of
 Technology
E52-252F
Cambridge, MA 02139

Julian R. Franks
6350B Anderson Graduate School of
 Management
University of California
Los Angeles, CA 90024-1481

Devra L. Golbe
Department of Economics
Hunter College
City University of New York
695 Park Avenue
New York, NY 10021

Jerry R. Green
Chair, Department of Economics
Harvard University
200 Littauer Center
Cambridge, MA 02138

Joseph A. Grundfest
Commissioner
U.S. Securities and Exchange
 Commission
450 Fifth Street, NW, Room 6106
Washington, D.C. 20549

Bronwyn H. Hall
National Bureau of Economic
 Research
204 Junipero Serra Boulevard
Stanford, CA 94305

Robert S. Harris
School of Business
University of North Carolina
Carroll Hall
Chapel Hill, NC 27514

Oliver S. D'Arcy Hart
Department of Economics
Massachusetts Institute of
   Technology
Cambridge, MA 02139

Bengt Holmstrom
School of Organization and
   Management
Yale University
Box 1A
New Haven, CT 06520

Gregg Jarrell
The Alcar Group Inc.
5215 Old Orchard Road
Suite 600
Skokie, IL 60077

Michael C. Jensen
Harvard Business School
Cotting 215
Harvard University
Boston, MA 01234

Colin Mayer
London Business School
Sussex Place
Regents Park
London NWI 45A
England

James L. Medoff
Department of Economics
Harvard University
Littauer Center 115
Cambridge, MA 02138

Randall Mørck
Department of Finance
4-21D Faculty of Business
University of Alberta
Edmondton, Alberta
Canada

Ariel Pakes
Department of Economics
University of Wisconsin
1180 Observatory Drive
Madison, WI 53706

James M. Poterba
National Bureau of Economic
   Research
1050 Massachusetts Avenue
Cambridge, MA 02138

Artur Raviv
J. L. Kellogg Graduate School of
   Management
Northwestern University
Leverone Hall
2001 Sheridan Road
Evanston, IL 60201

David Reishus
U.S. Joint Committee on Taxation
315 Constitution Avenue, NE
Washington, DC 20002

Richard S. Ruback
Alfred P. Sloan School of
   Management
Massachusetts Institute of
   Technology
E52-243A
Cambridge, MA 02139

Steven C. Salop
Law Center
600 New Jersey, NW
Georgetown University
Washington, DC 20001

Andrei Shleifer
Graduate School of Business
University of Chicago
1101 East 58th Street
Chicago, IL 60637

John B. Shoven
Department of Economics
Stanford University
Encina Hall, 4th Floor
Stanford, CA 94305

Lawrence H. Summers
Department of Economics
Littauer Center 229
Harvard University
Cambridge, MA 02138

Robert A. Taggart, Jr.
School of Management
Finance/Economics Department
Boston University
704 Commonwealth Avenue
Boston, MA 02215

Robert W. Vishny
Graduate School of Business
University of Chicago
1101 East 58th Street
Chicago, IL 60637

Lawrence J. White
Federal Home Loan Bank Board
1700 G Street, NW
Washington, DC 20552

Oliver E. Williamson
Law School
Yale Law School
127 Wall Street
New Haven, CT 06520

Name Index

Subject Index

341